HOLT

AFRICAN AMERICAN LITERATURE

Senior Consultants

Dr. Alfred W. Tatum Dr. Eric Cooper

On the Cover: *Mullet Friday* by Jonathan Green,
Original limited edition lithograph (1997), Collection of the McKissick Museum
Photography by Tim Stamm

Blocks by China Pettway
circa 1975, corduroy and cotton hopsacking, 83"x70"

Cover Quote: Quote is an excerpt from *I Know Why the Caged Bird Sings* by Maya Angelou. Copyright © 1969 and renewed © 1997 by Maya Angelou. Reproduced by permission of Random House, Inc., www.randomhouse.com.

HOLT, RINEHART AND WINSTON
A Harcourt Education Company
Orlando • Austin • New York • San Diego • London

Senior Consultants

Dr. Alfred W. Tatum
Associate Professor,
Department of Literacy Education
University of Illinois
Chicago, IL

Dr. Eric Cooper
Distinguished Service Professor
Computer Science Department
Carnegie Mellon University

Program Reviewers

Dr. Elizabeth Primas
Director of Literacy
Washington, DC

Carla Ranger, Director
African American Read-In
Dallas County Community Colleges
Dallas, TX

Traci Saxton
Language Arts Supervisor
East Orange School District, NJ

Dr. Linda E. Young
Clark County School District
Equity and Diversity Education
Las Vegas, NV

Printed in the United States of America

ISBN 978-0-55-400030-5
ISBN 0-55-400030-X
3 4 5 6 7 0868 11
4500313854

AFRICAN AMERICAN LITERATURE
CONTENTS

UNIT 2 THE SEARCH FOR FREEDOM (1750–1865) 64

UNIT 3 CHALLENGES AND CHANGE (1865–1945) 146

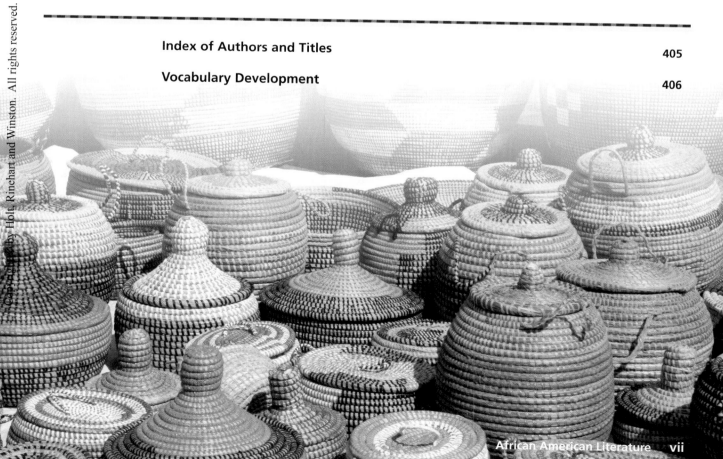

Perspectives on African American Literature

Knowledge of Our Past Enriches Our Present and Future

by Alfred W. Tatum

From the beginning of time to the present, Africans and African Americans have made significant contributions that have shaped the world. Unfortunately, many of these contributions and experiences have been overlooked across several generations for a variety of reasons. One of the main reasons is that many people saw and experienced a world based on racial differences, a world in which whites were viewed as superior and blacks were viewed as inferior. The manifestation of these racial differences, although not to the same extent as in the past, continues to exist and to haunt us in today's society.

Overlooking the experiences and contributions of Africans and African Americans affected our world in many ways. First, it robbed us of a memory of our rich past. Secondly, it shaped negative images of African and African American people that were largely based on the spread of false information by the framers of American society. Ultimately, many of the hopes and desires of African Americans wilted in the United States because there were very few images that provided them with a source of encouragement or confidence to do great things.

Fortunately, many African Americans, both male and female, were resilient. They found the strength to overcome legal, economic, institutional, and social barriers to provide a source of cultural strength and knowledge for future generations. Much of this cultural strength and knowledge can be found in African American literature—in essays, short stories, novels, poems, song lyrics, and political documents. These writings allow us to become familiar with or to reconnect with historical events as well as modern-day events such as the civil rights movement or the influence of the hip-hop generation. By reading African American literature, we are also able to meet and learn more about scientists, writers, politicians, athletes, religious leaders, and educators who have blazed trails to improve the world, not just for African Americans but for everyone. Additionally, we can learn more about racial and social conditions that are still in need of improvement.

Our reading of African American literature not only enables us to restore the rich lineage and history of a group of people but also empowers us all. Through African American literature we can develop an appreciation of the past as we strive toward a better future. Without such literature, we are all deprived of the knowledge of who we are and who we came to be, no matter our race or the color of our skin. It is my hope that you will read the texts in this collection with great intensity and passion. If you do so, these authors and their writings will become a part of you throughout your life, as you shape your existence in an ever-changing society.

Alfred W. Tatum

Literature, History, and the Promise of America

by Eric Cooper

Some teachers have told me that, when they ask their students to read selections that show institutionalized racism, the students react somewhat negatively. They ask, for example: "Why do we always have to read about black people struggling to survive or succeed?" According to these teachers, many students respond by saying those struggles were "back in days past." They see no connection between what they are reading and their own lives.

So, why is it important for us to study history and to study literature of the past as well as the present? Many great leaders have answered this question. Dr. Asa Hilliard, III, who worked and inspired thousands of students during his lifetime, said that to know our history provides a frame of reference for our identity and our aspirations. The philosopher Santayana has suggested that to ignore the past is to fall victim to its undertow. And James Baldwin wrote that history is "literally present in all that we do" and that we "are unconsciously controlled by it in many ways."

In the United States we use history as a pathway toward a unified vision of America, a unified vision that includes equal opportunity and equal protection under law for all of our country's citizens. And yet, many also recognize the feelings expressed by W.E.B. Du Bois, that an African American "ever feels his two-ness—an American, a Negro; two souls, two thoughts, two unreconciled strivings." For many of us there is also a "two-ness" of cultural norms—those of the neighborhood and those of the school. To reconcile the two, we must learn to channel our energy, intellect, and imagination and to accept the educational offerings of our schools and learn from them. These educational offerings are designed to enable us to succeed, to prosper, and to earn a position in the nation.

The African American experience captured in the literature in this book provides a lens through which to view the values and vision of America's promise for its citizens. Through this literature, we can see the promise of equal opportunity for all American citizens and the rich contributions of their different cultures. In particular, this literature will reveal the strengths, beauty, and brilliance of African American history and culture, a history and a culture that shapes, and is shaped by, the larger culture of our country.

Howard University's Moorland-Spingarn Research Center

Holt, Rinehart and Winston is proud to partner with **Howard University's Moorland-Spingarn Research Center**, home to one of the largest collections of materials chronicling the history and culture of people of African descent. The center is dedicated to preserving, protecting, and providing access to a range of resources that trace the black experience in Africa, the Americas, and other parts of the world.

Space shuttle pilot Colonel Frederick Drew Gregory carried this Spingarn Medal (shown above) into space.

World War II poster featuring a Tuskegee airman

Ceremonial Oba mask

Mod Mekkawi, Director, University Libraries at Howard University

Howard University emphasizes leadership and diversity.

THE CONNECTION

Together with the Moorland-Spingarn Research Center, Holt presents Connecting to Our Past. This exciting new online feature brings African American history and culture to life through rarely seen artifacts from the collection at Howard University's Moorland-Spingarn Research Center.

go.hrw.com
Program Home Page
Keyword: SAAH STUDENT

Museum exhibits (left to right): The March on Washington; Rosa Parks refusing to give up her seat; the Freedom Ride

National Civil Rights Museum

Holt, Rinehart and Winston proudly partners with the **National Civil Rights Museum** to bring you *Holt African American Literature and Holt African American History*. The primary mission of the National Civil Rights Museum is to document the history of the American civil rights movement. Established at the historic Lorraine Motel in Memphis, Tennessee, the Museum aims to advance the legacy of the civil rights movement by inspiring ongoing participation in civil and human rights movements worldwide.

go.hrw.com
Program Home Page
Keyword: SAAH STUDENT

Experience the civil rights movement as you visit the many exhibits in the museum.

Educational Programs

The educational focus of the National Civil Rights Museum is designed to increase awareness and promote active participation in the ongoing struggle for civil and human rights throughout the world. To accomplish this goal, the Museum's educational programs and initiatives utilize the histories contained in the permanent exhibitions as a springboard for learning. For more information on the National Civil Rights Museum, please visit www.civilrightsmuseum.org.

UNIT 1 FROM AFRICA TO THE NEW WORLD (prehistory to 1750)

Engraved map of the Atlantic Ocean, 1650, by Jan Jansson from his "Novus Atlas."
The Granger Collection, New York

LITERARY FOCUS FOR UNIT 1

What do you know about the cultures of Africa before the nineteenth century? The selections in this unit present modern and historical perspectives on African heritage.

You will analyze modern poems that use **imagery** to explore relationships with Africa. African proverbs reveal an oral tradition of societal values that were passed on from generation to generation. The **trickster in folk tales** uses cunning to outwit opponents but also teaches moral lessons. An ancient **epic** draws you in to the heroic exploits that gave rise to an empire. A modern epic honors ancestors who endured the Middle Passage—the horrendous journey that carried African captives across the Atlantic into bondage—and a famous **slave narrative** gives voice to the countless unheard victims of that journey.

As you read this unit, think about the legacy of the first Africans who arrived in the New World and what this legacy means to people in the United States today.

BEFORE YOU READ

20th-Century Poets on African Heritage

Countee Cullen

Naomi Long Madgett

Lucille Clifton

Three modern poets share their ideas about Africa, which include feelings of closeness and of separation.

LITERARY FOCUS: IMAGERY

An image is a representation of a thing or an experience. **Imagery** is the use of words to create these representations in a reader's mind. It helps the reader see, smell, taste, hear, or feel something in his or her imagination.

Imagery can appeal to our senses through literal meaning and through figurative meaning. For example, Countee Cullen begins "Heritage" with a series of literal images of the sun, sea, sky, and earth. Naomi Long Madgett's "First Man" is "sculpted from the clay of Africa," a non-literal image that not only implies a close connection to the land, but also evokes the creation myths of several cultures.

Poets use the meanings, sounds, and rhythms of words to convey ideas and emotions. Imagery lets us share sensory experiences, and we can interpret the meaning of these experiences in concrete and symbolic ways.

READING SKILLS: READING ALOUD

Sound and rhythm play important roles in poetry. Since poems are intended to be heard, **reading aloud** is one of the best ways to fully experience them.

- To begin, read through the poem to make sure you know the meanings and pronunciations of any unfamiliar words.
- Read the poem very slowly. Poets choose each word very carefully. Reading slowly will help you give each word the attention it deserves.
- Try to identify the speaker and the setting of the poem. This will influence the tone of your reading.
- Pause for punctuation or for dramatic effect.

After you have read and analyzed the three poems in this lesson, try reading them aloud.

Literary Focus
Understand imagery.

Reading Skills
Read aloud.

from Heritage

by Countee Cullen

What is Africa to me:
Copper sun or scarlet sea,
Jungle star or jungle track,
Strong bronzed men, or **regal** black
Women from whose loins I sprang
When the birds of Eden sang?
One three centuries removed
From the scenes his fathers loved,
Spicy grove, cinnamon tree,
What is Africa to me?

©DLILLC/CORBIS

MEET THE WRITER

Countee Cullen (1903–1946) was a major figure in the Harlem Renaissance. He began publishing poetry while he was still in high school, *Color* (1925), his first book of poetry, was published while he was in college. Cullen wrote in traditional verse forms and did not experiment with dialect or blues rhythms. Although he was determined to be known as a poet, not a "Negro poet," many of his poems do deal with themes that are of special concern to African Americans. The first ten lines of "Heritage" with its final question, "What is Africa to me?" go to the heart of the African American experience. (For more on Countee Cullen, see page 177.)

VOCABULARY

regal (rēg′əl) *adj.:* like or suitable for a king or a queen; majestic.

LITERARY FOCUS

Re-read lines 1–6. Think about the imagery the poet creates. To which sense do most of the images appeal? Which image do you find most striking, and why?

INTERPRET

Re-read lines 7 and 8. To what do the words *three centuries* refer?

INFER

Why do you think the poet changes the text to italic in lines 7 through 10?

First Man

by Naomi Long Madgett

Sculpted from the clay of Africa,
first man in all the universe,
you were created in the image of a tree.
Transplanted now to foreign soil,
you are still wondrous in your towering **vigor**
and amplitude,° and in the shade you give.

Tender birch or seasoned oak, mahogany or cedar,
baobab or ebony, you are the joy of a new Eden,
crested with leaves as varied
as fades and dreadlocks.

Your **countenance,** like rings of a **stalwart** trunk,
tells the unmatched story
of how you **persevered** and flourished
in spite of bitter storms.

Majestic man, enduring man of myriad visages,°
continue to grow strong and tall
within the circle of my love.

VOCABULARY

vigor (vig′ər) *n.:* active energy or strength.

countenance (koun′tə·nəns) *n.:* facial features, or the facial expression that shows a person's feelings.

stalwart (stôl′wərt) *adj.:* strong and sturdy; immoveable.

persevered (pʉr′sə·vird′) *v.:* continued with an action or effort in spite of difficulties.

ANALYZE

"First Man" uses a central metaphor that compares a man to a tree. How does the poet extend this metaphor in lines 9 and 10?

DRAW CONCLUSIONS

What does the poet mean by "bitter storms" in line 14?

6. **amplitude** (am′plə·to͞od′) *n.:* the quality of having great size or abundance.
15. **myriad visages** (mir′ē·əd·viz′ij·əs) *n.:* very many faces.

The Creation, oil on masonite by Aaron Douglas, 1935.
Photo by Jarvis Grant; Courtesy of Gallery of Art, Howard University

MEET THE WRITER

Naomi Long Madgett (1923–) was born in Norfolk, Virginia, but as a child, lived in East Orange, New Jersey, where her father was a Baptist minister. She began reading and writing poems early and was influenced by the poetry of Paul Laurence Dunbar and Countee Cullen.

In 1937, her family moved to St. Louis where Madgett entered a segregated school. She considered this, "the turning point in my life . . . for the better." Here her poetry writing was taken seriously and encouraged by teachers. In 1941, just as she graduated from high school, Madgett published her first book of poems, *Songs to a Phantom Nightingale.* Madgett graduated from Virginia State College in 1945. She then moved to Detroit and worked as a reporter for the *Michigan Chronicle,* an African American newspaper.

In 1955 she began teaching high school in Detroit, and soon realized that her students had little knowledge of famous black writers such as Langston Hughes or Countee Cullen. Madgett created and taught the first course in African American literature in Detroit public schools. In 1967 she was named Distinguished Teacher of the Year. In 1968 she began teaching at Eastern Michigan University. Madgett also continued to publish poetry depicting the black experience, such as *Star by Star* (1965) that contains her famous poem "Midway."

NOTES

EVALUATE

Why did Madgett enter a segregated school when she moved to St. Louis in 1937?

INFER

Why do you think Madgett felt that going to a segregated school changed her life for the better?

INTERPRET

Where is *home*? Does it refer to the place where the speaker lives?

INFER

What is the meaning of "the soul of your / variety"?

INFER

What emotion does "Africa" express? How does Lucille Clifton convey this emotion?

EXTEND

Write an analysis comparing and contrasting the three poems. Before you write, try reading the poems aloud to listen for similarities and differences in tone and style.

Africa

by Lucille Clifton

home
oh
home
the soul of your
variety
all of my bones
remember

MEET THE WRITER

Lucille Clifton (1936–) was born and raised in Depew, New York. She studied drama at Howard University and also studied at Fredonia State Teachers' College. Clifton raised six children, and says, "At home, I am wife and mama mostly. My family has always come first with me." However, despite family responsibilities, she has published more than twenty books of poetry, fiction, and children's literature.

About her poetic style, Clifton says, "I use a simple language. I have never believed that for anything to be valid or true or intellectual or 'deep' it had to first be complex."

Family history and relationships are an important element in Clifton's poetry. In *Generations* (1976), a poetic memoir, she describes five generations of her family, including her great-great-grandmother who was kidnapped in Africa and sold into slavery, and her great-grandmother Lucille—the first black woman lynched in Virginia. The scholar James A. Miller says of Clifton, "Clifton not only lays claim to an African past—a recurrent feature of many of her poems—she also defines herself as a poet whose task is to keep historical memory alive."

Clifton won the 2007 Ruth Lilly Poetry Prize, and she has been nominated twice for the Pulitzer Prize. She lives in Baltimore, Maryland.

SKILLS PRACTICE

20th-Century Poets on African Heritage

VOCABULARY AND COMPREHENSION

WORD BOX

regal
vigor
countenance
stalwart
persevered

A. Synonyms Write the word from the Word Box that is a synonym for each of the following words.

1. vitality ______________________
2. sturdy ______________________
3. persisted ______________________
4. royal ______________________
5. visage ______________________

B. Reading Comprehension Answer each question and write a poem.

6. In what ways does "Heritage" describe a person's connections with Africa?

____
____
____

7. What central image does Naomi Long Madgett use in "First Man?

____
____
____

8. What does the speaker of "Africa" mean by the phrase "all of my bones remember"?

____
____
____

9. Descriptions using vivid words and imagery can help readers understand a poem. Think about your heritage and write a poem on another sheet of paper that expresses some aspect of your thoughts and feelings. Include images to illustrate your ideas. Share your poem with your classmates or put it in your writing portfolio.

Vocabulary Skills
Identify synonyms.

BEFORE YOU READ

from Sundiata: An Epic of Old Mali

French translation by D. T. Niane
English translation by G. D. Pickett

As well as being an exciting tale of conflict and courage, this epic provides insight into the ancient Mali culture.

LITERARY FOCUS: EPIC

An **epic** is a long narrative poem that revolves around the deeds of a hero. Epics were passed down from generation to generation orally and helped to preserve the traditions and history of the culture from which they sprang.

An epic hero is distinguished by several characteristics, including the following:

- The hero character is usually of high status or noble lineage.
- The hero character performs courageous and sometimes superhuman deeds. These actions often decide the destiny of a nation or group of people.
- The hero character upholds the values of the culture.
- The hero character journeys great distances to fulfill his quest.

In this epic, the hero Sundiata shows these characteristics as he fights the evil king Soumaoro Kante. Through his actions, universal themes as well as the values of his Mali society are revealed.

READING SKILLS: ASKING QUESTIONS

One strategy to help you to get more out of what you read is **asking questions.** Getting into the habit of asking yourself *who, what, when, where, why,* and *how* questions after reading a paragraph or a passage can help you to focus your attention, locate and remember important details, and figure out what you don't understand.

Use a chart such as this one to record your questions and answers as you read the epic.

LINES	QUESTIONS	ANSWERS
Lines 1–9	Who is the narrator?	

Literary Focus
Understand the characteristics of epics and epic heroes.

Vocabulary Skills
Understand suffixes.

VOCABULARY DEVELOPMENT

PREVIEW SELECTION VOCABULARY

The following words appear in the excerpt from *Sundiata: An Epic of Old Mali.* Look them over before you begin to read.

eloquence (el′ə·kwəns) *n.:* persuasive, skillful speech.

*The griot prides himself on his **eloquence.***

oblivion (ə·bliv′ē·ən) *n.:* condition of being forgotten.

*History prevents the past from fading into **oblivion.***

exploits (ek′sploit′s) *n.:* brilliant or heroic deeds.

*The story of Sundiata's **exploits** lived on after him.*

grievances (grē′vənsez) *n.:* complaints.

*A king must declare his **grievances** against an enemy before waging war.*

ravenous (rav′ə·nəs) *adj.:* enormously hungry.

*Soumaoro had a **ravenous** appetite for power.*

boisterous (boi′stər·əs) *adj.:* rough and stormy.

*After the rain, the river was **boisterous** and high.*

calamity (kə·lam′ə·tē) *n.:* disaster; event that brings terrible affliction.

*The people of Sosso could not anticipate the **calamity** that would befall them.*

insolently (in′sə·lənt·lē) *adv.:* rudely and disrespectfully.

*Soumaoro **insolently** ignored Sundiata's reply.*

UNDERSTANDING SUFFIXES

Suffixes are word parts added to the end of root or base words. Notice in the chart below that different suffixes form different parts of speech. Knowing the part of speech and the meaning of the suffix can help you to define unfamiliar words. Look for words with these endings as you read the epic.

suffixes that form nouns	suffixes that form adjectives
–ance / –ence: condition; action *–ity:* state; quality *–ation / –ion:* action or process *–ness:* state; quality; condition; degree	*–able:* capable of an action *–ous:* possessing; characterized by *–ent:* performing or promoting a specified action *–ful:* full of; resembling
suffixes that form adverbs	**suffixes that form verbs**
–ly: like; resembling; in a specified manner	*–ate:* to act upon in a specified manner *–en:* to cause to be or become *–ize:* to cause to be or become; to treat as *–ify:* to make

WORD STUDY

A *griot* (line 1) is a storyteller. This term probably comes originally from the Latin *creatus,* which means "one brought up or trained."

ANALYZE

After reading lines 2–19, write some questions that you might ask to make sure that you understand the function and importance of a griot.

VOCABULARY

eloquence (el′ə·kwəns) *n.:* persuasive, skillful speech.

oblivion (əbliv′ē·ən) *n.:* condition of being forgotten.

exploits (ek′sploit′s) *n.:* brilliant or heroic deeds.

INTERPRET

What does the griot mean when he says in lines 21–22 that the "world is old, but the future springs from the past"?

from Sundiata: An Epic of Old Mali

French translation by D. T. Niane
English translation by G. D. Pickett

The Words of the Griot Mamoudou Kouyaté

I am a griot. It is I, Djeli Mamoudou Kouyaté, son of Bintou Kouyaté and Djeli Kedian Kouyaté, master in the art of **eloquence.** Since time immemorial the Kouyatés have been in the service of the Keita princes[1] of Mali; we are vessels[2] of speech, we are the repositories which harbour secrets many centuries old. The art of eloquence has no secrets for us; without us the names of kings would vanish into **oblivion,** we are the memory of mankind; by the spoken word we bring to life the deeds and **exploits** of kings for younger generations.

I derive my knowledge from my father Djeli Kedian, who also got it from his father; history holds no mystery for us; we teach to the vulgar just as much as we want to teach them, for it is we who keep the keys to the twelve doors of Mali.[3]

I know the list of all the sovereigns who succeeded to the throne of Mali. I know how the black people divided into tribes, for my father bequeathed to me all his learning; I know why such and such is called Kamara, another Keita, and yet another Sibibé or Traoré;[4] every name has a meaning, a secret import.

I teach kings the history of their ancestors so that the lives of the ancients might serve them as an example, for the world is old, but the future springs from the past.

1. **Keita princes:** a dynasty of rulers in Mali.
2. **vessels** (ves′əls) *n.:* here, people who are agents or receptacles for something.
3. **twelve doors of Mali:** Mali was originally composed of twelve provinces.
4. **Kamara . . . Traoré:** names of Mandingo tribes. Mali at first was a confederation of tribes.

My word is pure and free of all untruth; it is the word of my father; it is the word of my father's father. I will give you my father's words just as I received them; royal griots do not know what lying is. When a quarrel breaks out between tribes it is we who settle the difference, for we are the depositaries[5] of oaths which the ancestors swore.

Listen to my word, you who want to know; by my mouth you will learn the history of Mali.

By my mouth you will get to know the story of the ancestor of great Mali, the story of him who, by his exploits, surpassed even Alexander the Great;[6] he who, from the East, shed his rays upon all the countries of the West.

INFER

What is the griot's motive for the explanation that he gives in lines 23–34?

©Black Star/Alamy

5. **depositaries** (dē·päz′ə·ter′ēs) *n.:* trustees, people who are entrusted with something.
6. **Alexander the Great:** a famous military conqueror of the fourth century B.C., whose empire extended from the Mediterranean to India.

LITERARY FOCUS

Re-read lines 35–36. What do the animals associated with Sundiata's heritage foreshadow about his own traits?

VOCABULARY

grievances (grēv′ənsez) *n.:* complaints.

ANALYZE

Pause after reading lines 47–62. Ask yourself where each king is camped in relation to the other. Try drawing a simple map to help you answer your question.

PREDICT

Re-read lines 56–62. Note that both kings have magical powers. How might this fact be important later?

Listen to the story of the son of the Buffalo, the son of the Lion.[7] I am going to tell you of Maghan Sundiata, of Mari-Djata, of Sogolon Djata, of Naré Maghan Djata; the man of many names against whom sorcery could avail nothing.

Sundiata is the rightful heir of the king of Mali, but after his father's death, he is forced into exile by his father's first wife, who wants the throne for her own son. Sundiata soon becomes a master hunter and a powerful warrior. His mother, Sogolon, prepares him for the time when his destiny will be fulfilled and he will reclaim the kingdom of Mali. In the climax of the epic, he battles Soumaoro Kante, the evil sorcerer king of Sosso, who has invaded Mali.

from Krina

Sundiata went and pitched camp at Dayala in the valley of the Niger. Now it was he who was blocking Soumaoro's road to the south. Up till that time, Sundiata and Soumaoro had fought each other without a declaration of war. One does not wage war without saying why it is being waged. Those fighting should make a declaration of their **grievances** to begin with. Just as a sorcerer ought not to attack someone without taking him to task for some evil deed, so a king should not wage war without saying why he is taking up arms.

Soumaoro advanced as far as Krina, near the village of Dayala on the Niger and decided to assert his rights before joining battle. Soumaoro knew that Sundiata also was a sorcerer, so, instead of sending an embassy, he committed his words to one of his owls. The night bird came and perched on the roof of Djata's tent and spoke. The son of Sogolon in his turn sent his owl to Soumaoro. Here is the dialogue of the sorcerer kings:

7. **son . . . Lion:** According to D. T. Niane, Sundiata's mother had a buffalo as a totem; the lion is the totem and ancestor of the Keita. Through his mother, Sundiata is son of the Buffalo, and through his father, he is son of the Lion.

"Stop, young man. Henceforth I am the king of Mali. If you want peace, return to where you came from," said Soumaoro.

"I am coming back, Soumaoro, to recapture my kingdom. If you want peace you will make amends to my allies and return to Sosso where you are the king."

"I am king of Mali by force of arms. My rights have been established by conquest."

"Then I will take Mali from you by force of arms and chase you from my kingdom."

A terracotta figure of a man excavated in Djenne/Mopti, Mali (ca. 13th–14th CE).
Formerly Entwistle Gallery, London. Detroit Institute of Arts, Detroit, Michigan, U.S.A. Werner Forman/Art Resource, NY

CLARIFY

In long passages of dialogue, the speakers usually alternate. Note that Soumaoro says lines 63–64. Sundiata then replies in lines 65–67. Next to each pair of lines in the remainder of the dialogue, write the name of the speaker to help you keep them straight.

NOTES

DRAW CONCLUSIONS

What purpose does the exchange between the two kings serve?

VOCABULARY

ravenous (rav′ə·nəs) *adj.:* enormously hungry.

boisterous (bois′tər·əs) *adj.:* rough and stormy.

calamity (kə·lam′ə·tē) *n.:* disaster; event that brings terrible affliction.

ANALYZE

Re-read lines 95–102. Underline the words and phrases that help you to envision the setting of Sosso. Why do you think the poet includes such specific details as the number of fortresses?

"Know, then, that I am the wild yam of the rocks; nothing will make me leave Mali."

"Know, also that I have in my camp seven master smiths who will shatter the rocks. Then, yam, I will eat you."

"I am the poisonous mushroom that makes the fearless vomit."

"As for me, I am the **ravenous** cock, the poison does not matter to me."

"Behave yourself, little boy, or you will burn your foot, for I am the red-hot cinder."

"But me, I am the rain that extinguishes the cinder; I am the **boisterous** torrent that will carry you off."

"I am the mighty silk-cotton tree that looks on from high on the tops of other trees."

"And I, I am the strangling creeper that climbs to the top of the forest giant."

"Enough of this argument. You shall not have Mali."

"Know that there is not room for two kings on the same skin, Soumaoro; you will let me have your place."

"Very well, since you want war I will wage war against you, but I would have you know that I have killed nine kings whose heads adorn my room. What a pity, indeed, that your head should take its place beside those of your fellow madcaps."[8]

"Prepare yourself, Soumaoro, for it will be long before the **calamity** that is going to crash down upon you and yours comes to an end."

Sosso was a magnificent city. In the open plain her triple rampart with awe-inspiring towers reached into the sky. The city comprised a hundred and eighty-eight fortresses and the palace of Soumaoro loomed above the whole city like a gigantic tower. Sosso had but one gate; colossal and made of iron, the work of the sons of fire. Noumounkeba[9] hoped to tie Sundiata down outside of Sosso, for he had enough provisions to hold out for a year.

---

8. **madcaps** (mad′kaps′) *n.:* impulsive or rash people.
9. **Noumounkeba:** a tribal chief who is directing the defense of the city.

The sun was beginning to set when Sogolon-Djata appeared before Sosso the Magnificent. From the top of a hill, Djata and his general staff gazed upon the fearsome city of the sorcerer-king. The army encamped in the plain opposite the great gate of the city and fires were lit in the camp. Djata resolved to take Sosso in the course of a morning. He fed his men a double ration and the tam-tams beat all night to stir up the victors of Krina.

At daybreak the towers of the ramparts were black with sofas.[10] Others were positioned on the ramparts themselves. They were the archers. The Mandingoes[11] were masters in the art of storming a town. In the front line Sundiata placed the sofas of Mali, while those who held the ladders were in the second line protected by the shields of the spearmen. The main body of the army was to attack the city gate. When all was ready, Djata gave the order to attack. The drums resounded, the horns blared and like a tide the Mandingo front line moved off, giving mighty shouts. With their shields raised above their heads the Mandingoes advanced up to the foot of the wall, then the Sossos began to rain large stones down on the assailants. From the rear, the bowmen of Wagadou[12] shot arrows at the ramparts. The attack spread and the town was assaulted at all points. Sundiata had a murderous reserve; they were the bowmen whom the king of the Bolos had sent shortly before Krina. The archers of Bobo are the best in the world. On one knee the archers fired flaming arrows over the ramparts. Within the walls the thatched huts took fire and the smoke swirled up. The ladders stood against the curtain wall and the first Mandingo sofas were already at the top. Seized by panic through seeing the town on fire, the Sossos

10. **sofas** (sō′fəs) *n.:* infantrymen.
11. **Mandingoes:** inhabitants of Mali.
12. **Wagadou:** a name for Old Ghana.

ANALYZE

After reading lines 103–104, you might ask yourself who Sogolon-Djata is. Identify the passage in which you would find the answer.

COMPARE & CONTRAST

Draw a sketch of the battle scene described in lines 110–135. Compare your sketch with a partner and discuss similarities and differences.

LITERARY FOCUS

Re-read lines 113–130. What is revealed about Sundiata through his battle strategy?

ANALYZE

Re-read lines 129–135. What is the turning point of the battle?

INFER

Re-read lines 136–144. Why doesn't Sundiata kill Soumaoro's battle chief Noumounkeba?

NOTES

hesitated a moment. The huge tower surmounting the gate surrendered, for Fakoli's[13] smiths had made themselves masters of it. They got into the city where the screams of women and children brought the Sossos' panic to a head. They opened the gates to the main body of the army.

Then began the massacre. Women and children in the midst of fleeing Sossos implored mercy of the victors. Djata and his cavalry were now in front of the awesome tower palace of Soumaoro. Noumounkeba, conscious that he was lost, came out to fight. With his sword held aloft he bore down on Djata, but the latter dodged him and, catching hold of the Sosso's braced arm, forced him to his knees whilst the sword dropped to the ground. He did not kill him but delivered him into the hands of Manding Bory.[14]

Soumaoro's palace was now at Sundiata's mercy. While everywhere the Sossos were begging for quarter,[15] Sundiata, preceded by Balla Fasséké,[16] entered Soumaoro's tower. The griot knew every nook and cranny of the palace from his captivity and he led Sundiata to Soumaoro's magic chamber.

When Balla Fasséké opened the door to the room it was found to have changed its appearance since Soumaoro had been touched by the fatal arrow. The inmates of the chamber had lost their power. The snake in the pitcher was in the throes of death, the owls from the perch were flapping pitifully about on the ground. Everything was dying in the sorcerer's abode. It was all up with the power of Soumaoro. Sundiata had all Soumaoro's fetishes[17] taken down and before the palace were gathered together all Soumaoro's wives, all princesses taken from their families by force. The prisoners, their hands tied behind

13. **Fakoli:** Soumaoro's nephew. Soumaoro made an enemy of him by abducting his wife.
14. **Manding Bory:** Sundiata's brother.
15. **quarter** (kwôrt′ər) *n.:* mercy.
16. **Balla Fasséké:** Sundiata's griot.
17. **fetishes** (fet′ish·iz′) *n.:* objects believed to have magical power.

Horse and Rider, Djenne, Mali (terracotta), Private Collection.
Photo ©Heini Schneebeli/The Bridgeman Art Library International

their backs, were already herded together. Just as he had wished, Sundiata had taken Sosso in the course of a morning. When everything was outside of the town and all that there was to take had been taken out, Sundiata gave the order to complete its destruction. The last houses were set fire to and prisoners were employed in the razing of the walls. Thus, as Djata intended, Sosso was destroyed to its very foundations.

DRAW CONCLUSIONS

In line 161, why is it significant that Sundiata had "taken Sosso in the course of a morning" as he had wished?

CAUSE & EFFECT

What is the effect of Sundiata's actions?

VOCABULARY

insolently (in′sə·lənt·le) *adv.:* rudely and disrespectfully.

GENERALIZE

Re-read lines 167–185. What lesson for rulers might be drawn from the ironic fate of Sosso?

ANALYZE

Write questions that you still have about the epic in your chart. Work with a partner to find the answers.

EXTEND

Read an excerpt from another epic, such as the *Iliad,* the *Odyssey,* or *Gilgamesh.* Compare and contrast the traits of the hero with those of Sundiata. Discuss your insights with a partner who read the same epic.

Yes, Sosso was razed to the ground. It has disappeared, the proud city of Soumaoro. A ghastly wilderness extends over the places where kings came and humbled themselves before the sorcerer king. All traces of the houses have vanished and of Soumaoro's seven-storey palace there remains nothing more. A field of desolation, Sosso is now a spot where guinea fowl and young partridges come to take their dust baths.

Many years have rolled by and many times the moon has traversed the heaven since these places lost their inhabitants. The bourein,[18] the tree of desolation, spreads out its thorny undergrowth and **insolently** grows in Soumaoro's capital. Sosso the Proud is nothing but a memory in the mouths of griots. The hyenas come to wail there at night, the hare and the hind come and feed on the site of the palace of Soumaoro, the king who wore robes of human skin.

Sosso vanished from the earth and it was Sundiata, the son of the buffalo, who gave these places over to solitude. After the destruction of Soumaoro's capital the world knew no other master but Sundiata.

---

18. bourein (bo͝o′rān) *n.:* a dwarf shrub.

MEET THE WRITER

Djibril Tamsin Niane (1932–), a Guinean historian and playwright, researched oral sources of Mali history in the 1950s. He met Djeli Mamoudou Kouyaté, a griot and "one of the most authentic traditionists of Mali." Kouyaté recited *Sundiata* in Mandingo to Niane, who, in turn, translated it into French, from which it was then translated into English by **G. D. Pickett** (1939–1994). When Kouyaté related *Sundiata* to an audience, the listeners sat in respectful silence and awe, unlike listeners to folk tales.

BACKGROUND

Sundiata is an **epic,** a long narrative poem relating the actions and accomplishments of a hero. Older epics include *Gilgamesh* of the Babylonians and the *Iliad* and *Odyssey* of the Greeks. Recent works such as Derek Walcott's *Omeros,* which combines the traditions of the *Illiad* and the *Odyssey* with a Caribbean vision, show that the epic is one of the oldest, most enduring literary forms.

Sundiata is probably the best known African epic. Sundiata was a thirteenth-century leader who was founder of the Empire of Mali. The story *Sundiata* exists in many versions in Gambia, Guinea, Burkina Faso, Mali, and Senegal and was passed on orally from generation to generation by a griot, a storyteller obligated to faithfully preserve his peoples' traditions.

Other African epics include that of Askia Mohammed ruler of the Songhay Empire from 1493 to 1528. (It exists in oral tradition in numerous versions, as well as in the written accounts of Arab chroniclers.) The epic of Shaka (1795–1828), founder of the Zulu Empire, has been told by the African poet Mazizi Kunene in *Emperor Shaka the Great* (1979). (Though written, it is based on oral tradition, much of it retained in the author's own family.)

Sundiata, Askia Mohammed, and Shaka are all historical people who have become legendary, so that much of what is related about them in these epics cannot be taken to be "real." The purpose of these epics is not so much to convey factual history as it is to celebrate and instruct. *Sundiata,* for example, would be performed for the king and his attendants before battle as encouragement to bravery and daring. Hearing an epic should make the listener examine his own life and ask if he had done his utmost.

Skills Practice

from Sundiata: An Epic of Old Mali

EPIC HERO CHARACTERISTICS CHART

Fill in the blanks with examples of each characteristic.

Literary Focus
Demonstrate an understanding of an epic hero.

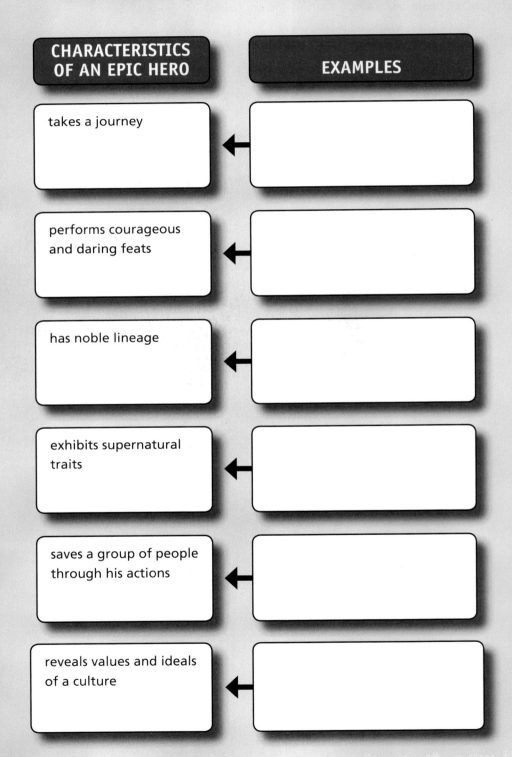

CHARACTERISTICS OF AN EPIC HERO	EXAMPLES
takes a journey	
performs courageous and daring feats	
has noble lineage	
exhibits supernatural traits	
saves a group of people through his actions	
reveals values and ideals of a culture	

from Sundiata: An Epic of Old Mali

VOCABULARY AND COMPREHENSION

WORD BOX
exploits
oblivion
ravenous
insolently
eloquence
grievances
calamity
boisterous

A. Suffixes Fill in the blank with the correct choice from the Word Box. Then identify its part of speech. Not all the words will be used.

1. Soumaoro had no inkling of the ______________ that would befall his city that day. **Part of Speech:** ______________

2. After listing their ______________ with each other, the two kings engaged in battle. **Part of Speech:** ______________

3. The ______________ wind helped to spread the flames through the city. **Part of Speech:** ______________

4. He looked ______________ at Sundiata, hoping to anger the king. **Part of Speech:** ______________

5. If history is not remembered, the past enters into ______________. **Part of Speech:** ______________

6. His ______________ quest for land led him to overextend his army. **Part of Speech:** ______________

B. Reading Comprehension Answer each question below.

7. What is the function of a griot in the Mali culture?

____

____

8. What are some of the comparisons that Soumaoro and Sundiata use when they threaten each other?

____

____

____

____

____

____

Vocabulary Skills
Understand suffixes.

BEFORE YOU READ

African Proverbs

Has someone ever said to you, "Better safe than sorry"? Or "Don't count your chickens before they hatch"? These short, clever expressions are called proverbs. Proverbs exist in all spoken languages around the world and use figurative language to communicate commonly held ideas or beliefs.

LITERARY FOCUS: PROVERB

The word ***proverb*** comes from the Latin *proverbium* (*pro* meaning "in front of, on behalf of" and *verbium* meaning "word"), suggesting that a proverb takes the place of ordinary words. Scholars are often unsure of the origins of proverbs, but believe they were passed down orally within a community to express codes of conduct. Many believe that proverbs containing similar wisdom or lessons exist in all parts of the world.

Proverbs are important in all traditional societies. They offer ideas about wisdom and moral and philosophical instruction reduced to a few carefully crafted words or phrases. For example, "Let the hawk perch and let the eagle perch" is a proverb meaning that different people with different beliefs can coexist peacefully. Because proverbs are short they can be easily memorized, which helps people remember lessons that are important and relevant in daily life. These lessons are then passed from person to person and generation to generation.

READING SKILLS: MAKE CONNECTIONS

When you **make connections,** you see a direct relationship between what is happening in the text and your own experiences. In this selection, you will probably read many items that can apply to your own life.

The way each proverb is written reflects its roots in traditional African culture, with references to animals, drums, and tribal values. However, you can make connections between the wisdom of the proverbs and your own observances and experiences. The references may change, but many of the values stay the same.

As you read these proverbs, make connections between the proverbs and the advice you can apply to your own life.

Literary Focus
Understand proverbs.

Reading Skills
Make connections to text.

African Proverbs

Ashanti (Ghana)

Only when you have crossed the river, can you say the crocodile has a lump on his snout.

One falsehood spoils a thousand truths.

When a man is wealthy, he may wear an old cloth.

Hunger is felt by a slave and hunger is felt by a king.

The ruin of a nation begins in the homes of its people.

When the cock is drunk, he forgets about the hawk.

By the time the fool has learned the game, the players have **dispersed.**

He who cannot dance will say: "The drum is bad."

It is the fool's sheep that break loose twice.

No one tests the depth of a river with both feet.

Buganda (Uganda)

He who hunts two rats, catches none.

When the master is absent, the frogs hop into the house.

INTERPRET

Read the first proverb on this page. Paraphrase what the proverb aims to express.

VOCABULARY

dispersed (di·spurst′) *v.:* broken up; scattered.

INTERPRET

Read the second proverb under Buganda. What does this expression mean to you?

42 proverbs from *African Proverbs,* compiled by Charlotte and Wolf Leslau. Copyright © 1962, 1985 by **Peter Pauper Press, Inc.** Reproduced by permission of the publisher.

Cameroon

By trying often, the monkey learns to jump from the tree.

Knowledge is better than riches.

Tso Elephant Mask from the Cameroon Grasslands (beaded textile), African/ Private Collection.
Photo ©Heini Schneebeli/The Bridgeman Art Library

Ethiopia

He who learns, teaches.

Confiding a secret to an unworthy person is like carrying grain in a bag with a hole.

The fool speaks, the wise man listens.

Advise and counsel him; if he does not listen, let **adversity** teach him.

Kenya

Do not say the first thing that comes to your mind.

Because a man has injured your goat, do not go out and kill his bull.

Absence makes the heart forget.

Home affairs are not talked about on the public square.

Madagascar

Indecision is like the stepchild: if he doesn't wash his hands, he is called dirty; if he does, he is wasting the water.

The end of an ox is beef, and the end of a lie is grief.

Cross the river in a crowd and the crocodile won't eat you.

LITERARY FOCUS

Read the first Cameroonian proverb. Explain its meaning as it relates to humans.

COMPARE & CONTRAST

Read the second Ethiopian proverb. What comparison is it making, both literally and figuratively?

VOCABULARY

adversity (ad·vur'sə·tē) *n.:* a state of hardship or misfortune.

INFER

Read the second Kenyan proverb. What feeling do you suppose the proverb warns against?

Mauritania

One must talk little, and listen much.

If you watch your pot, your food will not burn.

A cutting word is worse than a bowstring: a cut may heal, but the cut of the tongue does not.

Niger

A wise man who knows his proverbs can **reconcile** difficulties.

Ashes fly back into the face of him who throws them.

Nigeria

Fine words do not produce food.

Not to know is bad; not to wish to know is worse.

Senegal

It is better to travel alone than with a bad companion.

To spend the night in anger is better than to spend it in **repentance.**

Traditional story teller reciting tribal legends to young members of the Yaou Village. Côte d'Ivoire (Ivory Coast).
©Marc & Evelyne Bernheim/Woodfin Camp & Associates/IPN

INFER

In the second Mauritania proverb, what does the pot symbolize?

ANALYZE

Read the second Nigeria proverb. Why might not wishing to know be worse?

VOCABULARY

reconcile (rek′ən·sīl′) *v.:* to settle a quarrel.

repentance (ri·pen′təns) *v.:* a feeling of sorrow for wrongdoing.

VOCABULARY

disputed (di·spyo͞ot′id) *v.:* argued; debated.

ANALYZE

What is ironic about the third bird swooping in and stealing the kernel from the other two birds in the second Zairian proverb?

CONNECT

Which proverb is similar to the popular saying "The early bird catches the worm"?

Sierra Leone

To try and to fail, is not laziness.

Somalia

A thief is always under suspicion.

Wisdom does not come overnight.

Tanzania

Do not mend your neighbor's fence before looking to your own.

Zaire

You do not teach the paths of the forest to an old gorilla.

Two birds **disputed** about a kernel, when a third swooped down and carried it off.

To love someone who does not love you, is like shaking a tree to make the dew drops fall.

Zululand (South Africa)

The horse who arrives early gets good drinking water.

BACKGROUND

A well-chosen proverb can have a far more powerful impact than a lot of talk about vague ideas, which is why the Yoruba say, "Proverbs are the horses of words [ideas]. When a word is lost we use a proverb to look for it." Modern African writers such as Chinua Achebe are skillful in using proverbs as a means of conveying the deep reality of the African experience. Some Swahili short stories and novels are built around the essence of a single, unifying proverb. What is especially interesting about this use of proverbs is its suggestion of a movement from the written language back to the oral and the orator, a reminder that African literature may best be described as **lit/orature,** a combination of the two existing traditions.

SKILLS PRACTICE

African Proverbs

MAKE CONNECTIONS CHART

In the chart below, read the African proverb in the left-hand column. In the right-hand column, write how that proverb applies in your own life. The first one is done for you.

PROVERB	APPLICATION TO MY LIFE
One falsehood spoils a thousand truths.	One lie can ruin my reputation or cause people to doubt when I'm telling the truth.
By trying often, the monkey learns to jump from the tree.	
Because a man has injured your goat, do not go out and kill his bull.	
If you watch your pot, your food will not burn.	
Ashes fly back into the face of him who throws them.	

READING COMPREHENSION

Answer each question below.

1. What is a proverb?

____

____

____

2. How can proverbs be useful in everyday life?

____

____

____

Reading Skills
Make connections to proverbs.

BEFORE YOU READ

Spider's Bargain with God

A Tale from Ghana

The Son of Kim-ana-u-eze and the Daughter of the Sun and the Moon

by Julius Lester

Folk tales are stories that are passed from one generation to another through the oral tradition. As you read these selections, think about the terms used in speaking about literature in the oral tradition. The most general term used is **folklore.** Folklore includes **folk tales** and **folk songs.** Many **ballads** are also called folk songs. **Myths** and **legends** are sometimes also included in the category of folk tales.

LITERARY FOCUS: THE TRICKSTER IN FOLK TALES

These selections introduce you to the trickster, an archetypal figure that appears in folklore all over the world. The trickster often takes the form of a mischievous animal. Sometimes, as in the case of Ananse the spider and Mainu the frog, the trickster is a small and weak creature that uses cunning to outwit stronger and larger creatures.

- In "Spider's Bargain with God," Ananse cleverly manipulates creatures around his home to fulfill his goal of having all stories in the world told about him.
- The frog character in "The Son of Kim-ana-u-eze" is very clever, but different from Ananse since he unselfishly helps the son of Kim-ana-u-eze reach his goal of marrying the daughter of the Sun and the Moon. The character of Ananse appears in many folk tales and often is working to achieve only his own goals.

READING SKILLS: INFERRING CULTURAL BELIEFS

Although today folklore is read chiefly for entertainment, in earlier cultures folk tales were considered to be teaching tools. The themes, characters, plots, and other literary elements in folk tales and other forms of folklore were often tied to a people's cultural beliefs.

As you read "Spider's Bargain with God" and "The Son of Kim-ana-u-eze and the Daughter of the Sun and the Moon," consider the cultural beliefs and lessons that these two folk tales represent.

SKILLS FOCUS

Literary Focus
Understand the trickster in folktales.

Reading Skills
Infer cultural beliefs.

Vocabulary Skills
Use context clues.

VOCABULARY DEVELOPMENT

PREVIEW SELECTION VOCABULARY

The following words appear in "Spider's Bargain with God" and "The Son of Kim-ana-u-eze and the Daughter of the Sun and the Moon." Look them over before you begin the selection.

installment (in·stôl′mənt) *n.:* any of the parts of a debt to be paid over time.

*The payment of the debt required that each **installment** be delivered at a certain time.*

transported (trans·pôrt′·ed) *v.:* carried from one place to another over a long distance.

*Each person was **transported** from one place to another by the train headed across the countryside.*

suitor (sōōt′·ər) *n.:* a man who visits a woman over a period of time because he hopes to marry her.

*The **suitor** told the woman that he would like to marry her.*

virtue (vʉr′chōō) *n.:* good quality or feature.

*Kindness to others is considered a **virtue.***

USING CONTEXT CLUES

Context clues can help you understand what you are reading. A word's **context,** or the words, phrases, and sentences that surround it, often provide clues to the word's meaning. Read the sentences below and examine how the italicized context clues help you determine the meaning of the boldface words.

DEFINITION: The **earthenware** pot was *made from clay* that was then fired in a kiln to make it hard.

EXAMPLE: The frog **devoured** several meals at the home of the Lord Sun and Lady Moon which he *ate quickly* when they left the room.

COMPARISON: Ananse's **murmuring** sounded like the *low burble of a stream flowing over rocks.*

CONTRAST: *Instead of being truthful and direct,* Ananse prefers to use **trickery** to get others to do what he wants.

Spider's Bargain with God

A Tale from Ghana

Kwaku Ananse, the spider, went to Sky God Nana Nyamee and asked whether he could buy the stories told about Him so they would be told about Ananse instead. Nana Nyamee said, "Yes, provided you bring me the following things in payment."

Ananse said, "I am willing. Just name them."

Nana Nyamee said, "Bring me a live leopard, a pot full of live bees, and a live python." Ananse was afraid, but nevertheless he agreed to provide them. He went home and sat down and thought and thought.

At last he took a needle and thread, and set out toward the forest where the leopard lived. When he got to the stream where Leopard got his water, he sat down, took out the needle and thread, and sewed his eyelids together. He waited. When he heard the footsteps of Leopard coming to fetch water, he began to sing to himself: "Hmm. Nana Nyamee is wonderful. He sewed my eyes and took me to his palace. Then I began to see wonderful things, and I have been singing of them ever since. Beautiful women, palaces, rich and delicious food, and a wonderful life."

Leopard came up to him and asked Ananse, "What were you singing about?"

He replied, "Hmm. Nana Nyamee is wonderful. He sewed my eyes and took me to his palace. Then I began to see wonderful things, and I have been singing of them ever since. Beautiful women, palaces, rich and delicious food, and a wonderful life."

Leopard said, "Eh, Ananse, what is it, are you dreaming?"

"No," said Ananse, "there is a beautiful woman here."

Leopard said, "Please Ananse, sew my eyes shut, too, and lead me to Nana Nyamee so that I, too, may see all the wonderful things."

LITERARY FOCUS

The rivalry between Ananse and the Sky God appears in many folk tales. Why might Ananse want to buy the stories of the Sky God? What do his actions show about his character?

INFER

What can you infer about how Ananse intends to make the payments to Nana Nyamee when it says on lines 8–9 that he "sat down and thought and thought."

"No, I know you, Leopard, when you see her and all those other beautiful creatures you will kill them and eat them up."

"No, No, No," Leopard growled. "I shall not. Rather, I shall thank you."

Ananse took his needle and thread and sewed Leopard's eyes and led him to Nana Nyamee's palace. He said, "Nana Nyamee, here is the first **installment.** Keep it."

Next day Ananse took an earthenware pot and went to a place where he knew there were honey bees. As he came near the place he sang, "Oh bees! Oh bees!"

The bees said, "Ananse, what is all this murmuring about?"

Ananse replied, "I have had an argument with Nana Nyamee. He says all of you together won't fill this pot, but I say you will, and so I came to find out."

They said, "Oho, that is easy," and they flew into the pot, buzz, buzz, buzz, until the pot was full, and every bee had flown into it. Then Ananse quickly sealed the pot and carried it off to Nana Nyamee as his second installment.

For two days he could not think how to get the third—a live python. But at last he hit on a plan.[1] He went to the forest and cut a long stick, a stick as long as a tree. He carried this off to the forest, singing to himself, "I am right, he is wrong! He is wrong, I am right."

When Python saw him he said, "Ananse, what are you grumbling about?"

He answered, "How lucky I am to meet you here. I have had a long and bitter argument with Nana Nyamee. I have known you for a long time, and I know your measurements both when you are coiled, and when you are fully stretched out. Nana Nyamee thinks very little of you. He thinks you are only a little longer than the green mamba, and no longer than the cobra.

1. **hit on a plan:** to decide or find a plan that works.

VOCABULARY

installment (in·stôl′mənt) *n.:* any of the parts of a debt to be paid over time.

GENERALIZE

What human attributes do Ananse, Leopard, and the bees exhibit?

COMPARE & CONTRAST

What are the similarities and differences in the tricks that Ananse uses with the Leopard and the bees?

NOTES

DRAW CONCLUSIONS

Why does Python become angry in line 64?

Linguist staff with spider. Gold foil, wood, nails. African, Ghana: Asante group, Akan peoples. 19th–20th Century.
The Metropolitan Museum of Art. Gift of the Richard J. Faletti Family, 1986. (1986.475a–c)

I strongly disagree with him, and to prove my point I brought this pole to measure you."

Python was very angry, and he began stretching himself out to his greatest length along the stick.

And Ananse said, "You are moving! You are moving! Let me tie you to the stick so I can get the measurement exactly right."

And Python agreed. As Ananse tied Python up he sang a little song, and when he had Python securely fastened to the stick, Ananse carried him off to Nana Nyamee.

Nana Nyamee was very pleased with Ananse and forthwith beat the gong[2] throughout the world that all stories should be told about Ananse.

This is how Ananse became the leading figure in all Ananse stories.

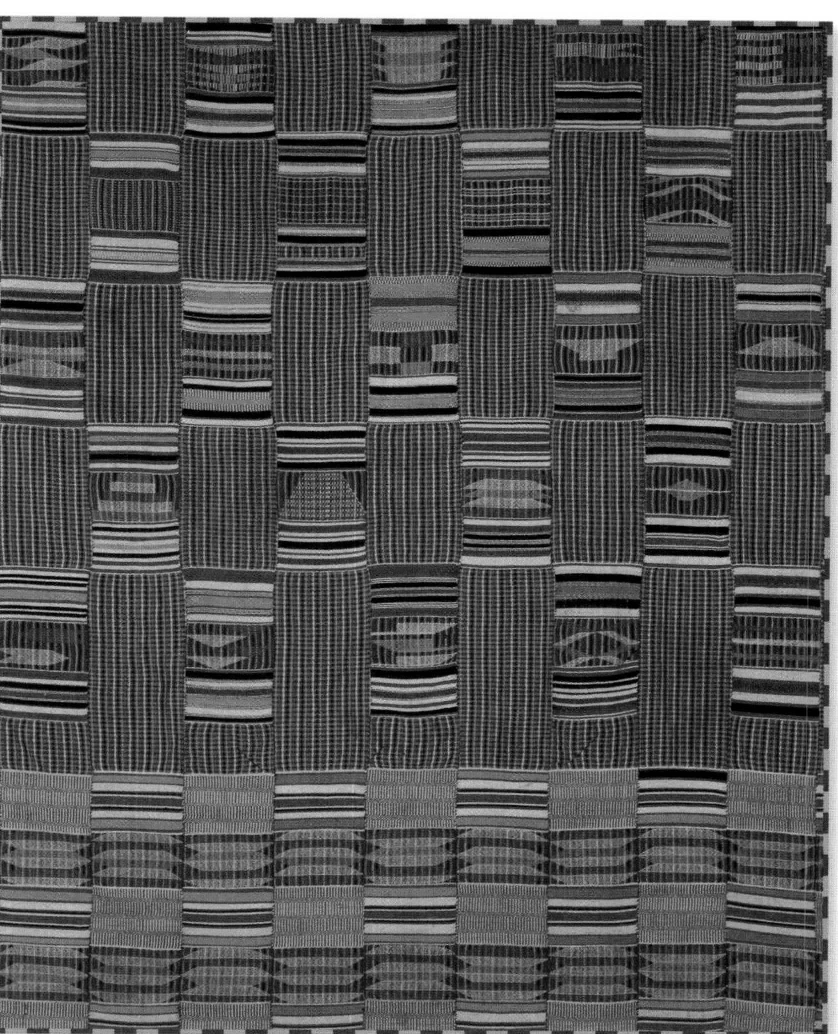

Kente Cloth, 20th c. Asante People, Ghana. 85 x 125 in.
Collection of The Newark Museum, Gift of Dr. Israel Samuelly and Michaela Samuelly, MD, 1993. Inv. 93.262. The Newark Museum, Newark, New Jersey, U.S.A. Photo Credit: The Newark Museum/Art Resource, NY

INFER

In line 14 of the story Ananse is singing. Here, in line 68 Ananse is also singing. For what reasons is he singing in each instance?

2. **beat the gong:** meaning to tell or spread the word

CLARIFY

In lines 14–15, what does the father mean when he says "it was his misfortune to have fathered such a son"?

INFER

What can you infer about the character of the son from lines 16–19?

The Son of Kim-ana-u-eze and the Daughter of the Sun and the Moon

by Julius Lester

When the son of Kim-ana-u-eze came to the age to marry, his father came to him and said, "Have you decided whom among the young girls of the village you wish to marry?"

"I will marry none of them, father."

"Then you love a girl of another village?"

"No. I will not marry any girl of this earth."

"Then whom will you marry?"

"I will marry the daughter of the Sun and the Moon."

The father looked at his son in amazement. "You have always been more of a dreamer than the other children, but this is ridiculous. No one can marry the daughter of the Sun and the Moon."

"But that is whom I want to marry, father."

And the father left him, wondering why it was his misfortune to have fathered such a son.

The son of Kim-ana-u-eze sat down and wrote a letter, asking Lord Sun and Lady Moon for permission to marry[1] their daughter. He gave it to the Deer and asked him to take it to Heaven. "But I cannot go to the sky," said the Deer.

He gave the letter to the Gazelle. "But I cannot go to the sky," was the answer.

He gave the letter to the Hawk. "You are the most magnificent of birds, Hawk. Surely you can fly to the sky."

"I can only go halfway," the Hawk told him. "Further than that is even too far for me."

1. **permission to marry:** in some cultures it is the custom for a man to ask the parents of a woman if he can marry her.

The son of Kim-ana-u-eze received the same answer from all of the animals he thought could deliver the letter. He was about to give up ever getting his letter to Lord Sun and Lady Moon when the Frog heard of his problem and went to him. He alone of the animals knew that the people of Lord Sun and Lady Moon came to earth each day to get water. "Give me your letter and I will deliver it, son of Kim-ana-u-eze."

Kim-ana-u-eze became angry. "I am in no mood for jokes, Frog. It is mean of you to come and make fun of me."

"I do not make fun of you. Give me the letter. I will deliver it."

"You are a frog. How can you deliver what the Hawk with his mighty wings cannot deliver?"

"Strength is not necessarily the answer for every task."

The son of Kim-ana-u-eze was impressed with this answer, and he gave the letter to the Frog. "But if you are seeking to make a fool of me," he warned, "you will be very unhappy."

"You will see."

The Frog went to the well where the people of Lord Sun and Lady Moon came to get water. He jumped down the well and waited. After a while, the people of Lord Sun and Lady Moon came. They put a pitcher into the water, and Frog swam into the pitcher. They took the pitcher from the well filled with water, not realizing that Frog was at the bottom. They returned to the Palace of Lord Sun and Lady Moon in the sky. There, they went into a room, placed the pitcher in a corner, and left.

Frog leaped out of the pitcher, and, looking around the room, he saw a table, placed the letter on it, then hid in the corner. Shortly, the Lord of the Sun came into the room and saw the letter on the table. He called his people and asked, "Where did this letter come from?"

"We do not know," they said.

He opened the letter and read it: "I, the son of Na Kim-ana-u-eze Kia Tumb'a Ndala, a man of earth, want to marry the daughter of Lord Sun and Lady Moon." Lord Sun put the

INFER

What can you infer about the character of the son of Kim-ana-u-eze from lines 27–29?

DRAW CONCLUSIONS

Re-read lines 33–38. Why doesn't the son of Kim-ana-u-eze trust Frog to deliver his letter?

LITERARY FOCUS

How do you know that Frog is the trickster in this folk tale?

VOCABULARY

transported (trans·pôrt′·ed) *v.:* carried from one place to another over a long distance.

FLUENCY

Read the boxed passage aloud, first alone and then with a partner. Use your voice to express the emotions that both Frog and the son are feeling as they speak.

INTERPRET

What do you think of the son's statement in lines 79–80? Is this a threat? How does Frog react?

letter away and told no one of its contents,[2] for he could not understand how a man of the earth had delivered a letter to him.

Frog leaped back in the jug, and, when it was emptied, the water girls returned to the earth to refill it. When they arrived at the well, Frog leaped quietly out and hid until the water girls returned to the sky.

Many days passed, and the son of Kim-ana-u-eze heard nothing from Frog. So he went to look for him. "Did you deliver my letter?"

"I did," Frog said, "but they sent no answer in return."

"You lie! You did not go! I knew you would deceive me!"

Frog was afraid. "Trust me. Perhaps the Lord of the Sun will respond to your next letter."

The son of Kim-ana-u-eze left Frog in anger. Six days passed before he decided he would give Frog one more chance, and he wrote another letter: "I wrote you, Lord Sun and Lady Moon. My letter was delivered, but you did not answer. You did not tell me whether you accept me or reject me." He went to Frog and gave him the letter. "I hope, for your sake, you return with an answer this time."

Frog went to the well, waited, and when the water girls came, he leaped into the jug and was thus **transported** to the sky where Lord Sun and Lady Moon lived. Once in the palace, he hid in the jug until the room was empty. Then he leaped out, placed the letter on the table, and returned to the corner.

Soon the Lord of the Sun passed through the room and saw the letter on the table. He opened it and read its contents.[2] He called the water girls. "Are you carrying letters when you go to get the water?"

"Oh, no," they told him.

2. **its contents:** the material or subject matter of a written text, such as a letter.

Lord Sun did not know whether he should believe them, but they had never given him the slightest cause to doubt their trustworthiness. So he decided to write a reply. "You may marry my daughter if you come with your first present. I wish to know you." He folded the letter and placed it on the table. Then he left the room.

Frog leaped to the table, got the letter, and leaped back into the jug. Shortly, someone came into the room and emptied the pitcher, and the water girls lifted it up and brought it back to earth.

Man talking to a frog by Tom Feelings, from *Black Folktales* by Julius Lester, Grove Press, 1991, with special permission of Kamili Feelings and the estate of Tom Feelings.

ANALYZE

Pause at line 96. What did the Lord Sun expect would happen with his letter?

WORD STUDY

The word *pitcher* in line 99 means "a vessel with a handle and lip that is used for liquids." What other meaning do you know for the word *pitcher*?

NOTES

VOCABULARY

suitor (so͞ot′·ər) *n.:* a man who visits a woman over a period of time because he hopes to marry her.

CONNECT

Parallelism is the use of words, phrases, clauses, or sentences that are similar in structure or in meaning. Parallelism is often found in texts handed down in the oral tradition. What is an example of parallelism on this page?

ANALYZE

The Lord Sun states in lines 94–95 that he wishes to know his daughter's suitor. Is this consistent with what is happening on this page? Why or why not?

Frog waited until evening and then took the letter to the son of Kim-ana-u-eze. "Who is it?" the son of Kim-ana-u-eze asked when he heard a knock at his door.

"It is I. Mainu, the frog."

"Come in."

Frog went in, gave him the letter, and left. The son of Kim-ana-u-eze opened the letter, and what he read made him happy. He took forty gold coins from his purse and wrote: "I have brought the first present. I await your word as to what you would find worthy of a wooing present.[3]" The son of Kim-ana-u-eze put the forty gold coins into a small pouch, sealed the letter, and waited until morning to give them to Frog.

Frog returned to the well, waited until the water girls came, and returned with them to the sky, hidden in the bottom of the water pitcher. They placed the pitcher in the corner, left the room, and Frog placed the letter and the pouch of money on the table and hid in the corner.

Soon Lord Sun came into the room, and when he read the letter and examined the gold coins, he was pleased. He looked all around the room for the one who had brought it, but saw no one. He smiled to himself, admiring the cleverness of his daughter's **suitor.** Lord Sun called Lady Moon, and when he showed her what their daughter's suitor had written and sent as a first present, she, too, was pleased. Lady Moon ordered a young hen to be cooked, so that he who sought their daughter would have something to eat. It was soon ready and was placed on the table. When the room was empty, Frog came out of the corner, ate the young hen, and returned to the corner.

Several hours later, Lord Sun came into the room and was pleased that the hen had been devoured, though he still had not seen who had devoured it. He sat down at the table and wrote

3. **wooing present:** a present given by someone who is wooing, or seeking the affection of another.

another letter: "Your present was received. The amount of your wooing present shall be a sack of gold coins." He sealed the letter, placed it on the table, and left the room. Frog came out of the corner, took the letter, and leaped in the jug and went to sleep.

The next morning, the water girls came into the room, lifted the jug, and took it to earth. Frog waited until evening and then went to the home of the son of Kim-ana-u-eze, gave him the letter, and departed.

The son of Kim-ana-u-eze read the letter and was pleased. Six days later he had gathered the sack of gold coins. "Here is the wooing present," he wrote. "Soon I will tell you on what day I will bring my wife to my home." He called Frog and gave him the letter and the sack of gold.

Frog went to the well, and soon he was in the pitcher of Lord Sun and Lady Moon being carried to the sky by the water girls. Once again, he waited until the room was empty and placed the letter and the sack of gold coins on the table.

Before long, Lord Sun came into the room and saw the letter and the sack of gold. He read the letter, examined the gold, and was pleased. He called Lady Moon, and she, too, was pleased. She ordered a young pig roasted for her daughter's husband-to-be. When it was ready, it was placed on the table. When the room was empty, Frog came out of the corner and ate it. Then he got back in the jug and went to sleep.

The next morning, the water girls returned to earth with the pitcher, Frog hiding quietly inside. That evening, he went to the home of the son of Kim-ana-u-eze and told him all that had happened. "Now you must choose the day when you wish to bring your bride home."

For twelve days, the son of Kim-ana-u-eze tried to find one of the animals who could go to the sky and bring his bride home. None of them could. The son of Kim-ana-u-eze went to Frog and told him. "There is nothing I can do, Frog."

"Leave it to me," Frog said.

COMPARE & CONTRAST

How is the attitude of the son of Kim-ana-u-eze different now from his attitude in lines 27–29?

“You have done much, Frog, and I thank you. But you cannot bring my bride home. You are too small.”

“Strength is not the only **virtue,** son of Kim-ana-u-eze.”

Frog went to the well and returned to the home of Lord Sun and Lady Moon as he had done many times before. He hid in the corner of the room until evening. When all was quiet, he quickly made his way through the palace until he came to the room where the daughter of the Sun and the Moon was sleeping. There he took out her eyes and tied them in a handkerchief. Then he went back to his corner and went to sleep.

The next morning, the Lord of the Sun was troubled when his daughter did not come to breakfast. He went to her room to see if she were ill.

“I cannot get up, father. I cannot see.”

Lord Sun called Lady Moon, and they could not understand what was the matter. The day before, their daughter’s eyes had sparkled like the night sky. Lord Sun called three messengers to him. “Go to Ngombo, the witch doctor, and tell him what has happened, and ask what we should do.”

Before evening, they returned and said, “Ngombo said that she is not yet married. He whom she is to marry has put a spell upon her and said that if she does not come to him, she will die.”

Lord Sun listened closely, and then he ordered everyone to get his daughter ready to meet her husband, and, come the morning, the messengers would take her to earth.

The next morning, Frog returned to earth in the pitcher of the water girls, and after they returned, he waited beside the well. That evening, the messengers descended to earth, the daughter of the Sun and the Moon with them. They left her beside the well and returned to the sky.

Frog returned the girl’s eyes and led her to the house of the son of Kim-ana-u-eze. And thus the son of Kim-ana-u-eze married the daughter of the Sun and Moon, and, while they lived, they lived happily.

VOCABULARY

virtue (vʉr′cho͞o) *n.:* good quality or feature.

PREDICT

In lines 165–166, the son of Kim-ana-u-eze says that Frog is too small to bring his bride home. Do you agree or disagree? Why?

CONNECT

Do you agree with Frog that strength is not the only virtue? Give an example to support your answer.

MEET THE WRITER

Julius Lester (1939–) has excelled in many fields: civil rights activist, musician, photographer, teacher, poet, novelist, and folklorist. He has written books for children and young adults. *The Long Journey Home: Stories from Black History* (1972) was a finalist for the National Book Award. Lester says, "Tales touch the best in us, and when we participate in a tale as teller and listener, we touch and share the best in each other."

BACKGROUND

Most African folk tales involve animal characters. The best known of these are Ananse the Spider, Tortoise, Elephant, Monkey, and Hare. So popular are these characters that one researcher collected more than two hundred stories dealing with Tortoise in Nigeria alone.

These animal tales traveled from Africa as oral stories that enslaved people carried with them on the Middle Passage, the route across the Atlantic from West Africa to the West Indies and America. Ananse became established as the main figure in Caribbean folklore. But in the United States, Hare, otherwise known as Brer Rabbit, is the central character in black folk tales. Monkey inhabits both regions, making mischief in Caribbean folklore as well as in the Signifying Monkey stories of the black oral tradition of the United States.

Among the Yoruba, the narrator of a folk tale first asks his audience several riddles that serve as an introduction. Then there will be a short dialogue between the narrator and audience and the story itself will be introduced: "My story is about the tortoise and his in-law the snail. Once upon a time. . . . " During the actual telling of the tale, there will be a song or two in which the narrator functions as soloist and the audience acts as the chorus in a call and response pattern. The tale ends with a closing formula to stress the moral, since these stories almost always have a particular lesson.

DRAW CONCLUSIONS

What are the lessons taught through this folk tale?

CONNECT

List other folk tales with which you are familiar that are related to the African tradition.

EXTEND

Write your own trickster tale using both the frog and the spider as characters. Try to show how these two unique characters would interact. Would they cooperate? Would they argue?

Spider's Bargain with God and The Son of Kim-ana-u-eze and the Daughter of the Sun and the Moon

Literary Focus Analyze the trickster characters in these folk tales.

TRICKSTER CHART

One way to decide the lessons in a folk tale is to think about the actions of the characters—in this case the trickster characters. Fill in the following chart for the two folk tales and then write a statement about the lessons you think you could apply to your life.

"SPIDERS BARGAIN WITH GOD"	"THE SON OF KIM-ANA-U-EZE"
What tricks did Spider use to achieve his goals?	What tricks did Frog use to achieve his goals?
What lessons might be learned from Spider's actions?	What lessons might be learned from Frog's actions?
What lessons from these folk tales might you apply to your own life?	

Spider's Bargain with God and

The Son of Kim-ana-u-eze and the Daughter of the Sun and the Moon

VOCABULARY AND COMPREHENSION

WORD BOX

virtues

suitor

installment

transported

A. Context Clues For each item below, fill in the blank with the appropriate word from the Word Box. Use the underlined context clues to help you.

1. Ananse needed to pay to Nana Nyamee over time, or in ________________ for the stories he wanted to buy.

2. Ananse ____________________ the python to Nana Nyamee by convincing Python to let Ananse tie him to a stick which made it easy to carry him.

3. Kim-ana-u-eze felt it was his misfortune to have a son who wanted to be a ____________________ to the daughter of the Sun and Moon in hopes of marrying her.

4. Frog seemed to think that strength was like a daisy among the many varieties of flowers possible in the garden, only one of many ____________ .

B. Reading Comprehension Answer the question below.

5. In the past folk tales were used as teaching tools. What media are used as teaching tools today? Are these tools effective?

____

____

____

____

____

____

____

____

Vocabulary Skills
Use context clues.

BEFORE YOU READ

from The Interesting Narrative of the Life of Olaudah Equiano
by Olaudah Equiano

Olaudah Equiano was kidnapped from his village and sold into slavery when he was about eleven years old. He was later able to purchase his freedom and eventually became an abolitionist. This excerpt is from his autobiography published in 1789.

In this excerpt from Chapter 2 of his *Narrative,* Olaudah Equiano describes arriving on the West African coast, where he is sold to European slave traders. He goes on to describe the horrors of the Middle Passage—the trade route that brought African captives across the Atlantic Ocean to be sold into slavery in the Americas.

LITERARY FOCUS: SLAVE NARRATIVE

An **autobiography** is a person's account of his or her own life. A **slave narrative** is an autobiographical account of a person who has experienced life under slavery. Olaudah Equiano pioneered the slave narrative as an important literary form, a strategic tool in publicizing the cruelties of slavery and rallying support for abolition, and a means to give voice to unheard victims of slavery. It is often a tale of emotional, spiritual, and physical endurance. Equiano's *Narrative* is characterized by vivid, flowing prose and a direct, unaffected style.

In a slave narrative, the narrator typically describes how he or she came to be enslaved and eventually attained freedom. For example, Equiano begins his *Narrative* by telling the reader about his African origins in present-day Nigeria, describing the daily life and customs among the people of his Igbo (or Ibo) village. He then recounts his capture by African raiders, his period of enslavement in Africa and the Americas, and purchasing his freedom ten years later.

READING SKILLS: FOLLOWING A SEQUENCE OF EVENTS

Think about how you might give a firsthand account of something you have witnessed or experienced. You would probably narrate the story following a **sequence of events** and include important details. Keeping track of the chronological order of events in a narrative can help you understand what you read.

As you read this excerpt from Equiano's *Narrative,* pay attention to the sequence of events and the descriptions of each event.

SKILLS FOCUS

Literary Focus Understand the characteristics of a slave narrative.

Reading Skills Follow a sequence of events.

Vocabulary Skills Understand synonyms.

VOCABULARY DEVELOPMENT

PREVIEW SELECTION VOCABULARY

The following words appear in Equiano's *Narrative.* Look them over before you begin the selection.

reviving (ri·vīv′iŋ) *v.:* bringing back to a healthy condition.

After fainting, the fresh air was ***reviving*** *him.*

consternation (kän′stər·nā′shən) *n.:* great fear or bewilderment.

His unfamiliar surroundings caused ***consternation.***

deprived (dē·prīvd′) *v.:* prevented from having.

The captives aboard the ship were ***deprived*** *of basic human rights.*

loathsomeness (lōth′səm·nəs) *n.:* disgusting state.

The ***loathsomeness*** *of the ship's interior made the passengers sick.*

pestilential (pes′tə·len′shəl) *adj.:* infectious, harmful, or deadly.

The filthy conditions were ***pestilential.***

improvident (im·präv′ə·dənt) *adj.:* lacking foresight.

The ***improvident*** *merchants should have realized the deadliness of the conditions.*

avarice (av′ə·ris) *n.:* greed for wealth.

The slave traders' ***avarice*** *led them to crowd the ship in an effort to maximize profits.*

rendered (ren′dərd) *v.:* caused to become.

The lack of ventilation ***rendered*** *the odor extremely unpleasant.*

UNDERSTANDING SYNONYMS

A **synonym** is a word that has the same meaning or close to the same meaning as another word. If you aren't satisfied with a word in your writing, try looking up its synonym. A **thesaurus** is a useful tool for finding synonyms. However, you must be careful to choose the synonym that is appropriate to its context. Look at all the choices given and follow the cross-references until you find the best synonym.

Not all words have synonyms, but try to remember the ones you discover when you read or when you look up the meaning of an unfamiliar word.

INFER

What does the word *cargo* refer to in line 3?

INTERPRET

Re-read lines 3–6. What was Equiano at a loss to describe and why?

WORD STUDY

The word *sound* has different meanings. What meaning (or meanings) does it have in line 7? Give several synonyms.

CLARIFY

What three different groups of people are on the ship?

from The Interesting Narrative of the Life of Olaudah Equiano

by Olaudah Equiano

The first object that saluted[1] my eyes when I arrived on the coast was the sea, and a slave ship, which was then riding at anchor, and waiting for its cargo. These filled me with astonishment, that was soon converted into terror, which I am yet at a loss to describe, and much more the then feelings of my mind when I was carried on board. I was immediately handled and tossed up to see if I was sound, by some of the crew; and I was now persuaded that I had got into a world of bad spirits, and that they were going to kill me. Their complexions too, differing so much from ours, their long hair, and the language they spoke, which was very different from any I had ever heard, united to confirm me in this belief. Indeed such were the horrors of my views and fears at the moment, that if ten thousand worlds had been my own, I would have freely parted with them all to have exchanged my condition with the meanest slave in my own country. When I looked round the ship too, and saw a large furnace or copper boiling and a multitude of black people, of every description, chained together, every one of their countenances expressing dejection and sorrow, I no longer doubted of my fate; and, quite overpowered with horror and anguish, I fell motionless on the deck, and fainted. When I recovered a little, I found some black people about me, who I believed were some of those who brought me on board, and had been receiving their pay: they talked to me in order to cheer me, but all in vain. I asked them if we were not to be eaten by those white men with horrible

1. **saluted** (sə·lo͞ot′ed) *v.:* here, met.

looks, red faces, and long hair. They told me I was not: and one of the crew brought me a small portion of spirituous[2] liquor in a wine glass; but, being afraid of him, I would not take it out of his hand. One of the blacks therefore took it from him and gave it to me, and I took a little down my palate, which, instead of **reviving** me, as they thought it would, threw me into the greatest **consternation** at the strange feeling it produced, having never tasted any such liquor before.

Soon after this the blacks who brought me on board went off, and left me abandoned to despair. I now saw myself **deprived** of all chance of returning to my native country, or even the least glimpse of gaining the shore, which I now considered as friendly; and I even wished for my former slavery, in preference to my present situation, which was filled with horrors of every kind, still heightened by my ignorance of what I was to undergo. I was not long suffered to indulge my grief. I was soon put down under the decks, and there I received such a salutation to my nostrils as I had never experienced in my life; so that, with the **loathsomeness** of the stench, and with my crying together, I became so sick and low that I was not able to eat, nor had I the least desire to taste any thing. I now wished for the last friend, death, to relieve me; but soon, to my grief, two of the white men offered me eatables; and, on my refusing to eat, one of them held me fast by the hands, and laid me across, I think, the windlass,[3] and tied my feet, while the other flogged me severely. I had never experienced any thing of this kind before, and although, not being used to the water, I naturally feared that element the first time I saw it, yet nevertheless, could I have got over the nettings, I would have jumped over the side, but I could not; and besides the crew used to watch us very closely, who were not chained down to the decks, lest we should leap into the

VOCABULARY

reviving (ri·vīv′iŋ) *v.:* bringing back to a healthy condition.

consternation (kän′stər·nāshən) *n.:* great fear or bewilderment.

deprived (dē·prīvd′) *v.:* prevented from having.

loathsomeness (lōth′səm·nəs) *n.*: disgusting state.

PREDICT

What does Equiano hint about his future in line 40?

COMPARE & CONTRAST

Notice how Equiano compares death to a friend in lines 46–47. How does this metaphor add meaning?

2. **spirituous** (spir′i·cho͞o·əs) *adj.:* containing alcohol.
3. **windlass** (wind′ləs) *n.:* a device for raising something such as an anchor.

INFER

Why would the crew whip the captives for not eating?

SUMMARIZE

What two developments helped improved Equiano's mood?

LITERARY FOCUS

Why do you think Equiano includes the description of the white man's beating in his description of his captor's "brutal cruelty"?

water. I have seen some of these poor African prisoners most severely cut for attempting to do so, and hourly whipped for not eating. This indeed was often the case with myself. In a little time after, amongst the poor chained men, I found some of my own nation,[4] which in a small degree gave ease to my mind. I inquired of these what was to be done with us. They gave me to understand we were to be carried to these white people's country to work for them. I was then a little revived, and thought if it were no worse than working, my situation was not so desperate. But still I feared I should be put to death, the white people looked and acted, as I thought, in so savage a manner; for I had never seen among any people such instances of brutal cruelty: and this is not only shewn[5] towards us blacks, but also to some of the whites themselves. One white man in particular I saw, when we were permitted to be on deck, flogged so unmercifully with a large rope near the foremast, that he died in consequence of it; and they tossed him over the side as they would have done a brute. This made me fear these people the more; and I expected nothing less than to be treated in the same manner. I could not help expressing my fearful apprehensions to some of my countrymen; I asked them if these people had no country, but lived in this hollow place, the ship. They told me they did not, but came from a distant one. "Then," said I, "how comes it, that in all our country we never heard of them?" They told me, because they lived so very far off. I then asked, where their women were: had they any like themselves. I was told they had. "And why," said I, "do we not see them?" They answered, because they were left behind. I asked how the vessel could go. They told me they could not tell; but that there was cloth put upon the masts by the help of the ropes I saw, and then the vessel went on; and the white men had some spell or magic they put in the water,

4. **some . . . nation:** Igbo (or Ibo) people.
5. **shewn** (shōn) *v.:* shown.

when they liked, in order to stop the vessel. I was exceedingly amazed at this account, and really thought they were spirits. I therefore wished much to be from amongst them, for I expected they would sacrifice me; but my wishes were in vain, for we were so quartered that it was impossible for any of us to make our escape.

While we stayed on the coast I was mostly on deck; and one day, to my great astonishment, I saw one of these vessels coming in with the sails up. As soon as the whites saw it, they gave a great shout, as which we were amazed; and the more so as the vessel appeared larger by approaching nearer. At last she came to an anchor in my sight, and when the anchor was let go, I and my countrymen who saw it, were lost in astonishment to observe the vessel stop, and were now convinced it was done by magic. Soon after this the other ship got her boats out, and they came on board of us, and the people of both ships seemed very glad to see each other. Several of the strangers also shook hands with us black people, and made motions with their hands,

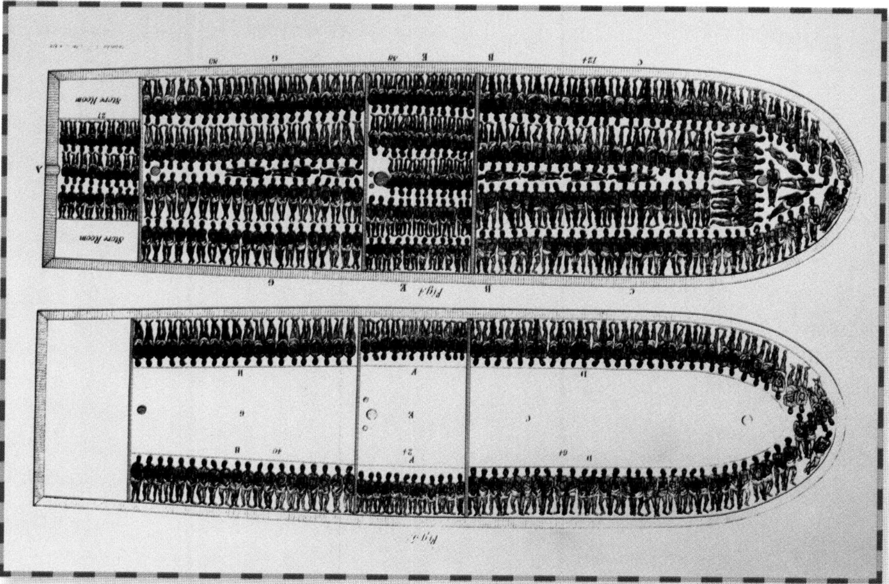

Plan of a slave ship's hold carrying enslaved Africans.

©Louie Psihoyos/CORBIS

ANALYZE

Re-read lines 93–102. What do you learn about the narrator based on his description of the ship?

SEQUENCE

In lines 94–102, underline words or phrases that indicate the sequence of events.

NOTES

signifying, I suppose, we were to go to their country; but we did not understand them. At last, when the ship, in which we were, had got in all her cargo, they made ready with many fearful noises, and we were all put under deck, so that we could not see how they managed the vessel.

But this disappointment was the least of my grief. The stench of the hold,[6] while we were on the coast, was so intolerably loathsome, that it was dangerous to remain there for any time, and some of us had been permitted to stay on the deck for the fresh air; but now that the whole ship's cargo were confined together, it became absolutely **pestilential.** The closeness of the place, and the heat of the climate, added to the number in the ship, being so crowded that each had scarcely room to turn himself, almost suffocated us. This produced copious perspirations, so that the air soon became unfit for respiration, from a variety of loathsome smells, and brought on a sickness among the slaves, of which many died, thus falling victims to the **improvident avarice,** as I may call it, of their purchasers. This deplorable situation was again aggravated by the galling[7] of the chains, now become insupportable; and the filth of necessary tubs,[8] into which the children often fell, and were almost suffocated. The shrieks of the women, and the groans of the dying, **rendered** it a scene of horror almost inconceivable.

6. hold (hōld) *n.:* the interior below the decks of a ship.
7. galling (gôl'iŋ) *adj.:* chafing or irritation.
8. necessary tubs: containers used as toilets.

VOCABULARY

pestilential (pes'tə·len'shəl) *adj.:* infectious, harmful, or deadly.

improvident (im·präv'ə·dənt) *adj.:* lacking foresight.

avarice (av'ə·ris) *n.:* greed for wealth.

rendered (ren'dərd) *v.:* caused to become.

INFER

Re-read lines 103–110. Why did the people from the other ship come aboard?

PARAPHRASE

Rewrite Equiano's description of the ship's hold in your own words.

Olaudah Equiano alias Gustavus Vassa, a slave, 1789 (mezzotint).
British Library, London, UK
©British Library Board. All Rights Reserved/ The Bridgeman Art Library International

MEET THE WRITER

Olaudah Equiano (1745–1797) wrote the first great black autobiography. *The Interesting Narrative of the Life of Olaudah Equiano, or Gustavus Vassa, the African, Written by Himself,* published in England in 1789, quickly became an international bestseller. Equiano tells how he grew up in Africa where, at eleven, he was kidnapped by traders and sold into slavery. He was shipped to Barbados in the West Indies, and his famous, detailed account of that voyage is a gripping and horrifying description of the slave trade in all its dehumanizing brutality.

From Barbados, he was taken to a Virginia plantation and later purchased by a British naval officer and given the name Gustavus Vassa. He served in the Seven Years' War, but instead of being freed, as promised, he was sold again. Equiano finally bought his freedom at age twenty-one. He then worked as a sailor and led an exciting and adventurous life, even traveling to the Arctic. He settled in England and actively supported the antislavery movement.

Scholar Vincent Carretta has raised doubts about Equiano's African origin in such works as *Equiano, the African: Biography of a Self Made Man* (University of Georgia Press, 2005). This Web site—http://www.brycchancarey.com/equiano/nativity.htm—presents both sides to the argument of whether Equiano was born in Africa or in South Carolina. In any event, Carretta maintains that the *Narrative* is "a great read, whether one approaches it as a slave narrative, spiritual autobiography . . . account of a self-made man, or adventure tale."

from The Interesting Narrative of the Life of Olaudah Equiano

Literary Focus Analyze the characteristics of a slave narrative.

Reading Skills Follow a sequence of events.

NARRATIVE CHART

The chart below lists events described by the narrator. For each event, add descriptive details from the excerpt.

EVENT	DESCRIPTION
Equiano arrives at the coast and is brought aboard a ship.	
Equiano faints on the deck.	
Equiano is beaten for refusing to eat.	
Equiano witnesses the murder of a white man on the ship.	
Another ship anchors alongside the slave ship to bring aboard more captives.	
All of the captives are forced into the ship's hold.	

from The Interesting Narrative of the Life of Olaudah Equiano

VOCABULARY AND COMPREHENSION

WORD BOX

unbearable
deplorable
copious
countenances

A. Synonyms For each item below, choose the best synonym from the word box to replace the underlined word.

1. Many fainted as a result of the intolerable heat.
   Synonym: ______________________

2. Each of the captives' faces expressed apprehension and fear.
   Synonym: ______________________

3. The gash on his head from the beating resulted in profuse bleeding.
   Synonym: ______________________

4. The awful state of disrepair in the building angered the tenants.
   Synonym: ______________________

B. Reading Comprehension Answer each question below.

5. How are the captives aboard the ship punished?
   ____
   ____

6. Why is Equiano slightly relieved after speaking with his countrymen?
   ____
   ____

7. Is this excerpt from Equiano's *Narrative* a compelling argument against the slave trade? Why or why not? Include details from the excerpt to support your answer.
   ____
   ____
   ____
   ____
   ____
   ____

Vocabulary Skills
Understand synonyms.

BEFORE YOU READ

from Omeros
by Derek Walcott

In "Omeros," author Derek Walcott has used the Greek version of Homer's name, *Omeros,* as the title of his epic, which reimagines the stories of the Greek epics in a Caribbean setting.

LITERARY FOCUS: EPIC

Centuries ago, the **epic** was an important way of telling stories and recounting history. Long, narrative, and sometimes exaggerated tales of heroic acts done by ancestors were repeated and orally passed down from one generation to the next to preserve their memory. Many ancient peoples could not read or write, so the spoken word was important to the survival of myth and legend, as well as fact.

Two of the most famous epic poems are the *Iliad* and the *Odyssey,* which were written by a Greek poet named Homer in the eighth century B.C. In this excerpt, Derek Walcott's character Achille hears about his African forbears who suffered through the horrendous voyage called the Middle Passage. It was this voyage that forced them into slavery in the West Indies—the new home to Achille.

READING SKILLS: PARAPHRASE

When you **paraphrase,** you restate a text or passage in another form but with the same meaning. Paraphrasing is different from summarizing, although both skills require that you restate ideas in your own words to aid in comprehension. When you summarize, you include only the most important ideas. When you paraphrase, you include all the information. For both, the connotation of the passage remains the same. As you read *Omeros*, paraphrase the speaker's description of the voyage to the Caribbean and his feelings toward the Middle Passage.

Sentence from the Text	Sample Paraphrase
"We were the color of shadows when we came down / with tinkling leg-irons to join the chains of the sea, / for the silver coins multiplying on the sold horizon,"	We were pale when we approached the sea in our chains—moving toward being sold far away for profit.

SKILLS FOCUS

Literary Focus
Understand epic poetry.

Reading Skills
Paraphrase text.

from Omeros

by Derek Walcott

Point of No Return Monument on the Route des Esclaves (Road of the Slaves) in Benin. ©Atlantide Phototravel/CORBIS

Now he heard the griot° muttering his **prophetic** song
of sorrow that would be the past. It was a note, long-drawn
and endless in its winding like the brown river's tongue:

"We were the colour of shadows when we came down
with tinkling leg-irons to join the chains of the sea,
for the silver coins multiplying on the sold horizon,

and these shadows are reprinted now on the white sand
of antipodal° coasts, your ashen ancestors
from the Bight of Benin,° from the margin of Guinea.

There were seeds in our stomachs, in the cracking pods
of our skulls on the scorching decks, the tubers
withered in no time. We watched as the river-gods

VOCABULARY

prophetic (pro·fet′ik) *adj.:* foretelling events.

INFER

Re-read lines 2–3. What is the theme in these lines?

LITERARY FOCUS

Note the quotation mark in line 4. How does the speaker's voice change? What new point of view does the speaker express?

1. **griot** (grē·ō′) *n.:* a professional historian, who may also be a poet, genealogist, teacher, musician, and storyteller.
8. **antipodal** (an·tip′ə·dəl) *adj.:* situated on opposite sides of the earth.
9. **Bight of Benin:** bay in northern section of the Gulf of Guinea.

PARAPHRASE

Re-read lines 13–19 and paraphrase them.

VOCABULARY

radiated (rā′dē·āt′id) *v.:* branched out in lines from a center.

perpetuate (pər·pech′o͞o·āt′) *v.:* to cause to continue indefinitely; to prolong.

reverberation (ri·vʉr′bə·rā′shən) *n.:* echoed or repeated sound.

INTERPRET

What do you think the author means by "each man was a nation in himself" in lines 32–33?

changed from snakes into currents. When inspected,
our eyes showed dried fronds in their brown irises,
and from our curved spines, the rib-cages **radiated**

like fronds from a palm-branch. Then, when the dead
palms were heaved overside, the ribbed corpses
floated, riding, to the white sand they remembered,

to the Bight of Benin, to the margin of Guinea.
So, when you see burnt branches riding the swell,°
trying to reclaim the surf through crooked fingers,

after a night of rough wind by some stone-white hotel,
past the bright triangular passage of the windsurfers,
remember us to the black waiter bringing the bill."

But they crossed, they survived. There is the epical splendour.
Multiply the rain's lances, multiply their ruin,
the grace born from subtraction as the hold's° iron door

rolled over their eyes like pots left out in the rain,
and the bolt rammed home its echo, the way that thunder-
claps **perpetuate** their **reverberation.**

So there went the Ashanti° one way, the Mandingo° another,
the Ibo° another, the Guinea. Now each man was a nation
in himself, without mother, father, brother.

---

20. swell (swel) *n.:* a long wave that moves steadily without breaking.
27. hold (hōld) *n.:* the interior part of a ship, where cargo is kept.
31. Ashanti (ə·shän′tē,-shan′-): a people from a region in central Ghana. **Mandingo** (man·diŋ′gō): a people from the region of the upper Niger River in western Africa.
32. Ibo (ē′bō′): a people of Nigeria.

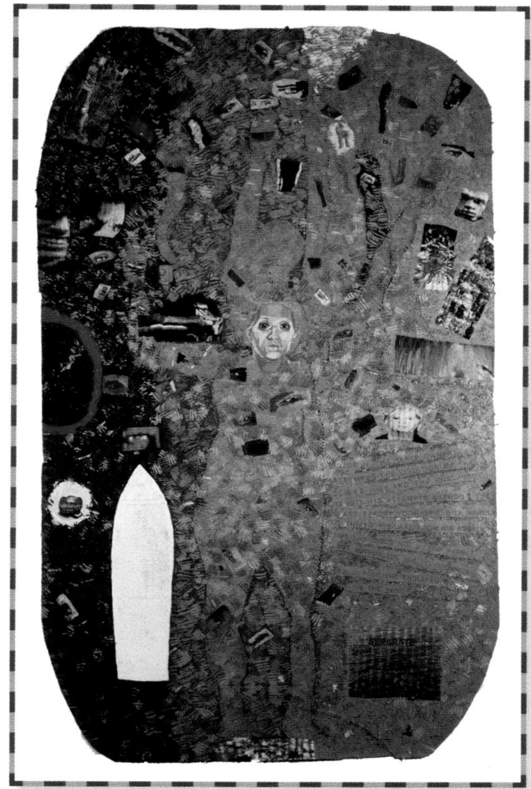

Autobiography: Water/ Ancestors/ Middle Passage/ Family Ghosts, mixed media by Howardena Pindell.
Wadsworth Atheneum, Hartford, CT. The Ella Gallup Sumner and Mary Catlin Sumner Collection Fund. ©Howardena Pindell

MEET THE WRITER

Derek Walcott (1930–) is a poet and playwright who was born in Saint Lucia in the West Indies where a French/English dialect is spoken. (He has used the dialect of his island home in his plays.) His mother was a teacher who introduced him to poetry and Shakespeare at an early age. Walcott attended college in Saint Lucia and Jamaica and has taught in the West Indies and at universities in the United States.

Walcott's work deals with his divided allegiance between his European and Caribbean culture and ancestry. He was raised in a colonial society and educated as a subject of Great Britain. At the same time, he learned the folk literature handed down through the oral culture of his ancestors.

Walcott also uses traditional forms of English poetry, often with classical allusions, and intricate metaphors and rhyme schemes. One critic said his "verse remains dense and elaborate, filled with dazzling complexities of style." *Omeros* (1990), a Caribbean *Odyssey,* is Walcott's epic masterpiece.

Walcott won the Nobel Prize in Literature in 1992. In his Nobel Laureate speech he said, "There is the buried language and there is the individual vocabulary, and the process of poetry is one of excavation and self-discovery."

SKILLS PRACTICE

from Omeros

EPIC CHART

Use the chart to record examples from *Omeros.* Think about how the elements of the epic help convey the author's message about the Middle Passage.

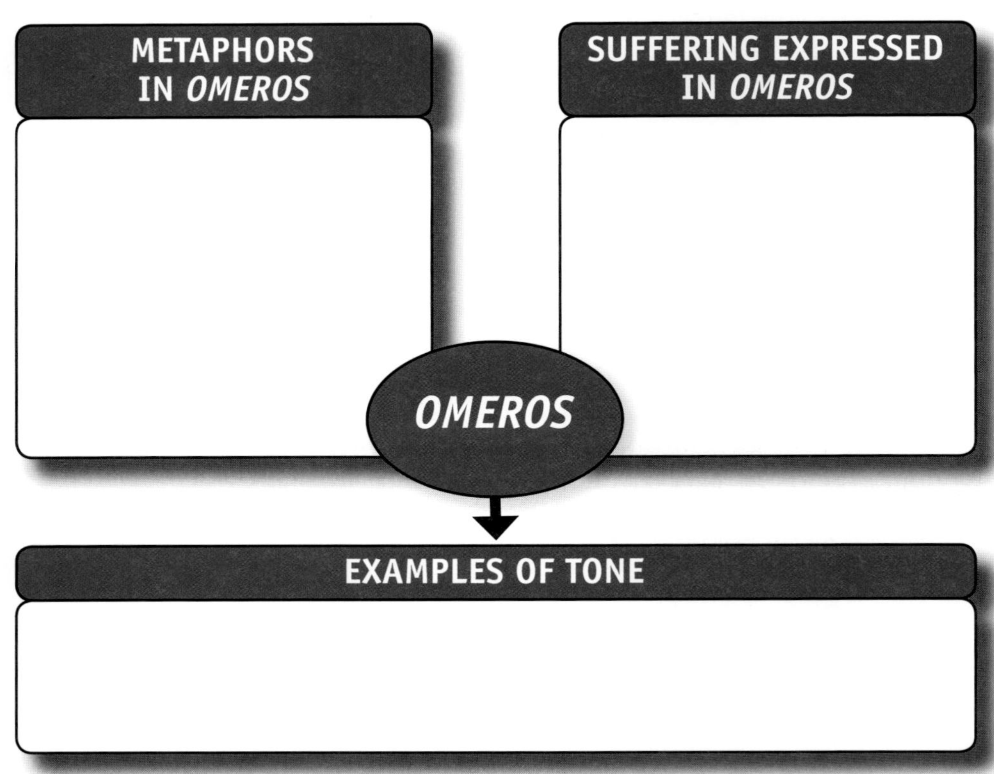

READING COMPREHENSION

Answer each question below.

1. What do you think is the meaning of the reference to the "black waiter" in line 24?

____

____

2. In lines 31–33, the narrator refers to the dispersion of African peoples during their enslavement. How does Walcott convey the terrible isolation endured by these displaced people?

____

____

____

Literary Focus Understand epic poetry.

Writer's Workshop
EXPOSITORY WRITING

ASSIGNMENT

Write an essay analyzing one of the selections in this book or another literary work of your choice.

PURPOSE

To think critically; to inform

AUDIENCE

Your teacher and your classmates

TRY IT OUT

With a partner, create a chart like the one on page 62 for "Spider's Bargain with God" (page 32).

ANALYZING LITERATURE

Have you ever taken something apart to see how it's put together? When you **analyze** a work of literature, you examine its literary elements and try to figure out how they interact to create meaning. In this workshop, you'll write an essay on one of the selections in this book or another literary work of your choice. You'll focus on important elements—such as **plot, character, setting, tone,** and **theme**—and discuss how they work together to create meaning.

PREWRITING

1. **Choose a Literary Work**—Look through the notes you've made on the selections in this book or think about another work of literature you've read recently. Choose a literary work that you feel strongly about. Is there one that stands out in your memory, maybe because it surprised you or touched your emotions or challenged your thinking?

2. **Do a Close Reading**—Re-read your selection and take notes. Focus on the important literary elements and think about the selection as a whole. Consider these questions as you read:
   - **Plot** Is there a **conflict** that sets the plot in motion? Is it an external conflict, an internal conflict, or both? Does the writer use **foreshadowing** to hint at what will happen? What is the **climax?** Is the **resolution** satisfying?
   - **Character** Who are the main **characters?** How does the author reveal their natures? What **motivates** these characters? Are their actions believable? Do they change? If so, what do they learn?
   - **Setting** Where and when does the story take place? Is the setting central to the conflict or theme? Does the setting evoke a particular **mood,** or **atmosphere?**
   - **Tone** How would you describe the author's attitude, and how is it revealed? Does the author use **satire** or **irony** to prove a point? What is the overall effect of the author's word choice and style?
   - **Theme** What central idea or insight into life or human nature does the literary work reveal? Does the author use **imagery** or other **figurative language** to reinforce meaning or provide clues to the theme? Is the theme stated directly by the author, or must it be inferred by the reader? Is the theme open to more than one interpretation?

Creating a chart like the one below can help you organize your essay ideas.

"The Son of Kim-ana-u-eze and the Daughter of the Sun and the Moon" by Julius Lester (page 35)		
ELEMENT	**EXAMPLES**	**IMPORTANCE**
Plot/Conflict	The son of Kim-ana-u-eze wants to marry the daughter of the Sun and the Moon, but his father and other animals tell him it is not possible. Frog uses wits and trickery to help him achieve his goal.	It is crucial to the story's theme.
Characters	The son of Kim-ana-u-eze: ambitious but despairs easily; Frog: clever, cunning	The son's weaknesses and Frog's strengths are central to the conflict and the theme.
Setting	A village on Earth; palace of Lord Sun and Lady Moon in the sky	The difficulty of going from Earth to the sky is central to the conflict and the theme.
Themes	Don't give up; don't underestimate or judge people; use your mind to solve problems.	The tale provides a moral lesson.

PATTERNS OF ORGANIZATION

- In your essay as a whole, organize your ideas in **order of importance** (from most important to least important, or vice versa).
- If your essay includes a plot summary, use **chronological order** (the order in which events occur) to relate what happens.
- If your essay describes a particular scene, use **spatial order** (in which objects are described left to right, near to far, and so on).

3. **State Your Main Ideas**—Look over your notes to decide which elements play the biggest role in revealing the selection's meaning. State your **main idea** about each element in one or two sentences; you can use these sentences later to write **topic sentences.** Next, draft a **thesis statement** that sums up your ideas about the selection.

4. **Elaborate; Back It Up**—Remember, there is no one correct analysis of a selection. Just be sure to back up your statements with specific details and examples. Here are some types of supporting evidence you can use to elaborate on your topic sentences:
   - references to specific events in the selection
   - descriptions of character traits with details to support them
   - details describing the setting
   - quotations from the selection
   - comparisons with other literary works or the real world

DRAFTING

1. **Start Writing**—With your notes, topic sentences, and thesis statement, you are ready to begin writing your analysis. In your **introduction,** identify the title and author of the story and present your **thesis statement.** In the **body** of the paper, elaborate on three or four main ideas. In your **conclusion,** restate the thesis and perhaps add a final personal observation or critical comment. You may want to begin by drafting your introduction, or you may prefer to begin with the body.

2. **Don't Summarize; Analyze**—As you write, check to make sure you are truly *analyzing* the story. Don't just summarize the plot and present your reaction to the story. Focus on interpreting the selection and revealing a level of meaning others may not have considered. Assume that your audience is familiar with the literary work, but provide enough context so that even a reader who hasn't read it would be able to follow along.

EVALUATING AND REVISING

1. **Self-Evaluation**—Re-read your draft to make sure that your ideas make sense and progress smoothly in a logical order. You may need to add transitional words or phrases (such as *first, second, finally, in addition, although,* and *as a result*) to signal where you're going and to show how your ideas are related.

2. **Peer Review**—Exchange drafts with a partner, and give each other constructive suggestions for revision. Focus on the evaluation criteria listed in the side column. In addition, point out unnecessary or overused words, irrelevant or unconvincing evidence, and confusing or awkward transitions. Comment on the points you agreed with or found most convincing and tell what you think about the content and organization of the essay as a whole.

EVALUATION CRITERIA

A good literary analysis

- includes the title, the author, and a thesis statement in the introduction
- discusses literary elements
- provides evidence (such as quotations and details from the text) to support main ideas
- includes transitional words and phrases
- concludes by restating the thesis

PROOFREADING & PUBLISHING

- If you are writing with a computer, use the spelling feature to check for words you often misspell.
- Share your literary analysis by reading it aloud to your class or writing group or by posting it on your school's Web site.

THE SEARCH FOR FREEDOM (1750–1865)

A Ride for Liberty — The Fugitive Slaves (c. 1862) by Eastman Johnson. Oil on board (22" x 26 1/4").
The Brooklyn Museum of Art, Gift of Miss Gwendolyn O.L. Conkling (40.59.A).

LITERARY FOCUS FOR UNIT 2

Have you ever had a goal that seemed far from reach? The selections in this unit show how desperation can breed hope and perseverance can quash boundaries. They represent some of the voices that helped carry the nation out of slavery.

First, a mathematical and scientific genius appeals to morality and reason in an **argument** against racism. Then a colonial poet uses **personification** to express affection toward those who held her in captivity—yet she, too, reminds her white audience of an intrinsic human equality. Through **allusion,** spirituals offer messages of hope and salvation. Two **slave narratives** transport us to a world of **conflict** that incited demands for justice. A modern **biography** honors those who risked everything to escape bondage. An old woman who journeyed from slavery to freedom delivers a stirring **speech** urging a younger generation forward on the long road ahead.

As you read, think about the challenges these authors faced and the rich literary tradition their words helped build.

BEFORE YOU READ

from Letter to Thomas Jefferson
by Benjamin Banneker

Born a free man, Benjamin Banneker was one of the small minority of blacks to receive an education in the American colonies. Banneker became an inventor, surveyor, mathematician, and astronomer. In 1791, Benjamin Banneker sent a copy of his first almanac with this letter to Thomas Jefferson, then Secretary of State under President George Washington. Previously, Jefferson had expressed the opinion that blacks were inferior to whites in reason and imagination. In fact, supporters of slavery published supposed scientific evidence to support this opinion. Banneker's letter tries to persuade Jefferson to rethink his negative views of blacks and help abolish slavery.

LITERARY FOCUS: ARGUMENT

The purpose of an **argument** is to persuade the intended audience (who might be listeners or readers) to act or think a certain way. A convincing argument is well organized, making it easy for the audience to follow and understand. It clearly presents the writer's **position,** or view on the issue, and supports it with logical reasons and evidence. It also includes a **counter-argument,** or rebuttal, that refutes reasons for an opposing view.

Benjamin Banneker's purpose in this letter is to convince Thomas Jefferson that society's perception of blacks is wrong and needs to be corrected. He hopes that if Jefferson is swayed by his words, he will act to improve the conditions of blacks and support the abolition of slavery. To accomplish his purpose, he develops his argument in a way that will appeal to Jefferson, reminding him of the ideals upon which the country was founded and the words that Jefferson himself wrote in the Declaration of Independence.

READING SKILLS: ANALYZING A WRITER'S ARGUMENT

When you **analyze a writer's argument,** you examine the reasons and evidence that the writer presents in support of his or her argument. **Reasons** are statements that explain why the audience should consider a particular point of view. Reasons should include counter-arguments and appeal to logic rather than emotion. Ideally, reasons should be backed up by evidence. **Evidence** consists of facts, examples, statistics, and direct quotations that prove the validity of a reason.

- As you read Benjamin Banneker's letter to Thomas Jefferson, evaluate the persuasiveness of his argument based on the evidence he uses to support his position.

SKILLS FOCUS

Literary Focus Recognize the characteristics of an argument.

Reading Skills Analyze a writer's argument.

Vocabulary Skills Use context clues to figure out the meaning of unknown words.

VOCABULARY DEVELOPMENT

PREVIEW SELECTION VOCABULARY

The following words appear in Banneker's letter to Thomas Jefferson. Look them over before you begin reading the selection.

dignified (dig′nə·fīd′) *adj.:* worthy of respect.

The Secretary of State holds a position that is seen as ***dignified*** *and important.*

prevalent (prev′ə·lənt) *adj.:* widespread.

Support for slavery was ***prevalent*** *in the South while it was less common in the North.*

eradicate (ē·rad′i·kāt′) *v.:* get rid of completely.

Banneker knew that the government could ***eradicate*** *slavery, if it so desired.*

diversified (də·vur′sə·fīd′) *adj.:* varied.

The ***diversified*** *population held different views about the issue.*

indispensable (in′di·spen′sə·bəl) *adj.:* necessary; essential.

Abolitionists believed that the economy could survive without slavery; plantation owners thought it was ***indispensable****.*

profound (prō·fo͞ond′) *adj.:* deep; heartfelt.

He proved to be a ***profound*** *thinker.*

benevolence (bə·nev′ə·ləns) *n.:* kindness.

His ***benevolence*** *led him to help enslaved Africans.*

impartial (im·pär′shəl) *adj.:* not favoring one side or another; unbiased.

He was ***impartial,*** *basing his judgments on the inner qualities of individuals, not their race.*

USING CONTEXT CLUES

Because Benjamin Banneker's letter was written in the eighteenth century, some of the words and phrases may be unfamiliar to a modern reader. To help figure out their meanings, use context clues. These are words or phrases around the unknown term that give hints about its definition. For example, sometimes a **synonym** or **antonym** precedes or follows an unknown word. Sometimes, a writer **restates** the meaning of a word or even includes a **definition.** Read this phrase from the letter:

"we have long been considered rather as *brutish* than human"

Notice that a contrast is set up between *brutish* and *human.* Therefore, *brutish* means the opposite of human. It might be defined as "resembling an animal."

As you read Banneker's letter, use context clues to help you decipher the meaning of words that you do not know.

from Letter to Thomas Jefferson

by Benjamin Banneker

VOCABULARY

dignified (dig′nə·fīd′) *adj.:* worthy of respect.

prevalent (prev′ə·lənt) *adj.:* widespread.

eradicate (ē·rad′i·kāt′) *v.:* get rid of completely.

ANALYZE

What tone does Banneker set in his opening paragraph by stressing the difference between his status and Jefferson's?

ANALYZE

Re-read lines 22–26. What is Banneker's purpose in writing this letter?

Maryland, Baltimore County
Near Ellicotts' Lower Mills, August 19th, 1791

Thomas Jefferson, Secretary of State.

Sir:—I am fully sensible of the greatness of that freedom, which I take with you on the present occasion, a liberty which seemed to me scarcely allowable, when I reflected on that distinguished and **dignified** station in which you stand, and the almost general prejudice and prepossession[1] which is so **prevalent** in the world against those of my complexion.

I suppose it is a truth too well attested to you, to need a proof here, that we are a race of beings who have long laboured under the abuse and censure of the world, that we have long been considered rather as brutish than human, and scarcely capable of mental endowments.

Sir, I hope I may safely admit, in consequence of that report which hath reached me, that you are a man far less inflexible in sentiments of this nature than many others, that you are measurably friendly and well disposed towards us, and that you are willing and ready to lend your aid and assistance to our relief, from those many distresses and numerous calamities, to which we are reduced.

Now, sir, if this is founded in truth, I apprehend[2] you will readily embrace every opportunity to **eradicate** that train of absurd and false ideas and opinions, which so generally prevails with respect to us, and that your sentiments are concurrent with mine, which are that one universal Father hath given Being to us

1. **prepossession** (prē′pə·zesh′ən) *n.:* an attitude formed beforehand; bias.
2. **apprehend** (ap′rē·hend′) *v.:* here, believe.

all, and that he hath not only made us all of one flesh, but that he hath also without partiality afforded us all the same sensations, and endued[3] us all with the same faculties,[4] and that however variable we may be in society or religion, however **diversified** in situation or colour, we are all of the same family, and stand in the same relation to him.

Sir, if these are sentiments of which you are fully persuaded, I hope you cannot but acknowledge, that it is the **indispensable** duty of those who maintain for themselves the rights of human nature, and who profess the obligations of Christianity, to extend their power and influence to the relief of every part of the human race, from whatever burden or oppression they may unjustly labour under, and this I apprehend a full conviction of the truth and obligation of these principles should lead all to.

(left) Wood-cut title page of Benjamin Banneker's 1795 *Almanac* and (right) a Benjamin Banneker stamp.
The Granger Collection, New York

3. **endued** (en·do͞od′) *v.:* endowed; provided.
4. **faculties** (fak′əl·tēz) *n.:* powers or abilities.

PARAPHRASE

State Banneker's view on African Americans and their place in society in your own words.

ANALYZE

What reason does Banneker offer in support of his position in lines 33–40?

VOCABULARY

diversified (də·vʉr′sə·fīd′) *adj.:* varied.

indispensable (in′di·spen′sə·bəl) *adj.:* necessary; essential.

INFER

Re-read lines 41–49. What does Banneker imply about the principles of Jefferson and others if they do not work for equality for all?

VOCABULARY

profound (prō·found′) *adj.:* deep; heartfelt.

EVALUATE

In lines 50–60, Banneker describes his status as a free black. Does this information strengthen his argument that all blacks should be free? Explain.

Sir, I have long been convinced that if your love for yourselves and for those inesteemable[5] laws, which preserve to you the rights of human nature, was found on sincerity, you could not but be solicitous that every individual of whatever rank or distinction, might with you equally enjoy the blessings thereof, neither could you rest satisfied, short of the most active diffusion of your exertions in order to their promotions from any state of degradation[6] to which the unjustifiable cruelty and barbarism of men have reduced them.

Sir, I freely and cheerfully acknowledge that I am of the African race, and in that colour which is natural to them of the deepest dye, and it is under a sense of the most **profound** gratitude to the Supreme Ruler of the universe that I now confess to you that I am not under that state of tyrannical thraldom[7] and inhuman captivity to which too many of my brethren are doomed; but that I have abundantly tasted of the fruition of those blessings which proceed from that free and unequalled liberty with which you are favoured and which, I hope you will willingly allow you have received from the immediate hand of that Being, from whom proceedeth every good and perfect gift.

Sir, suffer me[8] to recall to your mind that time in which the arms and tyranny of the British Crown were exerted with every powerful effort in order to reduce you to a State of Servitude, look back I entreat you on the variety of dangers to which you were exposed; reflect on that time in which every human aid appeared unavailable, and in which even hope and fortitude wore the aspect of inability to the conflict and you cannot but be led to a serious and grateful sense of your miraculous and providential preservation; you cannot but acknowledge that the present freedom and tranquility which you enjoy you have mercifully received and that it is the peculiar blessing of Heaven.

5. **inesteemable** (in·es′tē·mə·bəl) *adj.:* inestimable; invaluable (archaic).
6. **degradation** (deg′rə·dā′shən) *n.:* lowered rank.
7. **thraldom** (thrôl′dəm) *n.:* servitude.
8. **suffer me:** permit me.

This sir, was a time in which you clearly saw into the injustice of a state of slavery and in which you had just apprehensions of the horrors of its condition, it was now, sir, that your abhorrence thereof was so excited, that you publickly held forth this true and valuable doctrine, which is worthy to be recorded and remembered in all succeeding ages. "We hold these truths to be self-evident, that all men are created equal, and that they are endowed by their creator with certain unalienable[9] rights, that among these are life, liberty and the pursuit of happiness."

Here, sir, was a time in which your tender feelings for yourselves had engaged you thus to declare, you were then impressed with proper ideas of the great valuation of liberty and the free possession of those blessings to which you were entitled by nature; but, sir, how pitiable is it to reflect that although you were so fully convinced of the **benevolence** of the Father of mankind and of his equal and **impartial** distribution of those rights and privileges which he had conferred upon them, that you should at the same time counteract his mercies in detaining by fraud and violence so numerous a part of my brethren under groaning captivity and cruel oppression, that you should at the same time be found guilty of that most criminal act which you professedly detested in others with respect to yourselves.

Sir, I suppose that your knowledge of the situation of my brethren is too extensive to need a recital here; neither shall I presume to prescribe methods by which they may be relieved, otherwise than by recommending to you and all others to wean yourselves from those narrow prejudices which you have imbibed[10] with respect to them and as Job[11] proposed to his

LITERARY FOCUS

Why does Banneker draw an analogy between the tyranny of the British crown and slavery in lines 61–94?

VOCABULARY

benevolence (bə·nev′ə·ləns) *n.:* kindness.

impartial (im·pär′shəl) *adj.:* not favoring one side or the other; unbiased.

9. **unalienable** (un·āl′yən·ə·bəl) *adj.:* not to be separated.
10. **imbibed** (im·bībd′) *v.:* absorbed into the mind as ideas or principles.
11. **Job** (jōb): a well-known Biblical figure who endured great suffering but never lost his faith in God.

friends, "put your souls in their souls stead," thus shall your hearts be enlarged with kindness and benevolence towards them, and thus shall you need neither the direction of myself or others, in what manner to proceed herein.

Benjamin Banneker

Massachusetts Historical Society

EXTEND

Locate and read the text of Jefferson's reply to Banneker. Do you think it is an adequate response? Why or why not? List reasons and evidence to support your position.

MEET THE WRITER

Benjamin Banneker (1731–1806) was a major intellectual of the eighteenth century, a genius who excelled in astronomy, mathematics, and mechanical things. As a young man, he constructed a clock entirely of wood, without any model except a pocket watch. This remarkable clock continued to work until shortly after his death. Banneker's early education was in a one-room interracial school run by a Quaker in Baltimore County, Maryland. He went on to become a farmer and formed a friendship with George Ellicott, a wealthy Quaker, who lent Banneker books on scientific subjects. Soon he was able to predict a solar eclipse and began work on an almanac, a book full of practical information and predictions about weather and positions of the sun, moon, and planets.

In 1791, Banneker was appointed as a surveyor who would help define the boundaries and lay out streets for what would become the District of Columbia, our nation's capital. For the rest of his life he continued his scientific investigations and astronomical calculations.

SKILLS PRACTICE

from Letter to Thomas Jefferson

ARGUMENT ANALYSIS CHART

Complete the chart below with additional elements of Banneker's argument. Then use the details in the chart to help you evaluate the persuasiveness of his letter.

POSITION
Thomas Jefferson and others should rid themselves of their prejudices against blacks—consideration of the perspective of enslaved Africans will lead them to proceed justly. (lines 98–104)

REASON / COUNTER-ARGUMENT	REASON / COUNTER-ARGUMENT	REASON / COUNTER-ARGUMENT
If Thomas Jefferson believes as Banneker does that God "made us all of one flesh," then he must also believe all individuals deserve the same privileges and freedoms. As a Christian, it is Jefferson's duty to free the oppressed. (lines 26–40)		

EVALUATION

Literary Focus Analyze a writer's argument.

from Letter to Thomas Jefferson

VOCABULARY AND COMPREHENSION

WORD BOX

- dignified
- prevalent
- eradicate
- diversified
- indispensable
- profound
- benevolence
- impartial

A. Context Clues For each item below, fill in the blank with the appropriate word from the Word Box. Then, write the context clues on the line. Some words won't be used.

1. In contrast to the uniform ethnic make-up of my last town, my new city's population is quite ______________________.
   Context Clues: ______________________

2. I will ______________________ those weeds by pulling them up by the roots.
   Context Clues: ______________________________________

3. After the bad news was announced, a ______________________ and intense silence settled over the crowd.
   Context Clues: ______________________

4. Through her ______________________, she tries to make up for her husband's meanness. **Context Clues:** ______________________

5. The computer quickly became ______________________ to most business; now it is the most necessary piece of office equipment.
   Context Clues: ______________________

B. Reading Comprehension Answer each question below.

6. Why does Banneker choose to write to Thomas Jefferson?
   ____
   ____
   ____
   ____

7. Why does Banneker include direct quotations from the Declaration of Independence in his letter?
   ____
   ____
   ____
   ____

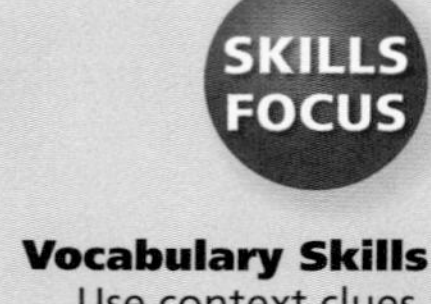

Vocabulary Skills
Use context clues.

BEFORE YOU READ

Two Poems by Phillis Wheatley
Poetry and Politics by Charles Johnson

The girl who came to be known as Phillis Wheatley was taken captive aboard a slave ship in Africa and sold in Boston, where she became a famous poet. In the poems in this selection, Wheatley expresses her deep love for her adopted home—the British colonies that would become the United States—despite the circumstances under which she came. In the short story that follows by contemporary author Charles Johnson, Wheatley and her former owner discuss whether she should try writing poetry that urges freedom for enslaved Africans.

LITERARY FOCUS: PERSONIFICATION

Personification is a figure of speech in which human qualities are given to something that is not human. Poets often use personification to describe something in a vivid and memorable way. For example, a writer would make a strong impression by saying that a house "threw open her arms and welcomed us in a warm embrace."

As you read Phillis Wheatley's poems, look for examples of personification.

- In the poem "On Being Brought from Africa to America," try to identify the personified virtue the speaker says revealed the Christian God to her. Why would she have chosen this particular virtue?
- In "To His Excellency General Washington," Wheatley uses the name *Columbia* to personify the American colonies. Think about the qualities she gives to Columbia and what this reveals about her attitude toward the colonies and the Revolutionary War.

READING SKILLS: INTERPRETING MEANING

Readers must pay attention to every word and detail in order to **interpret** the poem's message. Analyzing personification and other figurative language is one key to interpreting a poem. Also keep these tips in mind:

- Read any footnotes that explain difficult vocabulary and references.
- Be alert to unusual syntax, or word order. For example, a verb is usually followed by its object, but a poet might reverse this order.
- Expect to see some archaic words and contractions, such as *'twas,* ("it was"), *thou know'st* ("you know") and *ere* ("before").
- Pay attention to punctuation to see where sentences begin and end.
- Paraphrase, or restate in your own words, passages that are confusing.

Literary Focus Understand personification.

Reading Skills Interpret the meaning of specific lines of text.

Vocabulary Skills Use synonyms to figure out word meanings.

VOCABULARY DEVELOPMENT

PREVIEW SELECTION VOCABULARY

The following words appear in Wheatley's poems and in Johnson's short story. Look them over before you begin the selection.

pagan (pā′gən) *adj.:* not Christian, Muslim, or Jewish.

Wheatley abandoned the ***pagan*** *land of Senegal when she became a Christian.*

scornful (skôrn·fəl) *adj.:* showing contempt or disdain.

Some white people were ***scornful*** *of Wheatley because they considered all blacks to be inferior.*

diabolic (dī′ə·bäl′ik) *adj.:* of the Devil.

In the 1700s, Christians watched out for signs of the Devil and his ***diabolic*** *work.*

martial (mär′shəl) *adj.:* of or suitable for war.

The band played a ***martial*** *tune as the soldiers marched into battle.*

lament (lə·ment′) *v.:* to regret deeply.

Washington's enemies would ***lament*** *their decision to fight against such a strong and capable leader.*

biased (bī′əst) *v.* used as *adj.:* not objective; prejudiced.

Wheatley's friends had a ***biased*** *opinion of her poems; they liked everything she wrote.*

languishing (laŋ′gwish·iŋ) *v.* used as *adj.:* living in poor conditions; suffering.

In a rich country, no one should be ***languishing*** *in poverty.*

ostracized (äs′trə·sīzd′) *adj.:* banished or excluded.

Some black Christians were ***ostracized*** *rather than welcomed by white Christians.*

UNDERSTANDING SYNONYMS

Synonyms are words that have nearly the same meaning. When you write, it's important to select the best synonym for the context. For example, both of the following sentences would make sense with the word *happy,* but the synonyms convey more precise meanings.

- Yvonne was *pleased* that her local library had a copy of the book she needed.
- Jerome was *ecstatic* to learn that he had won a million dollars.

Synonyms can also be helpful when you're reading. If you encounter unfamiliar words while reading the next three selections, try these strategies:

- Check the context to see if there's another word that's used in a similar way or has nearly the same meaning. Synonyms are a kind of **context clue** that can help you define unknown words.
- Try substituting words you know in place of the unknown word. If you can think of a synonym that works in the context, you'll be able to guess what the word means.

On Being Brought from Africa to America

by Phillis Wheatley

’Twas mercy brought me from my **pagan** land,
Taught my benighted soul to understand
That there’s a God, that there’s a Saviour° too:
Once I redemption neither sought nor knew.
Some view that sable° race with **scornful** eye:
“Their colour is a **diabolic** dye.”
Remember, Christians, Negroes black as Cain°
May be refined and join the angelic strain.

Phillis Wheatley, as pictured in her 1773 book.
Phillis Wheatley frontpiece engraving. ©Bettmann/CORBIS

3. **Savior:** a reference to Jesus Christ.
5. **sable** (sā′bəl) *adj.:* dark or black in color.
7. **Cain:** in the Bible, the first-born son of Adam and Eve. After Cain murders his brother, Abel, God condemns him to wander the earth.

VOCABULARY

pagan (pā′gən) *adj.:* not Christian, Muslim, or Jewish.

scornful (skôrn·fəl) *adj.:* showing contempt or disdain.

diabolic (dī′ə·bäl′ik) *adj.:* of the Devil.

LITERARY FOCUS

What idea or quality does Wheatley personify in lines 1–3? Circle the word that names this quality. Then summarize what the speaker says it has done for her.

INTERPRET

Draw a line to divide the poem into its two halves. Write two sentences that tell the main idea of each half.

LITERARY FOCUS

The name *Columbia* in line 2 represents the American colonies. As you re-read this page, underline words and phrases that describe Columbia. Overall, what impression does the poet create through her use of personification?

INTERPRET

In line 3, Wheatley uses inverted syntax, switching the order of the verb and its object. In prose writing, the line would more likely read, "While freedom's cause alarms her anxious breast." Look for other examples of inverted syntax on this page. Try rewriting these lines using regular word order to help you interpret the meaning.

To His Excellency General Washington

by Phillis Wheatley

Celestial° choir! enthron'd in realms of light,
    Columbia's scenes of glorious toils I write.
While freedom's cause her anxious breast alarms,
She flashes dreadful in refulgent° arms.
See mother earth her offspring's fate bemoan,
And nations gaze at scenes before unknown!
See the bright beams of heaven's revolving light
Involved in sorrows and the veil of night!

Bostonians on their housetops watching the Battle of Bunker Hill at Charlestown on 17th of June 1775: illustration, 1901, by Howard Pyle.
The Granger Collection, New York

1. **celestial** (sə·les′chəl) *adj.:* of the heavens.
4. **refulgent** (ri·ful′jənt) *adj.:* radiant; shining.

The goddess comes, she moves divinely fair,
Olive and laurel binds her golden hair:
Wherever shines this native of the skies,
Unnumber'd charms and recent graces rise.
Muse!° bow propitious° while my pen relates
How pour her armies through a thousand gates,
As when Eolus° heaven's fair face deforms,
Enwrapp'd in tempest and a night of storms;
Astonish'd ocean feels the wild uproar,
The refluent° surges beat the sounding shore;
Or thick as leaves in Autumn's golden reign,
Such, and so many, moves the warrior's train.
In bright array they seek the work of war,
Where high unfurl'd the ensign° waves in air.
Shall I to Washington their praise recite?
Enough thou know'st them in the fields of fight.
Thee, first in peace and honors,—we demand
The grace and glory of thy **martial** band.
Fam'd for thy valor, for thy virtues more,
Hear every tongue thy guardian aid implore!
One century scarce perform'd its destined round,
When Gallic° powers Columbia's fury found;
And so may you, whoever dares disgrace
The land of freedom's heaven-defended race!
Fix'd are the eyes of nations on the scales,
For in their hopes Columbia's arm prevails.

WORD STUDY

Note the word *tempest* in line 16. Can you find a synonym for this word in the surrounding text? Write the synonym below, and then look up *tempest* in a dictionary to check its definition.

____

VOCABULARY

martial (mär′shəl) *adj.:* of or suitable for war.

INTERPRET

This poem is written in rhyming couplets. The couplet in lines 29–30 could be paraphrased as "The colonies were only 100 years old when they defeated the French." Paraphrase lines 31–32 on the lines below.

____

____

____

____

____

---

13. Muse: a Greek goddess, in this case Erato, who is thought to inspire poets. She is one of nine muses presiding over literature, the arts, and the sciences. **propitious** (prō·pish′əs) *adj.:* favorably inclined or disposed.

15. Eolus (ē′ō·ləs): the Greek god of the winds.

18. refluent (ref′lo͞o·ənt) *adj.:* flowing back.

22. ensign (en′sīn′) *n.:* flag.

30. Gallic (gal′ik): French. The colonists, led by Washington, defeated the French in the French and Indian War (1754–1763).

VOCABULARY

lament (lə·ment′)
v.: to regret deeply.

CONNECT

If you were General Washington, how would reading this poem make you feel? Why?

Anon Britannia° droops the pensive° head,
While round increase the rising hills of dead.
Ah! cruel blindness to Columbia's state!
Lament thy thirst of boundless power too late.
    Proceed, great Chief, with virtue on thy side,
Thy ev'ry action let the goddess guide.
A crown, a mansion, and a throne that shine,
With gold unfading, WASHINGTON! be thine.

---

35. Britannia: England. **pensive** (pen′siv) *adj.:* thinking deeply or seriously.

MEET THE WRITER

Phillis Wheatley (c. 1753–1784), one of the earliest American poets and the first black writer to publish a book of poetry, was most likely born in Senegal. She was kidnapped while a child and shipped to Boston where she was sold to John Wheatley, a wealthy merchant-tailor. Unlike most enslaved Africans, she was taught to read and write. In 1770, she published a poem honoring the death of the evangelist George Whitefield. This poem made her famous. She traveled to London in 1773, met notable people, and published *Poems on Various Subjects, Religious and Moral,* which earned her the title of the "Sable Muse." She was given her freedom in that same year.

At the center of Patriot activity in the colonies, Wheatley began writing poems supporting the cause of the American Revolution. Her poetry was written for a white audience and imitates the style of eighteenth-century English writers. It uses rhymed couplets and contains many Biblical and mythological allusions.

Poetry and Politics

by Charles Johnson

"Phillis, Have You a moment to talk?"

"Of course, ma'am, but should you be up at this hour? The doctor said—"

"I *know* what he said. Pooh! You've been reminding me of it every day since you returned from England, which I wish you'd *not* done for my sake. I'm an old woman, and far poorer company, I would guess, than the Countess of Huntingdon[1] and Benjamin Franklin. He isn't *really* a nudist, is he?"

"To hear others tell it, yes! I swear I heard them say it! And you're *not* poor company. I'd rather be here, helping you and Master John, than riding in carriages from one court to another in London and being called the 'Sable Muse.' Isn't that *silly?* I've never seen so many people astonished—there and here—that an Ethiop[2] could write verse!"

"No, not an Ethiop. They're dazzled, and well should they be, at a girl barely thirteen translating Ovid[3] from the Latin and publishing her first book at twenty. I daresay you are a prodigy, probably the most gifted poet in New England."

"Oh my . . . Better than Michael Wigglesworth?"[4]

"Leagues beyond *him*, my dear."

"Perhaps you are . . . **biased.** Is that possible?"

"Not a'tall . . ."

"But Mr. Jefferson,[5] his opinion of my work is less than laudatory."

---

1. **Countess of Huntingdon:** Selina Hastings (1707–1791), a British aristocrat associated with the Methodist preacher George Whitefield. The countess supported writers like Wheatley who shared her religious beliefs.
2. **Ethiop:** a person of African descent.
3. **Ovid** (43 B.C.–A.D. 17): Roman poet whose Latin works include *Metamorphoses,* a collection of myths and legends.
4. **Michael Wigglesworth** (1631–1705): New England poet and Puritan preacher.
5. **Mr. Jefferson:** Thomas Jefferson (1743–1826), colonial legislator and early supporter of American independence. He was a harsh critic of Wheatley's work and did not believe blacks were capable of writing great poetry.

VOCABULARY

biased (bī'əst) *v.* used as *adj.:* not objective; prejudiced.

CLARIFY

Johnson's story is historical fiction—an imaginary story based on actual people and events. Re-read the first four paragraphs. What real-life events create the setting for the story?

INTERPRET

In lines 12–14, Phillis says people are amazed at her poetry simply because she is black. Her friend, Mrs. Susannah Wheatley, does not agree. Why does Mrs. Wheatley think people are so impressed with Phillis?

VOCABULARY

languishing (laŋ′gwish·iŋ) *v.* used as *adj.:* living in poor conditions; suffering.

ostracized (äs′trə·sīzd′) *adj.:* banished or excluded.

WORD STUDY

Find the word *piety* in line 48. What synonym is used later in the same paragraph? (Hint: Wheatley's poem "On Being Brought from Africa to America" expresses her piety.)

____

SUMMARIZE

Why is Phillis worried about what other blacks will think of her and her poetry?

____

____

____

____

____

____

____

____

____

____

____

"As is my opinion of him. Come now, show me what you're working on. That is a new poem, isn't it? Is that why you're up before cock's crow?"

"Oh, I couldn't sleep! But, no! Don't look! Give it back, *please.* I know it's not good. At least not yet. It could be years before it's ready—"

"I just want to see. May I? Well . . . this *is* a departure for you. 'On the Necessity of Negro Manumission.'[6] What prompted you to begin this?"

"You . . . and Master John."

"How so?"

"Just prior to sending me to London for medical treatment you granted me manumission—"

"We were worried. Your health has always been frail."

"—and when I was there I discovered that everyone of my color was free. Just a few months before I arrived, Chief Justice Mansfield passed a ruling that freed all the slaves in England.[7] I was thinking, would that we had such a ruling here!"

"But there *are* free black men and women in Boston."

"Yes, and they live miserably, ma'am! My contact with them is slight, but I've seen them **languishing** in poverty and **ostracized** by white Christians. I wonder sometimes what they think of *me.* I imagine some mock the models I've chosen—Alexander Pope[8]—and my piety and the patriotism of my verse, such as the poem to General Washington, which you know I labored long and hard upon, though he is a slaveholder (and who replied not at all to my gift), so that, the *hardest* work sometimes, at least for me, has been to honor in my verse the principles of the faith that brought me freedom, yet—and yet—I have not spoken of its failures, here in New England or in the

---

6. **manumission** (man′yo͞o·mish′ən) *n.:* freedom from slavery.
7. **Chief Justice Mansfield . . . slaves in England:** The ruling in the 1772 Somersett case said that "as soon as any slave sets foot upon English territory, he becomes free."
8. **Alexander Pope** (1688–1744): English poet and satirist.

slaveholding states that justify my people's oppression by twisting scripture."

"Must you speak of these things?"

"Yes, I think so . . ."

"Is this why you could not sleep last night?"

"Yes, ma'am."

"Phillis . . . are you . . . unhappy here?"

"No, no! That's *not* what I'm saying. I'm thankful for the blessing that brought me from Senegal to America. Thankful that you took on the sickly child that I was, carried me here to be a companion for you, taught me to write and read, and introduced me to Horace and Virgil,[9] associates with whom I can spend hours, and ne'er once have they rebuked me for my complexion—"

"The finest thoughts have no complexion."

"So I have believed, ma'am. I believe that *still.* But while the greatest thoughts and works of literature and the gatekeepers of heaven vouchsafe no distinctions based on color, the *worst* prejudices and passions of man reign throughout the colonies. Will it not be odd, a hundred years hence, when readers open *Poems on Various Subjects, Religious and Moral* by Phillis Wheatley, and discover that in not a single poem do I address the anguish of bondage, the daily horror that is happening around us, the evil of men bleeding their sable brethren for profit?[10] Will I not be *suspect*? Or censured? For it is our hope—isn't it?—that freedom will come to all? If it does, ma'am, what will free Negroes think of me? That I wrote nothing to further our cause?"

"Would you become a pamphleteer then? A writer of newspaper articles?"

"Well, no, but—"

---

9. **Horace and Virgil:** Horace (65–8 B.C.) was a Roman poet and satirist. Virgil (70–19 B.C.), another Roman poet, wrote the national epic the *Aeneid.*
10. **in not a single poem . . . for profit:** In fact, Wheatley's book does address the topic of slavery. In a poem to William, Earl of Dartmouth, she describes her kidnapping in Senegal as a "cruel fate" for both herself and her parents.

INFER

Why does Phillis like to spend time studying classical works by Horace and Virgil?

WORD STUDY

The word *vouchsafe* (line 72) means "to grant or allow." Phillis Wheatley would have recognized the word's Latin roots, which mean "to call" and "healthy."

EVALUATE

Do you think Phillis deserves criticism for focusing mostly on religious and patriotic topics instead of slavery? Explain.

NOTES

COMPARE & CONTRAST

What does Phillis say is the difference between writing a poem about slavery and writing a pamphlet or newspaper article on the same topic?

PHILLIS WHEATLEY (c. 1753–1784), African-American poet, bronze, 2003 by Meredith Bergmann for the *Boston Women's Memorial.*
The Granger Collection, New York

"And *why* not a pamphleteer?"

"It's obvious why, isn't it? At the end of the day one wraps garbage in newspapers. And while a pamphlet can be valuable and stir people to action, a hundred years hence it may be forgotten—as the injustice it assails is forgotten—or it will be preserved only as a historical document, interesting for what it reveals about a moment long past, but *never* appreciated as art. I'm speaking of writing *poems* about oppression."

"Is poetry the right means for that?"

"How do you mean?"

"Tell me, Phillis, what is it about Virgil, Pope, and Horace that you love? Come now, don't be shy."

"The beauty, which age does not wear—"

"And?"

"The truth . . ."

"Which is timeless, no?"

"Yes, that's right."

"May I suggest something?"

"Please."

"I cannot read tea leaves so I have no idea what the future will bring or how your poetry will be received in the colonies a century from now. But of one thing I can assure you: You can never be censured. You are the first internationally celebrated woman poet in the colonies. The first American poet of your people. I'm sure they will take pride in your achievement, as John and I do. And you, my dear, are—by nature and temperament—a poet, regardless of what Jefferson says. You are not a pamphleteer. Your job is simple. I did not say *easy*, for no one knows better than you how difficult it is to create even *one* line of verse worth passing along to the next generation, or a poem that speaks to the heart of Christendom—white and colored—on both sides of the Atlantic. It is a noble calling, Phillis, this creating of beauty, and it is sufficient unto itself."

"Is it? Sometimes I wonder if my people see me—my work—as useless."

"Useless?"

"It doesn't *serve* their liberation, does it?"

"Why? Because you do not catalog horrors? Only praise what on these shores is praiseworthy?"

"Yes, exactly."

"Dear, dear Phillis . . ."

"Why are you laughing? What did I say? Am I amusing?"

"Oh no, of course not! But would you call Benjamin Banneker's work useless?"

"Hardly! While still a boy, he built from wood the first clock made wholly in America. From what I hear, it keeps perfect time to this very day."

INTERPRET

What does Mrs. Wheatley mean when she says in line 112 that Phillis's job is simple but not easy?

WORD STUDY

What synonym could you substitute for the word *sufficient* in line 117?

HISTORICAL CONTEXT

Lines 129–131 describe the clock that Benjamin Banneker made from hand-carved wooden parts. At the time this story takes place, the clock was Banneker's most notable achievement.

INTERPRET

According to Mrs. Wheatley, in what way is Phillis herself a "broadside" against slavery?

FLUENCY

Read the boxed passage aloud two times. First read it for clarity. Then read it again, using your voice to express the emotions that Phillis is feeling.

CONNECT

In lines 150–154, Phillis describes her difficulty writing poetry about things she hates. Can you relate to her experience? What kinds of activities come naturally to you, and what kinds are a struggle?

"What, then, of Santomee?"

"Who?"

"He was a slave in New York, one trained in Holland, who practiced medicine among the Dutch and English, probably saving many lives. And there is Onesimus, who in 1721 came up with an antidote for the smallpox. All of them proved the genius of your people. All of them enriched others through their deeds, thereby providing in the example of their persons, and the universal value of their products, the most devastating broadside[11] against the evils of Negro bondage imaginable. And you have done no less."

"You think so?"

"I *know* so."

"Thank you, ma'am. You are most kind."

"Will you continue, then, with this bristling, new poem?"

"Perhaps, if I can find my way into it. The *problem* is not that I don't feel outrage whenever I read or see or hear of injustice, it's rather that I fear I have no real talent for that sort of writing and rhetoric. For things I hate. I think I can compose passably well a hymn to morning, but as soon as I turn my pen to painting a portrait of a slave suffering beneath the lash, I cut myself off from what flows most easily from me—the things I love—and the words fall woodenly, unconvincingly, onto the page."

"No, it's not your best work."

"You're not supposed to *say* that!"

"Sorry! I was just agreeing with you, that's all. You needn't bite my head off!"

"You're supposed to tell me it's good."

"Fine, it's good."

"You don't *mean* that."

11. **broadside** (brod′sīd′) *n.:* a large sheet of paper printed on one side, often with a news bulletin, a political statement, or an advertisement. Broadsides were meant to be read quickly and either passed along or discarded.

"You're right, I don't, but I'm in no mood for an argument before breakfast. And it's not why I wanted to talk to you."

"Why did you?"

"You know how yesterday I felt poorly and stayed in bed?"

"Yes?"

"Well, I didn't bother with the post. All the mail, scented and sealed with candle wax, sat on a wig stand until I awoke this morning. I began looking through it, and I found a letter addressed to you. Perhaps I shouldn't give it to you if you're planning now on starting a new life as a composer of pamphlets."

"Oh, please! Who is it from?"

"Phillis, I think you should sit down."

"*Who?*"

"May I read it to you?"

"*I* can read!"

"But I would enjoy it so!"

"All right, then! Read!"

"Ahem . . .

"*Miss Phillis,*

Your favor of the 26th of October[12] *did not reach my hands till the middle of December. Time enough, you will say, to have given an answer ere this. Granted. But a variety of important occurrences, continually interposing to distract the mind and withdraw the attention, I hope will apologize for the delay, and plead my excuse for the seeming but not real neglect. I thank you most sincerely for your polite notice of me, in the elegant lines you enclosed; and however undeserving I may be of such encomium and panegyric, the style and manner exhibit a striking proof of your poetical talents; in honor of which, and as a tribute justly due to you, I would have published the poem, had I not been*

12. **26th of October:** Wheatley wrote to Washington in the fall of 1775. His reply was dated February 28, 1776.

ANALYZE

This story unfolds in a conversation rather than a series of events. Still, it has a conflict and a resolution. What conflict does Phillis face, and how does Washington's letter resolve this conflict?

WORD STUDY

The words *encomium* (line 188) and *panegyric* (line 189) are synonyms. Use context clues to predict what they mean. Then look them up in a dictionary to see if your prediction is correct. Write three more synonyms below.

INTERPRET

What does Phillis mean when she says, "This is a complicated time" (line 203)?

NOTES

apprehensive that, while I only meant to give the world this new instance of your genius, I might have incurred the imputation of vanity. This, and nothing else, determined me not to give it place in the public prints. . . . If you should ever come to Cambridge, or near headquarters, I shall be happy to see a person so favored by the Muses, and to whom nature has been so liberal and beneficent in her dispensations. I am with great respect . . .

Your obedient, humble servant,

George Washington"

"He said . . . *servant?*"

"Here, see for yourself."

"This [is] a complicated time, isn't it?"

"Yes, dear, I think it is."

MEET THE WRITER

Charles Johnson (1948–) is a novelist and short story writer. He was born in Evanston, Illinois, and graduated from Southern Illinois University where he studied the craft of writing with the novelist John Gardner. In 1990 Johnson won the National Book Award for his novel *Middle Passage*. It depicts the adventures of a free black who stows away aboard a slave ship complete with a power-mad captain and kidnapped Africans who are wizards. Johnson says his novels often deal with characters who are "adventurers of ideas, truth-seekers . . . and hunger for wisdom." This story about Phillis Wheatley seeking the right purpose for her poetry comes from Johnson's *Soulcatcher and Other Stories* (2001).

SKILLS PRACTICE

Two Poems • Poetry and Politics

Literary Focus
Analyze examples of personification.

PERSONIFICATION CHART

The chart below lists examples of personification from Phillis Wheatley's poems. For each thing that is personified, describe the human qualities that Wheatley gives it and explain the meaning or message of the personification.

"On Being Brought from Africa to America"	
Example: mercy	
Human qualities:	Meaning or message:
"To His Excellency General Washington"	
Example: American colonies (Columbia)	
Human qualities:	Meaning or message:
Example: England (Britannia)	
Human qualities:	Meaning or message:

WORD BOX

- pagan
- scornful
- diabolic
- martial
- lament
- biased
- languishing
- ostracized

Two Poems • Poetry and Politics

VOCABULARY AND COMPREHENSION

A. Synonyms Write the word from the Word Box that is a synonym of each given word or phrase. Use a thesaurus for help if necessary.

1. mourn ____________________
2. disparaging ____________________
3. soldierly ____________________
4. spurned ____________________
5. heathen ____________________
6. partial ____________________
7. wasting away ____________________
8. evil ____________________

B. Reading Comprehension Answer each question below.

9. Based on her poems, how does Phillis Wheatley feel about living in America?

____

____

____

____

10. In Charles Johnson's story, why is Phillis Wheatley worried about the poetry she has written? How is her concern put to rest by the end of the story?

____

____

____

____

____

____

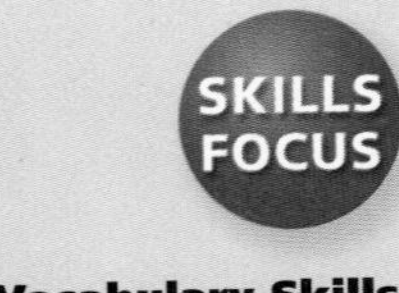

Vocabulary Skills
Identify synonyms.

BEFORE YOU READ

Address to the First Annual Meeting of the American Equal Rights Association

by Sojourner Truth

Sojourner Truth was born into slavery around 1797. She never learned to read or write but became a powerful and inspirational speaker for the abolitionist cause and for women's rights. Sojourner Truth delivered this speech at an equal rights convention in New York City in 1867. In it, she alludes to important historical events that were occurring at that time. Slavery had been abolished, and the process of extending the vote to free black males was underway.

LITERARY FOCUS: SPEECH

When you prepare a speech, always consider two important elements—**purpose** and **audience.** Purpose refers to the reason for a speech. Do you want to convince, inform, or entertain the audience? The audience is anyone who may be listening to or reading a speech. Do the listeners or readers know a lot or a little about the subject? Do they have specific attitudes that you need to address or take into account?

Keeping both purpose and audience in mind helps you decide what kinds of details to include and how to organize them. It also helps you choose the language and tone of the speech.

As you read Sojourner Truth's speech, notice how her awareness of her audience and her purpose influences her content and style.

READING SKILLS: DISTINGUISHING FACT FROM OPINION

In this speech, Sojourner Truth includes both facts and opinions. A **fact** is a statement that can be proven by personal observation or by looking it up in a reliable source. For example, Sojourner Truth states that enslaved Africans "have got their liberty." This statement can be proven true or false by checking the date that slavery was abolished in an encyclopedia or history book.

An **opinion** is a statement that expresses someone's personal beliefs, feelings, or thoughts. It cannot be proven true or false. For example, Sojourner Truth says that "there ought to be equal rights now more than ever."

Look for both facts and opinions as you read. Think about which contribute more to the effectiveness of her speech.

SKILLS FOCUS

Literary Focus
Understand purpose and audience in speeches.

Reading Skills
Distinguishing fact from opinion.

Vocabulary Skills
Recognizing figurative language.

VOCABULARY DEVELOPMENT

PREVIEW SELECTION VOCABULARY

The following words appear in "Address to the First Annual Meeting of the American Equal Rights Association." Look them over before you begin reading the selection.

strutting (strut′tiŋ) *v.:* swaggering; walking proudly.

*Sojourner Truth thought that instead of **strutting** about the house, the men should be out looking for jobs.*

consolation (kän′sə·lā′shən) *n.:* act of being comforted; comfort.

*It would be a **consolation** to know that she helped women gain equal rights.*

legion (lē′jən) *n.:* a large number.

*They brought out a **legion** of arguments in favor of equal rights for women.*

RECOGNIZING FIGURATIVE LANGUAGE

Throughout Sojourner Truth's speech, she uses **figurative language,** words and phrases not meant to be interpreted literally. By including figurative language in her speech, Sojourner Truth adds emphasis to her points and helps her listeners understand her meaning.

- A **metaphor** is a type of figurative language that makes a comparison between two unlike things without using any connective words that set up the comparison. For example, Truth uses a metaphor to compare slavery to a tree or plant when she says, "I want it [slavery] root and branch destroyed." This helps her audience to envision the complete destruction of the institution in their minds.
- A **simile** is another type of figurative language. In a simile, a comparison is made using connective words such as *like* or *as.* For example, Sojourner Truth uses the phrase "cuts like a knife."
- **Idioms** are another type of figurative language. They are common expressions that most people understand to mean something different from the literal meaning. For example: *Time flies.*

As you read Sojourner Truth's speech, look for metaphors, similes, and idioms that help convey her meaning to her audience.

Address to the First Annual Meeting of the American Equal Rights Association

by Sojourner Truth

My Friend, I Am Rejoiced That You Are Glad, But I Don't know how you will feel when I get through. I come from another field—the country of the slave. They have got their liberty—so much good luck to have slavery partly destroyed; not entirely. I want it root and branch destroyed. Then we will all be free indeed. I feel that if I have to answer for the deeds done in my body just as much as a man, I have a right to have just as much as a man. There is a great stir about colored men gettin' their rights, but not a word about the colored women; and if colored men get their rights, and not colored women theirs, you see the colored men will be masters over the women, and it will be just as bad as it was before. So I am for keeping the thing going while things are stirring; because if we wait till it is still, it will take a great while to get it going again. White women are a great deal smarter, and know more than colored women, while colored women do not know scarcely anything. They go out washing, which is about as high as a colored woman gets, and their men go about idle, **strutting** up and down; and when the women come home, they ask for their money and take it all, and then scold because there is no food. I want you to consider on that, chil'n.[1] I call you chil'n; you are somebody's chil'n, and I am old enough to be mother of all that is here. I want women to have their rights. In the courts women have no right, no voice; nobody speaks for them. I wish woman to have her voice there among the pettifoggers.[2] If it is not a fit place for women, it is unfit for men to be there.

1. **chil'n:** children.
2. **pettifoggers** (pet′i·fog′ərs) *n.:* petty, quibbling lawyers.

IDENTIFY

What is Sojourner Truth warning her audience about in lines 1–2?

INFER

Re-read lines 14–16. Is this statement a fact or opinion? What is her purpose in saying this?

VOCABULARY

strutting (strut′tiŋ) *v.:* swaggering; walking proudly.

LITERARY FOCUS

Based on lines 1–23, what is her purpose in this speech?

ANALYZE

Why does Sojourner Truth include the example from her own life in lines 31–36?

INTERPRET

What does Truth mean by the phrase "the ice is cracked" in line 39?

ANALYZE

To whom is Truth speaking in lines 40–44? Why?

Sojourner Truth.
Library of Congress

I am above eighty years old; it is about time for me to be going. I have been forty years a slave and forty years free, and would be here forty years more to have equal rights for all. I suppose I am kept here because something remains for me to do; I suppose I am yet to help to break the chain. I have done a great deal of work; as much as a man, but did not get so much pay. I used to work in the field and bind grain, keeping up with the cradler;[3] but men doing no more, got twice as much pay; so with the German women. They work in the field and do as much work, but do not get the pay. We do as much, we eat as much, we want as much. I suppose I am about the only colored woman that goes about to speak for the rights of the colored women. I want to keep the thing stirring, now that the ice is cracked. What we want is a little money. You men know that you get as much again as women when you write, or for what you do. When we

3. **cradler** (krād′lər) *n.:* a field hand that uses a scythe to cut the grain.

get our rights we shall not have to come to you for money, for then we shall have money enough in our own pockets; and may be you will ask us for money. But help us now until we get it. It is a good **consolation** to know that when we have got this battle once fought we shall not be coming to you any more. You have been having our rights so long, that you think, like a slave-holder, that you own us. I know that it is hard for one who has held the rein for so long to give up; it cuts like a knife. It will feel all the better when it closes up again. I have been in Washington about three years, seeing about these colored people. Now colored men have the right to vote. There ought to be equal rights now more than ever, since colored people have got their freedom. . . .

I am glad to see that men are getting their rights, but I want women to get theirs, and while the water is stirring I will step into the pool. Now that there is a great stir about colored men's getting their rights is the time for women to step in and have theirs. I am sometimes told that "Women ain't fit to vote. Why, don't you know that a woman had seven devils in her:[4] and do you suppose a woman is fit to rule the nation?" Seven devils ain't no account; a man had a **legion** in him. The devils didn't know where to go; and so they asked that they might go into the swine.[5] They thought that was as good a place as they came out from. They didn't ask to go into the sheep—no, into the hog; that was the selfish beast; and man is so selfish that he has got women's rights and his own too, and yet he won't give women their rights. He keeps them all to himself. . . .

I have lived on through all that has taken place these forty years in the anti-slavery cause, and I have plead with all the force I had that the day might come that the colored people might own their soul and body. Well, the day has come, although it came through blood. It makes no difference how it came—it

4. **a woman had seven devils in her:** an allusion to Mary Magdalene who is described in the Bible as having seven demons cast out of her.
5. **a man had a legion . . . might go into the swine:** in Mark's gospel, numerous demons from a possessed man rush into two thousand pigs, which then jump into the water and are drowned.

VOCABULARY

consolation (kän'sə·lā'shən) *n.:* act of comforting; comfort.

legion (lē'jən) *n.:* a large number.

DRAW CONCLUSIONS

Why does Truth include references to the Bible in lines 58–63?

NOTES

INTERPRET

Re-read lines 78–80. What point is Truth making by talking about the tax she must pay?

NOTES

did come. I am sorry it came in that way. We are now trying for liberty that requires no blood—that women shall have their rights—not rights from you. Give them what belongs to them; they ask it kindly too. I ask it kindly. Now, I want it done very quick. It can be done in a few years. How good it would be. I would like to go up to the polls myself. I own a little house in Battle Creek, Michigan. Well, every year I got a tax to pay. Taxes, you see, be taxes. Well, a road tax sounds large. . . . There was women there that had a house as well as I. They taxed them to build a road, and they went on the road and worked. It took'em a good while to get a stump up. Now, that shows that women can work. If they can dig up stumps they can vote. It is easier to vote than dig stumps. It doesn't seem hard work to vote, though I have seen some men that had a hard time of it . . . I don't want to take up your time, but I calculate to live. Now, if you want me to get out of the world, you had better get the women votin' soon. I shan't go till I can do that.

New York, May 9, 1867

MEET THE WRITER

Although **Sojourner Truth** (c. 1797–1883) was illiterate all of her life, she became one of the most eloquent orators of her time. Born into slavery in Ulster County, New York, she escaped to freedom, in 1827 and worked as a household servant in New York City. Here she came under the influence of an evangelical preacher and began to experience mystical visions. In one of these visions, she received her name, "Sojourner Truth" along with her mission—to travel, or sojourn, throughout the country speaking the truth. She became a firm abolitionist and supporter of women's rights, touring the West, moving audiences with her speeches and gospel songs. In 1850, she published *The Narrative of Sojourner Truth,* an autobiography that she had dictated to Olive Gilbert. Sales of the book provided money for her travels.

Truth's "Ain't I a Woman" speech, given in 1851, is probably her most famous. After hearing male speakers cite women's frailty as a reason to deny them rights, she challenged them with this well known speech. "Nobody ever helps me into carriages, or over mud-puddles, or gives me any best place. And ain't I a woman? . . . I have ploughed and planted . . . ! And ain't I a woman?" Although not as fiery, her later speeches also relied upon humor, allusions, and personal experience to convey their messages.

SKILLS PRACTICE

Address to the First Annual Meeting of the American Equal Rights Association

Literary Focus
Analyze a speech for purpose.

Reading Skills
Distinguish fact from fiction.

FACT AND OPINION CHART

In the chart below, list facts and opinions from Sojourner Truth's speech in the appropriate column. Then use the details in the chart to evaluate which contribute more to the persuasiveness of her speech.

FACTS	OPINIONS

EVALUATION

Address to the First Annual Meeting of the American Equal Rights Association

VOCABULARY AND COMPREHENSION

WORD BOX

strutting

consolation

legion

A. Figurative Language For each item below, fill in the blank with the appropriate word from the Word Box. Then, identify the type of figurative language used in the sentence.

1. The last person who could offer ______________________ was Sara, who is known to be a sore loser.

   Figurative Language: ______________________

2. Sam was ______________________ around that gym like a rooster.

   Figurative Language: ______________________

3. When the nest was disturbed, a ______________________ of ants poured out in a stream onto the parched ground.

   Figurative Language: ______________________

B. Reading Comprehension Answer each question below.

4. What does Sojourner Truth say will happen if "colored men get their rights" but "colored women" don't get theirs?

   ____

   ____

   ____

5. What does Sojourner Truth mean by her statement, "If they can dig up stumps they can vote"?

   ____

   ____

   ____

6. At the end of her speech, Sojourner Truth threatens not to die until women get equal rights. Why do you think she ends her speech with humor?

   ____

   ____

   ____

Vocabulary Skills
Recognize figurative language.

BEFORE YOU READ

from Narrative of the Life of Frederick Douglass, An American Slave
by Frederick Douglass

Frederick Douglass was a writer and orator who spoke out widely against slavery. He was born into slavery in Maryland but taught himself to read and write. After escaping from slavery at the age of twenty, Douglass quickly achieved prominence as a leader of the abolitionist movement. In this excerpt from his autobiography, Frederick Douglass explores a significant turning point in his life. At the same time, he paints a graphic and horrifying picture of the institution of slavery.

LITERARY FOCUS: CONFLICT

Conflict is the struggle between two opposing forces. It may be **internal,** taking place within a person, or **external.** External conflict can be against the forces of nature, against another person, or against society.

In this nonfiction account, narrator Frederick Douglass experiences internal conflict as he struggles with the condition of being enslaved. However, most of the action arises from his external conflict with Covey, a farmer to whom he has been leased.

Both types of conflict heighten the tension and suspense and lead up to the turning point, or **climax** of the narrative.

READING SKILLS: ANALYZING CAUSE AND EFFECT

Within a nonfiction narrative, events may be related by cause and effect. A **cause** is a situation or action that leads to another event. This outcome, the direct result of a previous action, is the **effect.** Sometimes, cause and effect relationships are evident. At other times, however, the relationship is implied, or you may need to look further back or ahead in the narrative to find the connection.

As you read Douglass's narrative, think about the relationship between the events. Analyzing the causes and effects will help you to understand more about his feelings, his motivations, and the meaning that he wants to convey through his writing.

Literary Focus
Understand conflict.

Reading Skills
Analyze cause and effect.

Vocabulary Skills
Recognize affixes and roots.

VOCABULARY DEVELOPMENT

PREVIEW SELECTION VOCABULARY

The following words appear in the excerpt from *Narrative of the Life of Frederick Douglass, An American Slave.* Look them over before you begin reading the selection.

circumstances (sur′kəm·stans′·ez) *n.:* conditions surrounding an event; determining factors.

*A combination of **circumstances** enabled Frederick Douglass to escape from slavery and flee to the North.*

immense (im·mens′) *adj.:* huge.

*Learning to read and write was an **immense** accomplishment for an enslaved person.*

comply (kəm·plī′) *v.:* to go along with; fulfill.

*If an enslaved person refused to **comply** with his master's wishes, he could be punished.*

resolved (ri·zälvd′) *adj.:* firmly decided.

*He was **resolved** not to give in this time but to fight back.*

persist (pər·sist′) *v.:* to hold to a purpose; to continue to do or believe something.

*Mr. Covey asked him if he meant to **persist** in his rebellion.*

gratification (grat′i·fi·kā′shən) *n.:* condition of being satisfied.

*He felt **gratification** at the outcome of the fight.*

compensation (käm′pən·sā′shən) *n.:* repayment; reimbursement.

*Enslaved Africans did not receive **compensation** for their labor.*

defiance (dē·fī′əns) *n.:* bold resistance to authority.

*His continued **defiance** in spite of harsh punishments inspired the other workers.*

RECOGNIZING AFFIXES AND ROOTS

Many words in the English language are formed by attaching an **affix,** or word part, to a base word or to a **root.** A root is the part of the word that tells what it means. If it is a whole word, such as *count,* it is called a base word. Most roots are parts of words, however, such as *liber,* which means "free."

- **Prefixes** are affixes placed at the beginning of a word to create a new word. For example, *ac–* added to *count* creates the word *account.* **Suffixes** are affixes added to the ends of roots or base words. They usually indicate the part of speech. For example, the suffix *–ation* signals a noun form, as in *compensation.*

Knowing the meanings of affixes and roots can help you determine the definitions and uses of unfamiliar words.

from Narrative of the Life of Frederick Douglass, An American Slave

by Frederick Douglass

I have already intimated that my condition was much worse, during the first six months of my stay at Mr. Covey's,[1] than in the last six. The **circumstances** leading to the change in Mr. Covey's course toward me form an epoch in my humble history. You have seen how a man was made a slave; you shall see how a slave was made a man. On one of the hottest days of the month of August, 1833, Bill Smith, William Hughes, a slave named Eli, and myself, were engaged in fanning wheat. Hughes was clearing the fanned wheat from before the fan. Eli was turning, Smith was feeding, and I was carrying wheat to the fan. The work was simple, requiring strength rather than intellect; yet, to one entirely unused to such work, it came very hard. About three o'clock of that day, I broke down; my strength failed me; I was seized with a violent aching of the head, attended with extreme dizziness; I trembled in every limb. Finding what was coming, I nerved myself up, feeling it would never do to stop work. I stood as long as I could stagger to the hopper with grain. When I could stand no longer, I fell, and felt as if held down by an **immense** weight. The fan of course stopped; every one had his own work to do; and no one could do the work of the other, and have his own go on at the same time.

Mr. Covey was at the house, about one hundred yards from the treading-yard where we were fanning. On hearing the fan stop, he left immediately, and came to the spot where we were. He hastily inquired what the matter was. Bill answered that I was sick, and there was no one to bring wheat to the fan. I had by this

INTERPRET

Re-read lines 4–6. What might be the distinction that Douglass makes between being a man and being enslaved?

VOCABULARY

circumstances (sur′kəm·stans′ez) *n.:* conditions surrounding an event; determining factors.

immense (im·mens′) *adj.:* huge.

ANALYZE

Re-read lines 12–16. What does Douglass try to do even after he becomes dizzy? Why?

1. **stay at Mr. Covey's:** In 1833 Douglass was hired out as a field hand to a man named Edward Covey, who had a reputation for breaking slaves.

time crawled away under the side of the post and rail-fence by which the yard was enclosed, hoping to find relief by getting out of the sun. He then asked where I was. He was told by one of the hands. He came to the spot, and, after looking at me awhile, asked me what was the matter. I told him as well as I could, for I scarce had strength to speak. He then gave me a savage kick in the side, and told me to get up. I tried to do so, but fell back in the attempt. He gave me another kick, and again told me to rise. I again tried, and succeeded in gaining my feet; but, stooping to get the tub with which I was feeding the fan, I again staggered and fell. While down in this situation, Mr. Covey took up the hickory slat with which Hughes had been striking off the half-bushel measure, and with it gave me a heavy blow upon the head, making a large wound, and the blood ran freely; and with this again told me to get up. I made no effort to **comply,** having now made up my mind to let him do his worst. In a short time after receiving this blow, my head grew better. Mr. Covey had now left me to my fate. At this moment I **resolved,** for the first time, to go to my master,[2] enter a complaint, and ask his protection. In order

Douglass Flogged by Covey, engraving from an almanac.
William Loren Katz

2. **my master:** Thomas Auld, son-in-law of Douglass's first master.

LITERARY FOCUS

Summarize the reason for the conflict between Frederick Douglass and Mr. Covey.

VOCABULARY

comply (kəm·plī′) *v.:* to go along with; fulfill.

resolved (ri·zälvd′) *v.:* firmly decided.

CAUSE & EFFECT

What decision does Douglass make in lines 44–45? What does he risk by doing this?

to do this, I must that afternoon walk seven miles; and this, under the circumstances, was truly a severe undertaking. I was exceedingly feeble; made so as much by the kicks and blows which I received, as by the severe fit of sickness to which I had been subjected. I, however, watched my chance, while Covey was looking in an opposite direction, and started for St. Michael's.[3] I succeeded in getting a considerable distance on my way to the woods, when Covey discovered me, and called after me to come back, threatening what he would do if I did not come. I disregarded both his calls and his threats, and made my way to the woods as fast as my feeble state would allow; and thinking I might be overhauled by him if I kept the road, I walked through the woods, keeping far enough from the road to avoid detection, and near enough to prevent losing my way. I had not gone far before my little strength again failed me. I could go no farther. I fell down, and lay for a considerable time. The blood was yet oozing from the wound on my head. For a time I thought I should bleed to death; and think now that I should have done so, but that the blood so matted my hair as to stop the wound. After lying there about three quarters of an hour, I nerved myself up again, and started on my way, through bogs and briers, barefooted and bareheaded, tearing my feet sometimes at nearly every step; and after a journey of about seven miles, occupying some five hours to perform it, I arrived at master's store. I then presented an appearance enough to affect any but a heart of iron. From the crown of my head to my feet, I was covered with blood. My hair was all clotted with dust and blood; my shirt was stiff with blood. My legs and feet were torn in sundry places with briers and thorns, and were also covered with blood. I suppose I looked like a man who had escaped a den of wild beasts, and barely escaped them. In this state I appeared before my master,

3. **St. Michael's:** a village in Talbot County, Maryland.

INFER

What is Douglass's state of mind as he struggles through the woods to St. Michael's?

WORD STUDY

Douglass uses the word *overhauled* in line 57 in a way that is different from its familiar usage. In this context, it means "caught up."

GENERALIZE

Underline the words and phrases in lines 71–76 that create a mental image of Douglass. What is the effect of this description?

CAUSE & EFFECT

What is the reason that Master Thomas forces Douglass to return to Covey? What do you learn about his character from his reaction to Douglass's plea?

INTERPRET

Why does Douglass say that his "behavior was altogether unaccountable" in line 105?

humbly entreating him to interpose his authority for my protection. I told him all the circumstances as well as I could, and it seemed, as I spoke, at times to affect him. He would then walk the floor, and seek to justify Covey by saying he expected I deserved it. He asked me what I wanted. I told him, to let me get a new home; that as sure as I lived with Mr. Covey again, I should live with but to die with him; that Covey would surely kill me; he was in a fair way for it. Master Thomas ridiculed the idea that there was any danger of Mr. Covey's killing me, and said that he knew Mr. Covey; that he was a good man, and that he could not think of taking me from him; that, should he do so, he would lose the whole year's wages; that I belonged to Mr. Covey for one year, and that I must go back to him, come what might; and that I must not trouble him with any more stories, or that he would himself *get hold of me.* After threatening me thus, he gave me a very large dose of salts, telling me that I might remain in St. Michael's that night, (it being quite late,) but that I must be off back to Mr. Covey's early in the morning; and that if I did not, he would *get hold of me,* which meant that he would whip me. I remained all night, and, according to his orders, I started off to Covey's in the morning, (Saturday morning,) wearied in body and broken in spirit. I got no supper that night, or breakfast that morning. I reached Covey's about nine o'clock; and just as I was getting over the fence that divided Mrs. Kemp's fields from ours, out ran Covey with his cowskin, to give me another whipping. Before he could reach me, I succeeded in getting to the cornfield; and as the corn was very high, it afforded me the means of hiding. He seemed very angry, and searched for me a long time. My behavior was altogether unaccountable. He finally gave up the chase, thinking, I suppose, that I must come home for something to eat; he would give himself no further trouble in looking for me. I spent that day mostly in the woods, having the alternative before me—to go home and be whipped to death, or stay in the woods and be starved to death. That night, I fell in with Sandy Jenkins, a slave with whom I was somewhat

Douglass Found in the Woods by Sandy.
The Granger Collection, New York

acquainted. Sandy had a free wife who lived about four miles from Mr. Covey's; and it being Saturday, he was on his way to see her. I told him my circumstances, and he very kindly invited me to go home with him. I went home with him, and talked this whole matter over, and got his advice as to what course it was best for me to pursue. I found Sandy an old adviser. He told me, with great solemnity, I must go back to Covey; but that before I went, I must go with him into another part of the woods, where there was a certain *root,* which, if I would take some of it with me, carrying it *always on my right side,* would render it impossible for Mr. Covey, or any other white man, to whip me. He said he had carried it for years; and since he had done so, he had never received a blow, and never expected to while he carried it. I at first rejected the idea, that the simple carrying of a root in my pocket would have any such effect as he had said, and was not disposed to take it; but Sandy impressed the necessity with much earnestness, telling me it could do no harm, if it did no good. To please him, I at length took the root, and, according to his

NOTES

PREDICT

Read lines 119–125. What is foreshadowed by Sandy giving the root to Douglass?

CAUSE & EFFECT

Re-read lines 130–138. What is puzzling about Mr. Covey's attitude toward Douglass? What does Douglass think may be the cause?

PREDICT

What is Covey most likely planning to do after he ties Douglass up?

ANALYZE

What happens to Douglass in line 151? Why do you think this occurs?

direction, carried it upon my right side. This was Sunday morning. I immediately started for home; and upon entering the yard gate, out came Mr. Covey on his way to meeting. He spoke to me very kindly, bade me drive the pigs from a lot near by, and passed on towards the church. Now, this singular conduct of Mr. Covey really made me begin to think that there was something in the *root* which Sandy had given me; and had it been on any other day than Sunday, I could have attributed the conduct to no other cause than the influence of that root; and, as it was, I was half inclined to think the *root* to be something more than I at first had taken it to be. All went well till Monday morning. On this morning, the virtue of the *root* was fully tested. Long before daylight, I was called to go and rub, curry, and feed, the horses. I obeyed, and was glad to obey. But whilst thus engaged, whilst in the act of throwing down some blades from the loft, Mr. Covey entered the stable with a long rope; and just as I was half out of the loft, he caught hold of my legs, and was about tying me. As soon as I found what he was up to, I gave a sudden spring, and as I did so, he holding to my legs, I was brought sprawling on the stable floor. Mr. Covey seemed now to think he had me, and could do what he pleased; but at this moment—from whence came the spirit I don't know—I resolved to fight; and, suiting my action to the resolution, I seized Covey hard by the throat; and as I did so, I rose. He held on to me, and I to him. My resistance was so entirely unexpected, that Covey seemed taken all aback. He trembled like a leaf. This gave me assurance, and I held him uneasy, causing the blood to run where I touched him with the ends of my fingers. Mr. Covey soon called out to Hughes for help. Hughes came, and, while Covey held me, attempted to tie my right hand. While he was in the act of doing so, I watched my chance, and gave him a heavy kick close under the ribs. This kick fairly sickened Hughes, so that he left me in the hands of Mr. Covey. This kick had the effect of not only weakening Hughes, but Covey also. When he saw Hughes bending over with pain, his courage quailed. He asked me if I meant to **persist** in my resistance. I told him I did, come what might; that he had used me like a brute for six months, and that I was determined to be used so no longer. With that, he strove to drag me to a stick that was lying just out of the stable door. He meant to knock me down. But just as he was leaning over to get the stick, I seized him with both hands by his collar, and brought him by a sudden snatch to the ground. By this time, Bill came. Covey called upon him for assistance. Bill wanted to know what he could do. Covey said, "Take hold of him, take hold of him!" Bill said his master hired him out to work, and not to help whip me; so he left Covey and myself to fight our own battle out. We were at it for nearly two hours. Covey at length let me go, puffing and blowing at a great rate, saying that if I had not resisted, he would not have whipped me half so much. The truth was, that he had not whipped me at all. I considered him as getting entirely the worst end of the bargain; for he had drawn no blood from me, but I had from him. The whole six months afterwards, that I spent with Mr. Covey, he never laid the weight of his finger upon me in anger. He would occasionally say, he didn't want to get hold of me again. "No," thought I, "you need not; for you will come off worse than you did before."

This battle with Mr. Covey was the turning-point in my career as a slave. It rekindled the few expiring embers of freedom, and revived within me a sense of my own manhood. It recalled the departed self-confidence, and inspired me again with a determination to be free. The **gratification** afforded by the triumph was a full **compensation** for whatever else might follow, even death itself. He only can understand the deep satisfaction which I experienced, who has himself repelled by force the bloody arm of slavery. I felt as I never felt before. It was a glorious resurrection, from the tomb of slavery, to the heaven of freedom. My long-crushed spirit rose, cowardice departed, bold

INTERPRET

Re-read lines 171–173. Why does Bill refuse to help Covey?

CAUSE & EFFECT

How does their fight change the relationship between Douglass and Covey?

VOCABULARY

persist (pər·sist′) *v.:* to hold to a purpose; to continue to do or believe something.

gratification (grat′i·fi·kā′shən) *n.:* condition of being satisfied.

compensation (käm′pən·sā′shən) *n.:* repayment; reimbursement.

VOCABULARY

defiance (dē·fī′əns) *n.:* bold resistance to authority.

INTERPRET

In lines 197–199, Douglass says that although he might "remain a slave in form, the day had passed forever when I could be a slave in fact." Explain his meaning.

NOTES

defiance took its place; and I now resolved that, however long I might remain a slave in form, the day had passed forever when I could be a slave in fact. I did not hesitate to let it be known of me, that the white man who expected to succeed in whipping, must also succeed in killing me.

From this time I was never again what might be called fairly whipped, though I remained a slave four years afterwards. I had several fights, but was never whipped.

Frederick Douglass.
National Portrait Gallery, Smithsonian Institution, Washington, D.C./Art Resource, NY

It was for a long time a matter of surprise to me why Mr. Covey did not immediately have me taken by the constable to the whipping post, and there regularly whipped for the crime of raising my hand against a white man in defence of myself. And the only explanation I can now think of does not entirely satisfy me; but such as it is, I will give it. Mr. Covey enjoyed the most unbounded reputation for being a first-rate overseer and negro-breaker. It was of considerable importance to him. That reputation was at stake; and had he sent me—a boy about sixteen years old—to the public whipping-post, his reputation would have been lost; so, to save his reputation, he suffered me to go unpunished.

FLUENCY

Read the boxed passage aloud. Try to convey Douglass's feelings of puzzlement and relief through your voice and expression.

CONNECT

Do you agree with Douglass's explanation for why Covey did not pursue a further punishment? Why or why not?

MEET THE WRITER

Frederick Douglass (1818–1895), who became an orator, writer, statesman, and diplomat, was born into slavery on a Maryland plantation. Though he was denied a formal education, Douglass taught himself to read and write. In 1838 he escaped to New York and then to Massachusetts. In 1841, he spoke at an abolitionist meeting, and his gifts as an orator were recognized immediately. One historian has written that "He was endowed with the physical attributes of an orator: a magnificent, tall body, a head crowned with a mass of hair, deep-set, flashing eyes, a firm chin, and a rich, melodious voice." In 1845 he traveled overseas to help win British support for abolition. He returned to the United States and worked for the Underground Railroad helping enslaved people escape to the North. He began publishing the *North Star* (later renamed *Frederick Douglass' Paper*), which became the most influential black newspaper of its time. He also supported equal rights for women. During the Civil War, he helped enlist black troops for the Union cause, and later in life he was appointed United States Consul General to Haiti.

Douglass's critics protested that a man of such eloquence could not possibly have been enslaved. He responded in 1845 with the *Narrative of the Life of Frederick Douglass, An American Slave,* his highly acclaimed autobiography. It showed his detractors that he had in fact endured the brutal hardships of slavery, and had survived and triumphed.

from Narrative of the Life of Frederick Douglass, An American Slave

SKILLS FOCUS

Literary Focus
Analyze conflict.

Reading Skills
Analyze cause and effect.

CAUSE AND EFFECT CHART

In the chart below, list an effect for each event from Douglass's narrative.

CAUSE: Douglass labored continually on one of the hottest August days.

↓

EFFECT:

CAUSE: Covey kicked Douglass and hit him with a board.

↓

EFFECT:

CAUSE: Douglass's master forced him to return to Covey.

↓

EFFECT:

CAUSE: When Douglass returned to Covey, Covey tried to beat him.

↓

EFFECT:

CAUSE: Douglass resolved to fight back and ended up beating Covey.

↓

EFFECT:

from Narrative of the Life of Frederick Douglass, An American Slave

VOCABULARY AND COMPREHENSION

WORD BOX

circumstances
immense
comply
resolved
persist
gratification
compensation
defiance

A. Affixes and Roots Write a word from the Word Box on the line next to its root and/or affix. Then write the meaning of the word. Not all words will be used.

1. *circum–,* "around"; *sta,* "stand"

   Word: ____________________

   Meaning: ____

2. *com–,* "with, together, jointly"; *pens,* "weigh or hang"

   Word: ____________________

   Meaning: ____

3. *grat,* "pleasing"

   Word: ____________________

   Meaning: ____

4. *im–,* "not"; *mens,* "measure"

   Word: ____________________

   Meaning: ____

5. *re–,* "again"; *solv,* "solve"

   Word: ____________________

   Meaning: ____

B. Reading Comprehension Answer each question below.

6. Why does Douglass consider his experience with Covey to be an "epoch" in his history?

   ____

   ____

   ____

7. What impression do you form of Douglass from this excerpt?

   ____

   ____

   ____

Vocabulary Skills
Recognize affixes and roots.

BEFORE YOU READ

SPIRITUALS

Four Spirituals
Go Down, Moses • Swing Low, Sweet Chariot • I Thank God I'm Free at Las' • Steal Away

A tradition of spirituals, religious folk songs, grew up among the enslaved Africans. On the surface, the words express a desire for salvation and spiritual freedom. Through the use of allusions and metaphors, however, the songs proclaim a deeper message—longing for escape from slavery.

Spirituals developed among enslaved people in the South before the Civil War, but the songs were not written or collected until the 1860s. The first systematic collection of spirituals, *Slave Songs of the United States,* appeared in 1867. This book helped to introduce the songs to a wide audience.

LITERARY FOCUS: ALLUSION

An **allusion** is an indirect reference to a work of literature or art or to a well-known person, place, or event. For example, a character might be described as having a "Mona Lisa smile." Anyone familiar with Leonardo da Vinci's famous painting knows instantly that the character's smile is mysterious. Allusions expand the meaning of a work, drawing on the readers' previous knowledge.

In these spirituals, the Biblical allusions add significance understood by enslaved Africans but not by the white slave owners. In this way, the songs could be used to send messages about freedom and encourage listeners to continue to hope without direct references. As a result, these spirituals also helped build community among the enslaved workers.

As you read the spirituals, think how the allusions contribute layers of meaning.

Literary Focus
Understand allusion.

Reading Skills
Explore listening.

READING SKILLS: LISTENING

These spirituals were meant to be sung or chanted aloud. As a result, they have strong rhythm. **Rhythm** is created by the pattern of stressed and unstressed syllables and is best heard when the work is read aloud. The spirituals also include other devices originally developed for the purpose of helping the singers or listeners to remember the words. One of these techniques is **repetition,** in which a word, phrase, line, or even a stanza is repeated throughout the song.

After you read each spiritual silently, read it aloud once or even twice to hear the rhythm and appreciate the meaning that the repetition helps to convey.

Go Down, Moses

Go down, Moses,
Way down in Egyptland
Tell old Pharaoh
To let my people go.

When Israel was in Egyptland
Let my people go
Oppressed so hard they could not stand
Let my people go.

Go down, Moses,
Way down in Egyptland
Tell old Pharaoh
"Let my people go."

"Thus saith the Lord," bold Moses said,
"Let my people go;
If not I'll smite your first-born dead
Let my people go."

Go down, Moses,
Way down in Egyptland,
Tell old Pharaoh,
"Let my people go!"

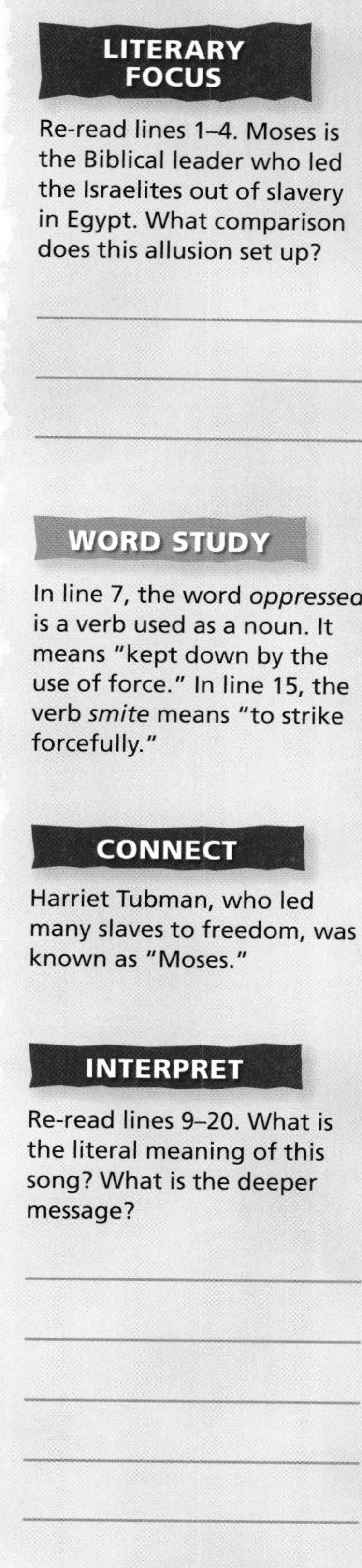

LITERARY FOCUS

Re-read lines 1–4. Moses is the Biblical leader who led the Israelites out of slavery in Egypt. What comparison does this allusion set up?

WORD STUDY

In line 7, the word *oppressed* is a verb used as a noun. It means "kept down by the use of force." In line 15, the verb *smite* means "to strike forcefully."

CONNECT

Harriet Tubman, who led many slaves to freedom, was known as "Moses."

INTERPRET

Re-read lines 9–20. What is the literal meaning of this song? What is the deeper message?

Swing Low, Sweet Chariot

INTERPRET

In the context of the poem, what are the two meanings of the word *home*?

ANALYZE

Some of the spirituals were used to send messages about secret meetings or escapes. What might line 11 be telling the right listener?

COMPARE & CONTRAST

Read the song aloud once or twice. What is the effect of the repetition?

Swing low, sweet chariot,
Coming for to carry me home,
Swing low, sweet chariot,
Coming for to carry me home.

I looked over Jordan and what did I see
Coming for to carry me home,
A band of angels, coming after me,
Coming for to carry me home.

If you get there before I do,
Coming for to carry me home,
Tell all my friends I'm coming too,
Coming for to carry me home.

Swing low, sweet chariot,
Coming for to carry me home,
Swing low, sweet chariot,
Coming for to carry me home.

Swing Low, Sweet Chariot, oil on board by William H. Johnson, c.1939.
The National Museum of American Art, Smithsonian Institution, Washington, D.C./Art Resource, NY

I Thank God I'm Free at Las'

Free at las',° free at las',
I thank God I'm free at las'.
Free at las', free at las',
I thank God I'm free at las'.

Way down yonder in de° graveyard walk,
I thank God I'm free at las'.
Me an' my Jesus gwineter° meet an' talk,
I thank God I'm free at las'.

On-a my knees when de light pass by,
I thank God I'm free at las'.
Thought my soul would arise and fly,
I thank God I'm free at las'.

Some o' dese° mornin's bright and fair,
I thank God I'm free at las'.
Gwineter meet my Jesus in de middle of de air,
I thank God I'm free at las'.

1. las': last.
5. de: the.
7. gwineter: going to.
13. some o' dese: some of these.

INFER

What is the feeling of the speaker? Why?

INTERPRET

According to the words of the speaker in lines 5–12, how has he attained his freedom? What is another way to interpret these lines?

CAUSE & EFFECT

What is the effect of the dialect?

Steal Away

Steal away, steal away, steal away to Jesus,
Steal away, steal away home,
I ain't got long to stay here.

My Lord, He calls me,
He calls me by the thunder,
The trumpet sounds within-a my soul,
I ain't got long to stay here.

Steal away, steal away, steal away to Jesus,
Steal away, steal away home,
I ain't got long to stay here.

Green trees a-bending,
Po' sinner stands a-trembling
The trumpet sounds within-a my soul,
I ain't got long to stay here.

Steal away, steal away, steal away to Jesus,
Steal away, steal away home,
I ain't got long to stay here.

WORD STUDY

The phrase "steal away" means to go somewhere quietly and without attracting attention.

PARAPHRASE

Re-read lines 4–10. In your own words, explain what the speaker is saying.

INFER

What is the speaker saying in the last line of each stanza?

BACKGROUND

Spirituals are a form of folk literature, like ballads. There are no known composers of these songs, and since they were transmitted orally, many of them exist in several different versions. Some spirituals were known as "signal" songs. They were used to carry messages. "Follow the Drinking Gourd," for instance, told enslaved Africans trying to escape to follow the Big Dipper in the night sky, which pointed to the North Star, the way to freedom.

Many writers have paid tribute to these beautiful and moving songs. In his poem "O Black and Unknown Bards," James Weldon Johnson says that the spirituals were born of oppression but became a poetry of hope, both for spiritual salvation and for freedom on earth.

SKILLS PRACTICE

Four Spirituals

Go Down, Moses • Swing Low, Sweet Chariot • I Thank God I'm Free at Las' • Steal Away

ALLUSIONS CHART

In the spirituals, the allusions to the Bible have a literal meaning and also a deeper significance. Explain the allusions in this chart.

ALLUSIONS	LITERAL MEANING	SIGNIFICANCE
Moses	leader of Israelites	
Egyptland	land of Egypt where the Israelites were enslaved	
Pharoah	ruler of Egypt who kept the Israelites enslaved	
my people	Israelites	
chariot	conveyance that will take the singer to heaven	
Jordan	river beyond which ancient Israel was located	

READING COMPREHENSION Answer each question below.

1. Why is Moses described as bold?

____

____

2. How does the Lord call the speaker in "Steal Away"? What impression of the Lord does the speaker convey?

____

____

____

3. Identify some of the major characteristics of the spiritual genre.

____

____

____

Literary Focus
Analyze allusions.

BEFORE YOU READ

from Incidents in the Life of a Slave Girl

by Harriet A. Jacobs

Although Harriet Jacobs suffered her share of harsh treatment while she was enslaved, this excerpt focuses more on the behaviors of the white members of the slave-owning society, rather than on her specific trials. The details she includes, however, are just as condemning of the institution, since they show how slavery destroys the humanity of those who profit from it even while inflicting suffering on those trapped by it.

LITERARY FOCUS: SLAVE NARRATIVE

Slave narratives are autobiographical accounts written by formerly enslaved people. By reading one of these narratives, you can learn more about the period of slavery in the United States, the society that kept it going, and the individuals who endured the hardships of being enslaved.

To help identify significant details, ask yourself these questions as you read the narrative:

- What is the specific setting, and how does it affect the action?
- What is the major conflict?
- What do the thoughts, actions, and words of Jacobs reveal about her character?
- What ideas are conveyed about the historical context?
- How does this narrative affect me?
- What are some themes brought out by the narrative?

READING SKILLS: DRAWING CONCLUSIONS

Drawing conclusions helps you to understand and appreciate the full meaning of what you read. When you draw conclusions, you use details in the text and your prior knowledge to make judgments or statements beyond what is written.

You draw conclusions frequently in your daily life. For example, if it is close to dinner time and appetizing smells are wafting from the kitchen, you might conclude that someone is cooking you a great dinner.

Paying close attention to details as you read will help you to draw accurate conclusions about the elements of this slave narrative.

Literary Focus Analyze elements of a slave narrative.

Reading Skills Draw conclusions based on details in a text.

Vocabulary Skills Use context clues to define unknown words.

VOCABULARY DEVELOPMENT

PREVIEW SELECTION VOCABULARY

The following words appear in the excerpt from *Incidents in the Life of a Slave Girl.* Look them over before you begin to read.

scourge (skurj) *v.:* afflict with suffering.

He used words as effectively as weapons to ***scourge*** *those under his authority.*

subserviency (səb·sur′vē·ən·sē) *n.:* behavior showing submissiveness or obedience to someone in authority.

The narrator does not show ***subserviency*** *to the white soldiers; rather she asserts her independence.*

appeased (ə·pēz′d) *v.:* satisfied or relieved.

The landowners were not ***appeased*** *until all the homes had been searched.*

USING CONTEXT CLUES

Reading a difficult text can become tedious if you're constantly reaching for a dictionary to define unknown words. When you use **context clues,** you look for surrounding words and phrases within the text that hint at meaning. Using context clues can make reading more enjoyable by keeping you immersed in the text. It can also help you improve your reading skills and build vocabulary.

The first step you may take in using context clues is to identify an unknown word's part of speech. This can tell you whether the word identifies a person, place, or thing, an action, or a description of something. Once you know what type of word you're trying to define, look for an **explanation, synonym, antonym,** or **example** that helps you gain a general sense of its meaning. Read the sentence below from the narrative:

> "Not far from this time Nat Turner's insurrection broke out; and the news threw our town into great commotion."

You may be unsure of the meaning of *insurrection,* but you can tell from its context that the word is a noun. You know that it is something that was led by a person named Nat Turner, it "broke out," and it caused commotion in the town. This can lead you to conclude that an insurrection is a rebellion.

As you read the selection, try this strategy of using context clues to help you understand any unfamiliar words.

ANALYZE

Supporters of slavery often tried to justify the practice by saying that enslaved people were happy and content. Read lines 1–4. How does the author suggest the opposite?

DRAW CONCLUSIONS

Read lines 12–16. What is the real purpose of the muster?

from Incidents in the Life of a Slave Girl

by Harriet A. Jacobs

Not far from this time Nat Turner's insurrection[1] broke out; and the news threw our town into great commotion. Strange that they should be alarmed, when their slaves were so "contented and happy"! But so it was.

It was always the custom to have a muster[2] every year. On the occasion every white man shouldered his musket. The citizens and the so-called country gentlemen wore military uniforms. The poor whites took their places in the ranks in every-day dress, some without shoes, some without hats. This grand occasion had already passed; and when the slaves were told that there was to be another muster, they were surprised and rejoiced. Poor creatures! They thought it was going to be a

Nat Turner (1800–1831), engraving, 19th century.
The Granger Collection, New York

1. **Nat Turner's insurrection:** In 1831, Nat Turner led a rebellion against slavery in Southampton County, Virginia, near Jacobs's owner's plantation.
2. **muster** (mus′tər) *n.:* military inspection.

From *Incidents in the Life of a Slave Girl* by Harriet A. Jacobs, 1861.

holiday. I was informed of the true state of affairs, and imparted it to the few I could trust. Most gladly would I have proclaimed it to every slave; but I dared not. All could not be relied on. Mighty is the power of the torturing lash.

By sunrise, people were pouring in from every quarter within twenty miles of the town. I knew the houses were to be searched; and I expected it would be done by country bullies and the poor whites. I knew nothing annoyed them so much as to see colored people living in comfort and respectability; so . . . I arranged every thing in my grandmother's house as neatly as possible. I put white quilts on the beds, and decorated some of the rooms with flowers. When all was arranged, I sat down at the window to watch. Far as my eye could reach, it rested on a motley crowd of soldiers. Drums and fifes were discoursing martial music. . . . Orders were given, and the wild scouts rushed in every direction, wherever a colored face was to be found.

It was a grand opportunity for the low whites, who had no negroes of their own to **scourge.** They exulted in such a chance to exercise a little brief authority, and show their **subserviency** to the slaveholders; not reflecting that the power which trampled on the colored people also kept themselves in poverty, ignorance, and moral degradation. Those who never witnessed such scenes can hardly believe what I know was inflicted at this time on innocent men, women, and children, against whom there was not the slightest ground for suspicion. Colored people and slaves who lived in remote parts of the town suffered in an especial manner. In some cases the searchers scattered powder and shot among their clothes, and then sent other parties to find them, and bring them forward as proof that they were plotting insurrection. Every where men, women, and children were whipped till the blood stood in puddles at

3. **nigh at hand:** near at hand.

LITERARY FOCUS

What do lines 20–22 reveal about Jacobs?

ANALYZE

What is the effect of "discoursing martial music" (lines 26–27) on the mood?

VOCABULARY

scourge (skurj) *v.:* afflict with suffering.

subserviency (səb·sur′vē·ən·sē) *n.:* behavior showing submissiveness or obedience to someone in authority.

DRAW CONCLUSIONS

Re-read lines 49–53. What picture emerges of many members of the white population?

VOCABULARY

appeased (ə·pēz′d) *v.:* satisfied or relieved.

CAUSE & EFFECT

What long-term effects did Nat Turner's rebellion have on the enslaved Africans living in this part of the South?

their feet. . . . The dwellings of the colored people, unless they happened to be protected by some influential white person, who was nigh at hand,[3] were robbed of clothing and every thing else the marauders thought worth carrying away. All day long these unfeeling wretches went round, like a troop of demons, terrifying and tormenting the helpless. At night, they formed themselves into patrol bands, and went wherever they chose among the colored people, acting out their brutal will. . . . The consternation was universal. No two people that had the slightest tinge of color in their faces dared to be seen talking together. . . .

The day patrol continued for some weeks, and at sundown a night guard was substituted. Nothing at all was proved against the colored people, bond or free. The wrath of the slaveholders was somewhat **appeased** by the capture of Nat Turner. The imprisoned were released. . . . Visiting was strictly forbidden on the plantations. The slaves begged the privilege of again meeting at their little church in the woods. . . . Their request was denied, and the church was demolished. They were permitted to attend the white churches, a certain portion of the galleries[4] being appropriated to their use.

4. **galleries** (gal′ər·ēz) *n.:* balconies.

MEET THE WRITER

Harriet A. Jacobs (1813–1897), was born into slavery in North Carolina. Her parents died when she was still a child, and she was taken in by her owner and taught to read and sew. This woman died when Jacobs was twelve, and she was sent to another owner who subjected her to abusive treatment. Ten years later, Jacobs escaped, went to her grandmother (a freedwoman who lived nearby), and hid in her tiny attic, infested with rats and mice. In the meantime, her two children were sent to live with her grandmother. Jacobs was able to watch them play in the street below through a small hole in the attic wall.

In 1842 Jacobs escaped to the North, where she was eventually reunited with her children. Nevertheless, she remained in constant danger because her owner continued searching for her, and after he died, his daughter continued the pursuit. Finally, a friend bought Jacobs's freedom from her owner's family.

Jacobs became active in the antislavery movement. On the advice of friends she wrote her autobiography, *Incidents in the Life of a Slave Girl* (1861). In her preface, she says that her purpose is "to arouse the women of the North to a realizing sense of the condition of two million of women at the South, still in bondage, suffering what I suffered, and most of them far worse."

EXTEND

Read another excerpt from *Incidents in the Life of a Slave Girl.* With a partner, analyze elements of her writing style and discuss your opinions about the selection.

SKILLS PRACTICE

from Incidents in the Life of a Slave Girl

Literary Focus
Analyze elements of a slave narrative.

Reading Skills
Draw conclusions based on details in a text.

DRAW CONCLUSIONS

Using details from the text and your prior knowledge, draw a conclusion that responds to each question.

HISTORICAL CONTEXT
What was the position of free blacks in society at the time this narrative is set?

↓

CONCLUSION

AUTHOR
Based on details in the narrative, what conclusions might you draw about the circumstances of the author at the time of the events?

↓

CONCLUSION

AUTHOR'S PURPOSE
Why did the author write this narrative?

↓

CONCLUSION

from Incidents in the Life of a Slave Girl

VOCABULARY AND COMPREHENSION

WORD BOX

scourge

appeased

subserviency

A. Context Clues Complete each sentence with the word from the Word Box. Then underline context clues that hint at the word's meaning.

1. The muster was eager to ______________________ potential rebels, and even tormented innocent people.

2. The muster would not be ______________________ until those involved were found and punished.

3. The ______________________ of the innocent victims did not seem to matter; they were treated as if they, too, had rebelled.

B. Reading Comprehension Answer each question below.

4. Why was a muster called?

____

____

____

____

5. Why were black people afraid to be seen speaking with each other during the weeks following the rebellion?

____

____

____

____

6. Identify an incident in which innocent people were targeted or threatened as a result of a conflict in which they were not involved. Compare and contrast this event with the aftermath of Nat Turner's rebellion as described by Jacobs.

____

____

____

____

Vocabulary Skills
Use context clues.

BEFORE YOU READ

from Harriet Tubman: Conductor on the Underground Railroad

by Ann Petry

In this excerpt from the Harriet Tubman biography, the author describes how the famous freer of enslaved people led a group of eleven runaways on a harrowing journey from a Maryland plantation to freedom in Canada. Harriet Tubman, who was born into slavery around 1820, escaped North in 1849. She then returned to the South nineteen times to help many enslaved people make the dangerous journey to freedom.

LITERARY FOCUS: BIOGRAPHY

Narratives are writings that tell a story. Narratives include both fiction (made-up stories) and nonfiction (true stories about real people and events). A **biography** is a nonfictional narrative, a true story about a person's life told by someone else. The selection you are about to read is excerpted from a biography of Harriet Tubman written by the contemporary author Ann Petry. In it, Petry relates one episode in the life of this courageous freedom fighter. To bring life to her characters, some dialogue has been recreated, but it is based on accounts Petry read while researching her subject.

Biographies of famous people in American history not only provide the opportunity to learn about the subject of the biography, but also about the daily life, customs, and issues of the time. As you read this selection, look for answers to these questions:

- What events take place in the selection?
- How did the Underground Railroad operate?
- What dangers and potential consequences did runaways risk?

Read about Harriet Tubman's character, and decide why you do or do not admire what she accomplished.

Literary Focus Understand the characteristics of a biography.

Reading Skills Identify author's purpose.

Vocabulary Skills Understand synonyms.

READING SKILLS: AUTHOR'S PURPOSE

In literature, an **author's purpose** is his or her intent in writing a particular work. Authors write literary works for a variety of reasons, including to inform, to entertain, to educate, to persuade, to explain, or to describe. Often, they accomplish more than one of these purposes in a literary work.

As you read the excerpt from the Harriet Tubman biography, think about the purpose or purposes that Ann Petry considered in her writing.

VOCABULARY DEVELOPMENT

PREVIEW SELECTION VOCABULARY

The following words appear in the excerpt from the Harriet Tubman biography. Look them over before you begin the selection.

intervals (in′tər·vəlz) *n.:* spaces between things; periods of time between events.

*The **intervals** between the classes were ten minutes—just enough time to get from one room to another.*

invariably (in·ver′ē·ə·blē) *adv.:* unchangingly; constantly.

*Though urged to shop at other stores, Linda **invariably** goes to her favorite boutique.*

incomprehensible (in′käm′prē·hen′sə·bəl) *adj.:* impossible to understand; unintelligible.

*Because the student could not read, he found the text **incomprehensible**.*

disheveled (di·shev′əld) *adj.:* not neat; rumpled; untidy.

*His uncombed hair and wrinkled clothing gave the professor a **disheveled** appearance.*

dispel (di·spel′) *v.:* drive away; get rid of.

*The teacher **dispelled** the students' hopes when she announced that no one had achieved a perfect score on the test.*

reluctance (ri·luc′təns) *n.:* unwillingness; hesitation.

*As she clutched the necklace tightly, the woman's **reluctance** to give it up was obvious.*

mutinous (myo͞ot′′n·əs) *adj.:* rebellious; disobedient to authority.

*The **mutinous** staff marched around the office building, chanting slogans to protest their low wages.*

indomitable (in·däm′i·tə·bəl) *adv.:* invincible; unyielding.

*The warriors displayed an **indomitable** spirit in refusing to surrender to their enemy.*

UNDERSTANDING SYNONYMS

A **synonym** is a word that has the same meaning or close to the same meaning as another word. Synonyms are always the same part of speech. If you aren't satisfied with a certain word in your writing, you can try to replace it with a synonym. A thesaurus is the most useful tool for finding synonyms. Most thesauri list synonyms based on a word's different shades of meaning, or connotations. When using a thesaurus, you should look at all the synonyms given and follow the cross-references until you find the exact meaning you would like to convey.

If you encounter a difficult word in reading the excerpt of the Harriet Tubman biography, think about synonyms that could be used to replace it.

from Harriet Tubman: Conductor on the Underground Railroad

by Ann Petry

INFER

Based on what you already know about this selection, who is Moses?

DRAW CONCLUSIONS

Re-read lines 13–16. What can you conclude about the sound of the whippoorwill call late at night out of season?

VOCABULARY

intervals (in′tər·vəlz) *n.:* spaces between things; periods of time between events.

invariably (in·vər′ē·a·blē) *adv.:* unchangingly; constantly.

Along the Eastern Shore of Maryland, in Dorchester County, in Caroline County, the masters kept hearing whispers about the man named Moses, who was running off slaves. At first they did not believe in his existence. The stories about him were fantastic, unbelievable. Yet they watched for him. They offered rewards for his capture.

They never saw him. Now and then they heard whispered rumors to the effect that he was in the neighborhood. The woods were searched. The roads were watched. There was never anything to indicate his whereabouts. But a few days afterward, a goodly number of slaves would be gone from the plantation. Neither the master nor the overseer had heard or seen anything unusual in the quarter.[1] Sometimes one or the other would vaguely remember having heard a whippoorwill call somewhere in the woods, close by, late at night. Though it was the wrong season for whippoorwills.

Sometimes the masters thought they had heard the cry of a hoot owl, repeated, and would remember having thought that the **intervals** between the low moaning cry were wrong, that it had been repeated four times in succession instead of three. There was never anything more than that to suggest that all was not well in the quarter. Yet when morning came, they **invariably** discovered that a group of the finest slaves had taken to their heels.

1. **in the quarter:** the area where enslaved people lived on the plantation.

Unfortunately, the discovery was almost always made on a Sunday. Thus a whole day was lost before the machinery of pursuit could be set in motion. The posters offering rewards for the fugitives could not be printed until Monday. The men who made a living hunting for runaway slaves were out of reach, off in the woods with their dogs and their guns, in pursuit of four-footed game, or they were in camp meetings saying their prayers with their wives and families beside them.

Harriet Tubman could have told them that there was far more involved in this matter of running off slaves than signaling the would-be runaways by imitating the call of a whippoorwill, or a hoot owl, far more involved than a matter of waiting for a clear night when the North Star was visible.

In December, 1851, when she started out with the band of fugitives that she planned to take to Canada, she had been in the vicinity of the plantation for days, planning the trip, carefully selecting the slaves that she would take with her.

She had announced her arrival in the quarter by singing the forbidden spiritual— "Go down, Moses, 'way down to Egypt Land" —singing it softly outside the door of a slave cabin, late at night. The husky voice was beautiful even when it was barely more than a murmur borne on the wind.

Once she had made her presence known, word of her coming spread from cabin to cabin. The slaves whispered to each other, ear to mouth, mouth to ear, "Moses is here." "Moses has come." "Get ready. Moses is back again." The ones who had agreed to go North with her put ashcake and salt herring in an old bandanna, hastily tied it into a bundle, and then waited patiently for the signal that meant it was time to start.

There were eleven in this party, including one of her brothers and his wife. It was the largest group that she had ever conducted, but she was determined that more and more slaves should know what freedom was like.

LITERARY FOCUS

What insights into Harriet Tubman's character does the author provide on this page?

INFER

Review the spiritual "Go Down, Moses" on page 113. Why would this song have been forbidden on plantations that held enslaved people?

VOCABULARY

incomprehensible (in'käm'prē·hen'sə·bəl) *adj.:* unintelligible; impossible to understand.

DRAW CONCLUSIONS

Based on the examples provided, what do you think was the basic intent of the Fugitive Slave Law as mentioned in lines 58–63?

INFER

Re-read lines 72–76. What was the monetary reward for capturing a person who had escaped from slavery?

PRICE, TWENTY-FIVE CENTS.
THE
BOSTON SLAVE RIOT,
AND
TRIAL
OF
Anthony Burns,
CONTAINING THE
REPORT OF THE FANEUIL HALL MEETING; THE MURDER OF BACHELDER; THEODORE PARKER'S LESSON FOR THE DAY; SPEECHES OF COUNSEL ON BOTH SIDES, CORRECTED BY THEMSELVES; VERBATIM REPORT OF JUDGE LORING'S DECISION; AND, A DETAILED ACCOUNT OF THE EMBARKATION.
BOSTON:
FETRIDGE AND COMPANY
1854.

Pamphlet informing people about the trial of Anthony Burns (1834–1862) conducted under the 1854 Fugitive Slave Law.
The Granger Collection, New York

She had to take them all the way to Canada. The Fugitive Slave Law was no longer a great many **incomprehensible** words written down on the country's lawbooks. The new law had become a reality. It was Thomas Sims, a boy, picked up on the streets of Boston at night and shipped back to Georgia. It was Jerry and Shadrach, arrested and jailed with no warning.

She had never been in Canada. The route beyond Philadelphia was strange to her. But she could not let the runaways who accompanied her know this. As they walked along she told them stories of her own first flight, she kept painting vivid word pictures of what it would be like to be free.

But there were so many of them this time. She knew moments of doubt when she was half-afraid, and kept looking back over her shoulder, imagining that she heard the sound of pursuit. They would certainly be pursued. Eleven of them. Eleven thousand dollars' worth of flesh and bone and muscle that belonged to Maryland planters. If they were caught, the eleven runaways would be whipped and sold South, but she—she would probably be hanged.

They tried to sleep during the day but they never could wholly relax into sleep. She could tell by the positions they assumed, by their restless movements. And they walked at night. Their progress was slow. It took them three nights of walking to reach the first stop. She had told them about the place where they would stay, promising warmth and good food, holding these things out to them as an incentive to keep going.

When she knocked on the door of a farmhouse, a place where she and her parties of runaways had always been welcome, always been given shelter and plenty to eat, there was no answer. She knocked again, softly. A voice from within said, "Who is it?" There was fear in the voice.

She knew instantly from the sound of the voice that there was something wrong. She said, "A friend with friends," the password on the Underground Railroad.

The door opened, slowly. The man who stood in the doorway looked at her coldly, looked with unconcealed astonishment and fear at the eleven **disheveled** runaways who were standing near her. Then he shouted, "Too many, too many. It's not safe. My place was searched last week. It's not safe!" and slammed the door in her face.

She turned away from the house, frowning. She had promised her passengers food and rest and warmth, and instead of that, there would be hunger and cold and more walking over the frozen ground. Somehow she would have to instill courage into these eleven people, most of them strangers, would have to feed them on hope and bright dreams of freedom instead of the fried pork and corn bread and milk she had promised them.

They stumbled along behind her, half-dead for sleep, and she urged them on, though she was as tired and as discouraged as they were. She had never been in Canada but she kept painting wondrous word pictures of what it would be like. She managed to **dispel** their fear of pursuit, so that they would not become hysterical, panic-stricken. Then she had to bring some of the fear back, so that they would stay awake and keep walking though they drooped with sleep.

Yet during the day, when they lay down deep in a thicket, they never really slept, because if a twig snapped or the wind sighed in the branches of a pine tree, they jumped to their feet,

DRAW CONCLUSIONS

What was the fate of a person who was caught trying to escape from slavery?

ANALYZE

Why do you think the author includes information about the reward for and fate of people trying to escape slavery?

VOCABULARY

disheveled (di·s·hev′əld) *adj.:* not neat; rumpled; untidy.

dispel (di·spel′) *v.:* drive away; get rid of.

SUMMARIZE

Summarize the ordeals that people suffered on their journey to escape from slavery.

INTERPRET

What words would you use to describe the mood the author creates in relating these ordeals?

EXTEND

Find out about Quaker beliefs and practices. Why would they have been inclined to help people who were trying to escape slavery?

Harriet Tubman, c. 1945, oil on paperboard by William H. Johnson (1901–1970).
Smithsonian American Art Museum, Washington, DC/Art Resource, NY

afraid of their own shadows, shivering and shaking. It was very cold, but they dared not make fires because someone would see the smoke and wonder about it.

She kept thinking, eleven of them. Eleven thousand dollars' worth of slaves. And she had to take them all the way to Canada. Sometimes she told them about Thomas Garrett, in Wilmington. She said he was their friend even though he did not know them. He was the friend of all fugitives. He called them God's poor. He was a Quaker[2] and his speech was a little different from that of other people. His clothing was different, too. He wore the wide-brimmed hat that the Quakers wear.

She said that he had thick white hair, soft, almost like a baby's, and the kindest eyes she had ever seen. He was a big man and strong, but he had never used his strength to harm anyone,

2. **Quaker:** a name used for a member of the Society of Friends, a Christian denomination that rejects violence.

always to help people. He would give all of them a new pair of shoes. Everybody. He always did. Once they reached his house in Wilmington, they would be safe. He would see to it that they were.

She described the house where he lived, told them about the store where he sold shoes. She said he kept a pail of milk and a loaf of bread in the drawer of his desk so that he would have food ready at hand for any of God's poor who should suddenly appear before him, fainting with hunger. There was a hidden room in the store. A whole wall swung open, and behind it was a room where he could hide fugitives. On the wall there were shelves filled with small boxes—boxes of shoes—so that you would never guess that the wall actually opened.

While she talked, she kept watching them. They did not believe her. She could tell by their expressions. They were thinking, New shoes, Thomas Garrett, Quaker, Wilmington—what foolishness was this? Who knew if she told the truth? Where was she taking them anyway?

That night they reached the next stop—a farm that belonged to a German. She made the runaways take shelter behind trees at the edge of the fields before she knocked at the door. She hesitated before she approached the door, thinking, suppose that he, too, should refuse shelter, suppose— Then she thought, Lord, I'm going to hold steady on to You and You've got to see me through—and knocked softly.

She heard the familiar guttural voice say, "Who's there?"

She answered quickly, "A friend with friends."

He opened the door and greeted her warmly. "How many this time?" he asked.

"Eleven," she said and waited, doubting, wondering.

He said, "Good. Bring them in."

He and his wife fed them in the lamplit kitchen, their faces glowing, as they offered food and more food, urging them to eat, saying there was plenty for everybody, have more milk, have more bread, have more meat.

COMPARE & CONTRAST

How is the description of Thomas Garrett's character and behavior consistent with principles that Quakers follow?

LITERARY FOCUS

What do you learn about Harriet Tubman lines 148–154?

VOCABULARY

reluctance (ri·luc′təns) *n.:* unwillingness; hesitation.

mutinous (myo͞ot′′n·əs) *adj.:* rebellious; disobedient to authority.

WORD STUDY

What synonym for the word *measure* comes closest to the intended meaning in the phrase *measure of contentment* in line 172? Explain the reason for your choice. Use a dictionary, if needed, to help you decide.

INFER

What is Harriet Tubman's purpose in telling the runaways about William Still, William and Ellen Craft, and Frederick Douglass?

They spent the night in the warm kitchen. They really slept, all that night and until dusk the next day. When they left, it was with **reluctance**. They had all been warm and safe and well-fed. It was hard to exchange the security offered by that clean warm kitchen for the darkness and the cold of a December night.

Harriet had found it hard to leave the warmth and friendliness, too. But she urged them on. For a while, as they walked, they seemed to carry in them a measure of contentment; some of the serenity and the cleanliness of that big warm kitchen lingered on inside them. But as they walked farther and farther away from the warmth and the light, the cold and the darkness entered into them. They fell silent, sullen, suspicious. She waited for the moment when some one of them would turn **mutinous**. It did not happen that night.

Two nights later she was aware that the feet behind her were moving slower and slower. She heard the irritability in their voices, knew that soon someone would refuse to go on.

She started talking about William Still and the Philadelphia Vigilance Committee[3]. No one commented. No one asked any questions. She told them the story of William and Ellen Craft and how they escaped from Georgia. Ellen was so fair that she looked as though she were white, and so she dressed up in a man's clothing and she looked like a wealthy young planter. Her husband, William, who was dark, played the role of her slave. Thus they traveled from Macon, Georgia, to Philadelphia, riding on the trains, staying at the finest hotels. Ellen pretended to be very ill—her right arm was in a sling, and her right hand was bandaged, because she was supposed to have rheumatism. Thus she avoided having to sign the register at the hotels for she could not read or write. They finally arrived safely in Philadelphia, and then went on to Boston.

No one said anything. Not one of them seemed to have heard her.

3. **Philadelphia Vigilance Committee:** local organization that helped people escaping along the Underground Railroad.

She told them about Frederick Douglass, the most famous of the escaped slaves, of his eloquence, of his magnificent appearance. Then she told them of her own first vain effort at running away, evoking[4] the memory of that miserable life she had led as a child, reliving it for a moment in the telling.

But they had been tired too long, hungry too long, afraid too long, footsore too long. One of them suddenly cried out in despair, "Let me go back. It is better to be a slave than to suffer like this in order to be free."

She carried a gun with her on these trips. She had never used it—except as a threat. Now as she aimed it, she experienced a feeling of guilt, remembering that time, years ago, when she had prayed for the death of Edward Brodas, the Master, and then not too long afterward had heard that great wailing cry that came from the throats of the field hands,[5] and knew from the sound that the Master was dead.

One of the runaways said, again, "Let me go back. Let me go back," and stood still, and then turned around and said, over his shoulder, "I am going back."

She lifted the gun, aimed it at the despairing slave. She said, "Go on with us or die." The husky low-pitched voice was grim.

He hesitated for a moment and then he joined the others. They started walking again. She tried to explain to them why none of them could go back to the plantation. If a runaway returned, he would turn traitor, the master and the overseer would force him to turn traitor. The returned slave would disclose the stopping places, the hiding places, the cornstacks they had used with the full knowledge of the owner of the farm, the name of the German farmer who had fed them and sheltered them. These people who had risked their own security to help runaways would be ruined, fined, imprisoned.

She said, "We got to go free or die. And freedom's not bought with dust."

---

4. **evoking** (ē·vok′iŋ) *v.:* to draw forth (the memory).
5. **field hands:** enslaved people who worked in the fields of a plantation.

INFER

What is the author's purpose in describing the stories that Tubman tells the runaways?

DRAW CONCLUSIONS

What do you learn from the text on this page?

ANALYZE

Re-read lines 217–228. Do you think Tubman's threat was real? Why or why not?

COMPARE & CONTRAST

How are the stories Tubman tells here different from the ones on the previous page? Why do you think she chooses these stories at this point?

VOCABULARY

indomitable (in·däm′i·tə·bəl) *adj.:* invincible; unyielding.

NOTES

This time she told them about the long agony of the Middle Passage on the old slave ships, about the black horror of the holds, about the chains and the whips. They too knew these stories. But she wanted to remind them of the long hard way they had come, about the long hard way they had yet to go. She told them about Thomas Sims, the boy picked up on the streets of Boston and sent back to Georgia. She said when they got him back to Savannah, got him in prison there, they whipped him until a doctor who was standing by watching said, "You will kill him if you strike him again!" His master said, "Let him die!"

Thus she forced them to go on. Sometimes she thought she had become nothing but a voice speaking in the darkness, cajoling,[6] urging, threatening. Sometimes she told them things to make them laugh, sometimes she sang to them, and heard the eleven voices behind her blending softly with hers, and then she knew that for the moment all was well with them.

She gave the impression of being a short, muscular, **indomitable** woman who could never be defeated. Yet at any moment she was liable to be seized by one of those curious fits of sleep, which might last for a few minutes or for hours.

Even on this trip, she suddenly fell asleep in the woods. The runaways, ragged, dirty, hungry, cold, did not steal the gun as they might have, and set off by themselves, or turn back. They sat on the ground near her and waited patiently until she awakened. They had come to trust her implicitly, totally. They, too, had come to believe her repeated statement, "We got to go free or die." She was leading them into freedom, and so they waited until she was ready to go on.

Finally, they reached Thomas Garrett's house in Wilmington, Delaware. Just as Harriet had promised, Garrett gave them all new shoes, and provided carriages to take them on to the next stop.

6. **cajoling** (kə·jōl′iŋ) *v.:* coaxing.

Thomas Garrett.
©Louie Psihoyos/CORBIS

By slow stages they reached Philadelphia, where William Still hastily recorded their names, and the plantations whence they had come, and something of the life they had led in slavery. Then he carefully hid what he had written, for fear it might be discovered. In 1872 he published this record in book form and called it *The Underground Railroad.* In the foreword to his book he said: "While I knew the danger of keeping strict records, and while I did not then dream that in my day slavery would be blotted out, or that the time would come when I could publish these records, it used to afford me great satisfaction to take them down, fresh from the lips of fugitives on the way to freedom, and to preserve them as they had given them."

CLARIFY

Re-read lines 259–268 and then explain the literal and figurative meanings of an *underground railroad.* Who were the "conductors"? What were the "station stops" along the way?

CONNECT

In lines 263–274, the text talks about how William Still recorded information about the escaping people. Why is this historically important?

EXTEND

Find out about the role John Brown (mentioned in line 287) played in the slavery issue. Why would Harriet Tubman have been a supporter of him?

WORD STUDY

Look up *fastidious* from line 296 in a dictionary if you do not know its meaning. Why would the runaways not have been fastidious about their food or shelter?

CONNECT

What kinds of feelings might the runaways have had as they traveled north?

William Still, who was familiar with all the station stops on the Underground Railroad, supplied Harriet with money and sent her and her eleven fugitives on to Burlington, New Jersey.

Harriet felt safer now, though there were danger spots ahead. But the biggest part of her job was over. As they went farther and farther north, it grew colder; she was aware of the wind on the Jersey ferry and aware of the cold damp in New York. From New York they went on to Syracuse, where the temperature was even lower.

In Syracuse she met the Reverend J. W. Loguen, known as "Jarm" Loguen. This was the beginning of a lifelong friendship. Both Harriet and Jarm Loguen were to become friends and supporters of Old John Brown.

From Syracuse they went north again, into a colder, snowier city—Rochester. Here they almost certainly stayed with Frederick Douglass, for he wrote in his autobiography:

"On one occasion I had eleven fugitives at the same time under my roof, and it was necessary for them to remain with me until I could collect sufficient money to get them to Canada. It was the largest number I ever had at any one time, and I had some difficulty in providing so many with food and shelter, but, as may well be imagined, they were not very fastidious in either direction, and were well content with very plain food, and a strip of carpet on the floor for a bed, or a place on the straw in the barnloft."

Late in December, 1851, Harriet arrived in St. Catharines, Canada West (now Ontario), with the eleven fugitives. It had taken almost a month to complete this journey; most of the time had been spent getting out of Maryland.

That first winter in St. Catharines was a terrible one. Canada was a strange frozen land, snow everywhere, ice everywhere, and a bone-biting cold the like of which none of them had ever experienced before. Harriet rented a small frame house in the town and set to work to make a home. The fugitives boarded with her. They worked in the forests, felling trees, and so did she. Sometimes she took other jobs, cooking or cleaning house for people in the town. She cheered on these newly arrived fugitives, working herself, finding work for them, finding food for them, praying for them, sometimes begging for them.

Often she found herself thinking of the beauty of Maryland, the mellowness of the soil, the richness of the plant life there. The climate itself made for an ease of living that could never be duplicated in this bleak, barren countryside.

In spite of the severe cold, the hard work, she came to love St. Catharines and the other towns and cities in Canada where black men lived. She discovered that freedom meant more than the right to change jobs at will, more than the right to keep the money that one earned. It was the right to vote and to sit on juries. It was the right to be elected to office. In Canada there were black men who were county officials and members of school boards. St. Catharines had a large colony of ex-slaves, and they owned their own homes, kept them neat and clean and in good repair. They lived in whatever part of town they chose and sent their children to the schools.

INFER

What challenges did the runaways face as they adjusted to life in Canada?

GENERALIZE

Write a generalization about the meaning of freedom based on the last paragraph on this page.

Harriet Tubman (far left), photographed with a group of people she helped escape from slavery.
©Bettmann/CORBIS

GENERALIZE

What generalization can you make about the rights granted to free blacks in Canada during the period of slavery in the United States?

DRAW CONCLUSIONS

What can you conclude about Harriet Tubman based on the work she pursued?

When spring came she decided that she would make this small Canadian city her home—as much as any place could be said to be home to a woman who traveled from Canada to the Eastern Shore of Maryland as often as she did.

In the spring of 1852, she went back to Cape May, New Jersey. She spent the summer there, cooking in a hotel. That fall she returned, as usual, to Dorchester County, and brought out nine more slaves, conducting them all the way to St. Catharines, in Canada West, to the bone-biting cold, the snow-covered forests—and freedom.

She continued to live in this fashion, spending the winter in Canada, and the spring and summer working in Cape May, New Jersey, or in Philadelphia. She made two trips a year into slave territory, one in the fall and another in the spring. She now had a definite crystallized purpose, and in carrying it out, her life fell into a pattern which remained unchanged for the next six years.

Harriet Tubman.
The Granger Collection, New York

MEET THE WRITER

Ann Petry (1908–1997) was born in Old Saybrook, Connecticut, where her father was a pharmacist. Petry graduated from the University of Connecticut and became a pharmacist in her family's drugstore.

During her years as a pharmacist Petry also began writing stories, and eventually made the decision to become a professional writer. In 1938 she moved to New York where she worked as a reporter for the *Amsterdam News,* a Harlem newspaper. She also published her own short stories and novels. In 1946 she published *The Street,* an extremely realistic novel about a black woman and her young son trying to survive racism and economic struggle in Harlem. Her novel was a best-seller, and Petry was compared to Richard Wright and his works of social protest. One reviewer said that *The Street* "deals with its Negro characters without condescension, without special pleading, without distortion of any kind."

Petry changed the setting of her other adult novels from the city to small towns in New England, but she still wrote about such themes as social class and doomed relationships. Her novel, *The Narrows* (1953), is now seen as being ahead of its time in depicting a tragic love affair between a well-educated African American man and a wealthy white woman.

Harriet Tubman: Conductor on the Underground Railroad (1955) and *Tituba of Salem Village* (1964) are two of Petry's works for young adults that include women who had been enslaved as main characters. Of these works, Petry has said, "I hoped that I had made them come alive, turned them into real people."

NOTES

SKILLS PRACTICE

Literary Focus Analyze biographical information.

Reading Skills Analyze author's purpose.

from Harriet Tubman: Conductor on the Underground Railroad

QUESTION/ANSWER AND AUTHOR'S PURPOSE CHART

The chart below lists questions about the Harriet Tubman biography. Write your answers in the second column. In the third column, explain why you think Ann Petry may have chosen to express each idea in her biography.

QUESTION	ANSWER	AUTHOR'S PURPOSE
How was Tubman able to gather runaways without getting caught?		
How did Tubman respond to her own feelings of doubt?		
How did Tubman respond to feelings of doubt among the runaways?		
Why did Tubman continue to make the dangerous journeys into the South after she had gained her own freedom?		

from Harriet Tubman: Conductor on the Underground Railroad

VOCABULARY AND COMPREHENSION

A. Synonyms Complete each sentence with the correct vocabulary word from the Word Box. Then fill in the line after each sentence with the correct synonym from the Synonym Box. Some words will not be used.

WORD BOX

intervals
invariably
incomprehensible
disheveled
dispel
reluctance
mutinous
indomitable

1. The actions of the ______________________ crew led to disaster.
____

2. The messy writing was ______________________ to everyone who tried to read it. ______________________

3. We turned on the radio at regular ______________________ to check on the score of the game. ______________________

4. The thunderstorm proved to ______________________ all doubts about the accuracy of the forecast. ______________________

5. The child's ______________________ to cooperate forced us to discipline her. ______________________

6. Nick ______________________ chooses action movies when he wants to see a film. ______________________

SYNONYM BOX

unswerving
periods
rebellious
unintelligible
rumpled
remove
unwillingness
consistently

B. Reading Comprehension Answer each question below.

7. What were the potential consequences of being caught for Harriet Tubman, her passengers, and the people who helped them on their journey North?
____
____
____

8. Harriet Tubman took many risks in leading people to freedom. Identify a modern leader who took similar risks in fighting for justice. On a separate sheet of paper, write a brief essay comparing and contrasting his or her work with that of Harriet Tubman's.

Vocabulary Skills
Identify synonyms.

Writer's Workshop
PERSUASIVE WRITING

ASSIGNMENT

Write an essay stating your opinion on a topic based on a personal experience. Use a personal narrative to support your opinion.

PURPOSE

To persuade

AUDIENCE

Your teacher and your classmates; readers of a school or local newspaper; a group with power to act on your ideas

TRY IT OUT

Use sensory details to write a vivid description of the following:

1. a public building in need of renovation
2. the atmosphere at a cultural festival
3. a ride on a crowded subway

Topic Ideas

- *What is the important message in a piece of literature?*
- *Are there "correct" gender roles?*
- *How is stereotyping harmful?*
- *What are children's obligations to parents?*

PERSUADING THROUGH PERSONAL NARRATIVE

You often share stories about hilarious, exciting, or upsetting things that happen in your life. Occasionally you might tell a personal story to **persuade** someone to take your advice, follow your example, learn from your mistakes, or agree with you.

In this workshop, you will use a **personal narrative** in an essay to support your opinion about a piece of literature or another topic. You will be using your personal narrative to say, "Here's what I think about this. I feel strongly because this is what happened to me."

PREWRITING

1. **Choose a Topic**—Think about your own personal experiences (challenges that you have met, causes that you support, hobbies that are rewarding). If nothing comes to mind immediately, skim a newspaper or magazine, or watch or listen to a news program on the radio, TV, or Internet. You might choose a piece of literature that "speaks" to you or a problem or issue in your own community or school. Make sure you choose a topic with which you've had some personal experience.

2. **State Your Opinion**—The first thing you must do is take a stand on the topic. After you've formed your own opinion, do some research for **background information** on the topic. Talk to people who know something about the topic. Then, write an **opinion statement,** a single sentence that expresses your position on a subject or issue.

3. **Tell Your Story**—Next, focus on the story part of your essay—the personal narrative that relates your experience. Describe events in **chronological order,** the order in which they happened. You might create a time line to help you organize the events you want to include. Add notes describing how you felt or what you thought about your experience. What did you learn that might interest others? How, exactly, does your experience relate to the topic of your essay?

4. **Elaborate**—Review your notes on the narratives you've read in this book. Consider why the writers chose to include certain details and how those details served as an argument against slavery. Think about why your experience would motivate people. Use **sensory details**—sights, sounds, smells, tastes, and touch sensations—to make your experience come alive for your readers.

5. **Call to Action**—A good way to end a persuasive essay based on a personal narrative is with a **call to action,** a clear statement of what you want your readers to do. You might ask them to join an organization, write a letter, contribute to a cause, perform a service, or simply change their attitude.

DRAFTING

1. **Organize Your Essay**—Either of the following ways to organize your essay can work effectively. (The outline in the side column illustrates the first option below.)
   - Begin with your opinion statement. Follow it with your personal narrative. End with a call to action.
   - Begin with your personal narrative. Follow it with your opinion, explaining how it was formed from your experience. End with a call to action.

2. **Use Your Own Voice**—Write about your experience in your own words, as if you were talking to a friend. Avoid difficult words and complicated sentences. Find your own voice, and express yourself clearly and directly. This will give your essay a genuine quality with which readers will identify.

EVALUATING AND REVISING

1. **Self-Evaluation**—In a personal narrative, you use the first-person pronoun *I* to identify yourself. It is easy, however, to begin too many sentences with *I* ("I did this," "I did that," "I think . . ."). Try to eliminate as many of these sentence constructions as possible when you revise. Remember that sentences that vary in length, beginnings, and structure will help hold your readers' interest. Also, keep in mind that using your own voice does not mean you should ramble or "speak" in a disjointed way. Look for places that need transitions to connect ideas and help readers follow along.

2. **Peer Evaluation**—Working with a classmate, take turns reading each other's essays aloud. Use the Evaluation Criteria in the side column as a guide for suggesting improvements in your partner's essay. Focus on how the narrative relates to the issue and to the writer's position. Is the narrative interesting? Is the opinion clearly stated? Is the call to action convincing? Incorporate your partner's suggestions into your essay and correct any errors in grammar, usage, and mechanics before preparing your final draft.

OUTLINE FOR A PERSUASIVE PERSONAL NARRATIVE

I. **Introduction**
   A. Opinion statement
   B. Background information, if needed
II. **Personal Narrative** (elaborated with sensory details)
   A. What happened
   B. Thoughts, feelings, reactions
III. **Conclusion**
   A. Summary of experience or restatement of opinion
   B. Call to action

EVALUATION CRITERIA

A good persuasive personal narrative

- clearly states the writer's opinion
- provides background information, if needed
- relates a personal narrative that supports the writer's opinion
- concludes with a restatement of the writer's opinion and a call to action

CHALLENGES AND CHANGE (1865–1945)

Tuskegee Airmen in Italy during World War II, c.1944.
©Bettmann/CORBIS

LITERARY FOCUS FOR UNIT 3

How do changes in society affect your life? The selections in this unit trace the development of African American literature from post-Civil War Reconstruction through the Harlem Renaissance, a cultural flowering of the 1920s centered in a New York City neighborhood.

You will analyze the **tone** of a fiery journalist's crusade for justice. Examples of **lyric poetry** reflect the challenges of the late 1800s. Later, the **speakers** of twentieth century poems use **alliteration** and **metaphor** to explore ideas about roots, legacy, and hope for the future. You'll use a **biographical and historical approach** to evaluate an author's perspective on racial stereotypes. In a short story, you'll compare and contrast the **character traits** of two aging sisters resolved to live their last days to the fullest. **Stage directions** in a play help to convey the obstacles African Americans faced, and **blues poetry**—lyrics from a genre that has profoundly influenced contemporary music—expresses the need for change.

As you read this unit, think about how the authors were influenced by the events of their time and how this historical context gave rise to such a wide variety of perspectives.

BEFORE YOU READ

from Crusade for Justice
by Ida B. Wells

Ida B. Wells (1862–1931) was an advocate for the rights of African Americans and women. She spoke and wrote throughout her life to help these causes.

LITERARY FOCUS: TONE

The **tone** of a piece of writing reflects the writer's attitude, mood, and manner. Tone might be humorous or sad, angry or calm, ironic or neutral. Even when a writer's tone seems neutral, however, the choice of words and details can reveal his or her feelings toward the subject. As you read this excerpt from *Crusade for Justice,* look closely at how Ida B. Wells describes her experience on the train and the events that followed.

- Pay attention to the words Wells uses to describe her own actions and the actions of others. Note when she expresses emotion—or doesn't—and think about what this may reveal about her attitude toward the events.
- Note the details Wells chooses to include. How do they affect your understanding of what happens?

Bear in mind that a writer may shift from one tone to another. Tone in literature is not unlike tone of voice; close reading, like close listening, can help you to understand a story better.

READING SKILLS: UNDERSTANDING HISTORICAL CONTEXT

This selection takes place after the end of Reconstruction—the era following the Civil War when the U.S. government sought to reunite the nation. During Reconstruction, Congress passed various laws to advance African American civil rights, including a bill that banned racial segregation in public transport and other facilities. When Reconstruction ended in 1877, however, people who believed in the supremacy of whites moved to regain control of the South. Freed people in the South, such as Ida B. Wells, lived out the struggle for civil rights on a daily basis. Even the question of whether an African American could travel freely caused debate in Congress. This excerpt from Wells's autobiography describes how she took a stand against segregation on public transport, more than seventy years before Rosa Parks famously refused to give up her own seat on a bus.

Consider the people Wells describes and how she interacts with them. Who is on her side? Who is against her? Draw conclusions about how the historical context affects these interactions.

Literary Focus
Understand a writer's tone.

Reading Skills
Understand historical context.

Vocabulary Skills
Look at context clues.

VOCABULARY DEVELOPMENT

PREVIEW SELECTION VOCABULARY

The following words appear in the excerpt from *Crusade for Justice.* Look them over before you begin the selection.

proposed (prō·pōzd′) *v.:* expressed an aim or plan.

*Wells **proposed** that she would leave the train at the first station.*

engaged (en·gājd′) *v.:* entered into a contract to work with; hired.

*She **engaged** a lawyer to sue the railroad.*

compromise (käm′prə·mīz′) *v.:* to reach an agreement by giving up a point of argument.

*The railroad wanted Wells to **compromise** in her demand for equal treatment.*

plaintiff (plān′tif) *n.:* the party that begins a lawsuit.

*The **plaintiff** sued the railroad for violating her civil rights.*

precedent (pres′ə·dənt) *n.:* a legal decision used as a guide in later similar cases.

*If Wells won, it would set a **precedent** for later judicial decisions in cases of African Americans suing for equal treatment.*

grievances (grēv′ənsez) *n.:* events that are considered valid reasons for complaint.

*Wells explained her **grievances** in the circuit court.*

CLARIFY WORD MEANINGS: LOOK AT THE CONTEXT

Wells wrote her autobiography, *Crusade for Justice,* more than half a century ago. Some of the language Wells uses—or the way she uses it—may be less than familiar to you today. Whenever you encounter an unfamiliar word or phrase, try looking closely at the context to see if that can help to clarify its meaning.

Sometimes knowing other words in a sentence is enough to clarify meaning. For example, when Wells writes "the sleeves of my linen duster had been torn out," the word *sleeves* indicates that a duster is probably a type of coat. Other times, you must consider the meaning of the sentence as a whole. Wells writes that had she agreed to the demands of the railroad, "I would have been a few hundred dollars to the good *instead of having to pay out* over two hundred dollars." The comparison *instead of having to pay out* suggests that here, Wells uses "to the good" to mean money she would have saved.

As you read the excerpt from *Crusade for Justice,* look for clues in the context that might help you to better understand the meaning of an unfamiliar word or phrase.

from Crusade for Justice

by Ida B. Wells

I secured a school in Shelby County, Tennessee, which paid a better salary and began studying for the examination for city schoolteacher which meant an even larger increase in salary. One day while riding back to my school I took a seat in the ladies' coach of the train as usual. There were no jim crow cars[1] then. But ever since the repeal of the Civil Rights Bill by the United States Supreme Court in 1877[2] there had been efforts all over the South to draw the color line on the railroads.

When the train started and the conductor came along to collect tickets, he took my ticket, then handed it back to me and told me that he couldn't take my ticket there. I thought that if he didn't want the ticket I wouldn't bother about it so went on reading. In a little while when he finished taking tickets, he came back and told me I would have to go in the other car. I refused, saying that the forward car was a smoker, and as I was in the ladies' car I **proposed** to stay. He tried to drag me out of the seat, but the moment he caught hold of my arm I fastened my teeth in the back of his hand.

I had braced my feet against the seat in front and was holding to the back, and as he had already been badly bitten he didn't try it again by himself. He went forward and got the baggageman and another man to help him and of course they succeeded in dragging me out. They were encouraged to do this by the attitude of the white ladies and gentlemen in the car; some of them even stood on the seats so that they could get a good view and continued applauding the conductor for his brave stand.

By this time the train had stopped at the first station. When I saw that they were determined to drag me into the smoker,

INFER

Re-read lines 9–13. Do you think Wells believes that the conductor simply "didn't want the ticket"? Explain, citing the historical context.

VOCABULARY

proposed (prō·pōzd′) *v.:* expressed an aim or plan.

ANALYZE

Explain why some passengers felt the conductor was making a "brave stand." (line 27)

1. **jim crow cars:** segregated railroad cars. Laws that enforced racial segregation were known as Jim Crow laws.
2. **repeal . . . 1877:** This ruling occurred in 1883.

which was already filled with colored people and those who were smoking, I said I would get off the train rather than go in—which I did. Strangely, I held on to my ticket all this time, and although the sleeves of my linen duster had been torn out and I had been pretty roughly handled, I had not been hurt physically.

I went back to Memphis and **engaged** a colored lawyer to bring suit against the railroad for me. After months of delay I found he had been bought off by the road, and as he was the only colored lawyer in town I had to get a white one. This man, Judge Greer, kept his pledge with me and the case was finally brought to trial in the circuit court. Judge Pierce, who was an ex-union soldier from Minnesota, awarded me damages of five hundred dollars. I can see to this day the headlines in the *Memphis Appeal* announcing DARKY DAMSEL GETS DAMAGES.

A DARKY DAMSEL

Obtains a Verdict for Damages Against the Chesapeake and Ohio Railroad—What It Cost

To Put a Colored School-Teacher in a Smoking-Car—Verdict for $500.

Judge Pierce yesterday rendered his decision in the case of Ida Wells *vs.* the Chesapeake and Ohio railroad. The suit has attracted a good deal of attention, Judge Greer appearing for the plaintiff and Mr. Holmes Cummins for the railroad. From the testimony it appeared that the railroad company had on sale at the time of the grievance of but one kind of passenger tickets, and that plaintiff purchased one good until used from Memphis to Woodstock, paying full price. She took a seat in the ladies' coach, and when approached by the conductor after the train left the depot handed him the ticket. He refused to accept it, and ordered her to go to the other coach, which was similar to that in which she was seated, but which was occupied exclusively by white men and negroes, many of whom were smoking. The plaintiff refused to go, and the conductor seizing her by the arm, attempted to force her into the other coach. She continued

The Memphis Daily Appeal, *December 25, 1884.*

The *Memphis Daily Appeal*, December 25, 1884.
The Commercial Appeal, Memphis, TN. Used with permission.

INFER

Why might Wells have continued to hold on to her ticket (line 32)?

VOCABULARY

engaged (en·gājd′) *v.:* entered into a contract to work with; hired.

DRAW CONCLUSIONS

Why might a former Union soldier (line 40) be more likely to side with Wells?

VOCABULARY

compromise (käm′prə·mīz) *v.:* to reach an agreement by giving up a point of argument.

plaintiff (plān′tif) *n.:* the party that begins a lawsuit.

GENERALIZE

In general, how did Ida B. Wells feel about the decisions she made about the case? Why?

LITERARY FOCUS

Explain the statement, "Negroes were not wards of the nation but citizens of the individual states." (lines 56–57) What does the tone of this statement reveal?

The railroad appealed the case to the state's supreme court, which reversed the findings of the lower court, and I had to pay the costs. Before this was done, the railroad's lawyer had tried every means in his power to get me to **compromise** the case, but I indignantly refused. Had I done so, I would have been a few hundred dollars to the good instead of having to pay out over two hundred dollars in court costs.

It was twelve years afterward before I knew why the case had attracted so much attention and was fought so bitterly by the Chesapeake and Ohio Railroad. It was the first case in which a colored **plaintiff** in the South had appealed to a state court since the repeal of the Civil Rights Bill by the United States Supreme Court. The gist of that decision was that Negroes were not wards of the nation but citizens of the individual states, and should

Ida B. Wells
The Granger Collection/New York

therefore appeal to the state courts for justice instead of to the federal court. The success of my case would have set a **precedent** which others would doubtless have followed. In this, as in so many other matters, the South wanted the Civil Rights Bill repealed but did not want or intend to give justice to the Negro after robbing him of all sources from which to secure it.

The supreme court of the nation had told us to go to the state courts for redress of **grievances;** when I did so I was given the brand of justice Charles Sumner[3] knew Negroes would get when he fathered the Civil Rights Bill during the Reconstruction period.

VOCABULARY

precedent (pres′ə·dənt) *n.:* a legal decision used as a guide in later similar cases.

grievances (grēv′ənsez) *n.:* events that are considered valid reasons for complaint.

INTERPRET

What does Wells believe about the security of African American rights in the South (lines 60–63)? Explain.

---

3. **Charles Sumner:** United States senator from Massachusetts. He championed civil rights for enslaved people who had been freed.

MEET THE WRITER

Ida B. Wells (1862–1931) was born into slavery in Holly Springs, Mississippi, six months before the Emancipation Proclamation declared the freedom of enslaved people in the South. She became a teacher, a lecturer, and a journalist. From the start of her career, she fought against racial discrimination. When she was twenty-two, she moved to Memphis, Tennessee, where she eventually became part owner and reporter for *Free Speech,* a local newspaper. After she investigated the lynching of three black grocers and exposed the white men who were responsible, her printing press was wrecked and her safety was threatened.

In 1895 she moved to Chicago, Illinois, and married Ferdinand L. Barnett, a lawyer and journalist. Even while caring for a growing family, Wells continued her role as a crusader for the rights of blacks, women, and humanity. In 1898 she led a delegation to President McKinley to protest the lynching of a black postmaster. She founded the Alpha Suffrage Club, which was likely the first black woman suffrage group, and the Negro Fellowship League, which provided assistance to black migrants from the South. In 1909, she took part in organizing the civil rights group that became the National Association for the Advancement of Colored People (NAACP).

In his forward to her autobiography, *Crusade for Justice*, the scholar John Hope Franklin says, "Few documents written by an American woman approach this one in importance or interest."

EXTEND

Research the history of the NAACP. Write a paragraph on another sheet of paper describing the ways in which the NAACP is active today.

SKILLS PRACTICE

from Crusade for Justice

Literacy Focus
Analyze author's tone.

TONE CHART

For each excerpt from *Crusade for Justice,* identify the tone and then paraphrase the statement in order to modify the tone. Consider how Wells's word choice affects you and how you perceive her and the events she relates.

EXCERPT: "I refused, saying that the forward car was a smoker, and as I was in the ladies' car I proposed to stay."

TONE:

PARAPHRASE:

EXCERPT: "He tried to drag me out of the seat, but the moment he caught hold of my arm I fastened my teeth in the back of his hand."

TONE:

PARAPHRASE:

EXCERPT: "The railroad's lawyer had tried every means in his power to get me to compromise the case, but I indignantly refused."

TONE:

PARAPHRASE:

EXCERPT: "It was twelve years afterward before I knew why the case had attracted so much attention and was fought so bitterly."

TONE:

PARAPHRASE:

from Crusade for Justice

VOCABULARY AND COMPREHENSION

WORD BOX

- proposed
- engaged
- compromise
- plaintiff
- precedent
- grievances

A. Context Clues For each item below, fill in the blank with the appropriate word from the Word Box. Then underline a phrase in the sentence that helps to clarify the meaning of the word.

1. The ________________________, Ida B. Wells, took the railroad company to court in an effort to win damages.

2. The lawyer Wells ________________________ vowed to work hard for her in court.

3. The railroad feared that a courtroom victory for Wells would be a ________________________ used in future judicial decisions.

4. Racial discrimination in public transport, hotels, and restaurants were some of the serious ________________________ faced by African Americans in the South.

5. Wells stood by her demands and refused to ________________________ her case.

6. Wells ________________________ that she would seek justice in the courtroom.

B. Reading Comprehension Answer each question below.

7. What did the railroads accomplish by winning the lawsuit? What affect did this have on African Americans?

____

____

____

____

8. How have conditions changed for blacks since Ida B. Wells's experience? Do you think racial injustices still exist today? Explain your answer.

____

____

____

____

Vocabulary Skills
Use context clues.

BEFORE YOU READ

The Song of the Smoke
by W.E.B. Du Bois

We Wear the Mask • Life's Tragedy
by Paul Laurence Dunbar

In the these poems, two authors who came of age in the years after Reconstruction explore their sense of self and meaning in the world.

LITERARY FOCUS: LYRIC POETRY

Poetry that expresses the speaker's thoughts and feelings is called **lyric poetry.** Lyric poets may often use imagery and figurative language instead of literal description. This can heighten an emotion and make it more vivid. For example, rather than say,"We hide painful feelings behind a smile," the poet Paul Laurence Dunbar writes, "We wear the mask that grins and lies." Here are some tips for understanding a lyric poem.

- Start by reading the poem a couple of times in order to get a sense of the sound and rhythm of the words. Notice the pace of the poem—whether the words seem to move swiftly or linger softly. Then try to describe the feelings the sound of the poem suggests.
- Look for examples of imagery. Visual images may be the ones you notice first, but remember that imagery also includes sound, touch, and other sensations. Consider what the imagery adds to the poem's meaning.
- Pay special attention to figurative language. Simile, metaphor, idiom, personification, and symbolism can convey ideas and emotions and add depth to meaning.

READING SKILLS: PARAPHRASING

Paraphrasing means restating something in a way that makes it simpler or clearer. Unlike a summary, a paraphrase can be as long as—or longer than—the original. Paraphrasing is a good way to work toward understanding a poem.

When you paraphrase, think of familiar words you could use in place of unfamiliar ones. Then use these words to help you reorganize the sentence structure.

Literary Focus Understand the characteristics of a lyric poem.

Reading Skills Paraphrase text to aid in comprehension.

The Song of the Smoke

by W.E.B. Du Bois

I am the Smoke King
I am black!
I am swinging in the sky,
I am wringing worlds awry;°
I am the thought of the throbbing mills,
I am the soul of the soul-toil kills,
Wraith° of the ripple of trading rills;
Up I'm curling from the sod,
I am whirling home to God;
I am the Smoke King,
I am black.

I am the Smoke King,
I am black!
I am wreathing broken hearts,
I am sheathing love's light darts;
Inspiration of iron times
Wedding the toil of toiling climes,°
Shedding the blood of bloodless crimes—
Lurid lowering° 'mid the blue,
Torrid towering toward the true,
I am the Smoke King,
I am black.

I am the Smoke King,
I am black!
I am darkening with song,
I am hearkening to wrong!
I will be as black as blackness can—

4. **awry** (ə·rī′) *adj.:* out of line.
7. **Wraith** (rāth) *n.:* ghost or specter.
17. **climes** (klīms) *n.:* regions.
19. **lowering** (lou′ər·iŋ) *adj.:* appearing dark and threatening.

ANALYZE

Review lines 3–9, noting the description of the Smoke King's movements. What feeling does this convey?

INTERPRET

In lines 14–17, what does the Smoke King do? What does this suggest about the Smoke King's character?

FLUENCY

Practice reading the second stanza aloud until you can say the words smoothly and at a natural rate. Use your voice to give life to the speaker's feelings.

INFER

Based on lines 28–29, how does the speaker feel about blackness? Explain.

____

____

____

____

____

ANALYZE

How does the repetition of the phrase "I am" (lines 30–37) affect its emotional impact?

____

____

____

____

____

____

PARAPHRASE

Paraphrase the question the speaker asks in line 40. Bear in mind that *hide* is a multiple meaning word; here it means "skin."

____

____

____

____

The blacker the mantle, the mightier the man!
For blackness was ancient ere whiteness began.
I am daubing° God in night,
I am swabbing Hell in white:
I am the Smoke King
I am black.

I am the Smoke King
I am black!
I am cursing ruddy morn,
I am hearsing° hearts unborn:
Souls unto me are as stars in a night,
I whiten my black me—I blacken my white!
What's the hue of a hide to a man in his might?
Hail! great, gritty, grimy hands—
Sweet Christ, pity toiling lands!
I am the Smoke King
I am black.

---

5. **daubing** (dôb′·iŋ) *v.:* covering; smearing.
6. **hearsing** (hʉrs′·iŋ) *v.:* shrouding.

MEET THE WRITER

William Edward Burghardt Du Bois (do͞o bois′) (1868–1963) was born in Great Barrington, Massachusetts. He was the first African American to receive a Ph.D. in American history from Harvard University.

The Souls of Black Folk, which many readers consider his masterpiece, was published in 1903. It consists of fourteen chapters that blend history, sociology, economic theory, fiction, and political commentary. Here Du Bois announced that "the problem of the twentieth century is the problem of the color-line." He described the psychological experience of blacks as having "two souls," one "American" and one "Negro." He also rejected Booker T. Washington's advice to accept segregation in exchange for economic help from whites. Instead, Du Bois wanted higher education and full political and civil rights for African Americans.

Between 1910 and 1934 Du Bois edited *The Crisis,* the journal of the National Association for the Advancement of Colored People (NAACP), a civil rights organization he helped create. He also was active in the Pan African movement for an independent and united black Africa, free of white colonial powers. In 1961, he left for Ghana, where he became a citizen shortly before he died. Martin Luther King, Jr., called Du Bois "one of the most remarkable men of our time."

We Wear the Mask

by Paul Laurence Dunbar

We wear the mask that grins and lies,
It hides our cheeks and shades our eyes,—
This debt we pay to human **guile;**
With torn and bleeding hearts we smile,
And mouth with myriad **subtleties.**

Why should the world be over-wise,
In counting all our tears and sighs?
Nay, let them only see us, while
    We wear the mask.

We smile, but, O great Christ, our cries
To thee from tortured souls arise.
We sing, but oh the clay is **vile**
Beneath our feet, and long the mile;
But let the world dream otherwise,
    We wear the mask.

Les Fétiches (Fetishes), 1938, oil by Loïs Mailou Jones.
The National Museum of American Art, Smithsonian Institution, Washington, D.C./Art Resource, NY

ANALYZE

Re-read lines 1–5. What function does the mask serve? Why is this important?

VOCABULARY

guile (gīl) *n.:* deception.

subtleties (sut″l·tēs) *n.:* forms of expression that may be hard to detect; shades of meaning.

vile (vīl) *adj.:* horrible.

COMPARE & CONTRAST

Compare and contrast the theme of this poem with the theme of "The Song of the Smoke"?

LITERARY FOCUS

What feelings does the speaker express in lines 1–4?

CONNECT

Which would feel more tragic: to "come near" to perfection (line 5) but miss it, or never to come near at all? Why?

VOCABULARY

potent (pōt″nt) *adj.:* powerful.

vanity (van′ə·tē) *n.:* extreme pride.

mortals (môr′təls) *n.:* humans.

Life's Tragedy

by Paul Laurence Dunbar

It may be misery not to sing at all
And to go silent through the brimming day.
It may be sorrow never to be loved,
But deeper griefs than these beset the way.

To have come near to sing the perfect song
And only by a half-tone lost the key,
There is the **potent** sorrow, there the grief,
The pale, sad staring of life's tragedy.

To have just missed the perfect love,
Not the hot passion of untempered youth,
But that which lays aside its **vanity**
And gives thee, for thy trusting worship, truth—

This, this it is to be accursed indeed;
For if we **mortals** love, or if we sing,
We count our joys not by the things we have,
But by what kept us from the perfect thing.

MEET THE WRITER

Paul Laurence Dunbar (1872–1906) was born in Dayton, Ohio, to parents who had been enslaved. The only black student in his high school class, he became president of the literary society, editor of the school newspaper, and class poet. He hoped to attend college but was too poor, and supported himself as an elevator operator while he continued to write.

In 1893, Dunbar published his first collection of poems, *Oak and Ivy*. Other volumes of poetry followed and Dunbar was highly praised. But Dunbar soon realized that he was not valued for his poems in standard English that he considered his major work. His readers, who were mainly whites, preferred his dialect poems that reinforced the stereotypes of contented blacks living in harmony on Southern plantations. Dunbar said, "You know, of course, that I didn't start as a dialect poet. I simply came to the conclusion that I could write it as well, if not better than anybody else I knew of, and that by doing so I should gain a hearing. I gained the hearing, and now they don't want me to write anything but dialect." Dunbar also wrote essays, short stories and novels, but he is best remembered as a poet.

SKILLS PRACTICE

The Song of the Smoke • We Wear the Mask • Life's Tragedy

VOCABULARY AND COMPREHENSION

WORD BOX

potent

guile

vanity

vile

A. Context Clues Complete each sentence with the correct vocabulary word from the Word Box.

1. The customer found the salesperson's ________________ offensive and demanded her money back.

2. The workers' conditions were so ________________ that they went on strike.

3. The audience encouraged the musician's ________________ with their applause.

4. The pharmacist advised the patient to beware of the ______________ medicine's strong side effects.

B. Reading Comprehension Answer the question below.

5. Relate the theme of one of the poems to a specific individual or present-day circumstance. Explain how this person or situation embodies the theme of the poem.

____

____

____

____

____

____

____

____

____

____

____

____

____

____

____

Literary Focus Understand the characteristics of a lyric poem.

Vocabulary Skills Demonstrate an understanding of vocabulary in context.

POEMS

BEFORE YOU READ

O Black and Unknown Bards
by James Weldon Johnson

If We Must Die
by Claude McKay

Reapers
by Jean Toomer

Exploring ideas about roots, legacy, and agriculture, these three poems show the variety of themes addressed by writers during the Harlem Renaissance.

LITERARY FOCUS: ALLITERATION

The repetition of a sound among words or syllables that are close together is called **alliteration.** Alliteration can occur with the sound of a consonant ("*s*ongs of *s*orrow") or a grouping of consonants ("*th*an *th*is"). Poets use alliteration to create a musical quality that pleases the ears. Alliteration draws attention to particular words and may forge connections among them.

- The repetition of a sound at the beginning of words is called **initial alliteration,** as in "*h*ungry *h*earts."
- When alliteration occurs within words, it is called **internal** or **hidden alliteration,** such as "har*mon*ies . . . a*mon*gst the stars."
- Alliteration may also include the repetition of a sound at the end of words; this is called **terminal alliteration** ("touche*d* in chor*d*").

READING SKILLS: READING POETRY FOR SENTENCE SENSE

Although written in verse, poems are made up of sentences. **Reading poetry for sentence sense** means reading from sentence to sentence, rather than from line to line. Usually, you can do this by following the punctuation. Reading for sentence sense makes a poem easier to understand. Take the first two lines of "Reapers" as an example:

> "Black reapers with the sound of steel on stones
> Are sharpening scythes. I see them place the hones"

If you think of that first line break as the end of a phrase, the line doesn't make sense—that's because it's part of a sentence that continues on the next line. It makes sense when you ignore the line breaks and follow the punctuation. Try this technique to help you better understand the poems by Johnson, McKay, and Toomer.

Literary Focus
Recognize alliteration in poetry.

Reading Skills
Read poetry for sentence sense.

O Black and Unknown Bards

by James Weldon Johnson

O black and unknown bards of long ago,
How came your lips to touch the sacred fire?
How, in your darkness, did you come to know
The power and beauty of the minstrel's lyre?°
Who first from midst his bonds lifted his eyes?
Who first from out the still watch, lone and long,
Feeling the ancient faith of prophets rise
Within his dark-kept soul, burst into song?

Heart of what slave poured out such melody
As "Steal away to Jesus"? On its strains
His spirit must have nightly floated free,
Though still about his hands he felt his chains.
Who heard great "Jordan roll"? Whose starward eye
Saw chariot "swing low"? And who was he
That breathed that comforting, melodic sigh,
"Nobody knows de trouble I see"?

What merely living clod, what captive thing,
Could up toward God through all its darkness grope,
And find within its deadened heart to sing
These songs of sorrow, love and faith, and hope?
How did it catch that subtle undertone,
That note in music heard not with the ears?
How sound the **elusive** reed° so seldom blown,
Which stirs the soul or melts the heart to tears.

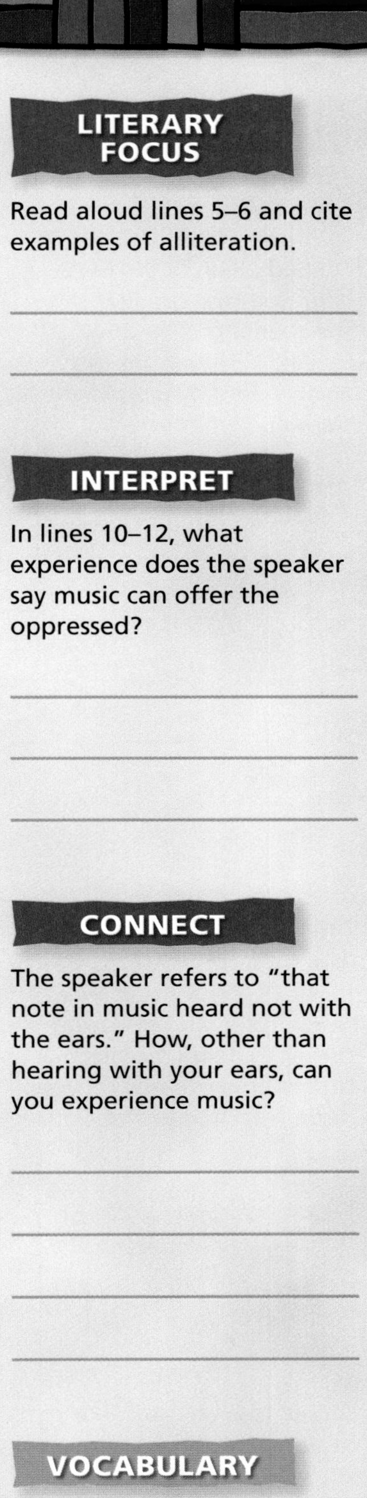

LITERARY FOCUS
Read aloud lines 5–6 and cite examples of alliteration.
INTERPRET
In lines 10–12, what experience does the speaker say music can offer the oppressed?
CONNECT
The speaker refers to "that note in music heard not with the ears." How, other than hearing with your ears, can you experience music?
VOCABULARY
elusive (ē·lo͞o′siv) *adj.:* hard to grasp or describe; baffling.

4. **minstrel's lyre:** In the Middle Ages, wandering poets called minstrels went from place to place, reciting poetry and accompanying themselves on musical instruments. The lyre is associated with poetry and song.
23. **reed** (rēd) *n.:* a wind instrument made from the hollow stem of a plant, associated with poetry and song.

CLARIFY

The speaker alludes to famous African American spirituals in lines 10, 13, 14, 16, and 28. In lines 25–28, how does the speaker say the theme of "Go down, Moses" differs from the music heard by a renowned German composer?

____

____

____

____

____

____

FLUENCY

Read aloud the fourth stanza (lines 25–32) for sentence sense, following punctuation rather than line breaks. Notice how this affects your understanding of the stanza.

VOCABULARY

degraded (dē·grād′id) *adj.:* lessened in value; made worse.

servile (sʉr′vəl) *adj.:* like that of servants or the enslaved.

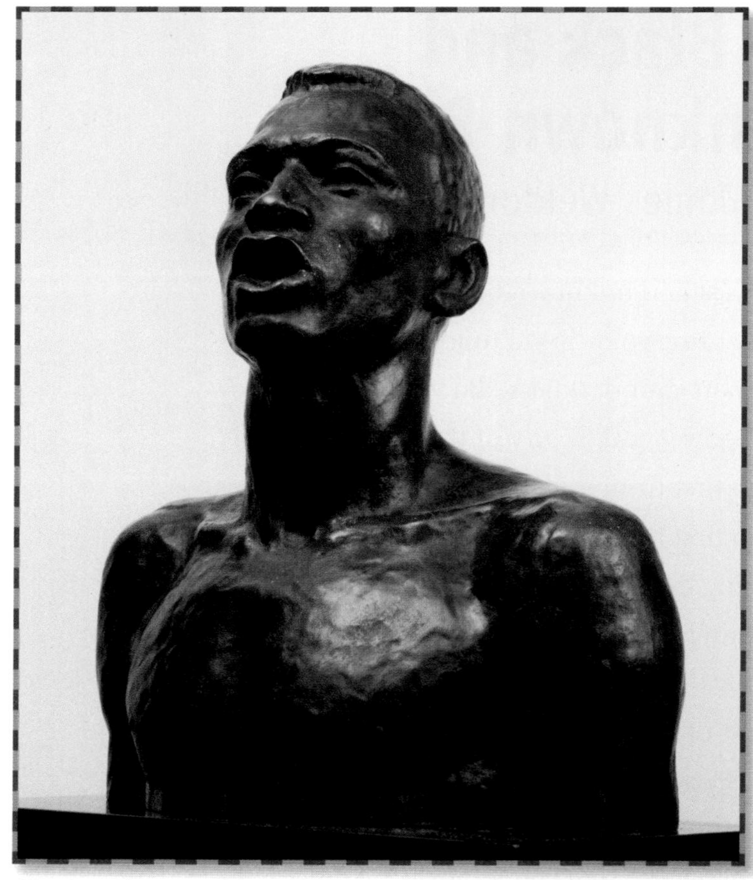

Singing Slave, sculpture by Richmond Barthé.
Art and Artifacts Division/The Schomburg Center for Research in Black Culture/New York Public Library

Not that great German master in his dream
Of harmonies that thundered amongst the stars
At the creation, ever heard a theme
Nobler than "Go down, Moses." Mark its bars
How like a mighty trumpet-call they stir
The blood. Such are the notes that men have sung
Going to valorous deeds; such tones there were
That helped make history when Time was young.

There is a wide, wide wonder in it all,
That from **degraded** rest and **servile** toil
The fiery spirit to the seer should call
These simple children of the sun and soil.
O black slave singers, gone, forgot, unfamed,
You—you alone, of all the long, long line
Of those who've sung untaught, unknown, unnamed,
Have stretched out upward, seeking the divine.

You sang not deeds of heroes or of kings;
No chant of bloody war, no exulting pean°
Of arms-won triumphs; but your humble strings
You touched in chord with music empyrean.°
You sang far better than you knew; the songs
That for your listeners' hungry hearts sufficed
Still live,—but more than this to you belongs:
You sang a race from wood and stone to Christ.

COMPARE & CONTRAST

How does the speaker contrast the works of the black and unknown bards with the poems of other bards in lines 41–44?

42. pean (pē'·ən) *n.:* a song of praise or joy, also spelled *paean.*
44. empyrean (em·pir'ē·ən) *adj.:* heavenly.

PARAPHRASE

Restate lines 45–48 in your own words.

MEET THE WRITER

James Weldon Johnson (1871–1938) was born in Jacksonville, Florida. After graduating from Atlanta University, he went on to excel in various fields. He was a school principal, a lawyer, a songwriter, a diplomat, a poet, a novelist, and a college professor.

Johnson began his literary career as a songwriter. He collaborated with his brother, a composer, to produce numerous hit songs. Their most famous composition, "Lift Every Voice and Sing," was first sung by a chorus of children on February 12, 1900, to celebrate the birthday of Abraham Lincoln. It has come to be known as the "Black National Anthem."

In 1912, Johnson's first novel, *The Autobiography of an Ex-Colored Man*, was published anonymously. This was one of the first novels to present a frank picture of the discrimination suffered by blacks in the United States.

To demonstrate the contributions that blacks had made to American culture, Johnson collected and published *The Book of American Negro Poetry* in 1922. Then he and his brother edited two collections of spirituals.

His best-known book of poetry, *God's Trombones*, was published in 1927. In this experiment with free verse, Johnson uses the rhythms, imagery, and oratorical style of traditional Southern preachers, rather than dialect.

Johnson's words continue to inspire people all over the world.

NOTES

If We Must Die

by Claude McKay

If we must die, let it not be like hogs
Hunted and penned in an inglorious spot,
While round us bark the mad and hungry dogs,
Making their mock at our accursed lot.
If we must die, O let us nobly die,
So that our precious blood may not be shed
In vain; then even the monsters we defy
Shall be **constrained** to honor us though dead!
O kinsmen! we must meet the common foe!
Though far outnumbered let us show us brave,
And for their thousand blows deal one deathblow!
What though before us lies the open grave?
Like men we'll face the murderous, cowardly pack,
Pressed to the wall, dying, but fighting back!

FLUENCY

Read aloud lines 1–2 for sense. Where did you pause in your reading? What verbs agree with the subject *hogs?*

VOCABULARY

constrained (kən·strānd) *v.:* forced by circumstances.

COMPARE & CONTRAST

Compare the speaker's ideas about what it means to die "like men" (line 13) and what it means to die "like hogs" (line 1).

MEET THE WRITER

Claude McKay (1890–1948) was born in Sunny Ville, Jamaica, in the West Indies. His love for his island home inspired his first two books of poetry, *Songs of Jamaica* and *Constab Ballads*, which were published in 1912. Most of these poems are written in Jamaican dialect.

In 1914 McKay moved to New York to pursue a literary career. He worked at menial jobs to support himself while he continued writing. In New York, McKay quickly found an American audience for his poetry through the *Liberator* and other notable publications.

McKay's best known poems are militant and angry sonnets, such as "If We Must Die," which urges people to fight against injustice. This poem was published in 1919, a year when race riots shook the nation. It expresses black America's mood of desperation and defiance.

In 1922 McKay published his most important collection of poems, *Harlem Shadows*. He also wrote novels, including *Home to Harlem* (1928). This novel was the first bestseller by a black author and won the Harmon Foundation Gold Medal Award for Literature.

Throughout his life, McKay traveled widely, living for extended periods in Europe, Russia, and North Africa. This may have led him to title his 1937 autobiography, *A Long Way from Home*.

Reapers

by Jean Toomer

Black reapers with the sound of steel on stones
Are sharpening scythes.° I see them place the hones°
In their hip-pockets as a thing that's done,
And start their silent swinging, one by one.
Black horses drive a mower through the weeds,
And there, a field rat, startled, squealing bleeds.
His belly close to ground. I see the blade,
Blood-stained, continue cutting weeds and shade.

Harvest Talk, 1953, charcoal drawing by Charles White.
Image reproduction ©The Art Institute of Chicago

ANALYZE

Which images in the poem create an ominous or menacing mood?

LITERARY FOCUS

What ideas in the poem are emphasized through alliteration?

COMPARE & CONTRAST

In what ways are the black reapers and the black horses similar and different?

2. **scythes** (sīthz) *n.:* tools with long blades, used for mowing or reaping.
hones (hōns) *n.:* hard stones used to sharpen cutting tools.

NOTES

Jean Toomer, c. 1925, oil pastel by Winold Reiss.
National Portrait Gallery, Smithsonian Institution/Art Resource, NY

MEET THE WRITER

Jean Toomer (1894–1967) was born in Washington, D.C., endured an unhappy childhood, and after high school, attended several colleges without earning a degree, and meanwhile began writing.

The poem "Reapers" comes from *Cane* (1923), which has been called the literary masterpiece of the Harlem Renaissance. The book is a mixture of fiction, poetry, and drama. The first third of *Cane* is set in rural Georgia. The characters experience frustration and tragedy, but despite this, their lives are touched by beauty. The second part has an urban setting where the characters find their lives corrupted by materialism. In the final section of the novel, a black intellectual returns to the South in search of his roots, but fails in his quest. The entire work is distinguished by the music of its language and its haunting imagery.

Cane's critical success did not especially please Toomer. Neither did his identification as a "Negro" writer. Toomer's racial heritage was mixed; he defined himself as "an American neither white nor black, rejecting these divisions, accepting all people as people."

Toomer continued to write to advance his political and spiritual beliefs, but little of his work was published. He died in 1967, the same year that *Cane* was reprinted for the first time.

Skills Practice

O Black and Unknown Bards • If We Must Die • Reapers

VOCABULARY AND COMPREHENSION

WORD BOX

servile
elusive
degraded
constrained

A. Context Clues Complete each sentence with the correct vocabulary word from the Word Box.

1. Even though they objected to many of the specifics, his argument was so convincing that the committee felt ______________________ to agree.

2. The ______________________ work that she was forced to do made her even more determined to try to escape.

3. He felt ______________________ when the teacher asked him to rewrite his essay.

4. The ______________________ creature emerged suddenly from the swamp but then quickly vanished.

B. Reading Comprehension Answer each question below.

5. "O Black and Unkown Bards" is an homage to the composers of spirituals. Identify a specific work, field of study, or form of expression that you think has had a positive impact on society. Then write a poem or essay in tribute on a separate sheet of paper.

6. Why might some people fighting against oppression or persecution today identify with the ideas in "If We Must Die"? Explain.

____

____

____

7. What literary elements in these poems did you find effective and interesting? Explain.

____

____

____

____

Reading Skills
Read poetry for sentence sense.

Vocabulary Skills
Demonstrate an understanding of vocabulary terms in context.

POEMS

BEFORE YOU READ

The Negro Speaks of Rivers • I, Too • Dreams • Dream Variations
by Langston Hughes

Langston Hughes emerged on the literary scene as a major figure of the Harlem Renaissance. These four poems convey feelings of hope, determination, and pride for African Americans.

LITERARY FOCUS: SPEAKER

The **speaker** is the voice that talks to the readers in a poem. "Dreams" uses the voice of a third-person speaker. Sometimes, first person is used, as in the other three poems. Whether the speaker is first or third person, he or she should not be confused with the poet. The speaker is a person created by the poet to convey the message of the work.

As you read these poems, think about what each speaker contributes to your understanding of the work.

READING SKILLS: MAKING INFERENCES ABOUT THE SPEAKER

When you make inferences, you form logical guesses based on evidence in the text and on what you already know. When you make inferences about the speaker of a poem, you look at the details included in the poem and consider what they show about the speaker's feelings, beliefs, traits, and background.

As you read, use a chart like the one below (see page 175) to help you collect evidence and make inferences about the speaker of each poem. An example is provided.

Literary Focus
Identify the speaker in poetry.

Reading Skills
Make inferences about the speaker of a poem.

POEM	TEXT EVIDENCE	WHAT THE TEXT REVEALS ABOUT THE SPEAKER
"I, Too"	The speaker talks about how people will be ashamed of how they have treated him and others.	The speaker is proud to be who he is.

The Negro Speaks of Rivers

by Langston Hughes

I've known rivers:
I've known rivers ancient as the world and older than the flow
of human blood in human veins.

My soul has grown deep like the rivers.

I bathed in the Euphrates° when dawns were young.
I built my hut near the Congo° and it lulled me to sleep.
I looked upon the Nile° and raised the pyramids above it.
I heard the singing of the Mississippi when Abe Lincoln went
down to New Orleans°, and I've seen its muddy bosom
turn all golden in the sunset.
I've known rivers:
Ancient, dusky rivers.

My soul has grown deep like the rivers.

---

4. **Euphrates** (yo͞o·frāt′ēz): a river in southwest Asia that is associated with several ancient civilizations.
5. **Congo** (käŋ·gō): a river in west-central Africa, the region of origin for most of the enslaved Africans that were taken to the Americas.
6. **Nile:** river near which pyramids of ancient Egypt were built.
7. **Mississippi . . . New Orleans:** Inspired to write this poem while viewing the Mississippi at sunset, Hughes "remembered reading how Abraham Lincoln had made a trip down the Mississippi on a raft to New Orleans, and how he had seen slavery at its worst, and had decided within himself that it should be removed from American life." Lincoln had traveled on the Mississippi as a youth and years later as president issued the Emancipation Proclamation, which declared the freedom of all enslaved people in the rebellious states during the Civil War.

GENERALIZE

Read the description of the ancient rivers in line 2. What do these rivers symbolize?

INTERPRET

Re-read lines 4–6. How did the Africans live before the arrival of slave traders?

WORD STUDY

The verb *lulled* in line 5 means "soothed" or "calmed." The adjective *dusky* in line 9 means "dark" or "shadowy."

DRAW CONCLUSIONS

Re-read line 7 and the footnote. Why would the Mississippi be singing when Lincoln traveled down to New Orleans?

I, Too

by Langston Hughes

I, too, sing America.

I am the darker brother.
They send me to eat in the kitchen
When company comes,
But I laugh,
And eat well,
And grow strong.

Tomorrow,
I'll be at the table
When company comes.
Nobody'll dare
Say to me,
"Eat in the kitchen,"
Then.

Besides,
They'll see how beautiful I am
And be ashamed—

I, too, am America.

©George Disario/CORBIS

"I, Too" from *The Collected Poems of Langston Hughes,* edited by Arnold Rampersad with David Roessel, Associate Editor. Copyright © 1994 by The Estate of Langston Hughes. Reproduced by permission of **Alfred A. Knopf, a division of Random House, Inc.** and electronic format by **Harold Ober Associates Incorporated.**

LITERARY FOCUS

Re-read lines 1–2. Who is the speaker in this poem?

INFER

Re-read lines 3–7. How does the speaker feel about his treatment?

INTERPRET

What is the extended metaphor developed in lines 3–10?

INFER

Re-read lines 8–18. What change does the speaker anticipate for the future?

Dreams

by Langston Hughes

Hold fast to dreams
For if dreams die
Life is a broken-winged bird
That cannot fly.

Hold fast to dreams
For when dreams go
Life is a barren field
Frozen with snow.

Dreams No. 2, tempera on fiberboard, 1965, by Jacob Lawrence (1917–2000). ©ARS, NY. Smithsonian American Art Museum, Washington, D.C./Art Resource, NY

INTERPRET

Re-read lines 1–4. To what does Hughes compare "a broken-winged bird that cannot fly"?

LITERARY FOCUS

Read the poem aloud. Why do you think Hughes chose a third-person speaker for this poem instead of creating a first-person speaker?

EVALUATE

Examine the metaphor used in the second stanza. How does it help to convey Hughes's theme?

ANALYZE

Re-read lines 1–9. The speaker is dark, like the night. Keeping this in mind, what might the desire to whirl and dance in the sun refer to?

INFER

Re-read lines 10–14. What do the verbs suggest about the speaker's approach to life?

INTERPRET

Examine lines 5–9 and 14–17. Both stanzas end similarly—with a description of the approaching night. What might the night symbolize within the context of this poem?

Dream Variations

by Langston Hughes

To fling my arms wide
In some place of the sun,
To whirl and to dance
Till the white day is done.
Then rest at cool evening
Beneath a tall tree
While night comes on gently,
    Dark like me—
That is my dream!

To fling my arms wide
In the face of the sun,
Dance! Whirl! Whirl!
Till the quick day is done.
Rest at pale evening . . .
A tall, slim tree . . .
Night coming tenderly
    Black like me.

MEET THE WRITER

Langston Hughes (1902–1967) was born in Joplin, Missouri, and grew up in Kansas and Ohio. He came to New York City to attend Columbia University because it was near Harlem. Hughes became the most famous writer of the Harlem Renaissance, even though much of the work for which he is internationally known was published long after the Renaissance ended. In 1921 he published "The Negro Speaks of Rivers," and he soon earned the title "poet laureate of Harlem." (For more on Hughes, see page 209.)

SKILLS PRACTICE

The Negro Speaks of Rivers • I, Too • Dreams • Dream Variations

INFERENCE CHART

Identify details from each of the poems that help you to make inferences about the speaker. Write your inferences in the last column.

POEM	TEXT EVIDENCE	WHAT THE TEXT REVEALS ABOUT THE SPEAKER
"The Negro Speaks of Rivers"		
"I, Too"		
"Dreams"		
"Dream Variations"		

Reading Skills
Make inferences about the speaker of a poem.

BEFORE YOU READ

Tableau
by Countee Cullen

In this poem, Harlem Renaissance writer Countee Cullen uses a simple image to make an important point about race relations.

LITERARY FOCUS: METAPHOR

A **metaphor** is a type of figurative language that makes a comparison between two unlike things without using a connective word such as *like, as, than,* or *resembles*. In a metaphor, the author is saying one thing is something else. The two items being compared may seem unrelated, but an essential quality in one is brought out by the comparison to the other. Read the following example:

"His eyes were chips of black marble."

By comparing the person's eyes to black marble, the idea of their color as well as their hardness is brought out. As you read the poem "Tableau," think about how Cullen's use of metaphor helps to bring out his theme.

READING SKILLS: ANALYZING WORD CHOICE

Poetry by nature is compressed. That means every word must be chosen carefully both for its denotation and for its connotation, or ideas associated with it. Read this example from the poem:

"The sable pride of the night."

The word *sable* in this line means "black." But, it has a connotation of richness and depth. The words *dark* and *black* have similar dictionary definitions but would not produce the same effect in the line. As you read "Tableau," look for words that have strong connotations.

Literary Focus Understand metaphor.

Reading Skills Analyze word choice.

Tableau°

by Countee Cullen

Locked arm in arm they cross the way,
The black boy and the white,
The golden splendor of the day,
The sable pride of night.

From lowered blinds the dark folk stare,
And here the fair folk talk,
Indignant that these two should dare
In unison to walk.

Oblivious to look and word
They pass, and see no wonder
That lightning brilliant as a sword
Should blaze the path of thunder.

° **tableau** (tab′lō′) *n.:* a striking dramatic scene or picture.

MEET THE WRITER

Countee Cullen (coun′tay) (1903–1946) was most likely raised by his grandmother and adopted by the pastor of a large Harlem church as a teen. He went to high school and college in New York, and earned a master's degree from Harvard. From around 1934 until he died, he taught French and English at the Frederick Douglass Junior High School in Harlem.

Cullen became a leading figure of the Harlem Renaissance, with books of poetry that included *Color* (1925) and *Copper Sun* (1927), as well as the novel *One Way to Heaven* (1931). Throughout his career, he was drawn to the subject of his racial heritage, "Somehow or other I find my poetry of itself treating of the Negro, of his joys and his sorrows—mostly of the latter—and of the heights and depths of emotion which I feel as a Negro." (For more on Cullen, see page 5.)

LITERARY FOCUS

Re-read lines 1–4. To what is each boy compared?

WORD STUDY

Use context clues to help you define *indignant* in line 7 as "outraged", as well as *oblivious* in line 9 as "unaware."

INTERPRET

Underline the words in the third stanza that show the effect of the boys' appearance. Why is the poem entitled "Tableau"?

INTERPRET

Read the poem aloud. In what way does the regularity of the rhythm and rhyme affect the meaning?

Tableau

METAPHOR CHART

Countee Cullen uses metaphors to describe the two boys and their impact on those who see them. Explain each metaphor in your own words and then discuss what it adds to the meaning of the poem.

LINES	METAPHOR	SIGNIFICANCE
1–4		
9–12		

SKILLS FOCUS

Literary Focus Analyze metaphors.

READING COMPREHENSION

Answer the question below.

In what ways may the theme of "Tableau" apply to relationships among all people?

BEFORE YOU READ

How It Feels to Be Colored Me
by Zora Neale Hurston

In this essay, Harlem Renaissance writer Zora Neale Hurston describes how she feels about being an African American woman, all the while poking fun at stereotypes held by both whites and blacks.

LITERARY FOCUS: BIOGRAPHICAL AND HISTORICAL APPROACH

When you take a **biographical approach** to literature, you consider how the writer's experiences affect the work. "How It Feels to Be Colored Me" is a **personal essay,** a nonfiction genre in which writers describe their experiences, emotions, and thoughts. Therefore, you know before you begin reading that the information will be biographical.

When you take a **historical approach** to literature, you consider how the historical context affects the work. In this essay, Hurston describes experiences from the early 1900s, so you know the historical context will be different from today. During the period Hurston is writing about, segregation was the norm in the South, and racial bigotry was common across the United States.

- Hurston's first historical setting is the all-black town of Eatonville, Florida, a place where Hurston was accepted as herself.
- Her next setting is a racially mixed community in which she is changed in the eyes of the world from her own self, Zora, to a racial stereotype of "a little colored girl."
- Next, Hurston moves to New York City, where she stands out in the white world of Barnard College.
- Finally, in a Harlem nightclub Hurston feels a connection to her African ancestry through the rhythms of jazz while her white companion sits unmoved.

READING SKILLS: COMPARE AND CONTRAST

When you **compare** two things, you look for *similarities,* or ways the things are alike. When you **contrast** two things, you look for *differences* between them.

As you read "How It Feels to Be Colored Me," compare and contrast Zora Neale Hurston's experience of being an African American in the various settings she describes.

Literary Focus Understand biographical and historical approaches to literary criticism.

Reading Skills Compare and contrast.

Vocabulary Skills Understand figurative language.

VOCABULARY DEVELOPMENT

PREVIEW SELECTION VOCABULARY

The following words appear in "How It Feels to Be Colored Me." Look them over before you begin the selection.

extenuating (ek·sten′yo͞o·āt′iŋ) *v.* used as *adj.:* making seem less serious by serving as an excuse or justification.

Hurston is African American and offers no ***extenuating*** *information that would make her seem more exceptional.*

deplored (dē·plôrd′) *v.:* strongly disapproved of; condemned.

The adults ***deplored*** *any showing off before the visitors.*

circumlocutions (sʉr′kəm·lō·kyo͞o′shənz) *n.:* roundabout ways of expressing something.

The music started without any fancy riffs or other ***circumlocutions*** *on the way to its heart.*

rambunctious (ram·buŋk′shəs) *adj.:* wild; disorderly.

As the music became more upbeat, the orchestra became downright ***rambunctious.***

exultingly (eg·zult′iŋ·lē) *adv.:* triumphantly.

The dancers snaked across the floor, following each other ***exultingly.***

veneer (və·nir′) *n.:* superficially attractive surface or appearance.

Polite behaviors form a ***veneer*** *we call civilization.*

UNDERSTANDING FIGURATIVE LANGUAGE

Figurative language compares one thing to another, very different thing and is not meant to be understood literally. Here are some common types of figurative language:

- A **simile** is a comparison that uses a connecting word such as *like, as, than,* or *resembles.* For example: *Her wit was as sharp as a tack.*
- A **metaphor** makes a comparison without a connecting word. Some metaphors say that something *is* something else: *His heart was a glowing ember.* Others imply the comparison: *His heart smoldered and burned.* An **extended metaphor** is one that is continued for several sentences.
- **Personification** gives human qualities to inanimate objects, ideas, animals, machines—in other words, to anything *not* human—to make its comparison: *The sky cried in pity for the parched land below.*
- An **idiom** is an expression common to a particular language that means something different from the literal meaning of the words. For example: *My heart is broken.*

As you read "How It Feels to Be Colored Me," look for the many ways in which Hurston uses figurative language to bring her message to the reader.

How It Feels to Be Colored Me

by Zora Neale Hurston

I am colored but I offer nothing in the way of **extenuating** circumstances except the fact that I am the only Negro in the United States whose grandfather on the mother's side was *not* an Indian chief.

I remember the very day that I became colored. Up to my thirteenth year I lived in the little Negro town of Eatonville, Florida. It is exclusively a colored town. The only white people I knew passed through the town going to or coming from Orlando. The native whites rode dusty horses; the Northern tourists chugged down the sandy village road in automobiles. The town knew the Southerners and never stopped cane chewing when they passed. But the Northerners were something else again. They were peered at cautiously from behind curtains by the timid. The more venturesome would come out on the porch to watch them go past and got just as much pleasure out of the tourists as the tourists got out of the village.

The front porch might seem a daring place for the rest of the town, but it was a gallery seat for me. My favorite place was atop the gatepost. Proscenium[1] box for a born first-nighter. Not only did I enjoy the show, but I didn't mind the actors knowing that I liked it. I usually spoke to them in passing. I'd wave at them and when they returned my salute, I would say something like this: "Howdy-do-well-I-thank-you-where-you-goin'?" Usually the automobile or the horse paused at this, and after a queer exchange of compliments, I would probably "go a piece of the way" with them, as we say in farthest Florida. If one of my family happened to come to the front in time to see me, of

1. **proscenium** (prō·sē′nē·əm) *n.* used as *adj.:* area separating the stage from the audience. A proscenium box is a good theater seat close to the stage.

VOCABULARY

extenuating (ek·sten′yo͞o·āt′iŋ) *v.* used as *adj.:* making seem less serious by serving as an excuse or justification.

INFER

Re-read lines 5–16. Why do you think Hurston did not feel "colored" while growing up in Eatonville, Florida?

INTERPRET

Underline the extended metaphor in lines 19–21. What does this figure of speech tell you about Hurston's character?

VOCABULARY

deplored (dē·plôrd′) *v.:* strongly disapproved of; condemned.

INFER

Why does Hurston become a racial stereotype—"a little colored girl"—when she goes to the city of Jacksonville?

WORD STUDY

The word *fast* (line 46) is a multiple-meaning word. It means "that won't fade."

INTERPRET

In line 55, Hurston uses a metaphor that alludes to a famous quote from Shakespeare's *The Merry Wives of Windsor:* "Why then, the world's mine oyster." What does Hurston mean by her figure of speech?

course negotiations would be rudely broken off. But even so, it is clear that I was the first "welcome-to-our-state" Floridian, and I hope the Miami Chamber of Commerce will please take notice.

During this period, white people differed from colored to me only in that they rode through town and never lived there. They liked to hear me "speak pieces" and sing and wanted to see me dance the parse-me-la, and gave me generously of their small silver for doing these things, which seemed strange to me, for I wanted to do them so much that I needed bribing to stop. Only they didn't know it. The colored people gave no dimes. They **deplored** any joyful tendencies in me, but I was their Zora nevertheless. I belonged to them, to the nearby hotels, to the county—everybody's Zora.

But changes came in the family when I was thirteen, and I was sent to school in Jacksonville. I left Eatonville, the town of the oleanders,[2] as Zora. When I disembarked from the riverboat at Jacksonville, she was no more. It seemed that I had suffered a sea change. I was not Zora of Orange County any more, I was now a little colored girl. I found it out in certain ways. In my heart as well as in the mirror, I became a fast brown—warranted not to rub nor run.

But I am not tragically colored. There is no great sorrow dammed up in my soul, nor lurking behind my eyes. I do not mind at all. I do not belong to the sobbing school of Negrohood who hold that nature somehow has given them a lowdown dirty deal and whose feelings are all hurt about it. Even in the helter-skelter skirmish that is my life, I have seen that the world is to the strong regardless of a little pigmentation more or less. No, I do not weep at the world—I am too busy sharpening my oyster knife.

Someone is always at my elbow reminding me that I am the granddaughter of slaves. It fails to register depression with me. Slavery is sixty years in the past.[3] The operation was successful

2. **oleanders** (ō′lē·an′dərz) *n.:* shrubs with fragrant flowers.
3. **Slavery . . . past:** Hurston wrote this essay as an adult in the mid-1920s. The Thirteenth Amendment officially ended slavery in 1865.

Zora Neale Hurston, c. 1935, Belle Glade, Florida.
Library of Congress

and the patient is doing well, thank you. The terrible struggle that made me an American out of a potential slave said, "On the line!" The Reconstruction[4] said, "Get set!" and the generation before said, "Go!" I am off to a flying start and I must not halt in the stretch to look behind and weep. Slavery is the price I paid for civilization, and the choice was not with me. It is a bully[5] adventure and worth all that I have paid through my ancestors for it. No one on earth ever had a greater chance for glory. The world to be won and nothing to be lost. It is thrilling to think—to know that for any act of mine, I shall get twice as much praise or twice as much blame. It is quite exciting to hold the center of the national stage, with the spectators not knowing whether to laugh or to weep.

The position of my white neighbor is much more difficult. No brown specter[6] pulls up a chair beside me when I sit down to eat. No dark ghost thrusts its leg against mine in bed. The game of keeping what one has is never so exciting as the game of getting.

HISTORICAL CONTEXT

At the time Hurston wrote this, her first essay, the social question aimed at African Americans was, essentially, "How does it feel to be a problem?" Hurston rejects this way of seeing herself. She claims her identity despite racism. In this essay she also seeks to resolve the incongruities between *colored me* and *real me,* much as all people seek to resolve the differences between other people's ideas of who they are and who they really are.

LITERARY FOCUS

Re-read lines 60–75. Why does Hurston consider the time she is living in a great time to be an African American? Why does she think that it is more exciting to be black than white?

---

4. **Reconstruction:** (1865–1877) period after the Civil War when the South was being rebuilt.
5. **bully** (bo͝ol′ē) *adj.:* (informal) excellent.
6. **specter** (spek′tər) *n.:* ghost.

INFER

Re-read lines 76–83. How does Hurston show that color consciousness is a socially constructed phenomenon?

INTERPRET

Why do you think Hurston uses stereotyped images of Africans to describe her reaction to the music?

VOCABULARY

circumlocutions (sʉr'kəm·lō·kyo͞o'shənz) *n.:* roundabout ways of expressing something.

rambunctious (ram·buŋk'shəs) *adj.:* wild; disorderly.

exultingly (eg·zult'iŋ·lē) *adv.:* triumphantly.

veneer (və·nir') *n.:* superficially attractive surface or appearance.

I do not always feel colored. Even now I often achieve the unconscious Zora of Eatonville before the Hegira.[7] I feel most colored when I am thrown against a sharp white background.

For instance at Barnard.[8] "Beside the waters of the Hudson" I feel my race. Among the thousand white persons, I am a dark rock surged upon, and overswept, but through it all, I remain myself. When covered by the waters, I am; and the ebb but reveals me again.

Sometimes it is the other way around. A white person is set down in our midst, but the contrast is just as sharp for me. For instance, when I sit in the drafty basement that is The New World Cabaret with a white person, my color comes. We enter chatting about any little nothing that we have in common and are seated by the jazz waiters. In the abrupt way that jazz orchestras have, this one plunges into a number. It loses no time in **circumlocutions,** but gets right down to business. It constricts the thorax and splits the heart with its tempo and narcotic harmonies. This orchestra grows **rambunctious,** rears on its hind legs and attacks the tonal veil with primitive fury, rending it, clawing it until it breaks through to the jungle beyond. I follow those heathen—follow them **exultingly.** I dance wildly inside myself; I yell within, I whoop; I shake my assegai[9] above my head, I hurl it true to the mark *yeeeeooww*! I am in the jungle and living in the jungle way. My face is painted red and yellow and my body is painted blue. My pulse is throbbing like a war drum. I want to slaughter something—give pain, give death to what, I do not know. But the piece ends. The men of the orchestra wipe their lips and rest their fingers. I creep back slowly to the **veneer** we call civilization with the last tone and find the white friend sitting motionless in his seat, smoking calmly.

7. **Hegira** (hi·jī'rə) *n.:* journey, especially one taken to escape danger. The word comes from Arabic, referring to Muhammad's flight from Mecca.
8. **Barnard:** liberal arts college for women in New York City, associated with Columbia University. Hurston studied anthropology there on scholarship and got her bachelor's degree in 1928.
9. **assegai** (as'ə·gī') *n.:* slender iron-tipped spear used in South Africa.

Zora Neale Hurston sitting on a porch in Eatonville, Florida, with musicians Rochelle French and Gabriel Brown, 1935.
©CORBIS

"Good music they have here," he remarks, drumming the table with his fingertips.

Music. The great blobs of purple and red emotion have not touched him. He has only heard what I felt. He is far away and I see him but dimly across the ocean and the continent that have fallen between us. He is so pale with his whiteness then and I am *so* colored.

At certain times I have no race. I am *me*. When I set my hat at a certain angle and saunter down Seventh Avenue, Harlem City, feeling as snooty as the lions in front of the Forty-Second Street Library, for instance. So far as my feelings are concerned, Peggy Hopkins Joyce on the Boule Mich[10] with her gorgeous raiment, stately carriage, knees knocking together in a most aristocratic manner, has nothing on me. The cosmic Zora emerges. I belong to no race nor time. I am the eternal feminine[11] with its string of beads.

NOTES

COMPARE & CONTRAST

Compare and contrast Hurston's reaction to the music with that of her companion.

10. Peggy . . . Mich: Peggy Hopkins Joyce (1893–1957), flamboyant actress who appeared on stage and in silent films. *Boule Mich* is short for Boulevard St. Michel, a famous avenue in Paris.

11. eternal feminine: from the last lines of the eighteenth-century German writer Goethe's play *Faust:* "The eternal feminine leads us upward."

FLUENCY

Read the boxed passage aloud, first for smoothness and then to characterize the feelings behind the text. Hurston's voice in this passage is different from her voice when she is making fun. Try, with your own voice, to illustrate that difference.

INTERPRET

Notice the extended metaphor of people as bags of different colors in lines 128–142 and the individual metaphors of the different bits of jumble. What do these metaphors tell you about the human condition? How does the metaphor relate to the theme of Hurston's essay?

I have no separate feeling about being an American citizen and colored. I am merely a fragment of the Great Soul that surges within the boundaries. My country, right or wrong.

Sometimes, I feel discriminated against, but it does not make me angry. It merely astonishes me. How *can* any deny themselves the pleasure of my company? It's beyond me.

But in the main, I feel like a brown bag of miscellany propped against a wall. Against a wall in company with other bags, white, red, and yellow. Pour out the contents, and there is discovered a jumble of small things priceless and worthless. A first-water diamond,[12] an empty spool, bits of broken glass, lengths of string, a key to a door long since crumbled away, a rusty knife blade, old shoes saved for a road that never was and never will be, a nail bent under the weight of things too heavy for any nail, a dried flower or two still a little fragrant. In your hand is the brown bag. On the ground before you is the jumble it held—so much like the jumble in the bags, could they be emptied, that all might be dumped in a single heap and the bags refilled without altering the content of any greatly. A bit of colored glass more or less would not matter. Perhaps that is how the Great Stuffer of Bags filled them in the first place—who knows?

12. first-water diamond: diamond of the highest quality.

MEET THE WRITER

Zora Neale Hurston (1891–1960) grew up in Eatonville, Florida, where her father was a carpenter, preacher, and sometime mayor. Her mother died in 1904. After her father remarried, Hurston left home to join a traveling theater company. She later enrolled in high school at Morgan Academy in Baltimore and attended Howard University in Ohio. After beginning to publish her fiction, she moved to New York City in 1924, where she studied anthropology at Barnard College and became an acclaimed member of the Harlem Renaissance. Hurston published short stories, novels, essays, an autobiography, and books based on her anthropological research in the South and in the Caribbean. Her work fell out of favor in the 1940s, and Hurston died in poverty. In 1973, the writer Alice Walker found her unmarked grave and erected a gravestone for her.

SKILLS PRACTICE

How It Feels to Be Colored Me

HISTORICAL CONTEXT CHART

The chart below lists the settings from "How It Feels to Be Colored Me." For each setting, describe the historical context and its influence in Zora Neale Hurston's essay.

SETTING	HISTORICAL CONTEXT
Eatonville, Florida	
Jacksonville, Florida	
Barnard College, New York City	
New World Cabaret, Harlem, New York City	

Literary Focus Analyze historical context. Take a historical approach to literary criticism.

How It Feels to Be Colored Me

VOCABULARY AND COMPREHENSION

WORD BOX

extenuating
rambunctious
exultingly
veneer

A. Figurative Language For each item below, fill in the blank with the appropriate word from the Word Box. Then, underline the figure of speech and identify it as a **simile,** a **metaphor,** an **idiom,** or **personification.**

1. There were no ______________ circumstances to excuse her for driving them all out of their minds.
   Figure of speech: ______________

2. The ______________ students were a herd of buffalo stampeding into the classroom.
   Figure of speech: ______________

3. The ______________ of new paint turned the ugly old house into a palace.
   Figure of speech: ______________

4. The painted house thought to itself ______________, "I am now the best-looking house on the block."
   Figure of speech: ______________

B. Reading Comprehension Answer the question below.

5. In what ways do you think Hurston's perspective might differ if she had stayed in Eatonville? Do you think she still would have become a writer? Use details from the essay to support your answer.
   ____
   ____
   ____
   ____
   ____
   ____

6. On a separate sheet of paper, describe an experience you have had, such as visiting or moving to a new city, that has had a significant impact on your life outlook.

Vocabulary Skills Identify figurative language.

Before You Read

The Richer, the Poorer

by Dorothy West

Dorothy West (1907–1998) was a writer connected with the Harlem Renaissance. In this short story, she recounts how two sisters who have lived very different lives are reunited.

LITERARY FOCUS: CHARACTER TRAITS

Characters are the people, animals, or things presented in a work of literature. They may be described as **flat**—one-sided and stereotypical— or **round**—many-sided and true to life. In some stories, the minor characters are flat characters, serving simply to advance the plot. Main characters are almost always round characters. Characters may also be described as **dynamic** or **static**. A dynamic character changes in some fundamental way during the course of a story. A static character remains the same.

Character traits are the special qualities unique to a character, including that person's values, likes and dislikes, habits, and outlook on life. You can learn about a character's traits by paying attention to the details that the narrator of a story gives you. The author/narrator may reveal a character's traits directly or indirectly. In **direct characterization**, the author/narrator simply tells the reader what the character is like. In **indirect characterization**, the author/narrator reveals a character's personality by describing his or her appearance, speech, private thoughts, and actions and also by how others react to the character. As you read "The Richer, the Poorer," ask yourself these questions: are the main characters dynamic or static, flat or round? What are their traits? Are these traits revealed directly, indirectly, or both directly and indirectly?

READING SKILLS: COMPARING AND CONTRASTING CHARACTERS

When you **compare** two things, you look for similarities—the ways the things are alike. When you **contrast** two things, you look for differences—the ways the things are not alike. When you **compare and contrast characters**, you compare which traits the characters have in common and which traits differ. As you read "The Richer, the Poorer," compare Lottie and Bess. In what ways are they alike? In what ways are they different?

Literary Focus
Understand character traits.

Reading Skills
Compare and contrast.

Vocabulary Skills
Use context clues.

VOCABULARY DEVELOPMENT

PREVIEW SELECTION VOCABULARY

The following words appear in "The Richer, the Poorer." Look them over before you begin the selection.

frivolous (friv′ə·ləs) *adj.:* lacking in seriousness; silly; trivial.

The girl thought her sister was ***frivolous*** *because she never saved her money or worried about the future.*

frugally (fro͞o′gəl·lē) *adv.:* done in a manner that avoids waste or unnecessary spending.

Having lived through a difficult childhood, she was conditioned to manage her income ***frugally****.*

sentimental (sən′tə·ment″l) *adj.:* having or showing much tender feeling.

She didn't have time to have ***sentimental*** *and caring thoughts about her sister.*

inefficient (in′e·fish′ənt) *adj.:* wasteful of time or energy; incapable.

To increase productivity, the ***inefficient*** *workers were asked to eliminate activities that distracted them.*

transformed (trans·fôrm′d) *v.:* changed.

People are sometimes ***transformed*** *when they experience new places and new ideas.*

lavish (lav′ish) *adj.:* extravagant; very abundant.

The meal seemed very ***lavish*** *and abundant when compared to her usual small dinners.*

wistfully (wist′fəl·lē) *adv.:* longingly; yearningly.

The hungry child gazed ***wistfully*** *at the rich pastries in the window of the bakery.*

USING CONTEXT CLUES

When you come across an unfamiliar word, look at the **context**—the words, phrases, or sentences surrounding the word—for clues to its meaning. Often, writers use a **definition**, a **restatement**, a **synonym**, or an **example** near the word that helps to explain its meaning. Read the following sentence from "The Richer, the Poorer":

> "By the time [Lottie] was twelve, she was clerking after school in a small variety store. Saturdays she worked as long as she was wanted. She decided to keep her money for clothes. When she entered high school, she would wear a wardrobe that neither she nor anyone else would be able to match."

If you did not know the meaning of *wardrobe,* what clues surrounding the word would help you determine it? Notice that a wardrobe is something you wear and that in the previous sentence Lottie decides to save her money for clothes. From this context, you might guess that the definition of *wardrobe* is "a collection of clothes."

As you read "The Richer, the Poorer," look at the context to help you determine the meaning of any unfamiliar words.

The Richer, the Poorer
by Dorothy West

Over the years Lottie had urged Bess to prepare for her old age. Over the years Bess had lived each day as if there were no other. Now they were both past sixty, the time for summing up. Lottie had a bank account that had never grown lean. Bess had the clothes on her back, and the rest of her worldly possessions in a battered suitcase.

Lottie had hated being a child, hearing her parents' skimping and scraping. Bess had never seemed to notice. All she ever wanted was to go outside and play. She learned to skate on borrowed skates. She rode a borrowed bicycle. Lottie couldn't wait to grow up and buy herself the best of everything.

As soon as anyone would hire her, Lottie put herself to work. She minded babies, she ran errands for the old.

She never touched a penny of her money, though her child's mouth watered for ice cream and candy. But she could not bear to share with Bess, who never had anything to share with her. When the dimes began to add up to dollars, she lost her taste for sweets.

Shadow and Sunlight, 1941, oil on canvas by Allan Rohan Crite.
Smithsonian American Art Museum, Washington D.C./Art Resource, NY

COMPARE & CONTRAST

What do you learn about Lottie and Bess in the first paragraph?

LITERARY FOCUS

What character traits does Lottie's behavior reveal about her in lines 14–17?

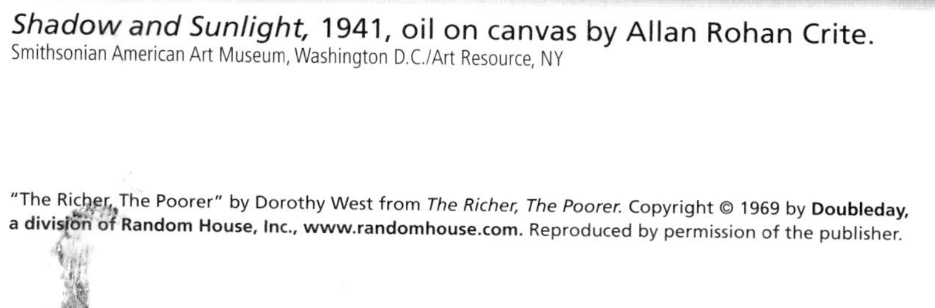

"The Richer, The Poorer" by Dorothy West from *The Richer, The Poorer.* Copyright © 1969 by **Doubleday, a division of Random House, Inc., www.randomhouse.com.** Reproduced by permission of the publisher.

VOCABULARY

frivolous (friv′ə·ləs) *adj.:* lacking in seriousness; silly; trivial.

INFER

What values does Lottie reveal in choosing to drop out of school to work full time?

COMPARE & CONTRAST

Why is it not surprising that Bess got married right out of high school and Lottie never married at all?

ANALYZE

Study lines 42–46. From whose point of view does the narrator tell the story? How do you know?

By the time she was twelve, she was clerking after school in a small variety store. Saturdays she worked as long as she was wanted. She decided to keep her money for clothes. When she entered high school, she would wear a wardrobe that neither she nor anyone else would be able to match.

But her freshman year found her unable to indulge so **frivolous** a whim, particularly when her admiring instructors advised her to think seriously of college. No one in her family had ever gone to college, and certainly Bess would never get there. She would show them all what she could do, if she put her mind to it.[1]

She began to bank her money, and her bankbook became her most private and precious possession.

In her third year of high school she found a job in a small but expanding restaurant, where she cashiered from the busy hour until closing. In her last year of high school the business increased so rapidly that Lottie was faced with the choice of staying in school or working full time.

She made her choice easily. A job in hand was worth two in the future.[2]

Bess had a beau in the school band, who had no other ambition except to play a horn. Lottie expected to be settled with a home and family while Bess was still waiting for Harry to earn enough to buy a marriage license.

That Bess married Harry straight out of high school was not surprising. That Lottie never married at all was not really surprising either. Two or three times she was halfway persuaded, but to give up a job that paid well for a homemaking job that paid nothing was a risk she was incapable of taking.

1. **put her mind to it:** idiom meaning to concentrate on or to act in a determined way about achieving a goal.
2. **a job in hand was worth two in the future:** a variation of the idiom *a bird in the hand is worth two in the bush* meaning that something available today is of more worth than something that may or may not be available in the future.

Bess's married life was nothing for Lottie to envy. She and Harry lived like gypsies, Harry playing in second-rate bands all over the country, even getting himself and Bess stranded in Europe. They were often in rags and never in riches.

Bess grieved because she had no child, not having sense enough to know she was better off without one. Lottie was certainly better off without nieces and nephews to feel sorry for. Very likely Bess would have dumped them on her doorstep.

That Lottie had a doorstep they might have been left on was only because her boss, having bought a second house, offered Lottie his first house at a price so low and terms so reasonable that it would have been like losing money to refuse.

She shut off the rooms she didn't use, letting them go to rack and ruin.[3] Since she ate her meals out, she had no food at home, and did not encourage callers, who always expected a cup of tea.

Her way of life was mean and miserly, but she did not know it. She thought she lived **frugally** in her middle years so that she could live in comfort and ease when she most needed peace of mind.

The years, after forty, began to race. Suddenly Lottie was sixty, and retired from her job by her boss's son, who had no **sentimental** feeling about keeping her on until she was ready to quit.

She made several attempts to find other employment, but her dowdy appearance made her look old and **inefficient**. For the first time in her life Lottie would gladly have worked for nothing, to have some place to go, something to do with her day.

Harry died abroad, in a third-rate hotel, with Bess weeping as hard as if he had left her a fortune. He had left her nothing but his horn. There wasn't even money for her passage home.

---

3. go to rack and ruin: idiom meaning to fall into disrepair or decay.

VOCABULARY

frugally (fro͞o′gəl·lē) *adv.:* done in a manner that avoids waste or unnecessary expense.

sentimental (sən′tə·ment″l) *adj.:* having or showing much tender feeling.

inefficient (in′e·fish′ənt) *adj.:* wasteful of time or energy; incapable.

WORD STUDY

Miserly and *frugally* have similar denotations but different connotations. Look up *miser* and *miserly* in a dictionary. Which word—*frugally* or *miserly*—describes Lottie's attitude toward money better? Why?

ANALYZE

What is Lottie discovering about her life in lines 73–74?

PREDICT

What do you think Lottie will have to do for her sister because of Harvey's death?

VOCABULARY

transformed (trans·fôrm'd) *v.:* changed.

LITERARY FOCUS

What transformation is beginning to take place in Lottie's personality?

DRAW CONCLUSIONS

What conflicting emotions does Lottie feel while redecorating? Is she aware of this conflict?

Lottie, trapped by the blood tie, knew she would not only have to send for her sister, but take her in when she returned. It didn't seem fair that Bess should reap the harvest of Lottie's lifetime of self-denial.

It took Lottie a week to get a bedroom ready, a week of hard work and hard cash. There was everything to do, everything to replace or paint. When she was through the room looked so fresh and new that Lottie felt she deserved it more than Bess.

She would let Bess have her room, but the mattress was so lumpy, the carpet so worn, the curtains so threadbare that Lottie's conscience pricked her. She supposed she would have to redo that room, too, and went about doing it with an eagerness that she mistook for haste.

When she was through upstairs, she was shocked to see how dismal downstairs looked by comparison. She tried to ignore it, but with nowhere to go to escape it, the contrast grew more intolerable.

She worked her way from kitchen to parlor, persuading herself she was only putting the rooms to rights to give herself something to do. At night she slept like a child after a long and happy day of playing house. She was having more fun than she had ever had in her life. She was living each hour for itself.[4]

There was only a day now before Bess would arrive. Passing her gleaming mirrors, at first with vague awareness, then with painful clarity, Lottie saw herself as others saw her, and could not stand the sight.

She went on a spending spree from the specialty shops to beauty salon, emerging **transformed** into a woman who believed in miracles.

She was in the kitchen basting a turkey when Bess rang the bell. Her heart raced, and she wondered if the heat from the oven was responsible.

4. **living each hour for itself:** Lottie is enjoying each hour as it happens instead of worrying about what will happen in the future.

Woman Ironing, 1944, by William H. Johnson (1901–1970).
Smithsonian American Art Museum, Washington D.C./Art Resource, NY

She went to the door, and Bess stood before her. Stiffly she suffered Bess's embrace, her heart racing harder, her eyes suddenly smarting[5] from the onrush of cold air.

"Oh, Lottie, it's good to see you," Bess said, but saying nothing about Lottie's splendid appearance. Upstairs Bess, putting down her shabby suitcase, said, "I'll sleep like a rock tonight," without a word of praise for her lovely room. At the **lavish** table, top-heavy with turkey, Bess said, "I'll take light and dark, both," with no marveling at the size of the bird, or that there was turkey for two elderly women, one of them too poor to buy her own bread.

With the glow of good food in her stomach, Bess began to spin stories. They were rich with places and people, most of them lowly, all of them magnificent. Her face reflected her telling, the joys and sorrows of her remembering, and above all, the love she lived by that enhanced the poorest place, the humblest person.

5. **smarting** (smär′tiŋ) *v.:* to feel sudden sharp or stinging pain.

VOCABULARY

lavish (lav′ish) *adj.:* extravagant; very abundant.

INFER

What emotions do you think Lottie is feeling when her heart races and her eyes smart? Is she aware of these feelings? How do you know?

COMPARE & CONTRAST

How does Lottie's life compare to the life that Bess describes in lines 121–125? What might Lottie be feeling in hearing the stories?

VOCABULARY

wistfully (wist′fəl·lē) *adv.:* longingly; yearningly.

INFER

What can you infer from the sentence "Tonight she [Bess] saw only what she had come seeking, a place in her sister's home and heart"?

COMPARE & CONTRAST

At the end, has Lottie changed? Has Bess changed? Explain.

Then it was that Lottie knew why Bess had made no mention of her finery, or the shining room, or the twelve-pound turkey. She had not even seen them. Tomorrow she would see the room as it really looked, and Lottie as she really looked, and the warmed-over turkey in its second-day glory. Tonight she saw only what she had come seeking, a place in her sister's home and heart.

She said, "That's enough about me. How have the years used you?"

"It was me who didn't use them," said Lottie **wistfully**. "I saved for them. I saved for them. I forgot the best of them would go without my ever spending a day or a dollar enjoying them. That's my life story in those few words, a life never lived.

"Now it's too near the end to try."

Bess said, "To know how much there is to know is the beginning of learning to live. Don't count the years that are left us. At our time of life it's the days that count. You've too much catching up to do to waste a minute of a waking hour feeling sorry for yourself."

Lottie grinned, a real wide-open grin, "Well to tell the truth, I felt sorry for you. Maybe if I had any sense I'd feel sorry for myself, after all. I know I'm too old to kick up my heels, but I'm going to let you show me how. If I land on my head, I guess it won't matter; I feel giddy already, and I like it."

©Richard Howard/Time & Life Pictures/Getty Images

EXTEND

In the library find and read another work by Dorothy West. Write a short essay on another sheet of paper comparing Dorothy West's character development in "The Richer, the Poorer" with the other work.

NOTES

MEET THE WRITER

Dorothy West (1907–1998) was born into a prosperous family in Boston, Massachusetts, where her father ran a fruit company. She began writing stories when she was seven and was published in the *Boston Post* while she was in her teens. After entering an *Opportunity* writing contest, she decided to settle in New York City. *Opportunity* published West's story "The Typewriter" in 1926. This story is about a man who becomes obsessed with pretending to be a wealthy financier and was included in *The Best Short Stories of 1926*.

In New York, West became acquainted with many writers of the Harlem Renaissance, including Zora Neale Hurston and Langston Hughes. In the early 1930s, she started the literary magazine *Challenge*. This magazine lasted only a few issues. Thereafter, she started *New Challenge* which published the work of such writers as Richard Wright and Ralph Ellison, but it too folded.

Although her magazine ventures failed, West continued to publish her own stories. In 1945, she moved to Martha's Vineyard, where she wrote her novel, *The Living is Easy* (1948). Its main character is a strong-willed black woman (based on West's mother) who rules her Boston family. In 1995, West published her long-awaited second novel, *The Wedding*. It takes place on Martha's Vineyard where a wealthy young black woman prepares for her marriage. West writes so well that one reviewer said, "At the end, it's as though we've been invited not so much to a wedding as to a full-scale opera, only to find that one great artist is belting out all the parts. She brings down the house." *The Wedding* was a best-seller that was also made into a movie.

The Richer, the Poorer

VENN DIAGRAM

Compare and contrast the characters of Bess and Lottie in the Venn diagram below. List their differences in the outer rings and their similarities in the center.

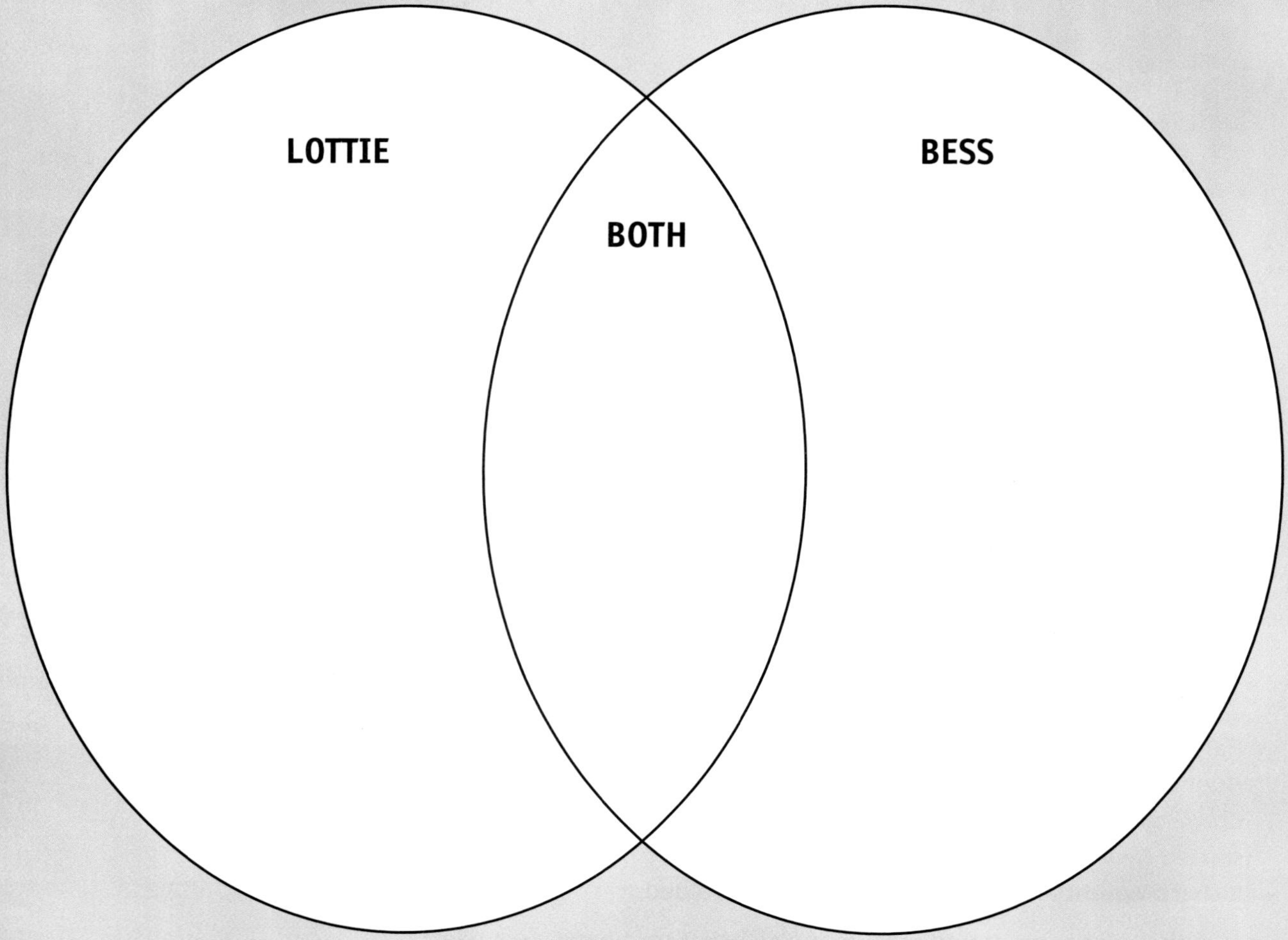

LOTTIE

BOTH

BESS

Literary Focus
Analyze character traits.

Reading Skills
Compare and contrast.

The Richer, the Poorer

VOCABULARY AND COMPREHENSION

WORD BOX
frivolous
frugality
sentimental
inefficient
transformed
lavish
wistfully

A. Context Clues Complete each sentence with the correct vocabulary word from the Word Box.

1. Being a ______________________ person, Colin felt a lump in his throat when the separated friends were reunited at the end of the movie.

2. Seeing the children laughing and playing outside the nursing home, the lonely resident reflected ______________________ on the happy times of her youth.

3. The child behaved ______________________, saving her money instead of buying treats.

4. The sister accepted the ______________________ dinner and did not appear to worry about the cost.

5. The worker was obsessed with saving money and thought most purchases were ______________________ and silly.

6. After viewing the documentary, the student found herself ______________ into a person who wanted to help others lead better lives.

7. Washing each item of clothing one at a time by hand is an ______________ way to do the laundry.

B. Reading Comprehension Answer each question below.

8. What do Lottie's thoughts reveal about her attitude toward Bess throughout most of the story?

____

____

9. What does Bess's behavior at the end of the story reveal about her attitude toward Lottie?

____

____

____

Vocabulary Skills
Use context clues.

Before You Read

from Don't You Want to Be Free? From Slavery through the Blues to Now—and Then Some! With Singing, Music, and Dancing

by Langston Hughes

Poet, playwright, and author Langston Hughes was a major voice of African Americans in the United States during the mid-twentieth century. In this play, Hughes conveys his central message through a series of vignettes, or short scenes, that show the obstacles that African Americans faced in the 1930s.

LITERARY FOCUS: STAGE DIRECTIONS

Stage directions are a playwright's instructions to the actors, telling them how to move and how to speak their lines. When you read a play, you need to pay close attention to the stage directions, which are italicized and in parentheses. Stage directions may be used to:

- identify the setting
- describe characters' appearances and their actions
- indicate characters' emotions and relationships
- fill in necessary background

Read this example from the play:

> *(The Overseer backs away and puts on a waiter's apron. Woman begins to peel potatoes, Young Man to study.)*

Notice how the stage directions tell you what each character is doing. This prepares you for the setting of the next vignette and the changing roles of the characters.

Literary Focus Understand the purpose of stage directions.

Reading Skills Make valid generalizations about situations presented in a play.

Vocabulary Skills Understand connotation and denotation.

READING SKILLS: MAKING GENERALIZATIONS

A **generalization** is a broad statement about a group of people, ideas, or things based on observations or facts. It usually identifies characteristics of a group. For example, "Most dogs have a keen sense of smell" is a generalization drawn from factual evidence and observation.

Generalizations might be valid or false. Valid generalizations contain words such as *most, many,* and *usually.* False generalizations, which include stereotypes, are often signaled by words such as *always, never, all,* and *none.*

In this play, Hughes shows the ways in which generalizations, or stereotypes, affect African Americans. As you read, also consider what valid generalizations you might make, based on the situations that he presents.

VOCABULARY DEVELOPMENT

PREVIEW SELECTION VOCABULARY

The following words appear in the play. Look them over before you begin to read.

trudging (truj′iŋ) *v.:* walking heavily; plodding.

He was discouraged, and it showed in the way he was ***trudging*** *up the street.*

despair (di·spār) *n.:* complete loss of hope.

Each setback brought her closer to ***despair****.*

impel (im·pel′) *v.:* push or urge forward.

The mother hoped her dreams would ***impel*** *her son to keep going and not give up.*

radical (rad′i·kəl) *n.:* revolutionary or rebel.

Because he demanded justice, he was labeled a ***radical****.*

UNDERSTANDING DENOTATIONS AND CONNOTATIONS

The **denotation** of a word is its dictionary definition. The denotations of the four vocabulary words from the selection appear above. **Connotation,** however, refers to the ideas associated with a word. For example, the word *gold* has a connotation of "precious" or "rare" or "valuable." Authors choose words carefully, keeping in mind both denotations and connotations. Read this example from the play:

"Remember how the strong in struggle and strife
Still bar you the way, and deny you life—
But march ever forward, breaking down bars."

Consider how different the meaning of the statement would be if the words *walk*, *go*, or even *trudge* replaced *march*. *March* has a connotation of power and determination that helps to convey the playwright's meaning.

As you read the play, be aware of the connotations of the words that Hughes chose. Think about how they contribute to the overall impact of the play.

INFER

Re-read the play's title and the poem "The Negro Speaks of Rivers" (page 171). In what ways do you think the theme of the poem might relate to the play?

DRAW CONCLUSIONS

Read the cast of characters. What does the lack of proper names suggest about the characters?

ANALYZE

This part of the play is set in 1930s Harlem. What do the props on the stage suggest?

from Don't You Want to Be Free? From Slavery through the Blues to Now—and Then Some! With Singing, Music, and Dancing

by Langston Hughes

Scene 1

Characters

Young Man
Woman
Overseer
Boy
Old Woman

Setting

Bare stage except for a lynch rope and an auction block.

The Beinecke Rare Book and Manuscript Library, Yale University Library

Woman: Good evening, son!

Young Man: Mom, I lost my job!

Woman: You lost your job?

Young Man: Yes! They laid me off tonight.

Woman: Well, honey, you'll find another one. Maybe.

Young Man: I don't know, Mom. Things is so tight, I done lost heart! Look how long I been a man now, and ain't never had a job that amounted to nothing. I've been all over and everywhere just the same. The dirty work for colored folks, the cheap work, underpaid work! I'm tired, Mom. Soon as I come here to be with you awhile and we get this little flat, first thing I do is lose my job. And the landlord's just sent us a notice about raising the rent, too. Mom, I'm about ready to give up. I swear I am!

Woman: Son, you ain't gonna give up no such a thing. Listen! You gonna keep right on just like I been keeping on. Did you ever stop to think about it, honey, about your mother, and all the rest of us colored women—what we been up against all through history, son. Sit down and lemme tell you, for *(Piano music.)*

I'm standing here today
Like a living story of that long dark way
That I had to climb, that I had to know
In order that our race might live and grow.
Look at my face, boy, dark as the night,
Yet shining like the sun with hope and light.
I'm the child they stole from the sand
Three hundred years ago in Africa's land.
I'm the dark girl who crossed the wide sea
Carrying in my body the seed of the Free.
I'm the woman who worked in the field,
Bringing the cotton and corn to yield.
I'm the one who labored as a slave,
Beaten and mistreated for the work that I gave—
Children sold away from me, husband sold, too.
No safety, no love, no respect was I due.
Three hundred years in the deepest South,

CLARIFY

What does the dialogue in lines 10–13 reveal about the setting of this vignette?

EVALUATE

Note that the stage directions in line 18 indicate the beginning of a song. Why do you think Hughes chose to incorporate music in the Woman's response to her son?

SUMMARIZE

What story does the Woman tell in lines 25–34?

INTERPRET

What is meant by "Love put a dream like steel in my soul" in line 37?

______

______

______

______

FLUENCY

Read aloud the boxed passage. Pause for punctuation and use voice inflection to help convey the meaning intended by the playwright.

VOCABULARY

trudging (truj′iŋ) *v.:* walking heavily; plodding.

despair (di·spār′) *n.:* complete loss of hope.

impel (im·pel′) *v.:* push or urge forward.

INTERPRET

What is the Woman's message? Underline figurative phrases in the boxed passage that convey this theme.

______

______

______

______

But love put a song and a prayer in my mouth.
Love put a dream like steel in my soul.
Now through my children, we're reaching the goal.
I couldn't read then. I couldn't write.
I had nothing back there in the night.
Sometimes the valley was filled with tears,
But I kept **trudging** on through the lonely years.
Sometimes the road was hot with sun.
But I had to keep on till my work was done.
I *had* to keep on! No stopping for me—
I was the seed of the coming Free.
I nourished our dream that nothing could smother
Deep in my breast—the Negro Mother.
I had only hope then, but now through you,
Dark child of today, my dreams must come true.
All you dark children in the world out there,
Remember my sweat, my pain, my **despair.**
Remember my years heavy with sorrow—
And make of those years a torch for tomorrow,
Make of my past a road to the light
Out of the darkness, the ignorance, the night.
Lift high my banner out of the dust.
Stand like free men supporting my trust.
Believe in the right, let none push you back.
Remember the whip and the slaver's track.
Remember how the strong in struggle and strife
Still bar you the way, and deny you life—
But march ever forward, breaking down bars.
Look ever upward at the sun and the stars.
Oh, my dark children, may my dreams and my prayers
Impel you forever up the great stairs—
For I will be with you till no white brother
Dares keep down the children of the Negro Mother.

'The Negro Mother and Other Dramatic Recitations,' illustrated and hand colored by Prentiss Taylor, 1931 / Langston Hughes. Book: 2 p.; 26 x 21cm. Prentiss Taylor papers.
Archives of American Art / Smithsonian Institution, Washington, D.C.

Overseer: *(Who is now a Landlord, coming to knock at their door, right):* Madam, did you get my notice about raising your rent, ten dollars a month more?

Woman: Yes, sir, I got the notice, but I am tired of that. I ain't gonna pay no more. We're paying enough.

Overseer: You'll pay it or move, and no smart talk about it, neither.

Young Man *(Rising):* Say, listen here! Who're you to speak to my mother like that?

Overseer: I'm the landlord. If you don't like it, get out of my place.

Young Man: Lemme see you get instead!

Overseer: What? This is my house!

Young Man: Yes, but you don't live in it! We live here! *(He towers above the Landlord.)* This is Harlem.

ANALYZE

The supervisor of enslaved workers on a plantation was known as an overseer. What idea does Hughes' reinforce by having the Overseer play the role of Landlord?

LITERARY FOCUS

What are the purposes of the stage directions in lines 69–70, 77, and 83?

CLARIFY

Why is the Boy astonished by the restaurant's refusal to serve African Americans in line 91?

LITERARY FOCUS

Note that the stage directions in lines 85–87 and 98–105 set up two separate vignettes. What social issues does Hughes address in each of these short scenes?

EVALUATE

Harlem is personified in line 95 and again in line 118. What point do you think Hughes is trying to make by attributing human qualities to the African American community?

(The Overseer backs away and puts on a waiter's apron. Woman begins to peel potatoes, Young Man to study. At the left a Boy holding a menu calls.)

Boy: Say, waiter! Where is the waiter? . . . Hey waiter! Give me an order of spaghetti and a bottle of beer, please.

Overseer: Sorry! We don't serve colored here.

Boy: What? You mean on 125th Street, and don't serve colored?

Overseer: Sure, this is a white place.

Boy *(Rising):* And you don't serve colored people?

Overseer: You heard me, big boy.

Boy: I might of heard you, but this is Harlem speaking now. Get me that spaghetti. I'm tired of this stuff! Talking about you don't serve colored people. Ain't I an American?

(Overseer backs away. Old Woman enters left as a picket carrying a sign that reads

Don't Buy Here!
This Store Does Not
Employ Negro Clerks

Slowly she walks back and forth in front of a store bearing the sign: MEAT MARKET. The Overseer rushes out in the white apron of a Butcher.)

Overseer: What you doing in front of my store? What I done to you? What for you walking up and down with that sign, destructing my business? Long as you trade with me, what is this?

Old Woman: You know what it is, Mr. Schultz! You know how long I been trading with you, don't you?

Overseer: More'n ten years, Mrs. Brown.

Old Woman: And all that time, I ain't never seen a colored clerk in this store, not one. My boy growed up and went through high school, and to college, and got more education than you ever had, but when one of your clerks died, and my boy come here to ask you for a job, you said: "No, you might give him a little janitor's job, but you got to have a white clerk." *(Loudly)* That's why I'm picketing out here, Mr. Schultz. Harlem is *tired*! No work! No money! I tell you, Harlem's tired!

Photograph from a production of *Don't You Want to Be Free?*
The Beinecke Rare Book and Manuscript Library, Yale University Library

(Old Woman brandishes her sign and the Butcher flees, to take off his apron and put on a coat and a pair of pince-nez[1] glasses with a flowing black ribbon. He is the editor of a daily paper and carries a handful of proofs. The Young Man enters.)

Young Man: You're the editor of the *Daily Scribe?*

Overseer: I am.

Young Man: I wrote a letter to your paper more'n two weeks ago about the hard times we colored folks've been having, and you didn't print it. I wish you'd tell me how come?

Overseer: Ah yes! I remember that letter. I'll tell you, boy, why we didn't print it. That letter would stir up trouble. I know times are hard, but you colored people have always been good citizens, peaceful and nice. Why get excited now? Just wait. Times'll be

1. **pince-nez** (pans′nā′) *n.:* reading glasses without sidepieces extending from the outer rim around the ears, supported on the bridge of the nose and often worn on a ribbon around the neck.

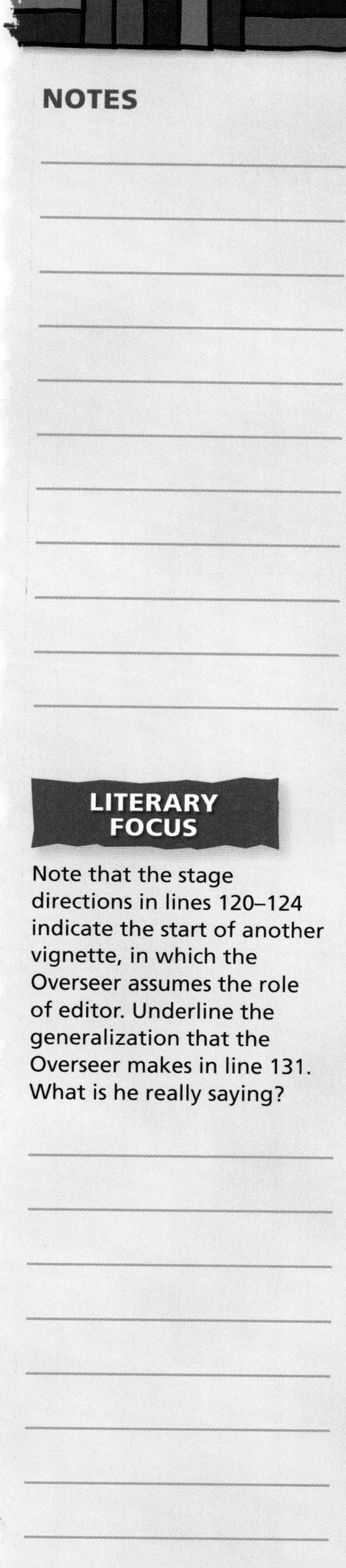

NOTES

LITERARY FOCUS

Note that the stage directions in lines 120–124 indicate the start of another vignette, in which the Overseer assumes the role of editor. Underline the generalization that the Overseer makes in line 131. What is he really saying?

CLARIFY

What point does the Young Man try to make by telling the editor what he has done for his country?

ANALYZE

Re-read lines 147–155. What is the purpose of the Young Man's references to Jim Crow Tennessee and Scottsboro?

better—the Republicans will be in again soon. Believe in God, boy, in the good old Stars and Stripes, and be loyal to your country.

Young Man:

But, Mr. Editor,
I've been loyal to my country
A long time, don't you see?
Now how about my country
Being loyal to me?
I fought in 1812 and 1863,
San Juan hill in Cuba,[2]
And for Democracy—
And fighting's not the only thing
I've done for liberty;
I've worked and worked a plenty,
Slave and free.
So when I pledge allegiance
To our flag so fair,
I keep looking at the stars and stripes
A-waving there,
And I'm wishing every star
Would *really* be a star
Like Jim Crow Tennessee—[3]
And no false convict's stripes such as
Scottsboro's[4] put on me.
I want that red and white and blue,
Mr. Editor,
To mean the same thing to me
As it does to you—
For I've been just as loyal

2. **1812 . . . Cuba:** the War of 1812, the Civil War, and the Spanish-American War.
3. **Jim Crow Tennessee:** Tennessee had numerous "Jim Crow laws" segregating and restricting the activities of African Americans.
4. **Scottsboro:** the site of a notorious Alabama case in which nine African American men were falsely accused of raping two white women.

To my country as you have,
Don't you see?
Now, how about my country
Being loyal to me?
Overseer: Why—er—uh—you're a **radical!**

VOCABULARY

radical (rad′i·kəl) *n.:* revolutionary or rebel.

Langston Hughes, 1932. Photo by Carl Van Vechten, published by permission of the Carl Van Vechten Trust. Gift of Prentiss Taylor.
National Portrait Gallery, Smithsonian Institution/Art Resource, NY

MEET THE WRITER

Langston Hughes (1902–1967) made many outstanding contributions as a poet, fiction writer, humorist, playwright, autobiographer, translator, and anthologist. He influenced writers in Africa and the Caribbean such as Léopold Sédar Senghor, Aimé Césaire, and Nicolás Guillén.

In his work, Hughes chose to identify with ordinary people. He once said that his poetry deals with "workers, roustabouts, and singers, and job hunters . . . people up today and down tomorrow, working this week and fired the next, beaten and baffled, but determined not to be wholly beaten." (For more on Hughes, see page 174.)

SKILLS PRACTICE

from Don't You Want to Be Free?

GENERALIZATIONS CHART

In the chart below, make a generalization about the social issues addressed in each mini scene of the play. Then make a valid generalization about the circumstances of African Americans in the 1930s, based on the ideas presented in the play.

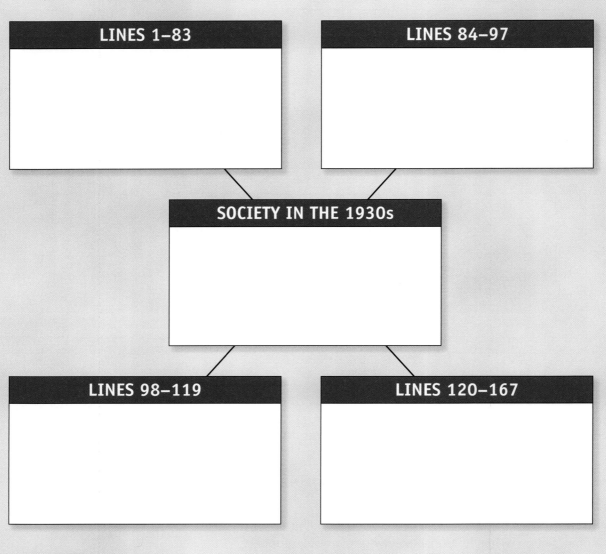

LINES 1–83	LINES 84–97

SOCIETY IN THE 1930s

LINES 98–119	LINES 120–167

Reading Skills
Make valid generalizations about situations presented in a play.

from Don't You want to Be Free?

VOCABULARY AND COMPREHENSION

WORD BOX

radical

despair

impel

trudging

A. Connotation and Denotation Write the word from the Word Box that correctly completes each sentence. Then explain its connotation.

1. She could hear him ______________________ up the stairs as if the weight of his body was too much to carry.

   Connotation ______________________

2. His ambition would ______________________ him to overcome the obstacles in his life.

   Connotation ______________________

3. The mother refused to give into ______________________, especially in front of her son.

   Connotation ______________________

4. Instead of listening to his grievances, they simply called him a ____________ and forgot about him.

   Connotation ______________________

B. Reading Comprehension Answer each question below.

5. Whom does the Woman represent when she tells the history of her people?

   ____

   ____

   ____

6. Why is Harlem "tired"?

   ____

   ____

   ____

7. Do you think the play's themes are still relevant in the United States today? Write your answer in a brief essay on a separate sheet of paper.

Vocabulary Skills
Demonstrate an understanding of connotation and denotation.

BLUES/SPEECH

BEFORE YOU READ

Backwater Blues
by Bessie Smith

Preaching Blues by Robert Johnson

from We, Too, Sing "America"
by Duke Ellington

In different ways, jazz and blues artists Bessie Smith, Robert Johnson, and Duke Ellington testify to the power of music to bring about change and transform what is personal into what is universal.

LITERARY FOCUS: BLUES POETRY

The **blues** is a type of vocal and instrumental music developed by African Americans. When you read blues poetry, you may notice the following characteristics:

- short stanzas
- melancholy tone
- use of nonstandard or vernacular English
- repetition of lines, sometimes with slight changes
- literary devices such as personification, metaphors, imagery

Look at the first stanza in "Backwater Blues." As you can see, the stanza is short, containing only three lines. The first is repeated. The third line helps to set the ominous tone by foreshadowing the conflict ahead.

READING SKILLS: RECOGNIZING SOCIAL AND HISTORICAL CONTEXT

Literature and the arts are often inspired or influenced by their historical or social contexts. **Historical context** refers to those events taking place in the world at the time a work is written. The **social context** may refer to the particular circumstances of a group in society. For example, the blues grew out of the experiences of African Americans, struggling to make something of their lives in the face of poverty and alienation.

As you read the selections, look for ways in which social and historical context influence the direction or content of each work.

Literary Focus Understand the characteristics of blues poetry.

Reading Skills Recognize social and historical context.

Backwater Blues

by Bessie Smith

When it rains five days and the skies turn dark as night,
When it rains five days and the skies turn dark as night,
Then trouble's takin' place in the lowlands at night.

I woke up this mornin', can't even get out of my door
I woke up this mornin', can't even get out of my door
That's enough trouble to make a poor girl wonder where she
want to go.

Then they rowed a little boat about five miles 'cross the farm.
Then they rowed a little boat about five miles 'cross the farm.
I packed all my clothes, throwed them in and they rowed me
along.

When it thunders and lightnin', and the wind begins to blow,
When it thunders and lightnin', and the wind begins to blow,
There's thousands of people ain't got no place to go.

Then I went and stood upon some high old lonesome hill.
Then I went and stood upon some high old lonesome hill.
Then I looked down on the house where I used to live.

Backwater blues done caused me to pack my things and go.
Backwater blues done caused me to pack my things and go.
'Cause my house fell down and I can't live there no more.

(Moan) . . . . I can't move no more,
(Moan) . . . . I can't move no more,
There ain't no place for a poor old girl to go.

INTERPRET

Re-read lines 4–9. What is the subject of the song?

INFER

How does the language in lines 10–18 reflect social context?

LITERARY FOCUS

What is the tone conveyed by the last three lines? How is this tone created?

EXTEND

Although "Backwater Blues" was written in the first person, it does not describe an event as experienced by Bessie Smith. Personalized lyrics allow blues artists to explore and convey the emotions associated with common types of tragedies or widespread social problems. Think about a problem or sad story you read about in the news or heard recently. Then write a blues song with personalized lyrics that tells about it and the feelings it has caused.

Bessie Smith, c. 1925.
©Bettmann/CORBIS

MEET THE WRITER

Bessie Smith (c.1894–1937), the "Empress of the Blues," was born in Chattanooga, Tennessee. She began her career with vaudeville legend Gertrude "Ma" Rainey and soon became the leading blues singer of her era. Record producer and music critic John Hammond said of Smith, "She was one of those rare beings, a completely integrated artist capable of projecting her whole personality into her music."

BACKGROUND

The **blues** has been called the "most popular musical style of the twentieth century." The blues became popular in rural regions of the South where it developed from spirituals, work songs such as "field hollers," and country ballads. The word *blues* began to appear in lyrics around 1900.

Blues lyrics are often personalized and deal with love, betrayal, revenge, poverty, natural disasters, wicked bosses, jail time, and "long lonesome roads." Rural blues musicians would play acoustic guitars on street corners or dance halls. The blues reached a wider audience when the African American composer and bandleader W. C. Handy (the "Father of the Blues") started writing and publishing blues songs. His "St. Louis Blues" (1914) is probably the most famous of all blues songs.

The 1920s were years made memorable by black women blues singers. "Crazy Blues," recorded by Mamie Smith in 1920, sold several million copies, and record company executives started frantically searching for new singers. Columbia records soon signed Bessie Smith, and the rest, as they say, is history.

Preaching Blues

by Robert Johnson

Mmmmmm mmmm
Got up this morning
The blues, walking like a man
Got up this morning
The blues walking like a man
Worried blues:
Give me your right hand

And the blues grabbed mama's child
And tore it all upside down
Blues grabbed mama's child
And they tore me all upside down
Travel on, poor Bob,
just can't turn you 'round

The blu-u-ues
Is a low down shaking chill
(yes) (I'm preaching 'em now)
Mmmm-mmmm
Is a low down shaking chill
You ain't never had 'em, I
Hope you never will

Well the blues
Is a aching old heart disease
(Do it now.
You gonna do it?
Tell me all about it.)

LITERARY FOCUS

Re-read lines 1–11. What is the effect of personifying the blues?

INTERPRET

Underline the comparison in lines 14–20. What mental image does it create?

ANALYZE

In lines 21–27, the artist says the blues is "a aching old heart disease." In what way does this metaphor further a listener's understanding of the suffering?

WORD STUDY

Consumption in line 28 is another name for tuberculosis, no longer in use. The disease was called consumption because the sufferer seemed to waste away, or be consumed by the illness.

CONNECT

What does the expression "gonna drive my blues away" mean to you?

____

____

____

____

____

The blues
Is a low down aching heart disease
And like consumption
Killing me by degrees

Now if it starts to raining
Gonna drive,
        gonna drive my blues
Now if it's startin' a-raining
I'm gonna drive my blues away
Going to the steel rig
Stay
  out
    there
      all
        day

MEET THE WRITER

Robert Johnson (1911–1938), the "King of the Delta Blues," was born in Hazelhurst, Mississippi. He was influenced by local blues artists Son House and Willie Brown, but soon developed his own unique style of singing and playing the guitar. Blues scholar, David Evans says of Johnson, "With only a guitar, Johnson is able to suggest the sound of a full band, including piano, drums and horns." Evans also says that "Johnson must be credited as the man who brought Deep South folk blues . . . into the mainstream of American music."

from We, Too, Sing "America"[1]

by Duke Ellington

First of all, I should like to extend my sincere appreciation to the Rev. Karl Downs for the opportunity to appear on this very fine program and express myself in a manner not often at my disposal. Music is my business, my profession, my life . . . but, even though it means so much to me, I often feel that I'd like to say something, have my say, on some of the burning issues confronting us, in another language . . . in words of mouth.

There is a good deal of talk in the world today. Some view that as a bad sign. One of the Persian poets, lamenting the great activity of men's tongues, cautioned them to be silent with the reminder that, "In much of your talking, thinking is half murdered." This is true no doubt. Yet, in this day when so many men are silent because they are afraid to speak, indeed, have been forbidden to speak, I view the volubility of the unrestricted with great satisfaction. Here in America, the silence of Europe, silent that is except for the harsh echoes of the dictators' voices,[2] has made us conscious of our privileges of free speech, and like the dumb suddenly given tongue, or the tongue-tied eased of restraint, we babble and bay to beat the band. Singly, as individuals, we don't say much of consequence perhaps, but put together, heard in chorus, the blustering half-truths, the lame and halting logic, the painfully-sincere convictions of Joe and Mary Doaks[3] . . . compose a powerful symphony which, like the small boy's brave whistle in the dark, serves notice on

WORD STUDY

The dictionary definition of *lamenting* in line 9 is "mourning" or "regretting." As it is used in this sentence, a closer definition might be "complaining about." *Volubility* in line 14 means "fluency." *Restraint* in line 19 means "controls" or "limits."

INTERPRET

Re-read lines 15–19. How does Ellington use the historical context of his speech to make his point?

PARAPHRASE

Lines 19–26 express Ellington's major thesis. State this claim in your own words.

1. **We, Too, Sing "America":** speech delivered on Annual Lincoln Day Services, Scott Methodist Church, Los Angeles, February 9, 1941.
2. **harsh . . . voices:** the lack of freedom under dictators such as Hitler, Stalin, and Mussolini; World War II had begun in Europe at the time of the speech.
3. **Joe and Mary Doaks:** names used to refer to an average man and woman.

NOTES

CONNECT

Recall the main idea of Langston Hughes's poem "I, Too" from page 172. How does Ellington extend and develop the idea?

WORD STUDY

Using context clues can help you define *valor* in line 33 as "courage" and *fervor* in line 44 as "intensity."

INTERPRET

What do both Hughes and Ellington mean when they say "sing America"?

Summer Madness, 1993, mixed media by Michael Escoffery.
Michael Escoffery/©ARS, NY/ Art Resource, NY

the hobgoblins that we are not asleep, not prey to unchallenged attack. And, so it is, with the idea in mind of adding my bit to the meaningful chorus, that I address you briefly this evening.

I have been asked to take as the subject of my remarks the title of a very significant poem, "We, Too, Sing America," written by the distinguished poet and author, Langston Hughes.

In the poem, Mr. Hughes argues the case for democratic recognition of the Negro on the basis of the Negro's contribution to America, a contribution of labor, valor, and culture. One hears that argument repeated frequently in the Race press,[4] from the pulpit and rostrum. America is reminded of the feats of Crispus Attucks,[5] Peter Salem,[6] black armies in the Revolution, the War of 1812, the Civil War, the Spanish-American War, the World War. Further, forgetful America is reminded that we sing without false notes, as borne out by the fact that there are no records of black traitors in the archives of American history. This is all well and good, but I believe it to be only half the story.

4. **Race press:** African American media sources.
5. **Crispus Attucks:** black man killed in the Boston Massacre.
6. **Peter Salem:** black soldier in the American Revolution.

We play more than a minority role, in singing "America." Although numerically but 10 per cent of the mammoth chorus that today, with an eye overseas, sings "America" with fervor and thanksgiving, I say our 10 per cent is the very heart of the chorus: the sopranos, so to speak, carrying the melody, the rhythm section of the band, the violins, pointing the way.

I contend that the Negro is the creative voice of America, is creative America, and it was a happy day in America when the first unhappy slave was landed on its shores.

There, in our tortured induction into this "land of liberty," we built its most graceful civilization. Its wealth, its flowering fields and handsome homes; its pretty traditions; its guarded leisure and its music, were all our creations.

We stirred in our shackles and our unrest awakened Justice in the hearts of a courageous few, and we recreated in America the desire for true democracy, freedom for all, the brotherhood of man, principles on which the country had been founded.

We were freed and as before, we fought America's wars, provided her labor, gave her music, kept alive her flickering conscience, prodded her on toward the yet unachieved goal, democracy—until we became more than a part of America! We—this kicking, yelling, touchy, sensitive, scrupulously-demanding minority—are the personification of the ideal begun by the Pilgrims almost 350 years ago.

It is our voice that sang "America" when America grew too lazy, satisfied and confident to sing . . . before the dark threats and fire-lined clouds of destruction frightened it into a thin, panicky quaver.

We are more than a few isolated instances of courage, valor, achievement. We're the injection, the shot in the arm, that has kept America and its forgotten principles alive in the fat and corrupt years intervening between our divine conception and our near tragic present.

SUMMARIZE

Re-read lines 48–54. Why was it a happy day when the first enslaved Africans arrived upon the shores of America?

ANALYZE

Re-read lines 59–65. How does this passage support Ellington's claim about the need for and importance of free speech?

HISTORICAL CONTEXT

In lines 67–69, Ellington refers to the circumstances of World War II that are threatening the nation's security.

Duke Ellington (on piano) and his orchestra, 1943.
©Michael Ochs Archives/CORBIS

MEET THE WRITER

Edward Kennedy "Duke" Ellington (1899–1974) was born in Washington, D.C. He began performing while still in high school and composed more than 6,000 pieces before he died. His band (Ellington played piano) started playing together in the 1920s and never broke up even after his death. Ellington's compositions were often innovative and experimental and sometimes lengthy: "Black, Brown and Beige" (1943) is fifty minutes long. He seemed to use every waking moment to create music, and once said, "You know how it is. You go home expecting to go right to bed. But then, on the way, you go past the piano and there's a flirtation. It flirts with you. So, you sit down and try out a couple of chords and when you look up, it's 7 A.M." In a funeral tribute, jazz vocalist Ella Fitzgerald said of Ellington, "It's a very sad day. A genius has passed."

SKILLS PRACTICE

Backwater Blues • Preaching Blues • *from* We, Too, Sing "America"

SOCIAL/HISTORICAL CONTEXT CHART

For each work, explain how the social or the historical context influences it.

SELECTION	SOCIAL OR HISTORICAL CONTEXT
"Backwater Blues"	
"Preaching Blues"	
"We, Too, Sing 'America'"	

Reading Skills
Explain how social or historical context influences literature.

Writer's Workshop

EXPOSITORY WRITING

ASSIGNMENT

Write an essay in which you state a generalization (a main idea or thesis) and then support it with details, such as facts, examples, reasons, and anecdotes.

PURPOSE

To inform

AUDIENCE

Your teacher and your classmates

NARROW YOUR TOPIC

Example:

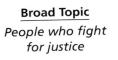

Broad Topic
People who fight for justice

↓

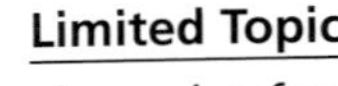

Limited Topic
Leaders who fought against slavery

↓

More Limited
Harriet Tubman's work on the Underground Railroad

SUPPORTING A GENERALIZATION

Each of the selections in this book has a central message, or **theme.** When you state the theme of a story or poem, you state it as a **generalization**—a broad statement that takes into account all the details in the text, not just one. In this workshop, you'll write an essay that begins with a generalization based on facts you've gathered about a topic. Then you'll back up your generalization with **supporting details.**

PREWRITING

1. **Tailor a Topic**—Find a topic that you want to know more about. It can be from any field—literature, history, science, math, art, music, and so on. Review your notes in this book or flip through a magazine to get ideas. Choose a broad topic that really interests you. After choosing a topic, narrow it down so that you will be able to cover it effectively within the confines of an essay. (See the example in the side column.)

2. **Make a Generalization**—After narrowing your topic, write down ideas that you may want to explore in your essay. Choose one of these ideas for your generalization, which will become the main idea or **thesis** of your essay. Be careful to select a generalization that you know you can support with specific facts or examples. State your generalization in a complete declarative sentence. For example, if you were to select Harriet Tubman's work on the Underground Railroad as your topic, you might create a generalization statement like this one: "Harriet Tubman was an invaluable member of the underground network that worked to help enslaved people escape to freedom."

3. **Gather Details to Support the Generalization**—Make a list of specific details that support your generalization, including facts, statistics, definitions, examples, anecdotes, quotations, reasons, opinions, or descriptions. You may need to do some research in the library or on the Internet to supplement what you already know about your topic.

4. **Impose Order**—Organize the supporting details in an order that makes sense for your topic.
   - If the details consist of events that take place over a period of time, use **chronological order,** arranging the events in the order in which they happen.

- If the details involve comparisons of one person or thing to another, use a **comparison-and-contrast** form of organization.
- If the details consist of reasons to persuade readers to adopt your opinion on a topic, you may want to organize them in **order of importance,** beginning with the least important or convincing detail and ending with the most important or convincing one. Keep in mind that readers tend to remember best what they read last.

DRAFTING

Start by just writing. Use your notes as a guide and keep going until you've turned all of them into sentences and paragraphs. You can go back and edit the content and organization later.

1. **The Introduction**—An effective introduction grabs readers' attention and clearly states the generalization. You might begin with a definition, a question, an anecdote, or an unusual piece of information.
2. **The Body**—Each paragraph in the body should develop a major point, which is stated in a **topic sentence.** All of these points should relate to the generalization stated in the introduction and be supported by specific examples.
3. **The Conclusion**—The conclusion should contain a summary of the key points and a restatement of the generalization. You may also include a final personal observation.

EVALUATING AND REVISING

1. **Peer Review**—Exchange first drafts with a classmate to evaluate each other's papers. Use the Evaluation Criteria in the side column to let your classmate know what you like about the essay and what you think can be improved.
2. **Self-Evaluation**—Revise your first draft, incorporating the suggestions you received from your classmate. Eliminate details that are irrelevant or that provide weak support. Rearrange any details that are out of order. Add **transition words,** if needed, to help readers follow the progression of your ideas. Finally, before writing or typing your final draft, correct any errors in grammar, usage, punctuation, and spelling.

TRY IT OUT

Think of three different ways to begin your essay. Write these three different introductions, and ask several classmates to give their opinion about the best one. Then choose the introduction you like best or the one that seems to work best for your essay.

EVALUATION CRITERIA

A good essay that supports a generalization

- states the generalization clearly in the introduction
- develops one major point in each body paragraph
- relates all major points to the generalization
- contains details that support the major point of each body paragraph
- is arranged in an order that makes sense
- restates the generalization in the conclusion

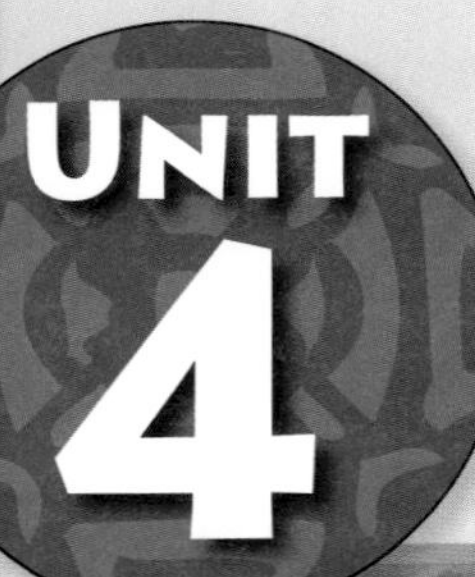

UNIT 4 BUILDING A NEW IDENTITY (1945–present)

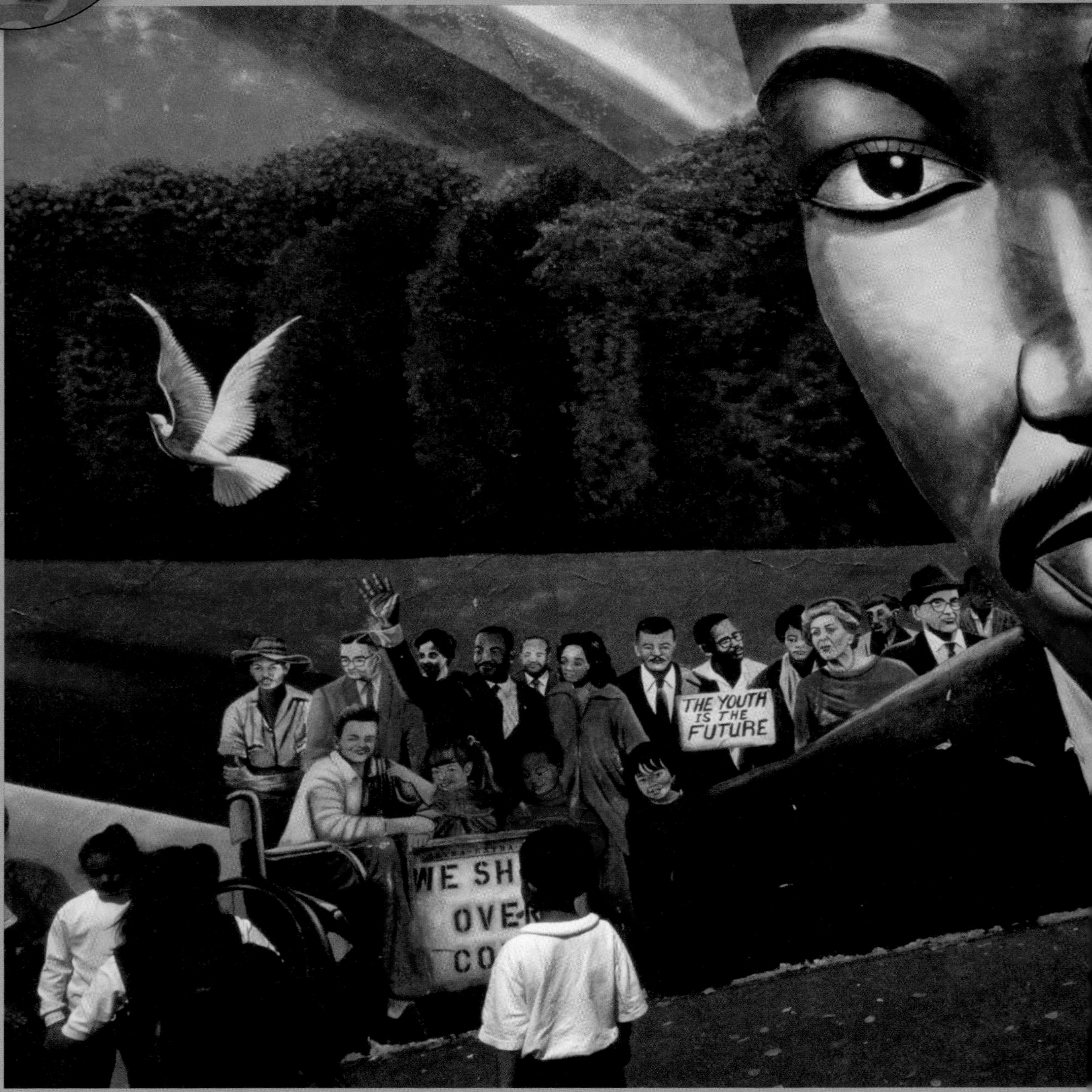

Students playing outside of Martin Luther King, Jr., Elementary School, San Diego, California.

LITERARY FOCUS FOR UNIT 4

Who do you think represents the voice of African American literature today? In this unit, you will examine the ideas of modern writers, musicians, politicians, and activists.

A short story told in the **first-person point of view** beckons you into mid-twentieth century urban life. **Autobiographies** by a civil rights leader and an award-winning author share memorable moments of their youth. An **informational essay** describes a Supreme Court case that helped advance the civil rights movement. **Techniques of emphasis** enliven one of history's most powerful speeches.

You'll analyze the **mood** of a memoir by a prominent politician. Essays raise cultural and social awareness and offer opportunities to study such literary elements as **tone, diction, voice,** and **simile.** You'll also interpret **text structure, free verse, theme,** and **simile** in poems and songs that connect you with writers' inner feelings and opinions.

As you read these selections, consider their contributions to African American literature and their messages of inspiration for the future.

BEFORE YOU READ

The First Day
by Edward P. Jones

In this short story by contemporary author Edward P. Jones, a young girl describes her reactions to being enrolled in kindergarten in Washington, D.C.

LITERARY FOCUS: FIRST-PERSON POINT OF VIEW

When a story is told in the **first-person point of view,** the narrator is one of the characters in the story. The use of the pronoun *I* (as in "I believe . . .," "I saw . . .," and so on) is a signal that tells you which character is telling the story. First-person point of view is also called a **limited point of view** because you directly learn only what the narrator sees, hears, thinks, and believes. You see the other characters through the narrator's eyes and therefore must **infer** what those characters are thinking and feeling, based on what the narrator says about them.

As you read "The First Day," pay attention to how the young girl describes her mother. Ask yourself these questions: What character traits does her mother possess? What character traits does the young girl possess? What is the young girl's attitude toward her mother? Do you share her attitude? Why or why not?

READING SKILLS: MAKING INFERENCES ABOUT CHARACTERS

An **inference** is an educated guess that you make based on the available evidence and your own knowledge and experience. You infer something when you use your reason and experience to guess at what an author does not directly tell you. **Making inferences about characters** involves arriving at conclusions based on what the characters say and do. As you read, use what you learn about the characters to help you make inferences about their traits, actions, motivations, and attitudes.

Literary Focus
Understand first-person point of view.

Reading Skills
Make inferences about characters.

Vocabulary Skills
Understand synonyms and antonyms.

VOCABULARY DEVELOPMENT

PREVIEW SELECTION VOCABULARY

The following words appear in "The First Day." Look them over before you begin the selection.

insistent (in·sis′tənt) *adj.:* urgent; pressing; persistent.

*The **insistent** weather-service warnings that interrupted the TV show made it impossible for us to ignore the approaching storm.*

vigorously (vig′ər·əs′lē) *adv.:* forcefully; energetically.

*When the shy student expressed his desire to register for advanced placement courses, his teacher nodded **vigorously** to show her approval.*

enunciates (ē·nun′sē·āts′) *v.:* pronounces distinctly; declares.

*Reading the list aloud, the head judge **enunciated** each rule to make sure the contestants understood all the ways in which they could be disqualified.*

quivering (kwiv′ər·iŋ) *v.:* trembling; shuddering.

*You could tell that the sad news had disturbed the child because her facial muscles were **quivering** uncontrollably.*

UNDERSTANDING SYNONYMS AND ANTONYMS

A **synonym** is a word that has the same or nearly the same meaning as another word. Synonyms are always the same part of speech. An **antonym** is a word that has the opposite or nearly the opposite meaning as another word. Synonyms and antonyms can be useful in many ways. If you aren't satisfied with a certain word in your writing, you can try to replace it with a synonym that either sounds better or more precisely conveys your intended meaning. Knowing a word's antonym can also help you determine whether the word you have selected conveys the appropriate intensity or nuance.

When you encounter a vocabulary word while reading "The First Day," think about synonyms and antonyms that could be used to replace the word. Do the synonyms work as well as the vocabulary word? If you replaced a vocabulary word with its antonym, how would the ideas expressed in the sentence change?

The First Day

by Edward P. Jones

In an otherwise unremarkable September morning, long before I learned to be ashamed of my mother, she takes my hand and we set off down New Jersey Avenue to begin my very first day of school. I am wearing a checkeredlike blue-and-green cotton dress, and scattered about these colors are bits of yellow and white and brown. My mother has uncharacteristically spent nearly an hour on my hair that morning, plaiting[1] and replaiting so that now my scalp tingles. Whenever I turn my head quickly, my nose fills with the faint smell of Dixie Peach hair grease. The smell is somehow a soothing one now and I will reach for it time and time again before the morning ends. All the plaits, each with a blue barrette near the tip and each twisted into an uncommon sturdiness, will last until I go to bed that night, something that has never happened before. My stomach is full of milk and oatmeal sweetened with brown sugar. Like everything else I have on, my pale green slip and underwear are new, the underwear having come three to a plastic package with a little girl on the front who appears to be dancing. Behind my ears, my mother, to stop my whining, has dabbed the stingiest bit of her gardenia perfume, the last present my father gave her before he disappeared into memory. Because I cannot smell it, I have only her word that the perfume is there. I am also wearing yellow socks trimmed with thin lines of black and white around the tops. My shoes are my greatest joy, black patent-leather miracles, and when one is nicked at the toe later that morning in class, my heart will break.

I am carrying a pencil, a pencil sharpener, and a small ten-cent tablet with a black-and-white speckled cover. My mother does not believe that a girl in kindergarten needs such things,

PREDICT

Re-read the first sentence. What clue tells you that the narrator's first day marked the beginning of a transformation in the relationship between her and her mother? Explain.

INFER

What can you infer from the fact that the mother spent an uncharacteristic amount of time plaiting her daughter's hair?

DRAW CONCLUSIONS

What is the girl's emotional state of mind on this day? How do you know?

---

1. **plaiting:** braiding.

Street scene, Washington, D.C., 1941, photograph by Edwin Rosskam.
Library of Congress

so I am taking them only because of my **insistent** whining and because they are presents from our neighbors, Mary Keith and Blondelle Harris. Miss Mary and Miss Blondelle are watching my two younger sisters until my mother returns. The women are as precious to me as my mother and sisters. Out playing one day, I have overheard an older child, speaking to another child, call Miss Mary and Miss Blondelle a word that is brand new to me. This is my mother: When I say the word in fun to one of my sisters, my mother slaps me across the mouth and the word is lost for years and years.

All the way down New Jersey Avenue, the sidewalks are teeming with children. In my neighborhood, I have many friends, but I see none of them as my mother and I walk. We cross New York Avenue, we cross Pierce Street, and we cross L and K, and still I see no one who knows my name. At I Street, between New Jersey Avenue and Third Street, we enter Seaton

VOCABULARY

insistent (in·sis′tənt) *adj.:* urgent; pressing; persistent.

LITERARY FOCUS

What character traits does the narrator convey about her mother in lines 37–39?

INFER

What do the girl's observations in lines 48–53 tell you about her background?

VOCABULARY

vigorously (vig′ər·əs′lē) *adv.:* forcefully; energetically.

LITERARY FOCUS

What inferences can you make about what the narrator reveals about her mother in lines 59–72?

DRAW CONCLUSIONS

Why do you think the mother wanted her daughter to attend Seaton?

Elementary School, a timeworn, sad-faced building across the street from my mother's church, Mt. Carmel Baptist.

Just inside the front door, women out of the advertisements in *Ebony*[2] are greeting other parents and children. The woman who greets us has pearls thick as jumbo marbles that come down almost to her navel, and she acts as if she had known me all my life, touching my shoulder, cupping her hand under my chin. She is enveloped in a perfume that I only know is not gardenia. When, in answer to her question, my mother tells her that we live at 1227 New Jersey Avenue, the woman first seems to be picturing in her head where we live. Then she shakes her head and says that we are at the wrong school, that we should be at Walker-Jones.

My mother shakes her head **vigorously**. "I want her to go here," my mother says. "If I'da wanted her someplace else, I'da took her there." The woman continues to act as if she has known me all my life, but she tells my mother that we live beyond the area that Seaton serves. My mother is not convinced and for several more minutes she questions the woman about why I cannot attend Seaton. For as many Sundays as I can remember, perhaps even Sundays when I was in her womb, my mother has pointed across I Street to Seaton as we come and go to Mt. Carmel. "You gonna go there and learn about the whole world." But one of the guardians of that place is saying no, and no again. I am learning this about my mother: The higher up on the scale of respectability a person is—and teachers are rather high up in her eyes—the less she is liable to let them push her around. But finally, I see in her eyes the closing gate, and she takes my hand and we leave the building. On the steps, she stops as people move past us on either side.

"Mama, I can't go to school?"

2. ***Ebony:*** a contemporary magazine published for the African American market.

She says nothing at first, then takes my hand again and we are down the steps quickly and nearing New Jersey Avenue before I can blink. This is my mother: She says, "One monkey don't stop no show."

Walker Jones is a larger, newer school and I immediately like it because of that. But it is not across the street from my mother's church, her rock, one of her connections to God, and I sense her doubts as she absently rubs her thumb over the back of her hand. We find our way to the crowded auditorium where gray metal chairs are set up in the middle of the room. Along the wall to the left are tables and other chairs. Every chair seems occupied by a child or adult. Somewhere in the room a child is crying, a cry that rises above the buzz-talk of so many people. Strewn about the floor are dozens and dozens of pieces of white paper, and people are walking over them without any thought of picking them up. And seeing this lack of concern, I am all of a sudden afraid.

"Is this where they register for school?" my mother asks a woman at one of the tables.

The woman looks up slowly as if she has heard this question once too often. She nods. She is tiny, almost as small as the girl standing beside her. The woman's hair is set in a mass of curlers and all of those curlers are made of paper money, here a dollar bill, there a five-dollar bill. The girl's hair is arrayed in curls, but some of them are beginning to droop and this makes me happy. On the table beside the woman's pocketbook is a large notebook, worthy of someone in high school, and looking at me looking at the notebook, the girl places her hand possessively on it. In her other hand she holds several pencils with thick crowns of additional erasers.

"These the forms you gotta use?" my mother asks the woman, picking up a few pieces of the paper from the table. "Is this what you have to fill out?"

The woman tells her yes, but that she need fill out only one.

SUMMARIZE

Summarize the narrator's description of Walker Jones school and her reaction to what she sees.

INFER

Re-read lines 102–104. Why do you think the girl puts her hand on the notebook?

ANALYZE

Re-read lines 116–119. Why does the mother look away after confiding that she can't read or write? What look has the narrator seen in her mother's face for the first time?

INFER

Re-read lines 120–121. Why do you think the other woman brightens when she realizes that the narrator's mother is asking for help?

INTERPRET

What does the narrator mean by saying "My mother is now diseased . . . ." in lines 123–124?

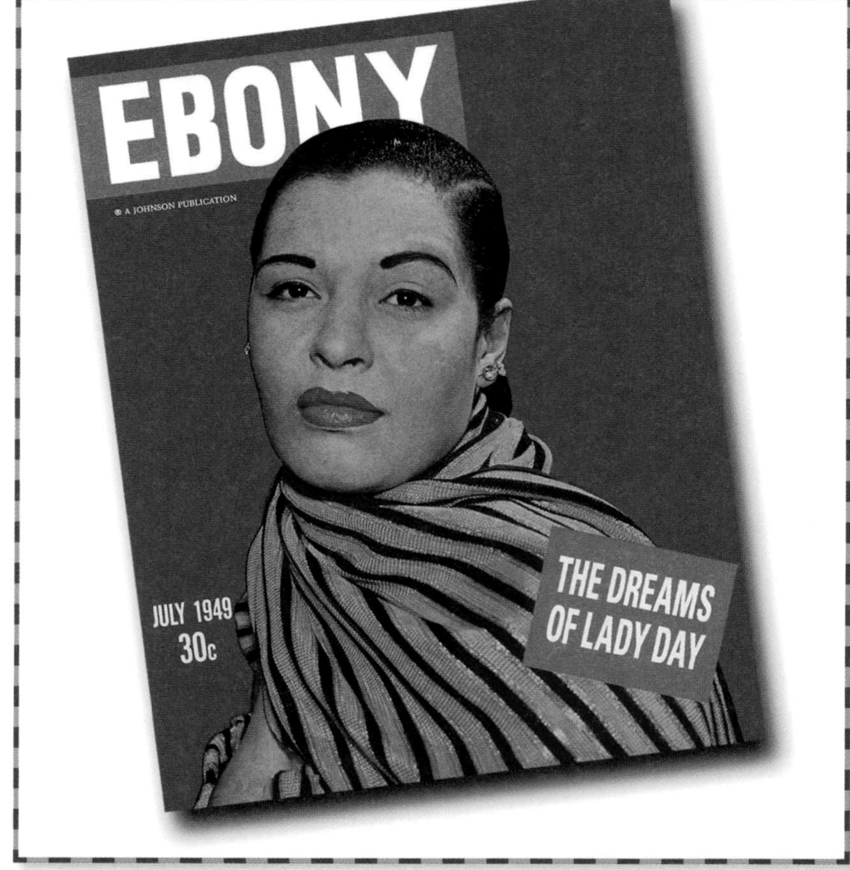

©Johnson Publishing Company, Inc.

"I see," my mother says, looking about the room. Then: "Would you help me with this form? That is, if you don't mind."

The woman asks my mother what she means.

"This form. Would you mind helpin me fill it out?"

The woman still seems not to understand.

"I can't read it. I don't know how to read or write, and I'm askin you to help me." My mother looks at me, then looks away. I know almost all of her looks, but this one is brand new to me. "Would you help me, then?"

The woman says Why sure, and suddenly she appears happier, so much more satisfied with everything. She finishes the form for her daughter and my mother and I step aside to wait for her. We find two chairs nearby and sit. My mother is now diseased, according to the girl's eyes, and until the moment her mother takes her and the form to the front of the auditorium, the girl never stops looking at my mother. I stare back at her.

"Don't stare," my mother says to me. "You know better than that."

Another woman out of the *Ebony* ads takes the woman's child away. Now, the woman says upon returning, let's see what we can do for you two.

My mother answers the questions the woman reads off the form. They start with my last name, and then on to the first and middle names. This is school, I think. This is going to school. My mother slowly **enunciates** each word of my name. This is my mother: As the questions go on, she takes from her pocketbook document after document, as if they will support my right to attend school, as if she has been saving them up for just this moment. Indeed, she takes out more papers than I have ever seen her do in other places: my birth certificate, my baptismal record, a doctor's letter concerning my bout[3] with chicken pox, rent receipts, records of immunization, a letter about our public assistance payments, even her marriage license—every single paper that has anything even remotely to do with my five-year-old life. Few of the papers are needed here, but it does not matter and my mother continues to pull out the documents with the purposefulness of a magician pulling out a long string of scarves. She has learned that money is the beginning and end of everything in this world, and when the woman finishes, my mother offers her fifty cents, and the woman accepts it without hesitation. My mother and I are just about the last parent and child in the room.

My mother presents the form to a woman sitting in front of the stage, and the woman looks at it and writes something on a white card, which she gives to my mother. Before long, the woman who has taken the girl with the drooping curls appears

3. **bout** (bout) *n.:* period of illness.

VOCABULARY

enunciates (ē·nun′sē·āts′) *v.:* pronounces distinctly; declares.

EVALUATE

What do you learn about the narrator's mother in lines 132–152?

INTERPRET

Note the metaphor comparing the mother's actions to those of a magician in lines 145–148. Why is this comparison ironic?

VOCABULARY

quivering (kwiv′ər·iŋ) *v.:* trembling; shuddering.

INFER

Why do you think the mother's lips quiver when she says goodbye to her daughter?

from behind us, speaks to the sitting woman, and introduces herself to my mother and me. She's to be my teacher, she tells my mother. My mother stares.

We go into the hall, where my mother kneels down to me. Her lips are **quivering**. "I'll be back to pick you up at twelve o'clock. I don't want you to go nowhere. You just wait right here. And listen to every word she say." I touch her lips and press them together. It is an old, old game between us. She puts my hand down at my side, which is not part of the game. She stands and looks a second at the teacher, then she turns and walks away. I see where she has darned one of her socks the night before. Her

Students with Books, 1966, Jacob Lawrence (1917–2000)
©ARS, NY Photo Credit: The Jacob and Gwendolyn Lawrence Foundation/Art Resource, NY

shoes make loud sounds in the hall. She passes through the doors and I can still hear the loud sounds of her shoes. And even when the teacher turns me toward the classrooms and I hear what must be the singing and talking of all the children in the world, I can still hear my mother's footsteps above it all.

MEET THE WRITER

Edward P. Jones (1950-), was raised by a single mother in Washington, D.C. The first eighteen years of his life were spent living in eighteen different apartments. Jones went on to graduate from Holy Cross College and the University of Virginia. He began writing and publishing short stories and his first collection *Lost in the City* (1992) earned a National Book Award nomination. The stories depict African Americans living in Washington D.C. One reviewer said, "It shouldn't come as a surprise—but it does as one reads these pages—that people perceived to be down and out can live such rich and varied lives."

Jones says that it took him more than ten years to complete his next work, *The Known World* (2003), a novel that deals with slaveholders in pre-Civil War Virginia. It is a world of irony and contradiction. A free black owns blacks, a white slaveholder falls in love with one of his slaves, and laws that sound laughable are deadly serious: "A runaway slave was, in fact, a thief since he had stolen his master's property—himself." One reviewer said, "This is slavery as it has never been written about or imagined before, and it is essential reading." For his novel, Jones won the Pulitzer Prize for fiction in 2004.

In 2006, Jones published *All Aunt Hagar's Children*, a collection of stories that returns to Washington and to the characters that appeared in *Lost in the City*.

DRAW CONCLUSIONS

Why do you think the narrator says she still remembers her mother's footsteps above everything else that she experienced on her first day at school?

EXTEND

Locate and read another short story from *Lost in the City*. Write a brief essay on another sheet of paper comparing a character in your selection to the narrator or the mother in "The First Day."

The First Day

Literary Focus Understand first-person point of view.

Reading Skills Make inferences about characters.

MAKING INFERENCES ABOUT CHARACTERS

The point of view of the narrator determined what you learned as you read "The First Day." In the chart below, fill in the point of view of the narrator in "The First Day." Then, tell what you have learned about the narrator and what you have learned about her mother. Finally, based on what you have learned, make some inferences about each character.

POINT OF VIEW

WHAT I LEARNED ABOUT	INFERENCES I CAN MAKE
The Narrator:	
The Mother:	

The First Day

VOCABULARY AND COMPREHENSION

WORD BOX

energetically
articulated
quaking
constant

A. Synonyms and Antonyms After each vocabulary word, write the letter of the correct antonym. Then read each sentence and write the correct synonym from the Word Box for the underlined vocabulary word.

1. insistent _______ a. intermittent
2. vigorously _______ b. remaining still
3. enunciate _______ c. weakly
4. quivering _______ d. slur
5. The insistent ringing of the telephone disturbed my sleep.

____

6. Our dog wagged his tail vigorously when he saw the treats.

____

7. The lecturer enunciated his ideas confidently. ______________________________
8. The frightened man was quivering from head to toe. ______________________

B. Reading Comprehension Answer each question below.

9. Why is the narrator turned away from the first school in which she attempts to enroll?

____
____
____

10. What is significant about the mother's gesture at the end of the story when she puts her daughter's hand down after her daughter pressed her lips together?

____
____
____
____

Vocabulary Skills
Identify synonyms and antonyms.

BEFORE YOU READ

from Black Boy

by Richard Wright

from The Autobiography of Malcolm X

by Malcolm X, with the assistance of Alex Haley

In these selections, author Richard Wright and civil rights activist Malcolm X reflect on the insight gained from memorable moments in their youth.

LITERARY FOCUS: AUTOBIOGRAPHY

An **autobiography** is a nonfictional narrative, a true story about a real person's life told by that person. The selections you are about to read are excerpted from autobiographical accounts written by Richard Wright and Malcolm X. Each selection relates a single event from the author's life that had a profound effect on his thinking.

An autobiography is written in the **first person**. Authors of autobiographies use the pronouns *I, me, my,* and *mine* to let readers know that they are writing about themselves from their own **point of view**. Readers "see" the events of an author's life through the eyes of the author as he or she observed and experienced those events. As you read the following selections, pay attention to the point of view revealed in each. What experience does each author relate? How does each author react to the experience? What insights does each author gain from the experience?

READING SKILLS: COMPARING AND CONTRASTING

When you **compare** two things, you look for similarities—the ways the things are alike. When you **contrast** two things, you look for differences—the ways the things are not alike. When you **compare and contrast** two texts, you note similarities and differences between those texts. You may compare and contrast the main characters, the ideas and messages, the authors' styles, or other elements. As you read the following two selections, pay attention to elements that you can compare and contrast. In what ways are the authors, their ideas, and their styles of writing similar? In what ways are they different?

Literary Focus
Understand the characteristics of an autobiography.

Reading Skills
Compare and contrast.

Vocabulary Skills
Review synonyms.

VOCABULARY DEVELOPMENT

PREVIEW SELECTION VOCABULARY

The following words appear in the excerpts from *Black Boy* and *The Autobiography of Malcolm X*. Look them over before you begin the selections.

conceivable (kən·sēv′ə·bəl) *adj.:* capable of being imagined, thought, understood, or believed.

Ned got a late start, but he thought that if he hurried it was ***conceivable*** *that he could get to the show on time.*

contemptuous (kən·temp′cho͞o·əs) *adj.:* manifesting or expressing disdain; scornful.

The celebrity's behavior at the party revealed her ***contemptuous*** *attitude toward everyone.*

speculate (spek′yo͞o·lāt′) *v.:* contemplate; theorize; think about.

Having no information on our new teacher, I began to ***speculate*** *about what she would be like.*

naïve (nä·ēv′) *adj.:* unaffected; childlike; artless.

When the ***naïve*** *country girl first arrived in the big city, she was an easy target for pickpockets.*

articulate (är·tik′yo͞o·lit) *adj.:* expressing oneself clearly; lucid.

The final speaker's rambling and incoherent talk was in stark contrast to the ***articulate*** *presentations that had preceded it.*

transformation (trans′fər·mā′shən) *n.:* a change in form, appearance, condition, or character.

His ***transformation*** *from a healthy, vibrant individual into an emaciated shell of a man was the result of a seriously debilitating illness.*

multitude (mul′tə·to͞od′) *n.:* a large number of persons or things.

Among the ***multitude*** *of concertgoers who packed the arena were long-time fans, as well as young people who had never seen the band live.*

mutilate (myo͞ot″l·āt) *v.:* maim, cripple, or damage, especially by removing an essential part.

The rare painting was protected by a glass shield to prevent troublemakers from attempting to spray slogans on it, slash the canvas, or ***mutilate*** *it in other ways.*

REVIEWING SYNONYMS

You have already learned that a **synonym** is a word that has the same meaning or nearly the same meaning as another word and that synonyms are always the same part of speech. Dictionaries often include synonym studies for some words, but a thesaurus is the most useful tool for finding synonyms.

When you encounter one of the vocabulary words listed above while reading the selections by Richard Wright and Malcolm X, think about synonyms that could be used to replace the word. Consult a thesaurus to help you find suitable replacements. Which ones convey the same connotation or shading of meaning? Which ones sound interchangeable, better, or awkward?

from Black Boy

by Richard Wright

LITERARY FOCUS

What does Wright say led him to write a story? What underlying desire may have prompted his decision? What does he do with the story?

HISTORICAL CONTEXT

This part of Wright's autobiography takes place in Jackson, Mississippi, during the 1920s. Consider the importance of the setting as you read.

The eighth grade days flowed in their hungry path and I grew more conscious of myself; I sat in classes, bored, wondering, dreaming. One long dry afternoon I took out my composition book and told myself that I would write a story; it was sheer idleness that led me to it. What would the story be about? It resolved itself into a plot about a villain who wanted a widow's home and I called it *The Voodoo of Hell's Half-Acre*. It was crudely atmospheric, emotional, intuitively psychological, and stemmed from pure feeling. I finished it in three days and then wondered what to do with it.

The local Negro newspaper! That's it . . . I sailed into the office and shoved my ragged composition book under the nose of the man who called himself editor.

"What is that?" he asked.

Thinking, 1990 (oil on board), Murrell, Carlton (Contemporary Artist) / Private Collection.
The Bridgeman Art Library International

"A story," I said.

"A news story?"

"No, fiction."

"All right. I'll read it," he said.

He pushed my composition book back on his desk and looked at me curiously, sucking at his pipe.

"But I want you to read it *now*," I said.

He blinked. I had no idea how newspapers were run. I thought that one took a story to an editor and he sat down then and there and read it and said yes or no.

"I'll read this and let you know about it tomorrow," he said.

I was disappointed; I had taken time to write it and he seemed distant and uninterested.

"Give me the story," I said, reaching for it.

He turned from me, took up the book and read ten pages or more.

"Won't you come in tomorrow?" he asked. "I'll have it finished then."

I honestly relented.

"All right," I said. "I'll stop in tomorrow."

I left with the conviction that he would not read it. Now, where else could I take it after he had turned it down? The next afternoon, en route[1] to my job, I stepped into the newspaper office.

"Where's my story?" I asked.

"It's in the galleys,"[2] he said.

"What's that?" I asked; I did not know what galleys were.

"It's set up in type," he said. "We're publishing it."

"How much money will I get?" I asked, excited.

"We can't pay for manuscript," he said.

"But you sell your papers for money," I said with logic.

WORD STUDY

What clues could help you guess the meaning of *relented* in line 33?

INFER

What logic does Wright employ to argue that he should be paid for his story?

1. **en route** (ən·ro͞ot′): on the way.
2. **galleys** (gal′ēz) *n.:* printer's proofs taken from type.

DRAW CONCLUSIONS

What do you think the newspaper editor's opinion is of Wright's story?

GENERALIZE

What generalization can you make about Wright's reaction to the editor's comments in lines 50–60?

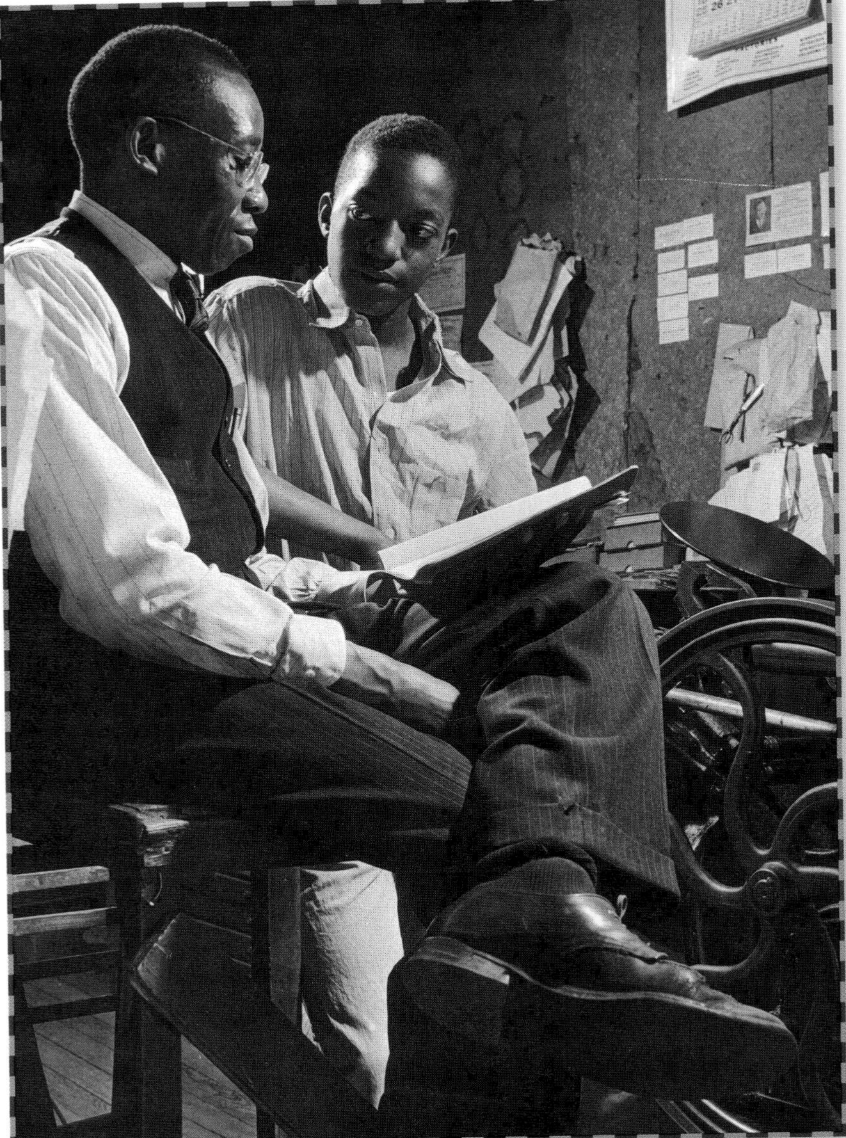

The editor of the local Negro newspaper runs Richard's story, from a 1945 *Life* magazine picture-dramatization of *Black Boy*.
©George Karger/Time & Life Pictures/Getty Images

"Yes, but we're young in business," he explained.

"But you're asking me to *give* you my story, but you don't *give* your papers away," I said.

He laughed.

"Look, you're just starting. This story will put your name before our readers. Now, that's something," he said.

"But if the story is good enough to sell to your readers, then you ought to give me some of the money you get from it," I insisted.

He laughed again and I sensed that I was amusing him.

"I'm going to offer you something more valuable than money," he said. "I'll give you a chance to learn to write."

I was pleased, but I still thought he was taking advantage of me.

"When will you publish my story?"

"I'm dividing it into three installments," he said. "The first installment appears this week. But the main thing is this: Will you get news for me on a space rate basis?"

"I work morning and evenings for three dollars a week," I said.

"Oh," he said. "Then you better keep that. But what are you doing this summer?"

"Nothing."

"Then come to see me before you take another job," he said. "And write some more stories."

A few days later my classmates came to me with baffled eyes, holding copies of the *Southern Register* in their hands.

"Did you really write that story?" they asked me.

"Yes."

"Why?"

"Because I wanted to."

"Where did you get it from?"

"I made it up."

"You didn't. You copied it out of a book."

"If I had, no one would publish it."

"But what are they publishing it for?"

"So people can read it."

"Who told you to do that?"

"Nobody."

"Then why did you do it?"

"Because I wanted to," I said again.

They were convinced that I had not told them the truth. We never had any instruction in literary matters at school; the literature of the nation or the Negro had never been mentioned.

INFER

How can you tell that the editor is not taking advantage of Wright?

INTERPRET

What reason does Wright give to explain why his classmates are mystified by his publishing a story?

EXTEND

Has something you've tried to do or achieve been misunderstood by others? Write a brief paragraph describing what it was, how the reactions of others made you feel, and what, if anything, you did about it?

VOCABULARY

conceivable (kən·sēv′ə·bəl) *adj.:* capable of being imagined, thought, understood, or believed.

CAUSE & EFFECT

What effect had Wright hoped his publishing a story would have on his classmates? What happened instead?

DRAW CONCLUSIONS

Why do you think Wright feared getting into a religious argument if he revealed his story's plot?

My schoolmates could not understand why anyone would want to write a story; and, above all, they could not understand why I called it *The Voodoo of Hell's Half-Acre*. The mood out of which a story was written was the most alien thing **conceivable** to them. They looked at me with new eyes, and a distance, a suspiciousness came between us. If I had thought anything in writing the story, I had thought that perhaps it would make me more acceptable to them, and now it was cutting me off from them more completely than ever.

At home the effects were no less disturbing. Granny came into my room early one morning and sat on the edge of my bed.

"Richard, what is this you're putting in the papers?" she asked.

"A story," I said.

"About what?"

"It's just a story, granny."

"But they tell me it's been in three times."

"It's the same story. It's in three parts."

"But what's it about?" she insisted.

I hedged, fearful of getting into a religious argument.

"It's just a story I made up," I said.

"Then it's a lie," she said.

"Oh, Christ," I said.

"You must get out of this house if you take the name of the Lord in vain," she said.

"Granny, please . . . I'm sorry," I pleaded. "But it's hard to tell you about the story. You see, granny, everybody knows that the story isn't true, but . . . "

"Then why write it?" she asked.

"Because people might want to read it."

"That's the Devil's work," she said and left.

My mother also was worried.

"Son, you ought to be more serious," she said. "You're growing up now and you won't be able to get jobs if you let people think that you're weak-minded. Suppose the superintendent of schools would ask you to teach here in Jackson, and he found out that you had been writing stories?"

I could not answer her.

"I'll be all right, mama," I said.

Uncle Tom, though surprised, was highly critical and **contemptuous.** The story had no point, he said. And whoever heard of a story by the title of *The Voodoo of Hell's Half-Acre*? Aunt Addie said that it was a sin for anyone to use the word "hell" and that what was wrong with me was that I had nobody to guide me. She blamed the whole thing on my upbringing.

In the end I was so angry that I refused to talk about the story. From no quarter, with the exception of the Negro newspaper editor, had there come a single encouraging word. It was rumored that the principal wanted to know why I had used the word "hell." I felt that I had committed a crime. Had I been conscious of the full extent to which I was pushing against the current of my environment, I would have been frightened altogether out of my attempts at writing. But my reactions were limited to the attitude of the people about me, and I did not **speculate** or generalize.

I dreamed of going north and writing books, novels. The North symbolized to me all that I had not felt and seen; it had no relation whatever to what actually existed. Yet, by imagining a place where everything was possible, I kept hope alive in me. But where had I got this notion of doing something in the future, of going away from home and accomplishing something that would be recognized by others? I had, of course, read my Horatio Alger[3] stories, my pulp stories,[4] and I knew my Get-Rich-Quick Wallingford[5] series from cover to cover, though I had sense

---

3. **Horatio Alger** (1832–1899): American writer known for stories in which penniless boys achieve fame and fortune.
4. **pulp stories:** sensational stories.
5. **Get-Rich-Quick Wallingford:** a character in a series of stories by George R. Chester. He makes a fortune through financial schemes.

VOCABULARY

contemptuous (kən·temp′cho͞o·əs) *adj.:* manifesting or expressing disdain; scornful.

speculate (spek′yo͞o·lāt′) *v.:* contemplate; theorize; think about.

CAUSE & EFFECT

What effect does his family's reactions to his story have on Wright?

INTERPRET

What does Wright dream of doing? What does he imply about the feasibility of his dream?

VOCABULARY

naïve (nä·ēv′) *adj.:* unaffected, childlike, artless.

articulate (är·tik′yo͞o·lit) *adj.:* expressing oneself clearly; lucid.

EXTEND

Research Jim Crow laws at the library or on the Internet and share what you learn with your classmates.

INFER

Do you think Wright would have made different choices in life if he told someone about his dreams? Explain.

enough not to hope to get rich; even to my naïve imagination that possibility was too remote. I knew that I lived in a country in which the aspirations of black people were limited, marked-off. Yet I felt that I had to go somewhere and do something to redeem my being alive.

I was building up in me a dream which the entire educational system of the South had been rigged to stifle. I was feeling the very thing that the state of Mississippi had spent millions of dollars to make sure that I would never feel; I was becoming aware of the thing that the Jim Crow laws[6] had been drafted and passed to keep out of my consciousness; I was acting on impulses that southern senators in the nation's capital had striven to keep out of Negro life; I was beginning to dream the dreams that the state had said were wrong, that the schools had said were taboo.

Had I been **articulate** about my ultimate aspirations, no doubt someone would have told me what I was bargaining for; but nobody seemed to know, and least of all did I. My classmates felt that I was doing something that was vaguely wrong, but they did not know how to express it. As the outside world grew more meaningful, I became more concerned, tense; and my classmates and my teachers would say: "Why do you ask so many questions?" Or: "Keep quiet."

I was in my fifteenth year; in terms of schooling I was far behind the average youth of the nation, but I did not know that. In me was shaping a yearning for a kind of consciousness, a mode of being that the way of life about me had said could not be, must not be, and upon which the penalty of death had been placed. Somewhere in the dead of the southern night my life

6. **Jim Crow laws:** laws that discriminated against African Americans.

had switched onto the wrong track and, without my knowing it, the locomotive of my heart was rushing down a dangerously steep slope, heading for a collision, heedless of the warning red lights that blinked all about me, the sirens and the bells and the screams that filled the air.

ANALYZE

Re-read lines 183–187. What is ironic about Wright's comment that his life had switched on to the wrong track?

MEET THE WRITER

Richard Wright (1908–1960) was born on a plantation near Natchez, Mississippi. Wright grew up in extreme poverty and the schools he attended did little to encourage him. Once, in order to borrow some books from a segregated library, he forged a note from a white borrower. Few American writers have had to overcome so many handicaps.

Wright's literary career began after he moved to Chicago. There, he became involved in radical politics, joined the Communist Party and began writing for political magazines. His interest soon turned to fiction, and by the time he moved to New York, he had begun *Uncle Tom's Children* (1938), a collection of short stories. His first major success came with his novel *Native Son* (1940). This book, which was the first written by an African American to be chosen by the book-of-the-month-club, vividly depicts the effects of racism in America.

Wright's ideas brought him into conflict with the ideology of communism, and in 1944 he withdrew from the party. The story of his early life, *Black Boy,* was published in 1945. Many readers consider this book to be his masterpiece. (*American Hunger,* the continuation of his autobiography, was published posthumously, in 1977.) Once when Wright was asked if the ideas in his works would make people happy, he replied, "I do not deal in happiness; I deal in meaning." In 1946, Wright moved to France, where he continued to write fiction and nonfiction until his death.

NOTES

from The Autobiography of Malcolm X

by Malcolm X, with the assistance of Alex Haley

WORD STUDY

The verb *conk* refers to a method of straightening tightly curled hair by applying a mixture of chemicals, or congolene. The noun *conk* refers to the resulting hairstyle, which was also called a "process." Work with a partner to make a list of slang terms that describe other hairstyles.

PREDICT

Based on what you've read about lye, what might be some other possible effects of the applying the congolene mixture besides straightening Malcolm's hair?

Shorty soon decided that my hair was finally long enough to be conked. He had promised to school me in how to beat the barbershops' three- and four-dollar price by making up congolene, and then conking ourselves.

I took the little list of ingredients he had printed out for me, and went to a grocery store, where I got a can of Red Devil lye,[1] two eggs, and two medium-sized white potatoes. Then at a drugstore near the poolroom, I asked for a large jar of vaseline, a large bar of soap, a large-toothed comb and a fine-toothed comb, one of those rubber hoses with a metal spray-head, a rubber apron and a pair of gloves.

"Going to lay on that first conk?" the drugstore man asked me. I proudly told him, grinning, "Right!"

Shorty paid six dollars a week for a room in his cousin's shabby apartment. His cousin wasn't at home. "It's like the pad's mine, he spends so much time with his woman," Shorty said. "Now, you watch me—"

He peeled the potatoes and thin-sliced them into a quart-sized Mason fruit jar, then started stirring them with a wooden spoon as he gradually poured in a little over half the can of lye. "Never use a metal spoon; the lye will turn it black," he told me.

A jelly-like, starchy-looking glop resulted from the lye and potatoes, and Shorty broke in the two eggs, stirring real fast—his own conk and dark face bent down close. The congolene turned pale-yellowish. "Feel the jar," Shorty said. I cupped my hand against the outside, and snatched it away. "Damn right, it's hot, that's the lye," he said. "So you know it's going to burn when I

1. **lye** (lī) *n.:* a highly concentrated solution of sodium hydroxide.

comb it in—it burns *bad.* But the longer you can stand it, the straighter the hair."

He made me sit down, and he tied the string of the new rubber apron tightly around my neck, and combed up my bush of hair. Then, from the big vaseline jar, he took a handful and massaged it hard all through my hair and into the scalp. He also thickly vaselined my neck, ears and forehead. "When I get to washing out your head, be sure to tell me anywhere you feel any little stinging," Shorty warned me, washing his hands, then pulling on the rubber gloves, and tying on his own rubber apron. "You always got to remember that any congolene left in burns a sore into your head."

The congolene just felt warm when Shorty started combing it in. But then my head caught fire.

I gritted my teeth and tried to pull the sides of the kitchen table together. The comb felt as if it was raking my skin off.

My eyes watered, my nose was running. I couldn't stand it any longer; I bolted to the washbasin. I was cursing Shorty with every name I could think of when he got the spray going and started soap-lathering my head.

He lathered and spray-rinsed, lathered and spray-rinsed, maybe ten or twelve times, each time gradually closing the hot-water faucet, until the rinse was cold, and that helped some. "You feel any stinging spots?"

"No," I managed to say. My knees were trembling.

"Sit back down, then. I think we got it all out okay."

The flame came back as Shorty, with a thick towel, started drying my head, rubbing hard. "*Easy, man, easy!*" I kept shouting.

"The first time's always worst. You get used to it better before long. You took it real good, homeboy. You got a good conk."

When Shorty let me stand up and see in the mirror, my hair hung down in limp, damp strings. My scalp still flamed, but not as badly; I could bear it. He draped the towel around my

DRAW CONCLUSIONS

What do Shorty's comments and the preparations he undertakes tell you about the risks involved in having one's hair conked?

INFER

Re-read lines 40–56. What do you think is Malcolm's purpose in describing the excruciating pain he endured to have his hair conked?

VOCABULARY

transformation (trans′fər·mā′shən) *n.:* a change in form, appearance, condition, or character.

CAUSE & EFFECT

After Shorty finishes his work, what causes Malcolm to forget about the pain he has endured?

COMPARE & CONTRAST

Re-read lines 68–78. How has Malcolm's view about conking changed?

shoulders, over my rubber apron, and began again vaselining my hair.

I could feel him combing, straight back, first the big comb, then the fine-tooth one.

Then, he was using a razor, very delicately, on the back of my neck. Then, finally, shaping the sideburns.

My first view in the mirror blotted out the hurting. I'd seen some pretty conks, but when it's the first time, on your *own* head, the **transformation,** after the lifetime of kinks, is staggering.

The mirror reflected Shorty behind me. We both were grinning and sweating. And on top of my head was this thick, smooth sheen of shining red hair—real red—as straight as any white man's.

Malcolm X.
©Robert Parent/Time Life Pictures/Getty Images

How ridiculous I was! Stupid enough to stand there simply lost in admiration of my hair now looking "white," reflected in the mirror in Shorty's room. I vowed that I'd never again be without a conk, and I never was for many years.

This was my first really big step toward self-degradation: when I endured all of that pain, literally burning my flesh to have it look like a white man's hair. I had joined that **multitude** of Negro men and women in America who are brainwashed into believing that the black people are "inferior"—and white people "superior"—that they will even violate and **mutilate** their God-created bodies to try to look "pretty" by white standards.

VOCABULARY

multitude (mul′tə·to͞od′) *n.:* a large number of persons or things.

mutilate (myo͞ot″l·āt) *v.:* maim, cripple, or damage, especially by removing an essential part.

INFER

Do you agree or disagree with Malcolm's view that by conking his hair he was joining people who believed that blacks are inferior to whites? Explain.

MEET THE WRITER

Malcolm X (1925–1965) became well known in the 1950s as a spokesperson for black separatism. His public appearances inspired many African Americans, but his rhetoric about violence—"the ballot or the bullet"—alienated others who sided with the nonviolent teachings of Martin Luther King, Jr. However, toward the end of his life, Malcolm X accepted the possibility of a worldwide multiracial brotherhood.

When Malcolm was young and living in Michigan, his father, a minister and organizer for the Marcus Garvey movement, was killed under suspicious circumstances. Malcolm was sent to live with an older sister, and gradually slipped into a life of crime. In 1946 he was arrested for robbery and sent to prison. There he converted to the Black Muslim religion, took the name Malcolm X, and began an intense program of self-education by copying every page in a dictionary and reading black history.

After his release, Malcolm became a minister at a mosque in Harlem. He was a superb orator and quickly gained prominence as a leader. As he rose in rank and influence, he grew increasingly critical of Elijah Muhammad, the founder of the Black Muslims. On a pilgrimage to Mecca he experienced a profound conversion, renamed himself El-Hajj Malik El-Shabazz and decided to work for unity and harmony among all blacks. But on February 21, 1965, while speaking to an audience in Harlem, he was shot and killed. He left a legacy of recorded speeches, and *The Autobiography of Malcolm X* was completed, with the assistance of Alex Haley, just before his death.

NOTES

SKILLS PRACTICE

Reading Skills Compare and contrast autobiographies.

from Black Boy
from The Autobiography of Malcolm X

COMPARING AND CONTRASTING CHART

Complete the chart below to compare and contrast the two selections you have just read.

from Black Boy	QUESTION	*from* The Autobiography of Malcolm X
	What life experience does each author relate?	
	How did each author react to the experience he relates?	
	What insights did each author gain from the experience?	

What similarities and differences exist between the two selections?

from Black Boy
from The Autobiography of Malcolm X

VOCABULARY AND COMPREHENSION

A. Synonyms Choose the correct synonym from the word box for the underlined vocabulary word in each sentence.

WORD BOX
disfigure
large quantity
imaginable
well-spoken
alteration
certainty
unsophisticated
scornful
guess

1. If we continue to buy souvenirs at every stop, it is conceivable that we will run out of money before the end of our vacation. ______

2. The judges were shocked and dismayed by the contemptuous disregard the winner displayed toward the prize he had won. ______

3. Mystified by the strange lights in the night sky, we began to speculate that they were coming from somewhere across the lake. ______

4. The articulate speaker voiced his opinions clearly and convincingly. ______

5. Her transformation from to hero surprised everyone. ______

6. The referees called only a few fouls against the home team but a multitude of infractions against the visitors. ______

7. The guards used hot iron spears to mutilate the prisoners, hoping to extract confessions from them. ______

B. Reading Comprehension Answer each question below.

8. When he was a student, what did Richard Wright dream of accomplishing?
______
______

9. As a young man, why was Malcolm X willing to endure intense pain in order to alter his appearance?
______
______
______

Vocabulary Skills
Understand synonyms.

BEFORE YOU READ

from Brown vs. Board of Education
by Walter Dean Myers

In this excerpt from his essay *"Brown vs. Board of Education,"* young-adult literature author Walter Dean Myers discusses the background and significance of the landmark Supreme Court case that helped fuel the movement to desegregate public places in the United States.

LITERARY FOCUS: ESSAY/INFORMATIONAL ARTICLE

Nonfiction is prose that deals with real, rather than imagined, events and people. An **essay** is a brief work of nonfiction that presents a particular point of view on a limited subject. A well-constructed essay includes an introduction that grabs the reader's attention and clearly states the author's subject and purpose, a body that develops the subject, and a conclusion that summarizes the author's main point and provides an insightful, concluding observation.

As its name implies, an **informational article** is a specific type of essay whose purpose is to **inform** readers about a particular subject. Informational articles can be found in a wide variety of print sources, including many, popular, general-interest magazines. Subject categories range from how-to and advice articles to travel literature, accounts of major historical events, and discussions of contemporary trends and issues. As you read *"Brown vs. Board of Education,"* pay attention to its structure. Identify the subject, note how the subject is developed, and evaluate the author's concluding observations.

READING SKILLS: IDENTIFYING AUTHOR'S PURPOSE

An **author's purpose** is his or her intent in writing a particular work. Authors write literary works for a variety of reasons, including to inform, to entertain, to educate, to persuade, to explain, or to describe. Often, they accomplish more than one of these purposes in a literary work. Walter Dean Myers's primary purpose in *"Brown vs. Board of Education"* is to inform readers about the Supreme Court case and its importance in African Americans' struggle for equality. As you read this selection, think about other possible purposes that he accomplishes.

Literary Focus Understand the characteristics of an essay/informational article.

Reading Skills Identify author's purpose.

Vocabulary Skills Use context clues to clarify word meanings.

ESSAY

VOCABULARY DEVELOPMENT

PREVIEW SELECTION VOCABULARY

The following words appear in *"Brown vs. Board of Education."* Look them over before you begin the selection.

segregated (seg′rə·gāt′id) *v.:* set apart from others or from the main group; isolated.

Fearing that the preschoolers would be alarmed by the roughhousing of the older children, we provided a ***segregated*** *facility for them to play by themselves in peace.*

intangible (in·tan′jə·bəl) *adj.:* unable to be touched; unable to be easily defined, formulated, or grasped.

The troubled woman was unable to identify a reason for her uneasiness, but she was aware that, though ***intangible****, it was very real.*

objectionable (əb·jek′shən·ə·bəl) *adj.:* justly liable to objection; disagreeable; offensive.

Anyone who knows about the dangers of secondhand smoke would agree that lighting a cigarette in enclosed, close quarters is an ***objectionable*** *practice.*

prohibitions (prō′i·bish′əns) *n.:* orders or laws forbidding something to be done; refusals to permit something.

In order to maintain order during the march, the leaders issued a list of ***prohibitions*** *to prevent individuals from getting out of line.*

CLARIFYING WORD MEANINGS: LOOK AT THE CONTEXT

When you come across an unfamiliar word, look at the context words, phrases, or sentences surrounding the word for clues to its meaning. Often, writers use a **definition, restatement, synonym,** or **example** near the word that helps to explain its meaning. For example, note this sentence from *"Brown vs. Board of Education"*:

> "For an African crouched in the darkness of a tossing ship, wrists chained, men with guns standing on the decks above him, freedom was a physical thing, the ability to move away from his captors, to follow the dictates of his own heart, to listen to the voices within him that defined his values and showed him the truth of his own path."

If you did not know the meaning of *freedom* as it is used in this sentence, you would have little difficulty figuring it out because it is followed by a definition. As you read *"Brown vs. Board of Education,"* look at the context to help you determine the meaning of any unfamiliar words.

from Brown vs. Board of Education

by Walter Dean Myers

There was a time when the meaning of freedom was easily understood. For an African crouched in the darkness of a tossing ship, wrists chained, men with guns standing on the decks above him, freedom was a physical thing, the ability to move away from his captors, to follow the dictates of his own heart, to listen to the voices within him that defined his values and showed him the truth of his own path. The plantation owners wanted to make the Africans feel helpless, inferior. They denied them images of themselves as Africans and told them that they were without beauty. They **segregated** them and told them they were without value.

It was Thurgood Marshall and a battery of N.A.A.C.P.[1] attorneys who began to challenge segregation throughout the country. These men and women were warriors in the cause of freedom for African Americans, taking their battles into courtrooms across the country. They understood the process of American justice and the power of the Constitution.

In *Brown vs. Board of Education of Topeka*, Marshall argued that segregation was a violation of the Fourteenth Amendment[2]—that even if the facilities and all other "tangibles" were equal, which was the heart of the case in *Plessy vs. Ferguson*,[3] a violation still existed. There were **intangible** factors, he argued, that made the education unequal.

Everyone involved understood the significance of the case: that it was much more than whether black children could go to school with white children. If segregation in the schools was

VOCABULARY

segregated (seg′rə·gāt′id) *v.* set apart from others or from the main group; isolated.

intangible (in·tan′jə·bəl) *adj.:* unable to be touched; unable to be easily defined, formulated, or grasped.

EVALUATE

How does the author gain the attention of readers in the introductory paragraph of this article?

LITERARY FOCUS

In your own words, state the subject of this article.

---

1. **N.A.A.C.P.:** National Association for the Advancement of Colored People.
2. **Fourteenth Amendment:** constitutional amendment that guaranteed due process and equal protection under the law.
3. ***Plessy vs. Ferguson:*** Supreme Court case that upheld racial segregation based on the idea that facilities could be "separate but equal."

Thurgood Marshall.
©Photo by Time Life Pictures/Time Magazine, Copyright Time Inc./Time Life Pictures/Getty Images

declared unconstitutional, then *all* segregation in public places could be declared unconstitutional.

Southerners who argued against ending school segregation were caught up, as then-Congressman Brooks Hays of Arkansas put it, in "a lifetime of adventures in that gap between law and custom." The law was one thing, but most Southern whites felt just as strongly about their customs as they did the law.

Dr. Kenneth B. Clark, an African-American psychologist, testified for the N.A.A.C.P. He presented clear evidence that the effect of segregation was harmful to African-American children. Describing studies conducted by black and white psychologists over a twenty-year period, he showed that black children felt inferior to white children. In a particularly dramatic study that he had supervised, four dolls, two white and two black, were presented to African-American children. From the responses of the children to the dolls, identical in every way except color,

COMPARE & CONTRAST

Contrast the opposing positions in the *Brown* vs. *Board* case.

GENERALIZE

What generalization did Dr. Clark make about black children? Why might this generalization be difficult to prove in court?

NOTES

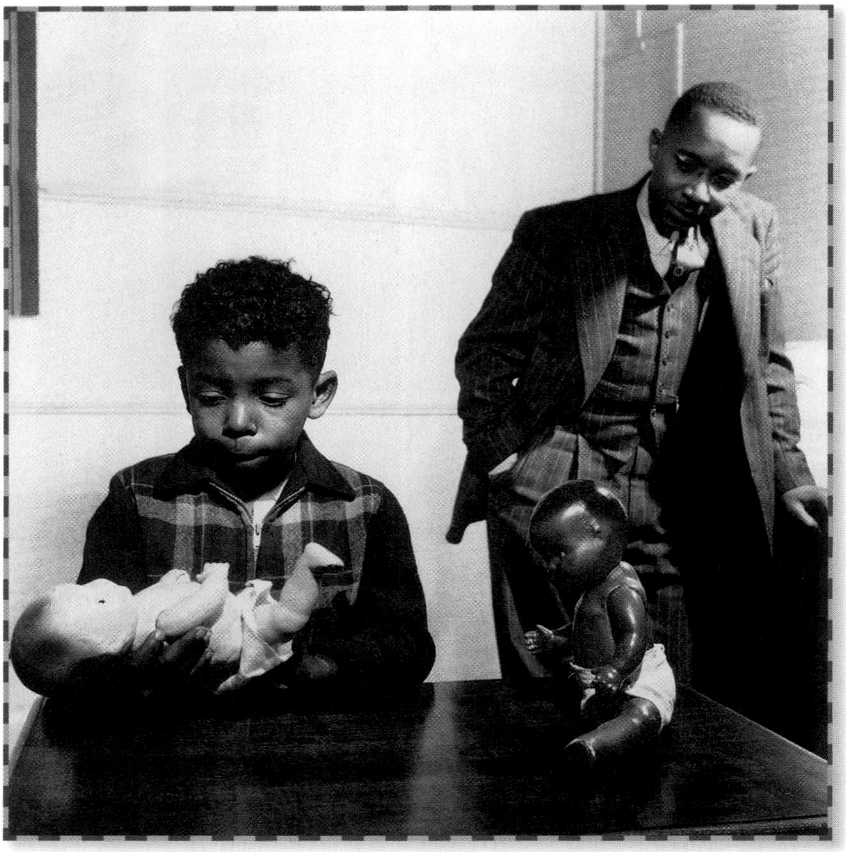

CAUSE & EFFECT

Identify the two cause-and-effect relationships in lines 47–53.

VOCABULARY

objectionable (əb·jek′shən·ə·bəl) *adj.:* justly liable to objection; disagreeable; offensive.

Dr. Kenneth B. Clark conducting "Doll Test."
Courtesy Estate of Gordon Parks / Library of Congress, #LC-USZ62-113572.

it was clear that the children were rejecting the black dolls. African-American children did not just feel separated from white children, they felt that the separation was based on their inferiority.

Dr. Clark understood fully the principles and ideas of those people who had held Africans in bondage and had tried to make slaves of captives. By isolating people of African descent, by barring them from certain actions or places, they could make them feel inferior. The social scientists who testified at *Brown vs. Board of Education* showed that children who felt inferior also performed poorly.

The Justice Department argued that racial segregation was **objectionable** to the Eisenhower Administration and hurt our relationships with other nations.

On May 17, 1954, after deliberating for nearly a year and a half, the Supreme Court made its ruling. The Court stated that it could not use the intentions of 1868, when the Fourteenth

Linda Brown sitting in a segregated classroom, 1953.
©Carl Iwasaki/Time Life Pictures/Getty Images

Amendment was passed, as a guide to its ruling, or even those of 1896, when the decision in *Plessy* vs. *Ferguson* was handed down. Chief Justice Earl Warren wrote:

> We must consider public education in the light of its full development and its present place in American life throughout the nation. We must look instead to the effect of segregation itself on public education.

The Court went on to say that "modern authority" supported the idea that segregation deprived African Americans of equal opportunity. "Modern authority" referred to Dr. Kenneth B. Clark and the weight of evidence that he and the other social scientists had presented.

The high court's decision in *Brown vs. Board of Education* signaled an important change in the struggle for civil rights. It signaled clearly that the legal **prohibitions** that oppressed African Americans would have to fall. Equally important was

INTERPRET

Re-read lines 63–66. Why didn't the "separate but equal" doctrine that guided the *Plessy* vs. *Ferguson* ruling apply to the Supreme Court's decision in *Brown* vs. *Board of Education*?

LITERARY FOCUS

Why do you think the author included the information in 67–71 about "modern authority"?

VOCABULARY

prohibitions (prō′i·bish′əns) *n.* orders or laws forbidding something to be done; refusals to permit something.

EXTEND

In lines 77–81, the author alludes to enslaved Africans and African Americans who participated in the struggle for freedom and equality. Select one of these references as a subject of further research and then write a brief report explaining the individual's or group's contributions.

NOTES

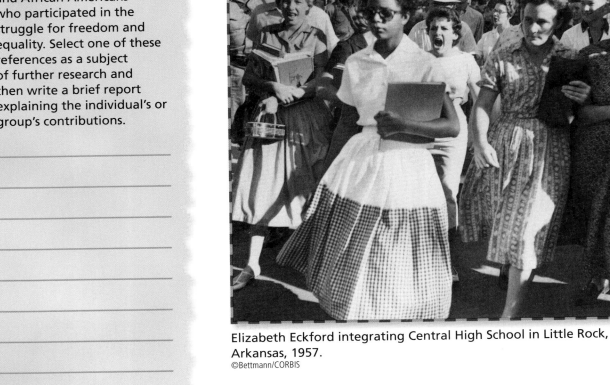

Elizabeth Eckford integrating Central High School in Little Rock, Arkansas, 1957.
©Bettmann/CORBIS

the idea that the nature of the fight for equality would change. Ibrahima,[4] Cinqué,[5] Nat Turner,[6] and George Latimer[7] had struggled for freedom by fighting against their captors or fleeing from them. The 54th[8] had fought for African freedom on the battlefields of the Civil War. Ida B. Wells[9] had fought for equality with her pen. Lewis H. Latimer[10] and Meta Vaux Warrick[11] had tried to earn equality with their work. In *Brown vs. Board of*

4. **Ibrahima:** Abdul Rahman Ibrahima Sori (1762–1829), African prince who was enslaved in the American South.
5. **Cinqué:** Joseph Cinqué (c.1813–c.1879), leader of a rebellion aboard the slave ship *Amistad*.
6. **Nat Turner** (1800–1831): leader of a rebellion against slavery in Virginia.
7. **George Latimer** (1820–1896): fugitive from slavery whose case helped fuel the abolition movement.
8. **54th:** the 54th Massachusetts Volunteer Infantry Regiment, African regiment in the Civil War known for their heroism and sacrifice.
9. **Ida B. Wells** (1862–1931): African American journalist and activist.
10. **Lewis H. Latimer** (1848–1928): African American inventor.
11. **Meta Vaux Warrick** (1877–1968): African American artist.

Education Thurgood Marshall, Kenneth B. Clark, and the lawyers and social scientists, both black and white, who helped them had won for African Americans a victory that would bring them closer to full equality than they had ever been in North America. There would still be legal battles to be won, but the major struggle would be in the hearts and minds of people and "in that gap between law and custom."

MEET THE WRITER

Walter Dean Myers (1937–) was born into an extremely poor family in Martinsburg, West Virginia. At three, he was adopted by a couple who moved to Harlem. Myers suffered from a speech impediment and turned to writing as a way to organize and communicate his thoughts and feelings. After high school and a three year tour of duty in the U.S. Army, Myers worked in various odd jobs. However, he also continued writing. Then, after working for seven years at a publishing firm, he decided to become a professional writer of young adult fiction and nonfiction.

Myers uses his own experiences as an African American to inform his readers and says, "I realized how few resources are available for black youngsters to open the world to them. I feel the need to show them the possibilities that exist for them that were never revealed to me as a youngster; possibilities that did not even exist for me then." For example, in his novel, *The Young Landlords* (1979), he shows how teenagers, who buy run-down apartment buildings, quickly take on adult responsibilities as they cope with repairs and tenant problems.

Myers's nonfiction includes works about Malcolm X, Muhammad Ali, and the Haitian revolutionary Toussaint L´Ouverture. This selection about the landmark Supreme Court case *Brown* vs. *Board of Education of Topeka* comes from *Now Is Your Time: The African American Struggle for Freedom* (1991). One reviewer said, "[Myers] tells a familiar story and shocks us with it all over again."

LITERARY FOCUS

Explain how the last two sentences of the article satisfy the requirements of a well-constructed essay.

EXTEND

Work with a partner to create a time line of important events in the struggle for civil rights. Based on your time line, did the "nature of the fight for equality" change after *Brown* vs. *Board of Education*? What factors do you think contributed to the changes that occurred?

from Brown vs. Board of Education

Reading Skills
Identify author's purpose.

AUTHOR'S PURPOSE CHART

The first column of the chart below lists questions about *"Brown vs. Board of Education."* In the second column, provide factual information from the selection to answer the questions. In the last column, identify the purpose or purposes (in addition to entertaining the reader) that Walter Dean Myers may have had in mind in presenting the information you listed to answer each question.

QUESTION	ANSWER	AUTHOR'S PURPOSE
What conditions did African captives endure on ships that brought them to America?		
What did plantation owners intend to accomplish by segregating enslaved Africans?		
What did Dr. Kenneth B. Clark conclude from the psychological tests he conducted on black children?		
What argument did social scientists use to convince the Supreme Court that segregation deprived African Americans of equal opportunity?		
What other individuals and groups who struggled for freedom and equality are mentioned in the article?		

from Brown vs. Board of Education

VOCABULARY AND COMPREHENSION

WORD BOX

- segregated
- intangible
- objectionable
- prohibitions

A. Context Clues Complete each sentence with the correct vocabulary word from the Word Box.

1. Shocked by the messages that people had painted on the fence, we rounded up some volunteers to scrub off the ______________________ material.

2. Herbie's charisma was ______________________ ; nobody knew how to describe it, but everyone knew he had it.

3. Being used to doing what she pleased at home, Lucy did not appreciate the ______________________ that her grandmother imposed on her.

4. The counselors ______________________ the two groups, housing the boys in one wing of the hotel and the girls in another.

B. Reading Comprehension Answer each question below.

5. What intangible factors were used as evidence to argue that schools needed to be desegregated?

____

____

____

6. What significant ramifications did people realize would occur if segregation in the schools was declared unconstitutional?

____

____

____

7. To whom was the Supreme Court referring when it cited "modern authority" as a basis for its decision?

____

____

____

Vocabulary Skills
Demonstrate an understanding of vocabulary in context.

Before You Read

My Dungeon Shook
by James Baldwin

In a letter to his fourteen-year old nephew, mid-twentieth-century author James Baldwin reveals his view of race relations in the United States and his philosophy about the way positive change might be effected.

LITERARY FOCUS: TONE AND DICTION IN PERSUASIVE WRITING

Persuasive writing is used to convince readers to think or act a certain way. How effective this persuasion is depends on both the content and the style of the writing.

Diction is one element of style. It refers to an author's choice of words and the arrangement of those words. For example, James Baldwin favors some challenging vocabulary and long sentences. His diction would be described as formal, although occasionally he interjects expressions that are more casual. Read this example from his letter:

> "The really terrible thing, old buddy, is that you must accept them. And I mean that very seriously. You must accept them and accept them with love."

In this example, the choice of the phrase "old buddy" helps him to convey a certain **tone**, or attitude. Departing from his more formal diction helps him to emphasize his sincerity.

Be sure to think about how tone and diction affect the persuasiveness of Baldwin's letter as you read.

READING SKILLS: ANALYZING A WRITER'S ARGUMENT

An effective argument includes a clear statement of the author's position on the topic and reasons and evidence that support this claim.

As you read Baldwin's letter, consider these questions to help you analyze his argument:

- What does he want you (the reader) to believe after reading his letter?
- What reasons or evidence does he give to help you agree with his view?
- Are you convinced?

Literary Focus
Analyze tone and diction in persuasive writing.

Reading Skills
Analyze a writer's arguement.

Vocabulary Skills
Use antonyms to understand unknown words.

VOCABULARY DEVELOPMENT

PREVIEW SELECTION VOCABULARY

The following words appear in "My Dungeon Shook." Look them over before you begin to read.

vulnerable (vul′nər·ə·bəl) *adj.:* susceptible to emotional or physical pain.

*A person can seem outwardly tough but still be **vulnerable** inside.*

perspective (pər·spek′tiv) *n.:* outlook.

*Because he was so much older than his brother, he had a different **perspective** on life.*

aspire (ə·spīr′) *v.:* work towards.

*For many years, African Americans were not encouraged to **aspire** to higher education.*

mediocrity (mē′dē·äk′rə·tē) *n.:* state of being ordinary or average.

*Baldwin encourages his nephew to strive for more than **mediocrity**.*

endure (en·door′) *v.:* carry on through hardships.

*Through much of their history, African Americans have had to **endure** numerous forms of discrimination and persecution.*

monumental (män′yoo·ment′′l) *adj.:* impressively large, sturdy, and enduring.

*His **monumental** strength enabled him to overcome obstacles and achieve success.*

REVIEWING ANTONYMS

Sometimes you can use **antonyms** to help you understand the meaning of unknown words. The presence of antonyms may be indicated by phrases such as *instead of, rather than, in contrast,* or by the structure of the sentence and context clues. Read this example from Baldwin's letter:

> "Like him, you are tough, dark, vulnerable, moody—with a very definite tendency to sound *truculent* because you want no one to think you are *soft.*"

The word *soft* is obviously intended to suggest the opposite of *truculent*. Therefore, you can guess that *truculent* means "tough" or "ready for a fight."

When you run across words that you don't know in Baldwin's letter, be sure to check the context to see if there are antonyms that you do know. This strategy will help you to improve your comprehension.

My Dungeon Shook

by James Baldwin

Dear James:

I have begun this letter five times and torn it up five times. I keep seeing your face, which is also the face of your father and my brother. Like him, you are tough, dark, **vulnerable,** moody—with a very definite tendency to sound truculent[1] because you want no one to think you are soft. You may be like your grandfather in this, I don't know, but certainly both you and your father resemble him very much physically. Well, he is dead, he never saw you, and he had a terrible life; he was defeated long before he died because, at the bottom of his heart, he really believed what white people said about him. This is one of the reasons that he became so holy. I am sure that your father has told you something about all that. Neither you nor your father exhibit any tendency toward holiness: you really are of another era, part of what happened when the Negro left the land and came into what the late E. Franklin Frazier[2] called "the cities of destruction." You can only be destroyed by believing that you really are what the white world calls a *nigger*. I tell you this because I love you, and please don't you ever forget it.

I have known both of you all your lives, have carried your Daddy in my arms and on my shoulders, kissed and spanked him and watched him learn to walk. I don't know if you've known anybody from that far back; if you've loved anybody that long, first as an infant, then as a child, then as a man, you gain a strange **perspective** on time and human pain and effort. Other people cannot see what I see whenever I look into your

INTERPRET

Re-read lines 2–14. Does Baldwin see the differences between his brother and his nephew and the grandfather as positive or negative?

LITERARY FOCUS

Re-read lines 17–19. How does Baldwin's language in this sentence affect his meaning?

VOCABULARY

vulnerable (vul′nər·ə·bəl) *adj.:* susceptible to emotional or physical pain.

perspective (pər·spek′tiv) *n.:* outlook.

1. **truculent** (truk′yə·lənt) *adj.:* eager to fight.
2. **E. Franklin Frazier** (1894–1962): a sociologist appointed to investigate the riots in Harlem during the Depression.

father's face, for behind your father's face as it is today are all those other faces which were his. Let him laugh and I see a cellar your father does not remember and I hear in his present laughter his laughter as a child. Let him curse and I remember him falling down the cellar steps, and howling, and I remember, with pain, his tears, which my hand or your grandmother's so easily wiped away. But no one's hand can wipe away those tears he sheds invisibly today, which one hears in his laughter and in his speech and in his songs. I know what the world has done to my brother and how narrowly he has survived it. And I know, which is much worse, and this is the crime of which I accuse my country and my countrymen, and for which neither I nor time nor history will ever forgive them, that they have destroyed and are destroying hundreds of thousands of lives and do not know it and do not want to know it. One can be, indeed one must strive to become, tough and philosophical concerning destruction and death, for this is what most of mankind has been best at since we have heard of man. (But remember: *most* of mankind is not *all* of mankind.) But it is not permissible that the authors of devastation should also be innocent. It is the innocence which constitutes the crime.

Now, my dear namesake, these innocent and well-meaning people, your countrymen, have caused you to be born under conditions not very far removed from those described for us by Charles Dickens[3] in the London of more than a hundred years ago. (I hear the chorus of the innocents screaming, "No! This is not true! How *bitter* you are!"—but I am writing this letter to *you*, to try to tell you something about how to handle *them*, for most of them do not yet really know that you exist. I *know* the conditions under which you were born, for I was there. Your countrymen were *not* there, and haven't made it yet. Your

3. **Charles Dickens** (1812–1870): English novelist whose works often served as a critique of the social conditions and poverty of nineteenth century London.

LITERARY FOCUS

What is Baldwin's attitude in lines 36–41? Underline the words that convey this tone.

ANALYZE

Why does Baldwin say that the innocents would call him bitter in lines 52–53?

WORD STUDY

In line 54, Baldwin uses the word *handle*. It has multiple meanings, but in this context, its denotation is "manage." What is the connotation?

James Baldwin and his nephew.
©Steve Schapiro/Black Star

CLARIFY

Re-read lines 70–73. Why does Baldwin say that "we were trembling"?

grandmother was also there, and no one has ever accused her of being bitter. I suggest that the innocents check with her. She isn't hard to find. Your countrymen don't know that she exists, either, though she has been working for them all their lives.)

Well, you were born, here you came, something like fourteen years ago; and though your father and mother and grandmother, looking about the streets through which they were carrying you, staring at the walls into which they brought you, had every reason to be heavyhearted, yet they were not. For here you were, Big James, named for me—you were a big baby, I was not—here you were: to be loved. To be loved, baby, hard, at once, and forever, to strengthen you against the loveless world. Remember that: I know how black it looks today, for you. It looked bad that day, too, yes, we were trembling. We have not stopped trembling yet, but if we had not loved each other none of us would have survived. And now you must survive because we love you, and for the sake of your children and your children's children.

This innocent country set you down in a ghetto in which, in fact, it intended that you should perish. Let me spell out precisely what I mean by that, for the heart of the matter is here, and the root of my dispute with my country. You were born where you were born and faced the future that you faced because you were black and *for no other reason*. The limits of you ambition were, thus, expected to be set forever. You were born into a society which spelled out with brutal clarity, and in as many ways as possible, that you were a worthless human being. You were not expected to **aspire** to excellence: you were expected to make peace with **mediocrity.** Wherever you have turned, James, in your short time on this earth, you have been told where you could go and what you could do (and *how* you could do it) and where you could live and whom you could marry. I know your countrymen do not agree with me about this, and I hear them saying, "You exaggerate." They do not know Harlem, and I do. So do you. Take no one's word for anything, including mine—but trust your experience. Know whence[4] you came. If you know whence you came, there is really no limit to where you can go. The details and symbols of your life have been deliberately constructed to make you believe what white people say about you. Please try to remember that what they believe, as well as what they do and cause you to **endure,** does not testify to your inferiority but to their inhumanity and fear. Please try to be clear, dear James, through the storm which rages about your youthful head today, about the reality which lies behind the words *acceptance* and *integration*. There is no reason for you to try to become like white people and there is no basis whatever for their impertinent assumption that *they* must accept *you*. The really terrible thing, old buddy, is that *you* must accept *them*. And I mean that very seriously. You must accept them and

4. **whence** (hwens) *adv.:* from where.

INTERPRET

Re-read lines 76–89. What does Baldwin believe about the lives of African Americans in the United States?

VOCABULARY

aspire (ə·spīr′) *v.:* work towards.

mediocrity (mē′dē·äk′rə·tē) *n.:* state of being ordinary or average.

endure (en·door′) *v.:* carry on through hardships.

LITERARY FOCUS

Underline words and phrases in lines 107–118 that create a tone of sympathy for white people. What is Baldwin's purpose here?

INTERPRET

What does Baldwin advocate as the means by which integration can be achieved in lines 130–134?

accept them with love. For these innocent people have no other hope. They are, in effect, still trapped in a history which they do not understand; and until they understand it, they cannot be released from it. They have had to believe for many years, and for innumerable reasons, that black men are inferior to white men. Many of them, indeed, know better, but, as you will discover, people find it very difficult to act on what they know. To act is to be committed, and to be committed is to be in danger. In this case, the danger, in the minds of most white Americans, is the loss of their identity. Try to imagine how you would feel if you woke up one morning to find the sun shining and all the stars aflame. You would be frightened because it is out of the order of nature. Any upheaval in the universe is terrifying because it so profoundly attacks one's sense of one's own reality. Well, the black man has functioned in the white man's world as a fixed star, as an immovable pillar: and as he moves out of his place, heaven and earth are shaken to their foundations. You, don't be afraid. I said that it was intended that you should perish in the ghetto, perish by never being allowed to go behind the white man's definitions, by never being allowed to spell your proper name. You have, and many of us have, defeated this intention: and, by a terrible law, a terrible paradox,[5] those innocents who believed that your imprisonment made them safe are losing their grasp of reality. But these men are your brothers—your lost, younger brothers. And if the word *integration* means anything, this is what it means: that we, with love, shall force our brothers to see themselves as they are, to cease fleeing from reality and begin to change it. For this is your home, my friend, do not be driven from it; great men have done great things here, and will again, and we can make America what America must become. It will be hard, James, but you come from sturdy, peasant stock,

5. **paradox** (par'ə·doks') *n.:* a statement that appears to be self-contradictory but is nonetheless true.

men who picked cotton and dammed rivers and built railroads, and, in the teeth of the most terrifying odds, achieved an unassailable and **monumental** dignity. You come from a long line of great poets, some of the greatest poets since Homer.[6] One of them said, "The very time I thought I was lost, My dungeon shook and my chains fell off."

You know, and I know, that the country is celebrating one hundred years of freedom[7] one hundred years too soon. We cannot be free until they are free. God bless you, James, and Godspeed.

YOUR UNCLE,

James

VOCABULARY

monumental (män'yo͞o·ment''l) *adj.:* impressively large, sturdy, and enduring.

INFER

Re-read lines 144–145. Baldwin is writing this letter in 1963, an active time in the civil rights movement. What does Baldwin's letter suggest he feels about the movement?

Aspiration, oil on canvas by Aaron Douglas.

©Fine Arts Museums of San Francisco, Museum purchase, the estate of Thurlow E. Tibbs Jr., the Museum Society Auxiliary, American Art Trust Fund, Unrestricted Art Trust Fund, partial gift of Dr. Ernest A. Bates, Sharon Bell, Jo-Ann Beverly, Barbara Carleton, Dr. And Mrs. Arthur H. Coleman, Dr. and Mrs. Coyness Ennix, Jr., Nicole Y. Ennix, Mr. and Mrs. Gary Francois, Dennis L. Franklin, Mr. and Mrs. Maxwell C. Gillette, Mr. and Mrs. Richard Goodyear, Zuretti L. Goosby, Marion E. Greene, Mrs. Vivian S. W. Hambrick, Laurie Gibbs Harris, Arlene Hollis, Louis A. and Letha Jeanpierre, Daniel and Jackie Johnson, Jr., Stephen L. Johnson, Mr. and Mrs. Arthur Lathan, Lewis & Ribbs Mortuary Garden Chapel, Mr. and Mrs. Gary Love, Glenn R. Nance, Mr. and Mrs. Harry S. Parker III, Mr. and Mrs. Carr T. Preston, Fannie Preston, Pamela R. Ransom, Dr. and Mrs. Benjamin F. Reed, San Francisco Black Chamber of Commerce, San Francisco Chapter of Links, Inc., San Francisco Chapter of the N.A.A.C.P., Sigma Pi Phi Fraternity, Dr. Ella Mae Simmons, Mr. Calvin R. Swinson, Joseph B. Williams, Mr. and Mrs. Alfred S. Wilsey, and the people of the Bay Area, 1997.84

6. **Homer:** Greek poet who is thought to have lived around 850 B.C. He is credited with creating two great epic poems, the *Iliad* and the *Odyssey.*
7. **celebrating . . . freedom:** the letter was written in 1963, one hundred years after President Lincoln issued the Emancipation Proclamation, which declared the freedom of all enslaved people in the Confederate states during the Civil War.

NOTES

Portrait of James Baldwin, 1963, by Beauford Delaney.
©National Portrait Gallery, Smithsonian Institution/Art Resource, NY

MEET THE WRITER

James Baldwin (1924–1987), a major American writer, produced a large body of work, including novels, essays, short stories, poetry, and plays. Born and raised in Harlem, Baldwin began writing in high school. When he was fourteen, he was appointed youth minister at Fireside Pentecostal Assembly. In a few years, he lost the desire to preach, but the oratorical style of that ministry found its way into his writings.

After graduating from high school in 1942, Baldwin wrote at night and supported himself by working at odd jobs during the day. He became friends with Richard Wright, who helped him get financial support with a Eugene F. Saxton fellowship in 1945. Literary magazines began accepting his essays and short stories. In 1948 he moved to Paris and remained in Europe until 1957. In 1953 he published his first and best-known novel, *Go Tell It on the Mountain*. This loosely autobiographical novel concerns a Harlem teenager's conflict with his repressive stepfather and the boy's religious conversion. (Much of Baldwin's fiction is autobiographical, and its major theme is black family life.)

Baldwin's national reputation as a writer and as a spokesperson for African American concerns was firmly established with two books of essays: *Nobody Knows My Name* (1961) and *The Fire Next Time* (1963). One recurring theme in his essays is the injustice he finds in American society. He once said, "The world changes according to the way people see it, and if you alter, even by a millimeter, . . . [how] people look at reality, then you can change it."

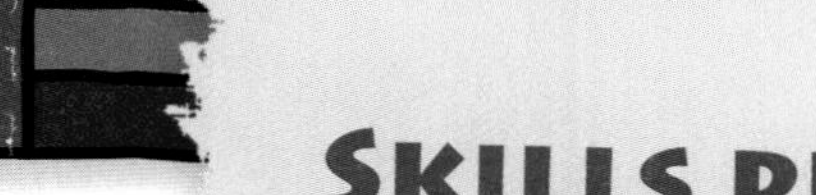

SKILLS PRACTICE

My Dungeon Shook

ELEMENTS OF AN ARGUMENT CHART

Baldwin develops an argument throughout his letter and reaches his conclusion at the end. Identify the elements of his argument in the chart below.

Literary Focus
Analyze tone and diction in persuasive writing.

Reading Skills
Analyze a writer's argument.

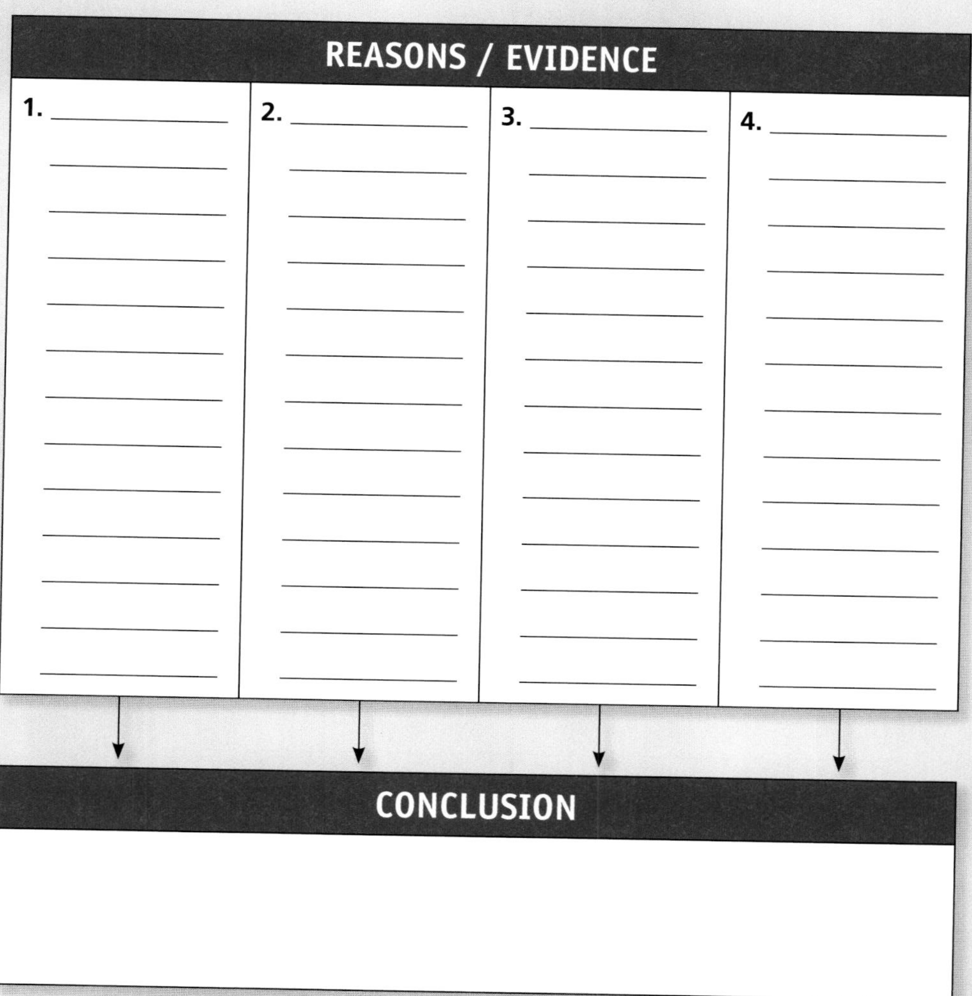

My Dungeon Shook

VOCABULARY AND COMPREHENSION

WORD BOX

monumental
mediocrity
aspire
vulnerable
endure

A. Antonyms Fill in the blank with the correct choice from the Word Box. Then underline the word's antonyms.

1. Baldwin advises his nephew that instead of giving up, he must continue to ______________________ the difficulties of his life.

2. Someone who is callous and hard cannot change as easily as a more ______________________ person can.

3. Baldwin believes that helping white people accept the change in society will not be a small task, but rather a ______________________ one.

4. It is easier to accept ______________________ than to strive for superiority.

5. He chose to ______________________ to his goals rather than relinquish them as some would have him do.

B. Reading Comprehension Answer each question below.

6. What is the purpose of James Baldwin's letter?

____

____

____

7. Why does Baldwin compare the United States to Dickens's London of one hundred years ago?

____

____

____

____

8. How does Baldwin define integration?

____

____

____

____

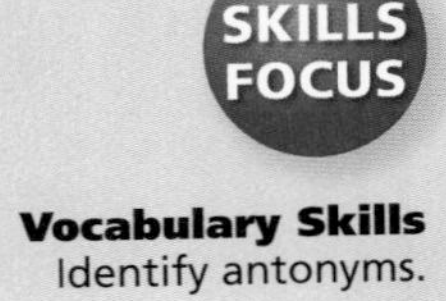

Vocabulary Skills
Identify antonyms.

BEFORE YOU READ

from Dreams from My Father
by Barack Obama

Barack Obama wrote *Dreams from My Father: A Story of Race and Inheritance* shortly before his political career began in the Illinois State Senate. In this excerpt from the memoir, Obama shares his experience of meeting his grandmother in Kenya for the first time. Though his visit feels like a homecoming, it leaves him feeling more uncertain than ever.

LITERARY FOCUS: MOOD

Mood is the atmosphere or feeling evoked by a passage or work. It is the emotional impact that writing has on readers. Mood may be described by words such as somber, frightening, suspenseful, sad, or peaceful.

The mood in a work of nonfiction is created by several elements, including setting, language (connotation of words, imagery, figurative language), and events. In this memoir, because Obama the author is also the first-person narrator, his thoughts, reactions, and feelings contribute to the mood. Read this example from the selection:

> "The market was full of women who sat on straw mats, their smooth brown legs sticking straight out in front of them from under wide skirts; the sound of their laughter as they watched me help Granny pick stems off collard greens . . . and the nutty-sweet taste of a sugarcane stalk that one of the women put in my hand."

The mood here is one of happiness. Obama describes a scene of warmth and conviviality, choosing incidents that convey the friendliness of the people and his own pleasure in being there.

As you read the selection, be aware of your feelings and consider why Obama might want you to experience these emotions.

Literary Focus
Understand mood in nonfiction.

Reading Skills
Identify author's purpose.

Vocabulary Skills
Understand synonyms.

READING SKILLS: IDENTIFYING THE AUTHOR'S PURPOSE

An author's **purpose** is his or her reason for writing a particular work. This purpose may be to inform or explain, to express thoughts or feelings, to persuade or to entertain. Sometimes a writer has more than one purpose. To help you determine Obama's purpose in this selection, keep these questions in mind as you read:

- What are the main ideas Obama wants to convey? Why?
- What kinds of details does Obama use to develop these ideas?
- What is his tone, or attitude toward his subject?

VOCABULARY DEVELOPMENT

PREVIEW SELECTION VOCABULARY

The following words appear in the excerpt from *Dreams from My Father.* Look them over before you begin to read.

exhumed (eks·hyo͞om′d) *verb used as adj.:* removed from a grave.

*The **exhumed** coffin still had dirt clinging to its sides.*

unceremoniously (un′ser·ə·mō′nē·əs′lē) *adv.:* abruptly; without formalities.

*Before Obama could react, the rooster had been **unceremoniously** slaughtered.*

mutual (myo͞o′cho͞o·əl) *adj.:* shared.

*Obama and his grandmother had a **mutual** affection for each other.*

ruefully (ro͞o′fəl′lē) *adv.:* sorrowfully or regretfully.

*He **ruefully** recognized that his trip created more questions than it answered.*

static (stat′ik) *adj.:* quiet, still, or at rest.

*He knew he could look forward to a dynamic, constantly changing life, rather than one that was **static**.*

SYNONYMS

A **synonym** is a word that has a similar meaning to another word. One word may have several synonyms. For example, in the memoir, Obama describes his grandmother's greeting:

> "[She] then turned to me and grabbed my hand in a hearty handshake."

Synonyms for "grabbed" include *took, seized, captured, snatched,* and *clutched*. Each one, however, has a different connotation, which changes the meaning of the sentence in which it is used. The original choice, *grabbed,* conveys enthusiasm and eagerness. The grandmother cannot wait to clasp the hand of her grandson. In contrast, *took* suggests none of that enthusiasm or force. Although *snatched* has a connotation of eagerness, it also suggests panic and creates the impression of an abrupt action.

Writers choose specific words to help them accomplish their purpose. As you read the memoir, think about how Obama's words impact his meaning and create a particular mood.

Sarah Hussein Obama, Barack Obama's grandmother.
©Evelyn Hockstein/ The New York Times/Redux

from Dreams from My Father

by Barack Obama

In the middle of the compound was a low, rectangular house with a corrugated-iron roof[1] and concrete walls that had crumbled on one side, leaving their brown mud base exposed. Bougainvillea, red and pink and yellow with flowers, spread along one side in the direction of a large concrete water tank, and across the packed earth was a small round hut lined with earthenware pots where a few chickens pecked in an alternating rhythm. I could see two more huts in the wide grass yard that stretched out behind the house. Beneath a tall mango tree, a pair of bony red cows looked up at us before returning to feed.

Home Squared.

LITERARY FOCUS

Read lines 1–10 aloud. What tone is created by this passage? Underline the words and phrases that develop this feeling.

ANALYZE

What does Obama mean by "Home Squared" in line 11?

1. **corrugated-iron roof:** a roof made of sheet iron panels with grooves and ridges for strength.

CLARIFY

Based on lines 12–23, what is the subject of this part of the memoir?

ANALYZE

Look at the descriptions of the photographs and other items on the wall in lines 28–38. Why are they significant to Obama?

BACKGROUND

The woman that Obama calls grandmother is, in fact, his step-grandmother. She was his grandfather's third wife and essentially raised Obama's father (the Old Man) after his own mother, Akuma, referred to in line 40, left the family. Roy and Auma are Obama's half-brother and half-sister by his father.

"Eh, Obama!" A big woman with a scarf on her head strode out of the main house drying her hands on the sides of her flowered skirt. She had a face like Sayid's, smooth and big-boned, with sparkling, laughing eyes. She hugged Auma and Roy as if she were going to wrestle them to the ground, then turned to me and grabbed my hand in a hearty handshake.

"Halo!" she said, attempting English.

"*Musawa!*" I said in Luo.[2]

She laughed, saying something to Auma.

"She says she has dreamed about this day, when she would finally meet this son of her son. She says you've brought her a great happiness. She says that now you have finally come home."

Granny nodded and pulled me into a hug before leading us into the house. Small windows let in little of the afternoon light, and the house was sparsely furnished—a few wooden chairs, a coffee table, a worn couch. On the walls were various family artifacts: the Old Man's Harvard diploma; photographs of him and of Omar, the uncle who had left for America twenty-five years ago and had never come back. Beside these were two older, yellowing photographs, the first of a tall young woman with smoldering eyes, a plump infant in her lap, a young girl standing beside her; the second of an older man in a high-backed chair. The man was dressed in a starched shirt and a *kanga*;[3] his legs were crossed like an Englishman's, but across his lap was what appeared to be some sort of club, its heavy head wrapped in an animal skin. His high cheekbones and narrow eyes gave his face an almost Oriental cast. Auma came up beside me.

"That's him. Our grandfather. The woman in the picture is our other grandmother, Akumu. The girl is Sarah. And the baby . . . that's the Old Man."

2. **Luo:** the largest ethnic group in Kenya; also the name of a group of languages spoken in the area.
3. ***kanga:*** a decorative rectangular cloth traditionally worn by people in East Africa.

I studied the pictures for some time, until I noticed one last picture on the wall. It was a vintage print, the kind that grace old Coca-Cola ads, of a white woman with thick dark hair and slightly dreamy eyes. I asked what the print was doing there, and Auma turned to Granny, who answered in Luo.

"She says that that is a picture of one of our grandfather's wives. He told people that he had married her in Burma[4] when he was in the war."

Roy laughed. "She doesn't look very Burmese, eh, Barack?"

I shook my head. She looked like my mother.

We sat down in the living room and Granny made us some tea. She explained that things were well, although she had given away some of the land to relatives, since she and Yusuf could not work it all by themselves. She made up the lost income by selling lunches to the children at the nearby school and bringing goods from Kisumu[5] to the local market whenever she had some spare cash. Her only real problems were with the roof of the house—she pointed to a few threads of sunlight that ran from the ceiling to the floor—and the fact that she hadn't heard anything from her son Omar in over a year. She asked if I had seen him, and I had to say no. She grunted something in Luo, then started to gather up our cups.

"She says when you see him, you should tell him she wants nothing from him," Auma whispered. "Only that he should come visit his mother."

I looked at Granny, and for the first time since our arrival, her age showed on her face.

After we unpacked our bags, Roy gestured for me to follow him out into the backyard. At the edge of a neighboring cornfield, at the foot of a mango tree, I saw two long rectangles of cement jutting out of the earth like a pair of **exhumed** coffins.

---

4. **Burma:** country in Southeast Asia, also known as Myanmar.
5. **Kisumu:** port city in western Kenya.

DRAW CONCLUSIONS

What image of the grandmother's character is created by the details she shares in lines 52–63?

EVALUATE

Re-read lines 64–68. How does this exchange help to bring out a main idea?

VOCABULARY

exhumed (eks·hyo͞om'd) *v. used as adj.:* removed from a grave.

There was a plaque on one of the graves: HUSSEIN ONYANGO OBAMA, B. 1895. D. 1979. The other was covered with yellow bathroom tiles, with a bare space on the headstone where the plaque should have been. Roy bent down and brushed away a train of ants that marched along the length of the grave.

"Six years," Roy said. "Six years, and there's still nothing to say who is buried here. I tell you now, Barack—when I die, you make sure that my name is on the grave." He shook his head slowly before heading back toward the house.

How to explain the emotions of that day? I can summon each moment in my mind almost frame by frame. I remember Auma and myself joining Granny at the afternoon market, the same clearing where the *matatu*[6] had first dropped us off, only now full of women who sat on straw mats, their smooth brown legs sticking straight out in front of them from under wide skirts; the sound of their laughter as they watched me help Granny pick stems off collard greens that she'd brought from Kisumu, and the nutty-sweet taste of a sugarcane stalk that one of the women put into my hand. I remember the rustle of corn leaves, the concentration on my uncles' faces, the smell of our sweat as we mended a hole in the fence bounding the western line of the property. I remember how, in the afternoon, a young boy named Godfrey appeared in the compound, a boy who Auma explained was staying with Granny because his family lived in a village where there was no school; I remember Godfrey's frantic steps as he chased a big black rooster through the banana and papaya trees, the knot in his young brow as the bird kept flapping out of his reach, the look in his eyes when finally Granny grabbed the rooster from behind with one hand and **unceremoniously** drew her knife across the bird's neck—a look that I remembered as my own.

6. *matatu:* taxi, usually a minibus.

INFER

Re-read lines 74–81. The second grave is that of Obama's father. How might Obama feel about the fact that the grave remains unmarked after six years?

FLUENCY

Read the boxed passage aloud several times. Work on conveying the mood as well as the emotions felt by Obama.

EVALUATE

Why do you think Obama records such specific details in lines 82–103?

VOCABULARY

unceremoniously (un'ser·ə·mo'nē·əs'lē) *adv.:* abruptly; without formalities.

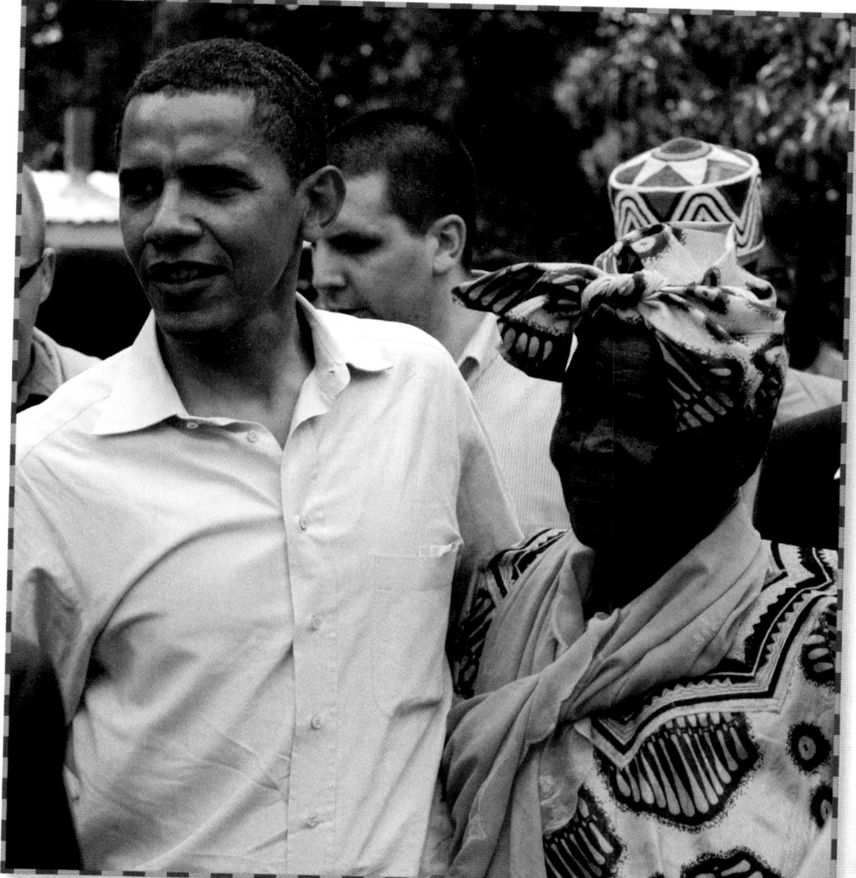

Obama and his grandmother in 2006.
©AFP/Getty Images

It wasn't simply joy that I felt in each of these moments. Rather, it was a sense that everything I was doing, every touch and breath and word, carried the full weight of my life; that a circle was beginning to close, so that I might finally recognize myself as I was, here, now, in one place. Only once that afternoon would I feel that mood broken, when, on our way back from the market, Auma ran ahead to get her camera, leaving Granny and me alone in the middle of the road. After a long pause, Granny looked at me and smiled. "Halo!" she said. "*Musawa!*" I said. Our **mutual** vocabulary exhausted, we stared **ruefully** down at the dirt until Auma finally returned. And Granny then turned to Auma and said, in a tone I could understand, that it pained her not to be able to speak to the son of her son.

"Tell her I'd like to learn Luo, but it's hard to find time in the States," I said. "Tell her how busy I am."

"She understands that," Auma said. "But she also says that a man can never be too busy to know his own people."

LITERARY FOCUS

Re-read lines 111–116. Note the use of words such as *exhausted, ruefully,* and *pained*. What feeling is communicated by this passage?

CONNECT

Re-read lines 119–120. How would Granny's comment make you feel if you were Obama?

VOCABULARY

mutual (myo͞o′cho͞o·əl) *adj.:* shared.

ruefully (ro͞o′fəl′lē) *adv.:* sorrowfully or regretfully.

VOCABULARY

static (stat'ik) *adj.:* quiet, still, or at rest.

NOTES

I looked at Granny, and she nodded at me, and I knew then that at some point the joy I was feeling would pass and that that, too, was part of the circle: the fact that my life was neither tidy nor **static,** and that even after this trip hard choices would always remain.

MEET THE WRITER

Barack Obama (1961–) was born in Honolulu, Hawaii. His father, from Kenya, and his mother, from Kansas, had met and married when they were students at the University of Hawaii. Obama's father left Hawaii to study at Harvard and then went back to Kenya to work as a government official. His mother remarried and the family moved to Indonesia, but in a few years Obama returned to Hawaii to live with his grandparents.

Obama went on to graduate from Columbia University in New York, and subsequently moved to Chicago to work with a church group seeking to improve living conditions in poor neighborhoods. In 1991, he graduated from Harvard Law School, where he became the first African American president of the Harvard Law Review. He returned to Chicago, worked as a civil rights lawyer, taught at the University of Chicago law school, and in 1997 began serving eight years in the Illinois State Senate. He was elected to the United States Senate in 2004 and declared his candidacy for President in 2007.

Dreams from My Father (1995) is a memoir of Obama's youth, his work in Chicago, and the trip he took to Kenya to explore his African heritage and visit the family of his father who had died in an automobile accident. Obama says that it is "a record of a personal, interior journey—a boy's search for his father, and through that search a workable meaning for his life as a black American." In 2006 Obama published *The Audacity of Hope*. In this book, he discusses politics, politicians, and his hopes for the future of America.

SKILLS PRACTICE

from Dreams from My Father

AUTHOR'S PURPOSE CHART

Complete the chart below to help you determine Barack Obama's purpose in writing his memoir.

Reading Skill
Identify author's purpose.

MAIN IDEAS	DETAILS	TONE

AUTHOR'S PURPOSE

from Dreams from My Father

VOCABULARY AND COMPREHENSION

WORD BOX

ruefully
static
exhumed
unceremoniously
mutual
endure

A. Synonyms Write the word from the Word Box that is a synonym of each given word. Use a thesaurus for help if necessary.

1. common ____________________
2. stationary ____________________
3. resurrected ____________________
4. informally ____________________
5. dolefully ____________________

B. Reading Comprehension Answer each question below.

6. How does Obama feel when he sees his grandmother's house for the first time?

____
____
____
____

7. What is the purpose of Obama's trip to Africa?

____
____
____
____

8. What realization does Obama arrive at on the afternoon of the market?

____
____
____
____

Vocabulary Skills Understand synonyms.

BEFORE YOU READ

from To A Young Jazz Musician
by Wynton Marsalis

In this excerpt, Wynton Marsalis offers valuable advice, gleaned from his own years of experience, to a new generation of jazz musicians.

LITERARY FOCUS: VOICE

Voice is a writer's distinctive use of language in a work. In nonfiction, the voice is often that of the writer. Readers are able to get a sense of the human personality of the writer through his or her voice.

Three elements contribute strongly to a writer's voice. These are sentence length, tone, and diction. **Tone** is the attitude the writer takes toward the subject; **Diction** refers to the writer's choice of words. Read this example from the selection:

> "I tell you I'm going to be a decathlete and my goal is the 2012 Olympics. And I'm forty-one years old. Man, I probably won't even get in shape, much less make the Olympic team."

Note Marsalis's use of the colloquial expression "man" and his relatively simple and short sentences. These facets of his writing help you to "hear" his voice.

READING SKILLS: IDENTIFYING AUDIENCE

The **audience** of a written work is whoever the author hopes is going to read it. In persuasive writing, the audience is particularly important. The writer has to consider the extent of readers' knowledge, their attitudes toward the topic, and their background. Understanding these aspects of the audience helps the writer choose the most convincing reasons and approach to his or her argument.

As you read this selection, look for the ways in which Marsalis shows his awareness of audience through his voice and the details he includes.

Literary Focus
Analyze a writer's voice.

Reading Skills
Identify audience.

Vocabulary Skills
Identify context clues.

VOCABULARY DEVELOPMENT

PREVIEW SELECTION VOCABULARY

The following words appear in the excerpt from "To a Young Jazz Musician." Look them over before you begin to read.

unique (yo͞o·nēk′) *adj.:* individual; only one of its kind.

Wynton Marsalis has a ***unique*** *gift for playing jazz.*

innovator (in′ə·vāt′ər) *n.:* one who introduces something new.

Marsalis might be called an ***innovator*** *who has brought jazz music to an entirely different level.*

philosophy (fə·läs′ə·fē) *n.:* system of values.

His ***philosophy*** *shaped his response to the setbacks that plagued his musical career.*

CONTEXT CLUES

When you are reading, you do not always have access to a dictionary to define unfamiliar words. There are several types of **context clues,** however, that you might use to help you figure out meanings of unknown terms. Sometimes writers use **comparisons, contrasts, cause-effect relationships, restatements,** and **examples**.

Read this passage from the selection:

> "Say I want to get back in shape but I don't articulate the goal that way, to you or myself. I tell you I'm going to be a decathlete . . ."

You may not know what the word *articulate* means. But, if you read further, the writer has restated the same idea in different words. You can then figure out that *articulate* has a meaning similar to *tell*.

As you read the selection, examine the sentences before and after each unfamiliar word to identify context clues that will help to reveal the meaning.

from To A Young Jazz Musician

by Wynton Marsalis

As jazz musicians, the great majority of us will not invent a new world of music inhabited by our disciples. Our challenge rests in something we already possess. Our own **unique** way of playing, as unique as our speaking voice. Now, does that mean you have the potential to be an **innovator** and create a unique world that becomes the norm for legions? Don't bank on it.

When a student can feel successful only if his or her work rivals the best work of the greatest artist ever, here comes depression, then a **philosophy** that attacks people who can play, then quitting. Two million people go to law school; you pull out the five greatest lawyers in history and say, "This is the standard of excellence by which you will be judged, pass or fail. If you

DRAW CONCLUSIONS

What does the title tell you about the intended audience and purpose of this work?

VOCABULARY

unique (yo͞o·nēk′) *adj.:* individual; only one of its kind.

innovator (in′ə·vāt′ər) *n.:* one who introduces something new.

philosophy (fə·läs′ə·fē) *n.:* system of values.

Wynton Marsalis performing at a jazz festival in 2002.
© Fabrice Coffrini/epa/CORBIS

Slightly adapted from "Moving It Forward: The New, New Thing" from *To a Young Jazz Musician* by Wynton Marsalis and Selwyn Seyfu Hinds. Copyright © 2004 by Wynton Marsalis Enterprises. Reproduced by permission of **Random House, Inc., www.randomhouse.com.**

EVALUATE

Re-read lines 16–18. How does the advice Marsalis gives reflect his understanding of his audience?

LITERARY FOCUS

Re-read lines 19–27. What is Marsalis's tone in this passage? How is this tone conveyed?

CONNECT

Do you agree with Marsalis's advice in lines 36–40? Why or why not?

are not equal to this level, you will not *pass* this course." Now, the first class may be eager to try that. But after the successive generations fail, who in their right mind will want to be a lawyer? So, first, don't think that you will move music anywhere. It's too heavy. And, second, don't feel that your basic level of success as a jazz musician is to be one of the great innovators of all time.

No one can teach you to be an innovator or even discourage you from being one. But someone can teach you to be a fine musician. How is it, given the near impossibility and the obvious absurdity of the goal, that thousands of jazz students all over the world think as you do, Anthony? I've heard that voiced in classes from Savannah to Sydney. "Yeah, we must do something new; must move the music somewhere to be successful." I've heard it for years. And in all those years, how many of those students moved the art form forward? Not one. Their goal killed them. Say I want to get back in shape but I don't articulate the goal that way, to you or myself. I tell you I'm going to be a decathlete and my goal is the 2012 Olympics. And I'm forty-one years old. Man, I probably won't even get in shape, much less make the Olympic team. Now, if I say, "I want to lose thirty pounds and tomorrow I'm going to get up and run a mile and a half, and I will try to go up a half mile every two weeks." Well, I might just lose ten of those thirty pounds in the next month.

What about redirecting your priorities? Instead of "I have to be one of these six great innovators or I'm not a success," you could say, "Hey, these are six great people. And I strive for that same level of power; at worst I would like to develop my own distinct sound."

Never quit. Because whether or not you reach your goal as a musician, you can always participate significantly in this music. Always act in accordance with what you know. Don't adjust your philosophy to your limitations or failures. Never quit. Focus on becoming a good musician. I want you to want that. Invest in your discipline, your practice, and your personal growth. Develop your soul by participating in the lives of other people in a positive way, through giving. You know, some people think the Boy Scouts are corny, but they have a community-service component. They might be focused on going for merit badges or winning jamborees, but a Scout has to go do something for the community as well. That's an important concept, because it means that activities must also have an objective of the soul. And that's what can heal our whole nation. We need *soul* objectives on a high level, a level higher than the pursuit of money and one-upmanship over another person.

As Art Blakey said, "You never see an armored car following a hearse." Be serious about these tasks and you'll earn the respect or jealousy of your peers. And if genius plans to meet you down the road, you won't miss the introduction, man.

In the Sweet By and By.

INTERPRET

Re-read lines 41–52. How do these ideas relate to being a jazz musician?

EXTEND

In an informal debate with your classmates, discuss whether or not you think Marsalis's argument is effective. Defend your viewpoint.

NOTES

MEET THE WRITER

Wynton Marsalis (1961–) was born in New Orleans. (His father, Ellis Marsalis, is a famous jazz teacher and pianist.) He started studying music early and by age eight was playing in a church band, and, at fourteen, he played his trumpet with the New Orleans Philharmonic. At seventeen he became the youngest musician to be admitted to Tanglewood's Berkshire Music Center and the Juilliard School. In 1980 he joined the Jazz Messengers and studied with the band's leader, Art Blakey. Marsalis then formed his own band.

He has earned nine Grammy Awards for both jazz and classical recording. In 1997, Marsalis became the first jazz musician to win a Pulitzer Prize for music. He has lectured, taught music workshops, and worked tirelessly to revitalize a wider interest in jazz. In 2001 he was a major commentator in *Jazz*, a PBS documentary miniseries that traced the history of jazz from its beginnings to the present. In "To a Young Jazz Musician" (2004), Marsalis expresses his opinions on the art of jazz and the art of living. He says, "Jazz speaks to a certain truth of the soul of our nation. And it will speak to the truth of your soul as a human being. When you contemplate the wisdom in jazz, eventually you see the objectives of the music as your objectives . . . . To improvise means to invent your own way of intelligently using what you have in order to improve your environment; to swing means to maintain equilibrium with elegance, to be resilient; and to play the blues means that no matter how tragic a situation may be, you have the capacity to conquer it with style."

SKILLS PRACTICE

from To A Young Jazz Musician

Literary Focus Analyze a writer's voice.

VOICE CHART

Fill in this chart with information about sentence length, diction, and tone to help you analyze Marsalis's voice.

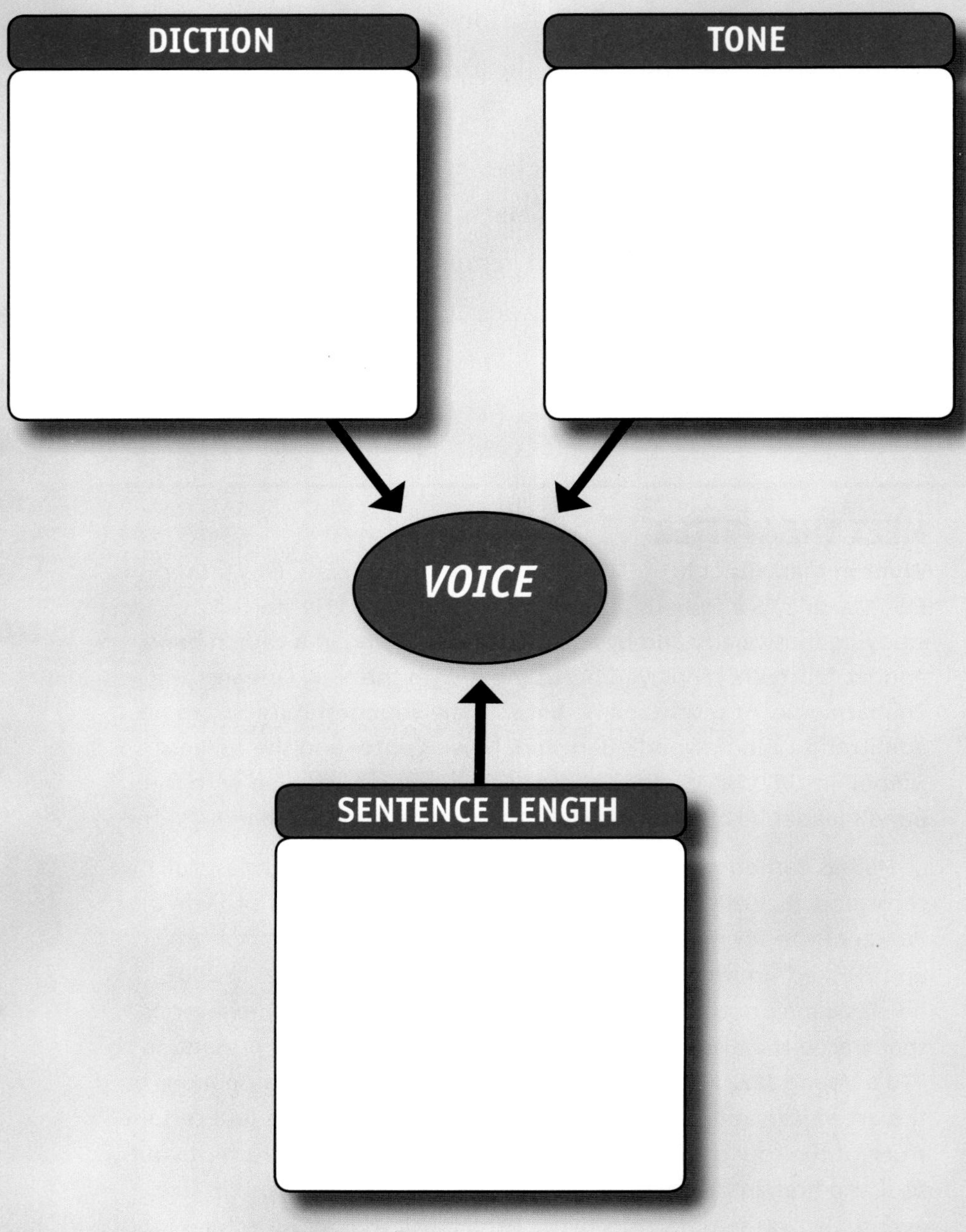

DICTION

TONE

VOICE

SENTENCE LENGTH

from To A Young Jazz Musician

VOCABULARY AND COMPREHENSION

WORD BOX

unique

philosophy

innovator

A. Context Clues Write the word from the Word Box that completes each sentence. Underline the context clue and identify it as restatement, comparison or contrast, cause-effect, or example.

1. His ______________________, which included such principles as striving to improve, made him a role model for many younger musicians.
   Context Clue: ______________________

2. Each writer's voice is like a fingerprint—it is ______________________.
   Context Clue: ______________________

3. Because he was a(n) ______________________, he was able to take jazz to a whole new level.
   Context Clue: ______________________

B. Reading Comprehension Answer each question below.

4. What is Marsalis's feeling about true innovators in the field of jazz music?
   ____

5. What is Marsalis's purpose in writing?
   ____
   ____
   ____

6. What is the point of his example about the 41-year-old decathlete?
   ____
   ____
   ____

7. What similarities and differences have you noticed about the messages and the tone of the selections by James Baldwin (pp. 226–271), Barack Obama (pp. 277–282), and Wynton Marsalis (pp. 287–289)? On a separate sheet of paper, write a short essay about your observations with examples from the selections.

Vocabulary Skills
Identify and use context clues.

BEFORE YOU READ

Before Hip-Hop Was Hip-Hop

by Rebecca Walker

Have you ever had the experience of looking back at a time in your life and realizing how significant it was to you? In this personal essay, author and activist Rebecca Walker reflects on the year that hip-hop transformed the world she knew—and changed how she saw herself.

LITERARY FOCUS: STYLE IN A PERSONAL ESSAY

Style is the particular way in which a writer uses language. While any essay can tell a story or explore an idea, the author of a **personal essay** uses his or her own life to do so. Style can determine how a reader reacts to a life experience the author relates. As you read "Before Hip-Hop Was Hip-Hop," consider how Walker's style shapes her piece and affects you as a reader.

- Pay attention to word choice—both vocabulary and figurative language. Does Walker use words and images that help you to understand her experience?
- Examine the length and structure of sentences and paragraphs. When does Walker use a long, complex description? When does she use a short, declarative sentence? Consider the effect of each.
- Notice when Walker uses the first-person point of view ("I") and when she uses the third-person ("we"). Make a guess about why she might choose one or the other.

READING SKILLS: EVALUATING WORD CHOICE

Evaluating word choice means determining how effective a word is. The right words help the reader visualize a scene or understand a feeling.

- Ask yourself whether words are specific enough to be effective. Walker writes of noticing her classmates' clothing—"razor sharp creases" on jeans, or a "fire engine red" sweatsuit. Can you picture what she describes?
- Notice whether words are interesting or flat. Walker writes of how her new school "crackled with energy" and was filled with "screaming self-expression." Do these phrases hold your interest?
- Consider whether figurative language is effective in creating an image or describing an emotion. Walker says that when she got to her new school, she "felt like a blank canvas." What does this tell you about her feelings?

Literary Focus
Analyze style in a personal essay.

Reading Skills
Evaluate word choice.

Vocabulary Skills
Understand word origins.

VOCABULARY DEVELOPMENT

PREVIEW SELECTION VOCABULARY

The following words appear in "Before Hip-Hop Was Hip-Hop." Look them over before you begin the selection.

indisputable (in·dis′pyo͞ot′ə·bəl) *adj.:* certain to be true; unquestionable.

At our school, DJ Marilinda was the ***indisputable*** *master of the turntable.*

inverted (in·vurt′əd) *v.:* turned upside down; changed to the opposite.

He ***inverted*** *the meaning of the word* sick *by using it to mean "great."*

palpable (pal′pə·bəl) *adj.:* able to be felt.

The excitement on the dance floor was ***palpable.***

cliques (kliks) *n.:* small groups that shut out others.

One of the snobbiest ***cliques*** *took over the best table in the lunchroom.*

transfixed (trans·fiks′d) *v.:* held still in wonder.

We stood there with wide eyes, ***transfixed*** *by the amazing performance.*

infused (in·fyo͞oz′d) *v.:* filled with a feeling or quality.

The performers in the poetry slam ***infused*** *every word with meaning.*

bravado (brə·vä′dō) *n.:* a display of bravery, perhaps false.

Malik claimed he wasn't nervous, but I think that was just a show of ***bravado.***

coveted (kuv′it′əd) *v.:* wished to possess; envied.

All that winter I ***coveted*** *my sister's silver boots and wished they were my own.*

UNDERSTANDING WORD ORIGINS

Some scholars believe that more than half of English words have French roots. After the Norman French conquered England in 1066, French became the language of England's ruling class. Thousands of French words entered Middle English—*government, religion, dance*—and the borrowing continues, though at a slower pace. French words adopted into English in recent centuries include the terms *clique* and *bravado* (originally *bravade*).

Learning about **word origins** can help you understand and remember the meanings of unknown words and build your vocabulary. For example, if you recognize the Latin root *vertere*, which means "to turn," in the word *inverted*, you can guess the meanings of related words such as *inverse* (reversed or opposite) and *versatile* (adaptable or able to turn easily). If you come across an unknown word in reading "Before Hip-Hop Was Hip-Hop," try considering its origin and any related words to help you understand its meaning.

Before Hip-Hop Was Hip-Hop

by Rebecca Walker

If you ask most kids today about hip-hop, they'll spit out the names of recording artists they see on TV: Eminem, P. Diddy, J. Lo, Beyonce. They'll tell you about the songs they like and the clothes they want to buy. They'll tell you about the **indisputable** zones of hip-hop like "EO" (East Orange, New Jersey), the "ATL" (Atlanta, Georgia), and the "West Side" (Los Angeles, California), neighborhoods they feel they know because they've seen them in all the glossiest, "flossiest" music videos. Hip-hop is natural to these kids, like air or water, just there, a part of the digital landscape that streams through their lives.

I watch this cultural sea change with fascination. It astounds me that hip-hop has grown into a global industry, a force that dominates youth culture from Paris to Prague, Tokyo to

VOCABULARY

indisputable (in·dis′pyo͞ot′ə·bəl) *adj.:* certain to be true; unquestionable.

CONNECT

Do you agree with Walker's idea that the media immerses kids in hip-hop culture?

WORD STUDY

The idiom *sea change* (line 11) originates from a Shakespearean quote. In its original context, the phrase described a "rich and strange" transformation caused by the sea. Over the years it evolved into an expression used to describe a profound transformation of any kind, and today it is often used to describe minor shifts in policy or trends.

Hip-hop dancers in Hangzhou, China.
©CLARO CORTES IV/Reuters/CORBIS

Timbuktu. I can't believe that in small, all-white towns like Lincoln, Nebraska, high school boys wear their clothes in the latest "steelo": pants sagging off their waists, sports jerseys hanging to their knees, baseball hats cocked to one side. Even in the pueblos of Mexico, where mariachi[1] bands and old school crooners still rule, it is hip-hop that sells cars, sodas, and children's toys on TV.

The vast empire of hip-hop amazes me because I knew hip-hop before it was hip-hop. I was there when it all began.

Way back then, in what today's ninth graders might call the ancient eighties, there was no MTV or VH-1. We found out about music by listening to the radio, flipping through the stacks at the record store, or buying "mix tapes" from local deejays at two dollars apiece. Back then, we carried combs in our back pockets and clipped long strands of feathers to the belt loops of our designer jeans. We wore our names in cursive gold letters around our necks or in big brass letters on our belt buckles. We picked up words and **inverted** them, calling something that we thought was really cool, "hot," and something that had a whole lot of life, "def."

We didn't know a whole new language was rolling off our tongues as we flipped English upside down and pulled some Spanish and even a few words from Africa into our parlance. We didn't know that young people for years to come would recycle our fashions and sample the bass lines from our favorite tracks. We thought we were just being kids and expressing ourselves, showing the grown-ups we were different from them in a way that was safe and fun. In fact we were at the epicenter of one

1. **mariachi** (mär'ē·ä'chē) *adj.:* a style of traditional Mexican dance music.

LITERARY FOCUS

What do you learn about Walker's viewpoint from her use of the metaphor that compares hip-hop to a "vast empire" (line 21)?

VOCABULARY

inverted (in·vurt'əd) *v.:* turned upside down; changed to the opposite.

LITERARY FOCUS

Why might Walker have chosen to use "we" instead of "I" in lines 24–39?

WORD STUDY

The word *parlance* (line 36), which means a way of speaking, comes from the French verb *parler*, "to speak."

INTERPRET

How has Walker's view of her hip-hop experience changed since she was a youth?

INFER

How did the young Walker feel about the "lanky, swanky" (lines 54–55) Bee Gees?

ANALYZE

Lines 65–67 contain one of several short paragraphs in this essay. Review lines 21–22 and line 44 as well. What purpose do these short paragraphs serve?

of America's most significant cultural revolutions, making it happen. Who knew?

Not me.

When I moved from Washington DC to the Bronx the summer before seventh grade, I had one box of records, mostly albums I had ordered from the Columbia Record Club. In 1982, if you promised to buy a record a month for one whole year, the Club sent you eight records for a penny. I had Bruce Springsteen's "The River," REO Speedwagon's "The Letter," "Belladonna" by Stevie Nicks. I had "Stairway to Heaven," by Led Zeppelin and the soundtrack from the movie *Saturday Night Fever*, which I played so many times I thought my mother would go crazy from listening to me belt out the lyrics with those lanky, swanky Bee Gees.

Along with my albums I had loads of 45s, what today we would call singles, little records with just two songs on them, that I bought at the record store near my school for just a dollar a piece. I had Chaka Khan's "I'm Every Woman," and Luther Vandross' "Never Too Much," and Chuck Brown and Soul Searcher's big hit, "Bustin' Loose." I had Michael Jackson's "Rock with You" and even Aretha Franklin's cover of "You Make Me Feel Like a Natural Woman" which I sang along to in the mornings as I styled my hair.

If you had asked me then about rap music I would have shrugged my shoulders and looked at you like you were crazy. Rap music? What's that?

But then I started seventh grade and my whole world turned upside down. At Public School 141, I went to classes with kids from all over the Bronx. There were kids whose families came from Puerto Rico and the Dominican Republic, and kids whose

©Atsuko Tanaka/CORBIS

families came from Russia and China. There were kids who were African-American and kids who were Irish-American, kids who were Italian-American and kids who were Greek-American. There were kids whose families were poor, kids whose families were well off, and kids whose families were somewhere in between. Some were Jewish, and others devout Catholics. Some were Muslim. Some of the Asian kids were even Buddhist.

The charge created by so many different elements coming together was **palpable**. The school crackled with energy, and as you can imagine, things weren't always smooth. There were some pretty entrenched **cliques,** and a few vicious fights on the schoolyard. But there was also so much "flavor." You could hear Spanish spoken with a thick "Nuyorican"[2] accent to a kid wearing a "yamulke."[3] A seemingly reserved Asian-American girl would get out of her parents' car, wait for them to drive off, and

LITERARY FOCUS

In lines 70–78, Walker could have just said that her classmates came from many different backgrounds. Why do you think she uses several sentences to describe them instead?

VOCABULARY

palpable (pal′pə·bəl) *adj.:* able to be felt.

cliques (kliks) *n.:* small groups that shut out others.

2. **Nuyorican** (no͞o′yô′rē′kan) *adj.:* a person of Puerto Rican descent who lives in New York; the term fuses the Spanish *Nueva York* with "Puerto Rican."

VOCABULARY

transfixed (trans·fiks′d) *v.:* held still in wonder.

infused (in·fyo͞oz′d) *v.:* filled with a feeling or quality.

bravado (brə·vä′dō) *n.:* a display of bravery, perhaps false.

INTERPRET

What is Walker's attitude toward her experience at Public School 141?

CONNECT

Re-read the boxed passage, underlining examples of imagery and figurative language. Then write a paragraph describing an experience of your own using a similar style.

then unzip her coat to reveal a fire engine red Adidas sweatsuit. A guy in a preppy, button down shirt would "sport" gold chains with pendants of every denomination: the Jewish Star of David, the Arabic lettering for Allah, and a shiny gold cross. He was everything, that was his "steelo," and everyone gave him "props" for it.

When I got to 141, I felt like a blank canvas. Nothing had prepared me for the dynamism, the screaming self-expression of the place and its students. For the first few weeks I secretly studied the habits of the seventh, eighth and ninth graders with whom I walked the halls and shared the cafeteria. I was **transfixed** by the way they **infused** their words with attitude and drama, moving their hands and heads as they spoke. I was captivated by the way many of them walked and ran and joked with each other with confidence and **bravado**. I noted what they wore and how they wore it: the razor sharp creases of their Jordache jeans, the spotless sneakers with the laces left loose and untied.

Slowly, I began to add some of what I saw into my "look." I convinced my grandmother to buy me a name chain to wear around my neck, and my stepmother to buy me dark dyed designer jeans. I bought my first pair of Nike sneakers, red, white and blue Air Cortez's, with money I saved from my allowance.

One by one, I started to make friends—Diane, Loida, James, Jesus, Maya. When James and Jesus weren't making fun of me for being so "square," they took me to parties on the Grand Concourse, the big boulevard lined with old apartment buildings and department stores that ran through the Bronx. The parties

3. **yamulke** (yäm′əl·kə) *n.:* a small cap worn by some Jewish men and boys; also spelled *yarmulke*.

were incredible, filled with young people who didn't drink, smoke or fight, but who just wanted to dance and laugh and ooh and ahhh over the "scratching" sounds and funky beats the DJ's coaxed out of their turntables.

A lot of the kids at the parties were "breakers" or "poppers and lockers," which meant they could breakdance, a style of movement that blends the Brazilian martial art of Capoeira with a dance called the Robot, and incorporates classical dance moves as well. The "breakers" moved in "crews" that competed against each other. Standing in a circle we watched as members of the different groups "moonwalked" into the center, and then hurled themselves to the floor, spinning on their heads, kicking their legs into the air, and making elaborate hand gestures, each more intricate and acrobatic than the last. Everyone at the party who wasn't "breaking" was a judge by default, and we registered our scores by clapping and yelling.

LITERARY FOCUS

Re-read the sentence in lines 124–128. How effective do you find Walker's word choice in this sentence? Why?

©Inti St Clair/Blend Images/CORBIS

VOCABULARY

coveted (kuv′it′əd) *v.:* wished to possess; envied.

INFER

Use context clues to infer the meaning of the slang in lines 131–132.

INTERPRET

How did Walker's social life seem to differ from the outside world?

When Loida and Diane weren't "capping on" or making fun of my clothes, they were "hipping" me to Kiss 98.7 and WBLS, the radio stations that had started to slip some of the songs we liked into their rotation. Songs like Planet Rock by Soul Sonic Force and Take Me Home by Lisa Lisa and the Cult Jam. After school and on the weekends, they took me to the street vendors that sold the accessories we all **coveted:** the big knockoff [4] Porsche sunglasses everybody wanted but not everybody could afford, and the heavy gold chains people collected around their necks like so many pieces of string. Loida and Diane also took me around the city on the bus, familiarizing me with the routes of the M1 and M3 and M7, showing me all the different neighborhoods like Little Italy and Chinatown, Bed-Stuy and Harlem.

I remember looking out the big sliding glass windows of the bus at the lines drawn in concrete and glass and thinking that while the world outside seemed so divided, inside, in my circle, amongst my friends, those lines didn't seem to exist. Loida was Dominican and Diane was Puerto Rican. Our friend Mary was Irish-American, and Lisa was Italian-American. Maya's family was from Haiti. Julius was Russian-American. We were different ages, with different likes and dislikes, but we were united in our love of hip-hop. We loved the "dope" beats, the ever changing and ever expanding lexicon,[5] the outrageous dance moves, the cocky swagger, the feeling that we were part of something dynamic and "fresh" that was bigger than any one of us. That world, that other realm that we created on the streets and in our minds, that streamed from the radio in the privacy of our bedrooms and coursed between us as we talked on the phone, that was where we lived.

4. **knockoff** *adj.:* an inferior copy of a designer brand.
5. **lexicon** (leks′i·kän′) *n.:* the vocabulary of a specific group.

That was where we felt free.

Looking back on it now, I can see that hip-hop was born of the diversity I found at 141. Unlike the hip-hop of today, it didn't come pre-packaged from a marketing department with millions of dollars to spend. Our hip-hop was the product of a bunch of kids from a bunch of different places trying to talk to each other, trying to create a common language that could cut through the many languages people spoke at home. Intuitively, kids were making a community where there was none; we were affirming our sameness in a world that seemed to only emphasize our difference. That desire to come together irrespective of superficial differences and sometimes in celebration of them, was what gave hip-hop authenticity, that was what kept it honest and as crucial to our well being as food. It's what kept it real.

Hip-Hop, A Piece of it's History by Johnny Myers.

EVALUATE

Walker seems to suggest that mass-marketed hip-hop can't be authentic. Do you agree? Explain.

EXTEND

Walker says that in her world, hip-hop felt "as crucial to our well-being as food" (line 174). Think of something you consider essential to happiness. Then use a simile or metaphor in a persuasive paragraph that expresses its importance.

I can't say much about hip-hop today, but I can say that old hip-hop, original hip-hop, changed my life forever. I only lived in the "Boogie Down Bronx" for a year, but those twelve months gave me so much. I learned that art could bring people together and make them forget their differences. I learned how good it could feel to move with a "posse," a group of friends who had my back no matter what. I learned that I could express myself and communicate with others through what I wore and how I walked and what music I liked. I learned that it doesn't take money or a special degree to transform the grit and drive and hardness of the city into something beautiful.

Loyalty. Community. Self-confidence. Creativity. Hip-hop taught me more about real life than anything I learned that year in class.

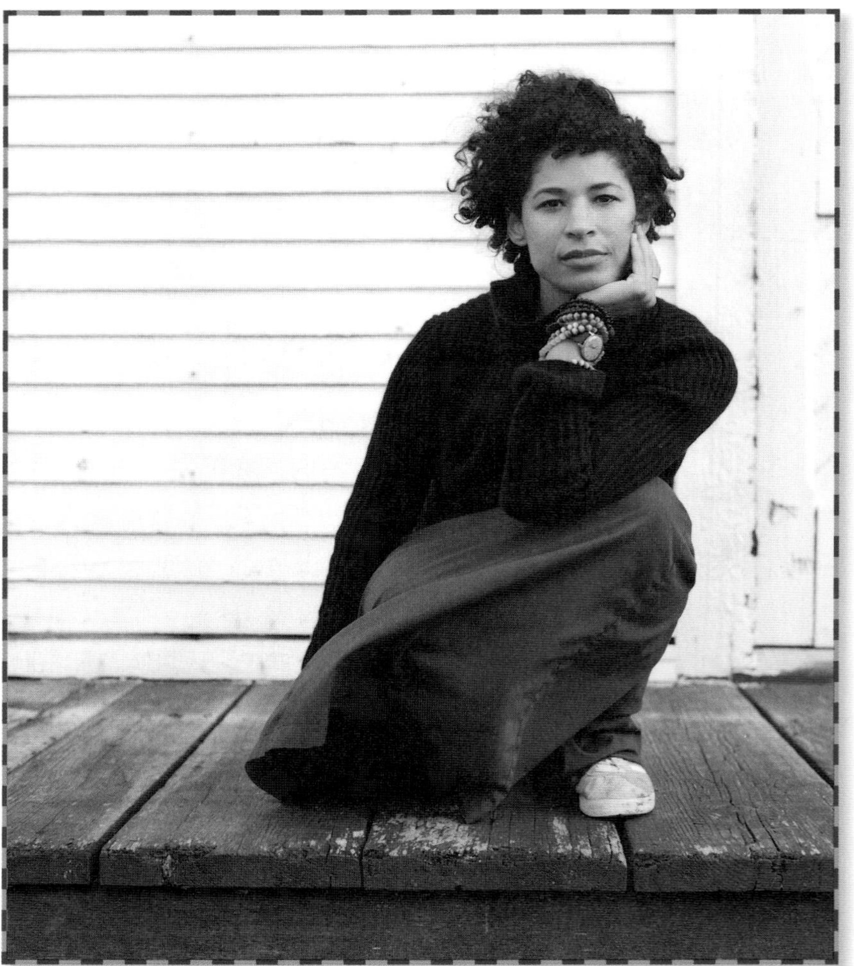
Rebecca Walker.
©John Fenton

LITERARY FOCUS

What is the effect of Walker's repetition of the phrase "I learned" in lines 178–187?

INFER

If not "money or a special degree" (lines 183–184), what does Walker think it takes to turn experience into art?

NOTES

I hope when young people today look at shiny videos by their favorite hip-hop artists, they will see through the expensive cars and exotic locations, the women in skimpy outfits and the men trying to approximate a "gangsta" lean. I hope they will remember that hip-hop was born without a formula and without a lot of expensive props or violent undertones. I hope they will marvel at the fact that in the early days of hip-hop, young people were making it up as they went along, following their hearts, following what felt good. I hope they will think about what it takes to create culture that is unique and transcendent and honest, and I hope they will begin to dream about creating a new world for themselves.

I hope hip-hop inspires you to make your own revolution.

MEET THE WRITER

Rebecca Walker (1969–) is the daughter of the writer Alice Walker and Mel Leventhal, a civil rights lawyer. Her parents divorced when Walker was eight years old and she then alternated between living with her mother in one city and her father in another. She describes this unsettling experience in *Black, White and Jewish* (2001). Walker had heartrending difficulty in reconciling her biracial identity. She also felt that her parents were absorbed in their own careers, and had left her to grow up on her own.

Walker experienced personal difficulties in her teenage years but graduated with honors from Yale University in 1992. She and a friend founded Third Wave Direct Action Corporation, a nonprofit organization to help female activists realize their goals. In 1995 Walker published *To Be Real: Telling the Truth and Changing the Face of Feminism*. It contains essays by young feminists responding to the question, "Is there more than one way to be a feminist?" Her recent book, a memoir, is *Baby Love: Choosing Motherhood after a Lifetime of Ambivalence* (2007). She says, "For me, having a baby has been the most transformational experience of my life." Walker also writes for magazines including *Ms.* and *Black Scholar*.

INTERPRET

Why do you think Walker means by "hip-hop was born without a formula" (line 192)?

LITERARY FOCUS

From lines 191–198, Walker repeats the phrase "I hope they" but switches in line 200 to "I hope . . . you." What effect does this create?

Before Hip-Hop Was Hip-Hop

SKILLS FOCUS

Literary Skills
Analyze style in a personal essay.

AUTHOR'S STYLE CHART

Use the following chart to explore how Walker's style affected you as a reader. The first column lists stylistic elements in "Before Hip-Hop Was Hip-Hop." In the second column, list **one** example of each element that you believe Walker used effectively (use ellipses in long examples). In the third column, briefly describe the effect this example had on you.

STYLISTIC ELEMENT	EXAMPLE	EFFECT
Word choice		
Figurative language		
Long description		
Short statement		
First-person point of view		
Third-person point of view		

Before Hip-Hop Was Hip-Hop

VOCABULARY AND COMPREHENSION

WORD BOX

inverted
palpable
cliques
bravado
coveted

A. Word Origins For each item below, fill in the blank with the appropriate word from the Word Box. Use what you know about the meaning of the word to match it with the statement about its origin.

1. This word comes from the Latin verb meaning to "touch."

____

2. This word came, via French, from the Latin verb meaning to "desire."

____

3. The root of this word comes from the Latin verb meaning to "turn."

____

4. This French word is used to describe a false display of courage.

____

5. This French word is used to mean small, exclusive groups.

____

B. Reading Comprehension Answer each question below.

7. According to Walker, why was the diversity at her school in the Bronx important to the development of hip-hop?

____

____

____

8. What did Walker and her friends love about hip-hop?

____

____

____

9. In what ways does Walker believe hip-hop is different today?

____

____

____

Vocabulary Skills
Understand word origins.

BEFORE YOU READ

Study on Young Blacks Reveals More Than Style

by Dawn Turner Trice

Dawn Turner Trice is a novelist, a newspaper columnist, and editor. In this opinion column, she discusses the prevalence and dangers of stereotyping.

LITERARY FOCUS: OPINION COLUMN

Newspapers are full of opinions, from movie reviews to editorials on political subjects. The opportunity to read thoughtful—and thought-provoking—opinions motivates many people who turn to newspapers day after day. An opinion column is a short piece that shares a writer's ideas about a timely subject. Because an **opinion column** is a kind of persuasive writing, it shares key features with that literary form. As you read "Study on Young Blacks Reveals More Than Style," look for these typical features.

- A "hook"—something at the start of the column that grabs the reader's attention, such as an anecdote, declaration, or surprising fact.
- A statement of opinion—this often occurs toward the beginning of the column.
- Supporting details—the writer shares evidence that supports the opinion; she or he may also note opposing viewpoints, or otherwise acknowledge complexity.
- Call to readers—the writer may ask readers to take positive action.

READING SKILLS: DISTINGUISHING FACT FROM OPINION

An opinion column usually includes both facts and opinions. A skillful persuasive writer often blends the two. In order to evaluate the accuracy of what you read, it is important to be able to **distinguish fact from opinion**.

- A **fact** is a statement about a subject that can be proven. Facts include dates, statistics, and other evidence that can be shown to be objectively true. When Trice writes that a team from the University of Chicago "surveyed nearly 1,600 black, white, and Hispanic youth," that is a statement of fact that can be proven.
- An **opinion** is a judgment or idea about a subject. It cannot be proven. Words that express judgment, such as *must, should,* and *certainly,* signal an opinion. When Trice writes that the results of the University of Chicago survey "should be required reading," that is a statement of opinion.

Literary Focus Understand structure of opinion columns.

Reading Skills Distinguish fact from opinion.

Vocabulary Skills Clarify word meanings.

VOCABULARY DEVELOPMENT

PREVIEW SELECTION VOCABULARY

The following words appear in "Study on Young Blacks Reveals More Than Style." Look them over before you begin the selection.

typecast (tīp′kast′) *v.:* to give an actor the same role again and again; to stereotype.

*Trice says that a young black man may be **typecast** as "a young thug."*

superficially (so͞o′pər·fish′əl·lē) *adv.:* in a way that is shallow or relates only to appearances.

*If you judge someone by their dress or manner, you are seeing them **superficially**.*

comprehensive (käm′prē·hen′siv) *adj.:* broad in content; including a large quantity.

*The survey was **comprehensive** because it included a wide range of respondents.*

prevailing (prē·vāl′·iŋ) *adj.:* dominant at present.

*It challenged the **prevailing** idea that kids don't question what they see in rap videos.*

CLARIFY WORD MEANINGS: RESTATEMENT

An opinion column is often written in an informal style. The writer may use language that sounds conversational, including short sentences, contractions, and the pronoun *I*. The writer may also use expressive words or figures of speech whose meanings may not immediately be clear to you. When that happens, try to guess what the word or phrase means. Then confirm that meaning through **restatement**, or saying it in a different way.

"The prevailing sentiment often is that the toothpaste is out of the tube . . ."

You know from the context that Trice isn't talking about toothpaste—she's talking about the possibility of social change. With this in mind, you may guess that she is using a metaphor about toothpaste to express the idea that "what is done can't be undone." Once you have a guess about the meaning, restate it to see whether it makes sense.

The prevailing sentiment often is that things can't be any different after this . . .

Study on Young Blacks Reveals More Than Style

by Dawn Turner Trice

Published February 26, 2007

I was on a train late in the evening recently when a young African-American man boarded. He was wearing a pair of those baggie jeans that tend to puddle around the gym shoes and sag relentlessly in the butt.

The hood of a dark jacket covered his head and he carried a cloth sack slung over his shoulder. He walked to the seat in front of me and sat down.

Several of us noticed the young man. More importantly, several of us thought we knew him. Not "knew him" in the sense that he was an acquaintance. But "knew him" in the sense that he fit a mold. He was a "type." He appeared to be a young thug type.

©Jerry Arcieri/CORBIS

EVALUATE

Re-read the first two paragraphs (lines 1–7). Do you think they are an effective "hook"? Explain.

CLARIFY

Use restatement to clarify what is meant by "fit a mold" (lines 10–11).

CONNECT

Have you observed people making assumptions about others based on their appearance? Why do you think people make these kinds of assumptions?

"Study on young blacks reveals more than style" by Dawn Turner Trice from *Chicago Tribune*, February 26, 2007 on www.chicagotribune.com/news/columnists/chi-0702260077feb26,1,5897004.column?coll=chi-news-col.

But after he sat, he pulled a laptop from his bag, along with a thick math book and a multi-buttoned calculator seemingly capable of rocket science calculations. He then started on what I would guess—since I'm so good at discernment[1]—was his homework.

I am not proud that I **typecast** this young man. But it happened and the story dovetails nicely with the point of this column, which is that often young people are viewed too **superficially.**

The University of Chicago recently released the results of a **comprehensive** survey on the attitude and behavior of young blacks.

It should be required reading for those of us who look at young people, more specifically young black people (and most specifically young black male people) and believe we know so much about them.

Having been so simplistically rendered in the media and even in statistics, young black men, possibly more than any other group, are readily typecast, often appearing as one-dimensional figures.

A team from the university's Black Youth Project (www.blackyouthproject.com)—led by political science professor Cathy Cohen—surveyed nearly 1,600 black, white and Hispanic youth, ages 15 to 25, from around the country.

The survey was taken over several months in 2005 and used methodology that allowed the respondents to be open and honest. Though the Black Youth Project surveyed an array of youths, the study's chief focus was on young blacks.

---

1. **discernment** (di·sʉrn′·mənt): the act of making a wise judgment.

VOCABULARY

typecast (tīp′kast′) *v.:* to give an actor the same role again and again; to stereotype.

superficially (so͞o′pər·fish′əl·lē) *adv.:* in a way that is shallow or relates only to appearances.

comprehensive (tīp′kast′) *adj.:* broad in content; including a large quantity.

ANALYZE

Is the sentence in lines 22–25 a statement of fact or opinion? How can you tell?

INTERPRET

Why does Dawn Turner Trice explain the parameters of the study in lines 29–36? How does this information help the reader?

Some of the findings may seem a bit counterintuitive.[2] Here's an example: What do young blacks really feel about the images they see in rap videos? If you think they're drinking the Kool-Aid, think again.

Although the survey showed that blacks listen to rap much more than their white and Hispanic counterparts, 66 percent of black females believe that rap videos portray women in negative and offensive ways. Fifty-seven percent of young black males believed similarly. A majority of young blacks also were greatly concerned about the violence in rap videos.

What does this suggest to me? The **prevailing** sentiment often is that the toothpaste is out of the tube and little can be done toward change. I despise that sentiment because it's defeatist. This isn't about going back to that non-existent time when life was perfect. It's about working with what we have.

It's clear that the majority of these young people are intelligent enough to see through rap music's misogynistic messages. For those who want to make sure that young people aren't getting their cues from videos, it's good to know or be reminded that many of them aren't.

The survey also examined these kids' ideas on safe sex, politics, racism, gender roles, crime and health care. Those findings were equally illuminating.

It's true that you don't have to convene a research team to know that there are some pretty weighty problems affecting

2. **counterintuitive** (kount'ər·in·to͞o'i·tiv): seeming to be against common sense.

HISTORICAL CONTEXT

"Drinking the Kool-Aid" (line 39) is an allusion to a 1978 event in which hundreds of cult members in Jonestown, Guyana, died by following their leader's orders to drink poisoned Kool-Aid. The phrase is used to mean "being brainwashed."

ANALYZE

Identify four facts presented in lines 41–46. How can you tell they are facts?

____

____

____

____

____

____

____

____

____

VOCABULARY

prevailing (prē·vāl'·iŋ) *adj.:* dominant at present.

WORD STUDY

The word *misogynistic* (line 53) means "hatred of women." It comes from the Greek word *misos*, "hatred," and the Greek root *gyno-*, "woman."

some segments of the black community. Even this survey cites a drumbeat of depressing statistics, from U.S. prison rates for young black males to poverty rates for black youth in general.

But the empirical[3] evidence helps us understand what's real and what isn't. That way, we're not just signing on to a stereotype that's been repeated so many times that it feels like we have the complete picture.

I grew up hearing that if you want to make a difference, you have to constantly examine that thing you're trying to change. Sometimes if you're too close, it may appear distorted. If you're too far away, you may not be able to appreciate the details.

When it comes to young people, this study draws a more accurate picture. It challenges us to see it from a different vantage point. Then it reminds us that we can't give up.

ANALYZE

Trice says that if people see a stereotype repeated often enough, they will believe it (lines 66–68). Where are stereotypes repeated? Identify a stereotype and make a list of places you have seen it repeated. Then list ideas for how this stereotype could be challenged.

3. **empirical** (em·pir'i·kəl): able to be proved by experience or observation; factual.

MEET THE WRITER

Dawn Turner Trice (1965–   ) grew up in Chicago in a family that loved storytelling. She is a columnist for the *Chicago Tribune* and writes about current political and social issues. She has also written two novels. *Only Twice I've Wished for Heaven* (1997) is a coming-of-age novel about an eleven-year-old black girl in Chicago who is befriended by a street-wise adult. *An Eighth of August* (2000), a novel with multiple narrators, takes place in an Illinois town that celebrates the signing of the Emancipation Proclamation each year. On being asked what advice she would give to young writers, Trice said, "Read everything. Not just a specific genre or a specific author or group of authors. Read and write. Do it! And do it as though your soul depends on it."

INFER

In lines 73–75, what does Trice say she wants readers to do?

SKILLS PRACTICE

Study on Young Blacks Reveals More Than Style

Reading Skills Distinguish fact from opinion.

CHART: DISTINGUISHING FACT FROM OPINION

List five facts from "Study on Young Blacks Reveals More Than Style" in the first column and five opinions in the second column. Before you write down each one, ask yourself: Is this statement a judgment or a fact that can be proven? Remember that even when you agree wholeheartedly with a judgment, it is still a statement of opinion.

FACTS	OPINIONS

Study on Young Blacks Reveals More Than Style

VOCABULARY AND COMPREHENSION

A. Clarify Word Meanings For each item below, clarify the meaning of the boldfaced word by restating it on the line that follows.

1. Without thinking, Trice **typecast** the young black man on the train.

____

2. Trice says that adults have a tendency to see young people **superficially**.

____

3. A **comprehensive** survey will collect the opinions of a wide range of people.

____

4. According to Trice, the **prevailing** idea among adults is that young people don't question what they see in rap videos.

____

B. Reading Comprehension Answer each question below.

5. What did the survey show about how young black people think about rap videos?

____

____

____

6. What does Trice believe adults could learn from the results of this survey?

____

____

____

7. For two days, record in a notebook instances of stereotyping that you observe in school or elsewhere. Also record instances when you find yourself making assumptions based on superficial characteristics. Discuss your findings in class. Is stereotyping common in your school or community based on the information gathered by the class? Are there ways that people can be encouraged to avoid stereotyping even if it isn't very common in your area?

Vocabulary Skills
Clarifying word meanings.

BEFORE YOU READ

Tavis Smiley: shares life lessons in new book 'What I Know For Sure'

by Clarence Waldron, *Jet,* October 30, 2006

The journalist Clarence Waldron presents a critical essay about a memoir written by TV talk-show host Tavis Smiley.

LITERARY FOCUS: CRITICAL ESSAY

You have probably read a variety of nonfiction, including essays, biographies and autobiographies, and informational articles. A **critical essay** is an informational article intended to entertain and inform readers about the writer's critical evaluation of a book, movie, play, concert, or other artistic work. The writer may also intend to persuade the reader to use the review as a basis for deciding whether or not to read the book, see the movie or play, or attend the concert.

A well-written critical essay of a book provides background information about the author, a brief synopsis of the contents, and an evaluation of the significance of the work and/or its potential interest to readers. As you read this critical essay, look for these features and think about your own reaction to what Clarence Waldron says about his subject.

READING SKILLS: EVALUATING A WRITER'S JUDGMENTS

Evaluating a writer's judgments involves forming your own opinion about the value of the writer's opinions on a subject. To evaluate a review of a book you have not yet read, you need to rely on what you already know about the subject of the book and your own assessment of what the writer says about the subject. As you read this review, ask yourself the following questions:

- What do I know about the subject?
- What is the writer's attitude toward the subject?
- What information or reasons does the writer provide to back up his opinions?
- What is my evaluation of his opinions?

Literary Focus
Understand critical essays.

Reading Skills
Evaluate a writer's judgements.

Vocabulary Skills
Clarify word meanings.

VOCABULARY DEVELOPMENT

PREVIEW SELECTION VOCABULARY

The following words appear in "Tavis Smiley: shares life lessons in new book 'What I Know For Sure.'" Look them over before you begin the selection.

dysfunction (dis′fuŋk′shən) *n.:* abnormal condition, trait, activity, or operation.

School authorities believe that a ***dysfunction*** *in the family—perhaps an unloving parent—is the cause of the child's depression.*

empower (em·pou′ər) *v.:* give official authority to; give legal power to; give faculties or abilities to.

His determination to finish the race ***empowered*** *the runner to continue despite his injury.*

cathartic (kə·thär′·tik) *adj.:* of, related to, or having the effect of cleansing or purifying.

Walking in the fresh air had the ***cathartic*** *effect of freeing her mind of the troubles that beset her family.*

catalyst (kat′ə·list′) *n.:* an agent that provokes or speeds significant change or action.

The luscious pastries displayed in the bakery window were the ***catalyst*** *that enticed us into the store.*

zeal (zēl) *n.:* ardent desire; impassioned eagerness; fervor; enthusiasm.

No one is more passionate about the welfare of our congregation than our pastor; his ***zeal*** *to help those in need is boundless.*

CLARIFY WORD MEANINGS

You have learned that the **context** in which an unfamiliar word appears often provides clues to its meaning. Writers sometimes use a **definition**, a **restatement**, a **synonym**, or an **example** near the word that helps to explain its meaning. Note, for example, the following sentence from the beginning of "Tavis Smiley: shares life lessons in new book 'What I Know For Sure'":

> "You can always count on Tavis Smiley to keep it real and tell it like it is."

If you weren't certain what Clarence Waldron means when he uses the expression "keep it real," the words that follow it would help you clarify its meaning, The expression "tell it like it is" explains the meaning of "keep it real."

As you read this critical essay, look at the context to help you determine the meaning of any unfamiliar words.

INTERPRET

What adjectives would you use to describe Waldron's characterization of Smiley's personality?

EVALUATE

Do you think Waldron admires Smiley? Why or why not?

PREDICT

In lines 22–23, it is clear that Smiley didn't want to write the book. Make a prediction about the reasons for his hesitation. Check your prediction as you continue to read.

Tavis Smiley: shares life lessons in new book 'What I Know For Sure'

by Clarence Waldron

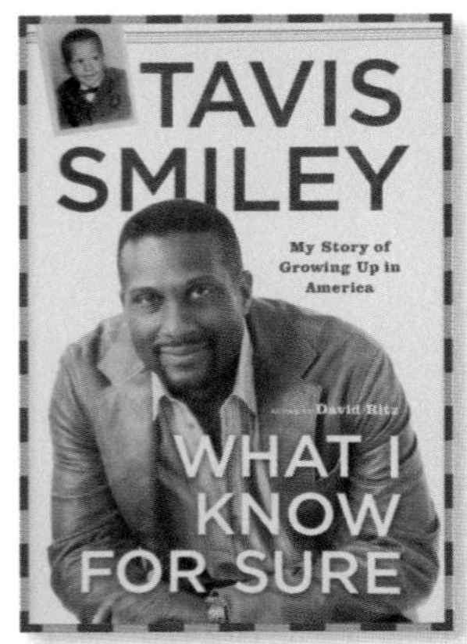

©The Doubleday Broadway Publishing Group, a Division of Random House, Inc., New York. Jacket photography by Kevin Foley

You can always count on Tavis Smiley to keep it real and tell it like it is. And that's what he does in his new book, *What I Know For Sure: My Story of Growing Up in America* (Doubleday, $21.95), his memoir of poverty, pain and ultimate triumph.

He talks candidly about his childhood, growing up poor and one of 10 children in a trailer in rural Indiana. He also opens up and reveals how his father once beat him and his sister with an electrical cord—a beating so brutal that he was hospitalized and then placed in a foster home. That beating forever changed his life, he writes.

Along the way, Smiley shares the life lessons he used to overcome hardships and made him one of the nation's leading TV and radio personalities and social advocates.

What I Know For Sure was written with author David Ritz, who has penned biographies with Aretha Franklin, Ray Charles, B.B. King and others.

Smiley admits that he didn't want to sit down and write his memoirs.

"Doubleday, my publisher, has been asking me to do this for five years and I kept telling them no. I didn't want to relive some of the painful parts of my life. Once you get through it, you don't want to relive it. I also felt that everybody has a story and I don't know a single Black family anywhere that does not have **dysfunction** in it. And finally, I am still relatively young, too young to write an autobiography."

But it was his life-calling commitment to help and uplift others that convinced him to share his story.

"I agreed to do it because my work is about enlightening, encouraging and empowering people, and I felt it could be helpful and could **empower** other people."

Smiley, 42, is the host of "Tavis Smiley" show on PBS and his radio show, "The Tavis Smiley Show from PRI." He is the first American to simultaneously host signature talk shows on both public television and public radio. He's been a commentator on "The Tom Joyner Morning Show" for 10 years. He's also celebrating his 15th year in the media at a major gala at the Museum of Television and Radio in Beverly Hills next month.

He is the author of nine best-sellers, including *Keeping the Faith, How To Make Black America Better* and *Never Mind Success . . . Go For Greatness!* He edited and wrote the introduction to *The Covenant with Black America*, which quickly rose to No. 1 spot on the *New York Times* bestseller list earlier this year.

In *What I Know For Sure*, he writes how his life changed when, in seventh grade, he was brutally beaten by his father. He and [his] sister were sent to separate foster homes after the state authorities learned of the beatings. It also made the local media.

"In the end, Phyllis was sent away to live in a White foster home . . . she was so scarred by what had happened that she never went back to the trailer (the Smiley home)," he writes.

VOCABULARY

dysfunction (dis'fuŋk'shən) *n.:* abnormal condition, trait, activity, or operation.

empower (em·pou'ər) *v.:* give official authority to; give legal power to; give faculties or abilities to.

ANALYZE

What does Smiley hope to accomplish by publishing his experiences? Do you think Waldron is sympathetic to this goal?

LITERARY FOCUS

Why do you think Waldron lists Smiley's professional achievements starting in line 36?

“Ironically I was assigned to a foster home of an elderly Black preacher and his wife who lived in a trailer on the opposite end of our trailer park.” Smiley eventually was sent back to live with his family after several months.

Smiley tells *Jet* how difficult it was to look back on the tragic beating that ripped his family apart. “I cried all through the conversation with David Ritz. It was painful, but in some ways it was therapeutic and **cathartic.**”

He admits that writing about the beating incident has caused some pain for his family. “It has caused some tension in my own family. My father did the beating, my sister was beaten as was I, and my mother didn’t stop it. Each of us has some difficulty in putting our business out in that way. They all read the book. Everyone gave me their permission and cooperation to talk about it. But once you see it in print it is another thing. But everybody understands that in the end, if we can empower other lives by the sharing of the story, then it is worth it.”

He says what he learned from that chapter of his life is that “you never close on those moments . . . you find a way to navigate through it and live with it. It was the defining moment that set me on the path of using every bit of skill, energy, passion that I can muster to turn my life into something meaningful. That moment was the **catalyst** that got me moving at age 13, and I’m still moving today.”

He notes, “It broke my sister’s spirit. She never came back. She has lived a life of pain and poverty and I have been blessed beyond measure. But that all started on how we processed that event. She allowed it to break her spirit. For me, it empowered me to say to myself and to my community, ‘I will not be defined

WORD STUDY

Explain in your own words the meaning of the expression *putting our business out* in line 67.

CAUSE & EFFECT

What effect did Smiley’s traumatic childhood experience have on him as described in lines 72–78?

VOCABULARY

cathartic (kə·thär′·tik) *adj.:* of, related to, or having the effect of cleansing or purifying.

catalyst (kat′ə·list′) *n.:* an agent that provokes or speeds significant change or action.

by this moment. I'm going to rise up here like a phoenix from the ashes[1] and make something of myself. When we raise Tavis' name in the future, it is not going to be about a beating, his father getting arrested, about it tearing his family apart, about him going into the hospital. That is not going to be the subject when my name is raised. We're going to talk about something else, 'like I saw you in *Jet* last week,'" he laughs.

Another life lesson he shares in the book is "love wins." "That's powerful because the story of Black people is a love story. We've come to love this country in spite of, not because of. What I know is whatever the dysfunction, whatever the setback, whatever the challenge, whoever the person. What matters is how deeply you love."

Smiley also teaches through his life story that while you can choose your friends, you can't choose your family. "I've learned that the three things that matter most in life I call the three Fs—faith, family and friends. You can't choose your family even when you have family members who are trifling."

He also recalls his triumphs at Indiana University and the people who helped him get admitted to the college and the financial aid he needed. "No one in this life gets ahead without the help of a lot of other people," he writes. He also recalls how he started his career as an aide to the late Los Angeles Mayor Tom Bradley, his rise to TV fame on BET and the highly publicized firing from the cable network.

"I've learned that when you are walking in your purpose, when you know what your vocation is, what your calling is, you must pursue that with relentless **zeal** and vigor. No one person, place or thing determines your success. When you are doing what you

1. **phoenix from the ashes:** a mythological bird that sets itself on fire after a long life and then rises from the ashes to live again.

COMPARE & CONTRAST

How did Smiley's sister's reaction to the family crisis differ from his?

INTERPRET

What do you think Smiley means when he says about fellow African Americans in line 93, "We've come to love this country in spite of, not because of"?

VOCABULARY

zeal (zēl) *n.:* ardent desire; impassioned eagerness; fervor; enthusiasm.

DRAW CONCLUSIONS

Why do you think Waldron includes quotations from prominent and respected black leaders?

CONNECT

How did you react to the opinions expressed in this review?

are supposed to do, you concentrate on perfecting your passion; the rest takes care of itself. In my case, there's no rule, there's no law that says my work must be done at BET or NPR. You do the work where you have the opportunity to do the work. And when that opportunity passes, you move on. The thing is, 'Are you committed to your craft?'"

His colleagues and friends describe his amazing appeal and commitment to empowering Black people.

Princeton University scholar Dr. Cornel West read *What I Know For Sure* and told *Jet:* "It's an instant classic by a historical figure still in his early 40s." He adds, "He's my brother. I've known him for over 20 years. I've seen him soar like an eagle. He's an exemplary figure when it comes to service to Black people and love of Black people."

Henry Louis Gates, director of the W.E.B. DuBois Institute at Harvard said: "He's reaching people emotionally and intellectually with a level of discourse that does not talk down to people. He's so compelling and so popular. If DuBois has two descendants, Tavis Smiley is the journalist-activist and Cornel West is the scholar."

Asked why he connects so well with the public, especially with Blacks, Smiley notes: "That's a question that you'll have to ask Black people. But I hope that the answer would be that they know that I love them. And that it pains me to see Black people living beneath their privilege. I thank God for the public support and try to keep my head down and stay focused on the work. I always try to enlighten, encourage and empower people."

MEET THE WRITER

Clarence Waldron is the senior staff editor for *Jet*, a weekly magazine devoted to African American issues. His responsibilities include writing and editing feature articles and training *Jet* writers. Waldron also teaches graduate journalism students at Northwestern University.

SKILLS PRACTICE

Tavis Smiley: shares life lessons in new book 'What I Know For Sure'

EVALUATING A WRITER'S JUDGMENTS CHART

The chart below lists questions about the critical essay you have just read. Use the right-hand column to answer these questions.

QUESTION	RESPONSE
What is the subject of Waldron's review, and what do I know about the subject?	
What is Waldron's attitude toward the subject?	
What information or reasons does he provide to back up his opinions about the subject?	
What is my evaluation of his opinions?	

Reading Skills
Evaluate a writer's judgements.

Tavis Smiley: shares life lessons in new book 'What I Know For Sure'

WORD BOX

dysfunction
empowered
cathartic
catalyst
zeal

VOCABULARY AND COMPREHENSION

A. Vocabulary in Context Complete each sentence with the correct vocabulary word from the Word Box.

1. The peace and tranquility that one can achieve through daily meditation is a truly ______________________ experience.

2. The relentless protests of the neighborhood residents served as a ______________________ in prodding the city council to approve repairs for the street.

3. Officials are convinced that the production slowdown is due to a ______________________ in the work relationships among the assembly-line crew.

4. The ______________________ with which the accomplished student pursues her studies is undeniable proof of her love for learning.

5. The constant encouragement of my coach ______________________ me to give my all at each practice session.

B. Reading Comprehension Answer each question below.

6. What persuaded Smiley to write about his own life experiences?

____

____

____

7. How does Tavis Smiley feel about his work? What does he think people should do if they know their vocation?

____

____

____

____

Vocabulary Skills
Clarify word meanings.

BEFORE YOU READ

Online Extra: A Talk with Oprah Winfrey

from Business Week, *November 29, 2004*

Talk-show host Oprah Winfrey discusses her commitment to funding global education projects in this online interview.

LITERARY FOCUS: INTERVIEW

An **interview** is a meeting in which information is exchanged. It is usually conducted face to face between two people, the person seeking information (interviewer) and the person providing the information (interviewee). Reporters, magazine writers, and radio or television commentators routinely conduct interviews to acquire information. Such interviews usually focus on individuals who are prominent in current events—elected officials, entertainers, professional athletes, health and safety officials, and others—and are intended to provide information about the interviewee, his or her work or activities, or his or her views on an issue or event.

A good interview focuses on the topic or issue to be discussed and includes a lead-in question that allows the interviewee to provide background information, follow-up questions that build on the interviewee's responses and amplify the topic, and a closing question that allows the interviewee to offer a final thought or observation. As you read "Online Extra: A Talk with Oprah Winfrey," look for elements of a good interview.

READING SKILLS: EVALUATING WEB SOURCES

The Internet can be a valuable research tool, providing access to a wide variety of Web sites worldwide, including government agencies, universities, libraries, online reference sources, data retrieval services, and commercial publications. When you use the Internet for a research project, it is important to **evaluate the web sources** in order to determine the reliability of the information by using questions such as the following:

- Is the sponsor of the Web site reputable—a recognized credible source?
- Is it regarded as an authority on the topic you are researching?
- Can you distinguish factual information on the Web site from matters of opinion, advertisements, or promotions?

The interview you are about to read first appeared online on a Web site sponsored by *Business Week* magazine. After you have read the interview, reflect on the questions above to help you evaluate the web source.

Literary Focus Understand the structure of interviews.

Reading Skills Evaluate web sources.

Vocabulary Skills Understand roots and affixes.

VOCABULARY DEVELOPMENT

PREVIEW SELECTION VOCABULARY

The following words appear in "Online Extra: A Talk with Oprah Winfrey." Look them over before you begin the selection.

philanthropy (fə·lan′thrə·pē) *n.:* goodwill towards one's fellow man expressed through active efforts to promote human welfare; humanitarianism.

Because our grandfather lives on a fixed income, he concentrates his ***philanthropy*** *on doing volunteer work rather than on funding the efforts of others.*

siblings (sib′liŋz) *n.:* persons who have the same parents or one common parent.

The strict parents impose the same curfew on all of their children, despite the fact that the ***siblings*** *are several years apart in age.*

globally (glō′bəl·lē) *adv.:* of, relating to, or involving the whole world; worldwide.

Our class is monitoring environmental crises ***globally****, tracking major industrial polluters in every corner of the world.*

UNDERSTANDING ROOTS AND AFFIXES

In the interview you are about to read, Oprah Winfrey says that the memory of Christmas gifts given to her by a group of nuns inspired her to fund an education project. The word *inspire* is composed of the prefix *in-* meaning "into" and the root *spire*, which comes from the Latin word *spirare* meaning "to breathe." Combined, the prefix and root mean "to breathe into," which suggests the meaning of *inspire:* "to put thought, feeling, or life into; to influence."

Understanding the root meaning of one word can often help you understand related words. Words related to the Latin root *spirare* include *aspire, conspire, inspiration, perspire, spirit,* and *spiritual*. Can you think of others?

As you read "Online Extra: A Talk with Oprah Winfrey," try analyzing the structure of any unfamiliar word you encounter to see if its parts provide you with clues to the word's meaning.

Online Extra: A Talk with Oprah Winfrey

The media mogul explains a key focus of her charity work: "Education is freedom. It provides the tools to affect one's own destiny."

from Business Week, *November 29, 2004*

Oprah Winfrey is the first African-American philanthropist to make the *BusinessWeek* Top 50 list. BW's Michelle Conlin recently asked Oprah to tell us a bit about her commitment to charity. Edited excerpts of their conversation follow:

Oprah and children benefiting from ChristmasKindness South Africa 2002. © AP IMAGES/Benny Gool

Q: Did you have a role model as a philanthropist growing up — someone who gave in perhaps even the tiniest of ways but who was instrumental in demonstrating the virtue of charity?

A: So many things in life inspire **philanthropy,** such as your faith in humanity and your belief in the human spirit to overcome. As far as a role model, I'd say there were moments with generous people that stand out for me. I will never forget when I was about 12, and my mother told my **siblings** and me that we would not be receiving Christmas gifts because there wasn't enough money.

VOCABULARY

philanthropy (fə·lan′thrə·pē) *n.:* goodwill towards one's fellow man expressed through active efforts to promote human welfare; humanitarianism.

siblings (sib′liŋz) *n.:* persons who have the same parent or one common parent.

EVALUATE

What kinds of articles would you expect to find in *BusinessWeek's* magazine and on their Web site?

LITERARY FOCUS

What purpose does the question on this page serve?

I remember at the time that I felt sad and thought: "What would I say when the other kids asked what I had gotten?" Just when I started to accept that there would not be a Christmas that year, three nuns showed up at our house with gifts for us. There was a turkey, a fruit basket, and some games, and for me, there was a doll.

I felt such a sense of relief that I would no longer have to be embarrassed when I returned to school. I remember feeling that I mattered enough to these nuns — who I had never met and to this day still don't know their names — and what it meant that they had remembered me.

My memory of the nuns' generosity that Christmas is what inspired me to create ChristmasKindness South Africa 2002 — an initiative that included visits to orphanages and rural schools in South Africa where 50,000 children received gifts of food, clothing, athletic shoes, school supplies, books, and toys.

Q: Do you foresee your philanthropy continuing to focus on kids, women, and education?

A: My foundation will continue to focus primarily on funding education projects **globally.** I believe that education is freedom. It provides the tools to affect one's own destiny. My gifts are more focused and directed toward making immediate change.

Right now, the single biggest project my foundation is working on is building The Oprah Winfrey Leadership Academy for Girls South Africa, which will cost somewhere in the neighborhood of $20 million and will educate close to 5,000 girls in a 10-year period. It's my vision that this academy will help to develop the future leaders of South Africa and be a source of pride for South Africans for generations to come.

VOCABULARY

globally (glōbəl·lē) *adv.:* of, relating to, or involving the whole world; worldwide.

CAUSE & EFFECT

What inspired Oprah to create ChristmasKindness South Africa 2002 (line 27)?

LITERARY FOCUS

Explain why the questions on this page are good follow-up questions.

Oprah at the opening of The Oprah Winfrey Leadership Academy for Girls in South Africa, 2007.
© Kim Ludbrook/CORBIS

Q: Do you foresee more of your philanthropy going global?

A: From the start, The Oprah Winfrey Foundation has been committed to empowering women, children, and families by furthering education and welfare for low-opportunity communities around the world. Through my Foundation, we have awarded hundreds of grants to organizations that carry out this vision. It provides teacher education and scholarships to students who are determined to use their education to give back to their communities in the U.S. and abroad. [It] contributes school supplies and builds schools to educate thousands of underserved children internationally.

EXTEND

With a partner do some research at the library or on the Internet. Find out how people can apply for a grant from The Oprah Winfrey Foundation and then determine whether any organizations or schools in your area have received grant monies from the Foundation. Write notes about your findings on the lines below or on another sheet of paper. Share your information in a class discussion.

ANALYZE

What purpose(s) might the first question on this page serve?

LITERARY FOCUS

What purpose does the last question serve?

EVALUATE

How would you rate the reliability of the web source? Why?

Q: One of the celebrity magazines claimed that you intend to bequest your fortune after you pass on. Is this true, or do you have a plan to give most of your wealth away during your lifetime?

A: You'll just have to wait and see.

Q: What has been more meaningful—making your money or giving it away?

A: Making other people happy is what brings me happiness. I have a blessed life, and I have always shared my life's gifts with others. I believe that to whom much is given, much is expected. So, I will continue to use my voice and my life as a **catalyst** for change, inspiring and encouraging people to help make a difference in the lives of others. I'm fortunate that the work I do in my life becomes more meaningful with every experience.

BACKGROUND

Oprah Winfrey (1954–) was born in Kosciusko, Mississippi. While in high school she became a reporter on a local radio station. After college, she moved to Baltimore and worked as a TV news reporter, then host for a morning program. In 1984 she moved to Chicago to host *A.M. Chicago*. Within a year her show was top rated, and in 1985 it became the *Oprah Winfrey Show*. Winfrey has written several books and discusses books on her show. She encourages her readers and viewers to make their dreams come true, "You can't accomplish anything worthwhile if you inhibit yourself. If life teaches you nothing else, know this for sure: When you get the chance, *go for it!*"

SKILLS PRACTICE

Online Extra: A Talk with Oprah Winfrey

EVALUATING AN INTERVIEW CHART

The structure of a good interview can be thought of as similar to the structure of a well-written essay. The outline shown in the left column of the chart below reflects this similarity. Use the middle column to describe the information you learn in each part of the interview, including the nature of the questions asked and a brief summary of the responses. In the last column, evaluate the effectiveness of each part.

OUTLINE	INFORMATION PROVIDED	MY EVALUATION
I. Introduction A. Background B. Purpose Statement		
II. Body A. First Question B. Second Question C. Third Question D. Fourth Question		
III. Conclusion Last Question		

Literary Focus
Analyze an interview.

WORD BOX

siblings

globally

philanthropic

Online Extra: A Talk with Oprah Winfrey

VOCABULARY AND COMPREHENSION

A. Root Words and Affixes Write the correct word from the Word Box on the line next to its root and affix. Beneath each item, write the meaning of the Word Box word.

1. *philos* "loving" + *anthropos* "man" ______________________
   Meaning: ______________________

2. *sibb–* "a relation" + *–ling* "little" ______________________
   Meaning: ______________________

3. *globus* "ball, sphere" + *–al* (adjective-forming suffix) + *–ly* (adverb-forming suffix) ______________________
   Meaning: ______________________

B. Reading Comprehension Answer each question below.

4. What inspired Oprah to create ChristmasKindness South Africa 2002?

____

____

____

5. What does Oprah mean when she says that her philanthropic work is global in nature?

____

____

____

6. In her response to the last question, what advice from the Bible does Oprah refer to in order to help explain her motivation for doing philanthropic work? Why do you think Oprah finds this advice meaningful?

____

____

____

____

____

____

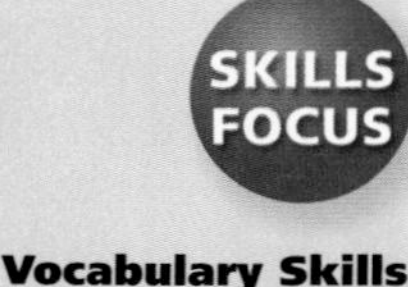

Vocabulary Skills
Recognize roots and affixes.

BEFORE YOU READ

I Have a Dream

by Martin Luther King, Jr.

Martin Luther King Jr.

by Gwendolyn Brooks

This speech by Martin Luther King, Jr., was delivered to a crowd of more than 200,000 civil rights protesters gathered for the March On Washington on August 28, 1963. The poem by Gwendolyn Brooks that follows pays tribute to King's life and legacy.

LITERARY FOCUS: TECHNIQUES OF EMPHASIS

To **emphasize** is to bring out the importance of something. Speakers have many ways to emphasize ideas. They can change their volume or tone. They can insert gestures. They can pause before or after a phrase or sentence. They can even repeat parts of their speech.

Martin Luther King, Jr., was a skilled orator. But, he did not just rely on his speaking ability to make his words effective. Rather, he also incorporated **techniques** such as repetition and parallelism into his speeches to help bring out important ideas. Repetition is repeating key words and phrases. Parallelism involves using words, phrases, clauses, or sentences that are similar in structure. Read this quote from "I Have a Dream":

> ". . . where they will not be judged by the color of their skin but by the content of their character."

Notice how the parallel structure helps to focus your attention on the distinction that King wishes to make.

As you read "I Have a Dream," look for the ideas emphasized by the use of both techniques.

Literary Focus Understand techniques of emphasis.

Reading Skills Read aloud for effect.

Vocabulary Skills Use context clues.

READING SKILLS: READING ALOUD FOR EFFECT

The speech and the poem in this group are both designed to be read aloud. By doing so, you can hear the devices that the authors use to emphasize important ideas. You can also hear the expression that they want to convey.

Before you read aloud, first read the passage silently. Practice words that might be difficult to pronounce. Note the placement of the punctuation. Then read it aloud once or twice to help you set your pace.

VOCABULARY DEVELOPMENT

PREVIEW SELECTION VOCABULARY

The following words appear in "I Have a Dream." Look them over before you begin to read.

prosperity (prä·sper′ə·tē) *n.:* condition of being financially well-off.

__Prosperity__ seems to be out of the grasp of many groups in society.

exile (eks′īl′) *n.:* outcast.

His status was that of an __exile__; he was forced to watch others enjoy opportunities that he could not.

legitimate (lə·jit′ə·mət) *adj.:* reasonable.

Those African Americans who were denied the right to vote had a __legitimate__ complaint.

creed (krēd) *n.:* a system of beliefs or principles.

Fortunately, they all shared the same __creed__, which enabled them to forge a strong government.

USING CONTEXT CLUES

Many words have multiple meanings. You may know all of the meanings. However, sometimes, the only way to determine which one the author intended is to read the phrases, clauses, or sentences around the word. Take the word *legitimate* from the list above, for example. Read the sentence in which it appears in "I Have a Dream":

> "This sweltering summer of the Negro's legitimate discontent will not pass . . ."

The word has several meanings, some of which might work in this sentence. It can mean "lawful" or "genuine" or "reasonable." So to decide, you look closely at the words around *legitimate.* You can eliminate "lawful or legal" since that definitely does not fit the context. Further examination helps you to figure out that the author most likely means it in the sense of "reasonable." In other words, the discontent is justified and logical.

As you read the speech and the poem, be aware of multiple-meaning words and use their context to help you define them correctly.

I Have a Dream

by Martin Luther King, Jr.

I am happy to join with you today in what will go down in history as the greatest demonstration for freedom in the history of our nation.

Five score years ago, a great American, in whose symbolic shadow we stand today, signed the Emancipation Proclamation. This momentous decree came as a great beacon light of hope to millions of Negro slaves, who had been seared in the flames of withering injustice. It came as a joyous daybreak to end the long night of their captivity. But one hundred years later, the Negro still is not free. One hundred years later, the life of the Negro is still sadly crippled by the manacles of segregation and the chains of discrimination.

One hundred years later, the Negro lives on a lonely island of poverty in the midst of a vast ocean of material **prosperity.** One hundred years later, the Negro is still languished in the corners of American society and finds himself an **exile** in his own land. So we've come here today to dramatize a shameful condition.

In a sense we have come to our nation's capital to cash a check. When the architects of our republic wrote the magnificent words of the Constitution and the Declaration of Independence, they were signing a promissory note[1] to which every American was to fall heir.

This note was a promise that all men, yes, black men as well as white men, would be guaranteed the unalienable[2] rights of life, liberty, and the pursuit of happiness.

It is obvious today that America has defaulted on this promissory note insofar as her citizens of color are concerned. Instead of honoring this sacred obligation, America has given the

1. **promissory note:** a written pledge to pay money at a specified time.
2. **unalienable** (un·āl′yən·ə·bəl) *adj.:* that cannot be taken away.

COMPARE & CONTRAST

Re-read lines 4–8. To what does King compare the Emancipation Proclamation?

LITERARY FOCUS

Why does King repeat "one hundred years later" in lines 13–18?

VOCABULARY

prosperity (prä·sper′ə·tē) *n.:* condition of being financially well-off.

exile (eks′īl) *n.:* outcast.

INTERPRET

What point is King making through the banking metaphor developed in lines 32–36?

ANALYZE

Read lines 40–45 aloud. How does the parallelism affect your reading?

VOCABULARY

legitimate (lə·jit′ə·mət) *adj.:* reasonable.

Martin Luther King, Jr., during his address to the crowd at the March on Washington.
©Francis Miller/TimeLife Pictures/Getty Images

Negro people a bad check; a check which has come back marked "insufficient funds."

But we refuse to believe that the bank of justice is bankrupt. We refuse to believe that there are insufficient funds in the great vaults of opportunity of this nation. So we have come to cash this check, a check that will give us upon demand the riches of freedom and the security of justice.

We have also come to this hallowed spot to remind America of the fierce urgency of Now. This is no time to engage in the luxury of cooling off or to take the tranquilizing drug of gradualism. Now is the time to make real the promises of democracy. Now is the time to rise from the dark and desolate valley of segregation to the sunlit path of racial justice. Now is the time to lift our nation from the quicksands of racial injustice to the solid rock of brotherhood. Now is the time to make justice a reality for all of God's children.

It would be fatal for the nation to overlook the urgency of the moment. This sweltering summer of the Negro's **legitimate** discontent will not pass until there is an invigorating autumn of freedom and equality. Nineteen sixty-three is not an end but a beginning. Those who hope that the Negro needed to blow off steam and will now be content will have a rude awakening if the nation returns to business as usual.

There will be neither rest nor tranquility in America until the Negro is granted his citizenship rights. The whirlwinds of revolt will continue to shake the foundations of our nation until the bright day of justice emerges.

But there is something that I must say to my people who stand on the warm threshold which leads into the palace of justice. In the process of gaining our rightful place we must not be guilty of wrongful deeds.

Let us not seek to satisfy our thirst for freedom by drinking from the cup of bitterness and hatred. We must ever conduct our struggle on the high plane of dignity and discipline. We must not allow our creative protest to degenerate into physical violence. Again and again we must rise to the majestic heights of meeting physical force with soul force.

The marvelous new militancy which has engulfed the Negro community must not lead us to a distrust of all white people, for many of our white brothers, as evidenced by their presence here today, have come to realize that their destiny is tied up with our destiny. They have come to realize that their freedom is inextricably bound to our freedom. We cannot walk alone.

And as we walk, we must make the pledge that we shall always march ahead. We cannot turn back. There are those who are asking the devotees of civil rights, "When will you be satisfied?" We can never be satisfied as long as the Negro is the victim of the unspeakable horrors of police brutality.

We can never be satisfied as long as our bodies, heavy with the fatigue of travel, cannot gain lodging in the motels of the highways and the hotels of the cities. We cannot be satisfied as long as a Negro in Mississippi cannot vote and a Negro in New York believes he has nothing for which to vote.

No, no, we are not satisfied and we will not be satisfied until justice rolls down like waters and righteousness like a mighty stream.

INTERPRET

In lines 46–56, what does King say will result if "the nation returns to business as usual"?

____

____

____

____

ANALYZE

What is the warning that King issues to his audience in lines 61–66? Why?

____

____

____

____

____

INTERPRET

Re-read lines 78–85. What are the goals of the members of the movement?

____

____

____

____

____

EVALUATE

In lines 86–92, how does King emphasize the sacrifices that his audience has had to endure in their fight to gain civil rights?

DRAW CONCLUSIONS

Take turns reading lines 101–126 aloud with a partner. Discuss the tone and impact of this section of the speech and the devices that King uses to create the effect.

VOCABULARY

creed (krēd) *n.:* a system of beliefs or principles.

I am not unmindful that some of you have come here out of great trials and tribulations. Some of you have come fresh from narrow jail cells. Some of you have come from areas where your quest for freedom left you battered by the storms of persecution and staggered by the winds of police brutality. You have been the veterans of creative suffering. Continue to work with the faith that unearned suffering is redemptive.

Go back to Mississippi, go back to Alabama, go back to South Carolina, go back to Georgia, go back to Louisiana, go back to the slums and ghettos of our northern cities, knowing that somehow this situation can and will be changed.

Let us not wallow in the valley of despair, I say to you today, my friends, so even though we face the difficulties of today and tomorrow. I still have a dream. It is a dream deeply rooted in the American dream.

I have a dream that one day this nation will rise up and live out the true meaning of its **creed**—we hold these truths to be self-evident that all men are created equal.

I have a dream that one day on the red hills of Georgia the sons of former slaves and the sons of former slave owners will be able to sit down together at the table of brotherhood.

I have a dream that one day even the state of Mississippi, a state sweltering with the heat of injustice, sweltering with the heat of oppression, will be transformed into an oasis of freedom and justice.

I have a dream that my four little children will one day live in a nation where they will not be judged by the color of their skin but by the content of their character.

I have a dream today.

I have a dream that one day, down in Alabama, with its vicious racists, with its governor[3] having his lips dripping with

3. **Alabama . . . governor:** Governor Wallace, who was a segregationist. In 1963, he stood in the doorway of the University of Alabama to block the enrollment of black students.

the words of interposition[4] and nullification;[5] one day right down in Alabama little black boys and black girls will be able to join hands with little white boys and white girls as sisters and brothers.

I have a dream today.

I have a dream that one day every valley shall be exalted, and every hill and mountain shall be made low, the rough places will be made plain and the crooked places will be straight and the glory of the Lord shall be revealed and all flesh shall see it together.[6]

Martin Luther King, Jr., with his son, Dexter.
©Flip Schulke/CORBIS

LITERARY FOCUS

Note the parallelism in lines 118–120. How does this device add meaning to King's words in this part?

INFER

Why does King reference this quotation from the Bible in lines 122–126?

4. **interposition** (in′tər·pə·zish′ən) *n.:* the doctrine that a state may reject a federal order that it considers to be trespassing on its rights.
5. **nullification** (nul′ə·fi·kā′shən) *n.:* the refusal of a state to recognize or enforce a federal law that it considers a violation of its sovereignty.
6. **every valley . . . together:** Compare Isaiah 40:4–5: Every Valley shall be exalted, and every mountain and hill shall be made low: and the crooked shall be made straight, and the rough places plain: And the glory of the Lord shall be revealed, and all flesh shall see it together: for the mouth of the Lord hath spoken *it*.

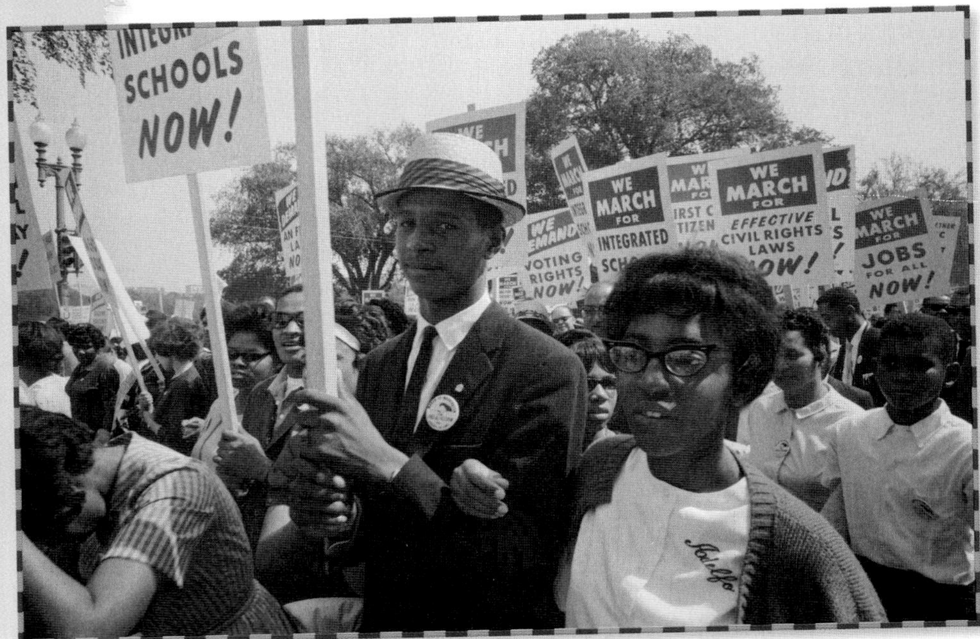

Protesters at the March on Washington.
©Wally McNamee/CORBIS

This is our hope. This is the faith that I will go back to the South with. With this faith we will be able to hew out of the mountain of despair a stone of hope. With this faith we will be able to transform the jangling discords of our nation into a beautiful symphony of brotherhood. With this faith we will be to work together, to pray together, to struggle together, to go to jail together, to stand up for freedom together, knowing that we will be free one day.

This will be the day, this will be the day when all of God's children will be able to sing with new meaning "My country 'tis of thee, sweet land of liberty, of thee I sing. Land where my fathers died, land of the Pilgrim's pride, from every mountainside, let freedom ring!" And if America is to be a great nation this must become true.

And so let freedom ring from the prodigious hilltops of New Hampshire.

Let freedom ring from the mighty mountains of New York.

Let freedom ring from the heightening Alleghenies of Pennsylvania.

Let freedom ring from the snow-capped Rockies of Colorado.

DRAW CONCLUSIONS

How does King want his listeners to feel when they hear lines 135–139?

GENERALIZE

Read lines 141–153 aloud to a partner. What is the tone of this passage? What techniques does King use to provide emphasis?

Let freedom ring from curvaceous peaks of California.

But not only that.

Let freedom ring from Stone Mountain of Georgia.

Let freedom ring from Lookout Mountain of Tennessee.

Let freedom ring from every hill and mole hill of Mississippi, from every mountainside, let freedom ring!

And when this happens, when we allow freedom to ring, when we let it ring from every village and every hamlet, from every state and every city, we will be able to speed up that day when all of God's children, black men and white men, Jews and Gentiles, Protestants and Catholics, will be able to join hands and sing in the words of the old Negro spiritual, "Free at last, free at last. Thank God Almighty, we are free at last."[7]

---

7. **"free at last":** The words "free at last" in this spiritual carry a double meaning. They refer to freedom from slavery as well as freedom from sin.

MEET THE WRITER

Martin Luther King, Jr., (1929–1968) became nationally known as the leader of a bus boycott protesting the arrest of Rosa Parks after she refused to give up her bus seat to a white man in Montgomery, Alabama in 1955. After the success of the boycott, King was elected president of the Southern Christian Leadership Conference. Its goals were to increase black voter registration in the South and to eliminate all forms of segregation. King led campaigns for voter registration and helped organize the massive march on Washington, D.C., in 1963.

King was born in Atlanta, Georgia, and nurtured in the Christian ideas of his father, a Baptist minister. He earned a PhD in theology from Boston University and was committed to the philosophy of nonviolent resistance, first learned from his Christian faith and then from the teachings of Mahatma Gandhi, a social reformer in India. Especially dedicated to King's cause were young people—even children—who endured attacks by dogs, firehoses, bombs, and club-wielding police. Images of these brutalities, broadcast by the media, stung the conscience of the nation and helped to defeat Southern segregation laws and encourage passage of the Civil Rights Act of 1964.

King's struggle for human dignity earned him many awards including the Nobel Peace Prize in 1964. King was assassinated in Memphis, Tennessee, on April 4, 1968. Robert Kennedy said, "Martin Luther King dedicated his life to love and to justice for his fellow human beings, and he died because of that effort." To honor his memory, King's birthday is now a national holiday.

CONNECT

Re-read the last paragraph. Do you think King's hope for the future has been realized? Why or why not?

NOTES

LITERARY FOCUS

What ideas does Brooks emphasize through alliteration and parallel structure?

ANALYZE

What ideas does the speaker convey through personification of Dream (lines 8–9) and Justice (lines 10–13)? How does this relate to the theme of the poem?

Martin Luther King Jr.

by Gwendolyn Brooks

A man went forth with gifts.

He was a prose poem.
He was a tragic grace.
He was a warm music.

He tried to heal the vivid volcanoes.
His ashes are
    reading the world.

His Dream still wishes to anoint°
    the barricades of faith and of control.

His word still burns the center of the sun,
    above the thousands and the
    hundred thousands.

The word was Justice. It was spoken.

So it shall be spoken.
So it shall be done.

---

8. anoint (ə·noint′) *v.:* to put oil on, often in a sacred ceremony.

©Bettmann/CORBIS

EXTEND

Find other poems about the civil rights movement. Compare and contrast their styles and themes. Draw a chart such as the one below (or a different one that you like). Record your observations on the chart. Then share your information in a class discussion.

Differences	Poem Titles	Similarities
________	1.	________
________	2.	________
________	3.	________
________	4.	________

NOTES

MEET THE WRITER

Gwendolyn Brooks (1917–2000), whose poetry earned her many honors and awards, was one of America's most imaginative and accomplished poets. Born in Topeka, Kansas, Brooks moved to Chicago at an early age and lived in the core of the city's black community. Brooks's first volume of poetry, *A Street in Bronzeville* (1945), depicts this experience. She said, "I wrote about what I saw and heard in the street. I lived in a small second-floor apartment at the corner, and I could look first on one side and then on the other. There was my material."

Brooks received the Pulitzer Prize for poetry in 1950 for *Annie Allen*. She was the first African American ever to be awarded this prize and also became the first black woman ever to be appointed Poetry Consultant to the Library of Congress. Throughout the 1950s, Brooks continued to write about the thousands of African Americans who had fled the rural South for Northern cities—only to discover that there was little difference between the two regions in terms of racism.

In her later work, Brooks began to change in response to the radical movements of the time. In 1967, she attended a conference of black writers at Fisk University, where she heard Amiri Baraka read. Of this experience she said, "I felt that something new was happening." Her poems became more political in content, more free in style, and more colloquial in language. She said, "If it hadn't been for . . . these young writers who influenced me, I wouldn't know what I know about this society. By associating with them I know who I am."

SKILLS PRACTICE

I Have a Dream • Martin Luther King Jr.

Literary Focus Analyze techniques of emphasis.

RHETORICAL DEVICE CHART

Give examples of repetition and parallelism that you find in Martin Luther King's speech. Explain what you think these devices contribute to his speech.

REPETITION	PARALLELISM

EFFECT

I Have a Dream •

Martin Luther King Jr.

VOCABULARY AND COMPREHENSION

A. Context Clues Read the definition of each word. Then use it in an original sentence that shows that meaning.

1. creed: a system of beliefs.

   Sentence: ________________________________

2. prosperity: condition of being financially well-off.

   Sentence: ________________________________

3. legitimate: reasonable.

   Sentence: ________________________________

4. exile: outcast.

   Sentence: ________________________________

B. Reading Comprehension Answer each question below.

5. Why does King say that America has "defaulted on this promissory note insofar as her citizens of color are concerned"?

   ____

   ____

6. What is King's dream?

   ____

   ____

7. What is the poet's purpose in writing "Martin Luther King Jr."?

   ____

   ____

8. On a separate sheet of paper, write an essay that compares and contrasts the messages and tone of "I Have a Dream" and "Martin Luther King Jr."

Vocabulary Skills
Use context clues.

BEFORE YOU READ

The Dancing Mind

by Toni Morrison

Toni Morrison (1931–) is an award-winning writer whose work is widely read. In this speech, she explores the power of books from the perspectives of both readers and writers.

LITERARY FOCUS: ANALYZING TEXT STRUCTURE

Analyzing text structure means examining how a text is organized. Understanding the structure helps you to understand a text. Common structures include chronology, or sequence of events; main idea and details; cause and effect; problem and solution; and comparison and contrast. A text may have more than one structure—for example, an essay that mainly uses chronology may also include a section with cause-effect structure. Consider these points as you read "The Dancing Mind."

- Look for the topic sentence or main idea of each paragraph. Notice how the details in that paragraph support its subject. For example, Morrison begins one paragraph, "Both of these stories are comments on the contemporary reading/writing life," and then explores this statement with details.
- Compare the subject of a paragraph with the subjects of the paragraphs before and after it. Ask yourself whether the topics follow in sequence, by cause and effect, or another overall structure.
- Analyzing text structure helps you to comprehend what the author considers most important. For this reason, text structure is tied closely to the author's purpose. Morrison states her purpose directly, as is common in a speech. As you read, think about her purpose for writing and what text structure might best serve that purpose.

Literary Focus Analyze text structure.

Reading Skills Understand anecdotes.

Vocabulary Skills Understand figurative language.

READING SKILLS: UNDERSTANDING ANECDOTES

An **anecdote** is a brief, true story that is used to illustrate an idea or express something noteworthy about a person, place, or thing. Anecdotes are used frequently in speeches and other oral presentations. They bring a subject to life and help to engage listeners.

- As you read each anecdote in this speech, consider what the anecdote reveals about the person at its center. Ask yourself: What did I learn about this person? What larger meaning might be gained from his or her experience? How does this meaning relate to Morrison's purpose?

VOCABULARY DEVELOPMENT

PREVIEW SELECTION VOCABULARY

The following words appear in "The Dancing Mind." Look them over before you begin the selection.

status quo (stat′əs kwō′) *n.:* the state of things as they are now.

An oppressive government may ban books of criticism to try to preserve the ***status quo****.*

sinister (sin′is·tər) *adj.:* threatening; likely to cause harm.

The knowledge that even one book has been banned may feel ***sinister*** *to all writers.*

literate (lit′ər·it) *adj.:* knowledgeable and well-read.

He was a ***literate*** *person—he had many years of education and had read widely.*

satiate (sā′shē·āt′) *v.:* satisfy completely.

Like many readers, Morrison has never been able to ***satiate*** *her hunger for new ideas.*

expediency (ek·spē′dē·ən·sē) *n.:* concern for what may achieve a goal, rather than for what is fair or honest.

He rewrote the letter for the sake of ***expediency****, fearing the truth would be unacceptable.*

conglomerate (kən·gläm′ər·it) *n.:* a united group of companies or other associations.

The bookstore ***conglomerate*** *included more than three hundred stores and a popular Web site.*

UNDERSTANDING FIGURATIVE LANGUAGE

Metaphors, similes, symbols, and personification are all types of **figurative language**—words and phrases that are used in a nonliteral sense. Writers use figurative language to communicate with greater vividness and power. Toni Morrison's writing is so rich in figurative language that you will find it in every paragraph of this speech.

- Ask yourself what figurative language adds to the author's meaning. For example, rather than saying, "I need to offer my thoughts to another," Morrison writes, "I need to offer the fruits of my own imaginative intelligence to another." Consider what it might mean to compare thoughts with fruit. Fruit is a product of a natural growth process; it is a living thing; it is nourishing and may be considered pleasing.

Although you can't know exactly why Morrison chose this metaphor, you can discover what ideas it stirs in you. This is part of the power of figurative language.

The Dancing Mind

by Toni Morrison

VOCABULARY

status quo (stat′əs kwō′) *n.:* the state of things as they are now.

sinister (sin′is·tər) *adj.:* threatening; likely to cause harm.

LITERARY FOCUS

How do you think the second paragraph (lines 11–14) relates to the one that came before?

INFER

Read lines 22–42 and consider the graduate student's achievements. Why might reading for his own benefit be "the hardest thing he ever had to do" (line 38)?

There is a certain kind of peace that is not merely the absence of war. It is larger than that. The peace I am thinking of is not at the mercy of history's rule, nor is it a passive surrender to the **status quo.** The peace I am thinking of is the dance of an open mind when it engages another equally open one—an activity that occurs most naturally, most often in the reading/writing world we live in. Accessible as it is, this particular kind of peace warrants vigilance. The peril it faces comes not from the computers and information highways that raise alarm among book readers, but from unrecognized, more **sinister** quarters.

I want to tell two little stories—anecdotes really—that circle each other in my mind. They are disparate,[1] unrelated anecdotes with more to distinguish each one from the other than similarities, but they are connected for me in a way that I hope to make clear.

The first I heard third- or fourth-hand, and although I can't vouch for its accuracy, I do have personal knowledge of situations exactly like it. A student at a very very prestigious university said that it was in graduate school while working on his Ph.D. that he had to teach himself a skill he had never learned. He had grown up in an affluent[2] community with very concerned and caring parents. He said that his whole life had been filled with carefully selected activities: educational, cultural, athletic. Every waking hour was filled with events to enhance his life. Can you see him? Captain of his team. Member of the Theatre Club. A Latin Prize winner. Going on vacations designed for pleasure and meaningfulness; on fascinating and educational trips and tours; attending excellent camps along with equally

1. **disparate** (dis′pə·rət) *adj.:* fundamentally different.
2. **affluent** (af′lo͞o·ənt) *adj.:* wealthy.

highly motivated peers. He gets the best grades, is a permanent fixture on the honor roll, gets into several of the best universities, graduates, goes on to get a master's degree, and now is enrolled in a Ph.D. program at this first-rate university. And it is there that (at last, but fortunately) he discovers his disability: in all those years he had never learned to sit in a room by himself and read for four hours and have those four hours followed by another four without any companionship but his own mind. He said it was the hardest thing he ever had to do, but he taught himself, forced himself to be alone with a book he was not assigned to read, a book on which there was no test. He forced himself to be alone without the comfort or disturbance of telephone, radio, television. To his credit, he learned this habit, this skill, that once was part of any **literate** young person's life.

The second story involves a first-hand experience. I was in Strasbourg[3] attending a meeting of a group called the

Aspects of Negro Life: Song of the Towers, 1934, Aaron Douglas (1899–1979).
©Copyright Schomburg Center for Research in Black Culture, The New York Public Library/Art Resource, NY

3. **Strasbourg:** a city in northeast France.

CONNECT

Think of a time when you or someone you know about made a strong effort to face a personal shortcoming or learn a new skill, as the graduate student did (line 36–37). Then write a one-paragraph anecdote that recalls this experience and what was gained from it.

VOCABULARY

literate (lit'ər·it) *adj.:* knowledgeable and well-read.

ANALYZE

What emotions are suggested in the description of the woman crying (lines 54–57)?

INTERPRET

What does the metaphor "alien in his own company" (line 64) tell you about the graduate student? The word *alien* is used here to mean something foreign.

Parliament of Writers. It is an organization of writers committed to the aggressive rescue of persecuted writers. After one of the symposia,[4] just outside the doors of the hall, a woman approached me and asked if I knew anything about the contemporary literature of her country. I said no; I knew nothing of it. We talked a few minutes more. Earlier, while listening to her speak on a panel, I had been awestruck by her articulateness, the ease with which she moved among languages and literatures, her familiarity with histories of nations, histories of criticisms, histories of authors. She knew my work; I knew nothing of hers. We continued to talk, animatedly, and then, in the middle of it, she began to cry. No sobs, no heaving shoulders, just great tears rolling down her face. She did not wipe them away and she did not loosen her gaze. "You have to help us," she said. "You have to help us. They are shooting us down in the street." By "us" she meant women who wrote against the grain. "What can I do?" I asked her. She said, "I don't know, but you have to try. There isn't anybody else."

Both of those stories are comments on the contemporary reading/writing life. In one, a comfortable, young American, a "successfully" educated male, alien in his own company, stunned and hampered by the inadequacy of his fine education, resorts to autodidactic[5] strategies to move outside the surfeit[6] and bounty and excess and (I think) the terror of growing up vacuum-pressured in this country and to learn a very old-fashioned skill. In the other, a splendidly educated woman living in a suffocating regime writes in fear that death may very well be the consequence of doing what I do: as a woman to write and publish unpoliced narrative. The danger of both environments is striking. First, the danger to reading that our busied-up,

4. **symposia** (sim·pō′zē·ə) *n.:* meetings that include presentations on a particular topic.
5. **autodidactic** (ôtō·dī′daktik) *adj.:* self-taught.
6. **surfeit** (sʉr′fit) *n.:* an excessive amount.

education-as-horse-race, trophy-driven culture poses even to the entitled; second, the physical danger to writing suffered by persons with enviable educations who live in countries where the practice of modern art is illegal and subject to official vigilantism[7] and murder.

I have always doubted and disliked the therapeutic claims made on behalf of writing and writers. Writing never made me happy. Writing never made me suffer. I have had misfortunes small and large, yet all through them nothing could keep me from doing it. And nothing could **satiate** my appetite for others who did. What is so important about this craft that it dominates me and my colleagues? A craft that appears solitary but needs another for its completion. A craft that signals independence but relies totally on an industry. It is more than an urge to make sense or to make sense artfully or to believe it matters. It is more than a desire to watch other writers manage to refigure the world. I know now, more than I ever did (and I always on some level knew it), that I need that intimate, sustained surrender to the company of my

The Libraries are Appreciated, 1943, by Jacob Lawrence.
©Philadelphia Museum of Art/CORBIS

DRAW CONCLUSIONS

Re-read lines 72–78. Is "the danger of both environments" external or internal? Explain.

EVALUATE

Re-read lines 79–87. Does Morrison view being a writer as a choice? How does this support her idea that threats to the writing life are very serious?

VOCABULARY

satiate (sā′shē·āt′) *v.:* satisfy completely.

7. **vigilantism** (vij′ə·lan′tiz′əm) *n.:* the actions of those who take the law into their own hands; vigilantism is usually associated with violence.

mind while it touches another's—which is reading: what the graduate student taught himself. That I need to offer the fruits of my own imaginative intelligence to another without fear of anything more deadly than disdain—which is writing: what the woman writer fought a whole government to do.

The reader disabled by an absence of solitude; the writer imperiled by the absence of a hospitable community. Both stories fuse and underscore for me the seriousness of the industry whose sole purpose is the publication of writers for readers. It is a business, of course, in which there is feasting, and even some coin; there is drama and high, high spirits. There is celebration and anguish, there are flukes and errors in judgment; there is brilliance and unbridled ego. But that is the costume. Underneath the cut of bright and dazzling cloth, pulsing beneath the jewelry, the life of the book world is quite serious. Its real life is about creating and producing and distributing knowledge; about making it possible for the entitled as well as the dispossessed to experience one's own mind dancing with another's; about making sure that the environment in which this work is done is welcoming, supportive. It is making sure that no encroachment of private wealth, government control, or cultural **expediency** can interfere with what gets written or published. That no **conglomerate** or political wing uses its force to still inquiry or to reaffirm rule.

Securing that kind of peace—the peace of the dancing mind—is our work, and, as the woman in Strasbourg said, "There isn't anybody else."

Toni Morrison
November 1996

INTERPRET

Think about how Morrison describes the exchange of ideas that takes place through reading and writing (lines 89–96). In what ways is this like a dance?

ANALYZE

What does the metaphor of the costume (lines 104–106) contribute to your understanding of how Morrison views the publishing industry?

VOCABULARY

expediency (ek·spē′dē·ən·sē) *n.:* concern for what may achieve a goal rather than for what is fair or honest.

conglomerate (kən·gläm′ər·it) *n.:* a united group of companies or other associations.

©Deborah Feingold/CORBIS

MEET THE WRITER

Toni Morrison (1931–   ) was born in Lorain, Ohio, on the shores of Lake Erie. She says, "I am from the Midwest so I have a special affection for it. My beginnings are always there." Lorain is the setting for her first novel, *The Bluest Eye* (1969), which one critic called, "a novel of growing up young and black and female in America."

Morrison graduated from Howard and Cornell universities, taught college, and worked as an editor at Random House for many years before publishing her first book. She is currently an emeritus professor at Princeton University. Morrison is known mainly as a novelist but has also written drama, essays, music lyrics, and children's books.

Her most well-known novel, *Beloved* (1987), won the Pulitzer Prize. It is set in Ohio and Kentucky before and after the Civil War and focuses on characters who must cope with their legacy of having been enslaved. A reviewer said that in it readers would see slavery "as one of the most viciously antifamily institutions human beings have ever devised." *Beloved* was later made into a movie starring Oprah Winfrey and Danny Glover.

Morrison believes that a novel should strongly affect readers: "It should be beautiful, and powerful, but it should also *work*. It should have something in it that enlightens; something in it that opens the door and points the way. Something in it that suggests what the conflicts are, what the problems are. But it need not solve those problems because . . . it is not a recipe."

In 1993 Morrison was awarded the Nobel Prize in Literature. The Nobel press release stated that Morrison, "who in novels characterized by visionary force and poetic import, gives life to an essential aspect of American reality."

The Dancing Mind

Literary Focus Analyze text structure.

TEXT STRUCTURE CHART

Use the following chart to explore how Morrison structured "The Dancing Mind." In the first column, summarize the subject of each paragraph of the speech. In the second column, briefly describe the purpose of the paragraph. Finally, identify the overall structure of the text. The answers for the first paragraph are given.

SUBJECT	PURPOSE
discusses the idea of the "dancing mind"	to introduce the central idea of the speech—the "dancing mind"

OVERALL STRUCTURE

The Dancing Mind

VOCABULARY AND COMPREHENSION

WORD BOX

status quo
sinister
literate
satiate
expediency
conglomerate

A. Figurative Language For each item below, fill in the blank with the appropriate word from the Word Box. Then underline the figurative language used in the sentence.

1. The mind of a highly ______________________ person is a fascinating country to visit.

2. The megastore of the ______________________ is a hungry whale that swallows its competition.

3. As a writer who did not fit the ______________________ , she felt like a square peg in a round hole.

4. He could not ______________________ his thirst for contemporary art.

5. Those who knew the power-hungry politician said that ______________ was her only guide.

6. My heart sank when I read of the ______________________ plan to ban foreign books.

B. Reading Comprehension Answer each question below.

7. In what way does the graduate student's struggle remind you of your own life or the life of someone you know?

____

____

____

8. Why is the struggle that the woman writer shared with Morrison important to people in this country and around the world?

____

____

____

9. In what ways have changes in technology affected the world of reading and writing? Write your answer in a brief essay on a separate sheet of paper.

Vocabulary Skills
Identify figurative language.

BEFORE YOU READ

Runagate Runagate

by Robert Hayden

For My People

by Margaret Walker

In the first poem, Robert Hayden brings to vivid life the feelings and experiences of traveling the Underground Railroad. In the second poem, Margaret Walker creates a uniquely intimate voice to chronicle the trials, tribulations, and hopes of African Americans past and present.

LITERARY FOCUS: FREE VERSE

Free verse does not follow the strict requirements of some other poetic forms. In contrast, major characteristics of free verse include the following:

- irregular line lengths—There will be some short and some long lines.
- no fixed rhyme scheme—There may be rhyme, but it will not occur in a pattern.
- irregular rhythm—The meter (arrangement of stressed and unstressed syllables) will not be uniform throughout.
- varied stanzas—The number of lines in each stanza may not be the same.

Also, the way the lines are arranged may differ from stanza to stanza. Free verse often sounds more like conversation than formal poetry. However, you will still find literary devices, such as metaphors, similes, personification, parallelism, symbolism, and imagery; and sound devices, such as repetition, alliteration, and onomatopoeia.

Try reading both of these poems aloud to help you understand how their free verse forms their meaning.

Literary Focus Understand free verse.

Reading Skills Identify the speaker.

Vocabulary Skills Identify word origins.

READING SKILLS: IDENTIFYING THE SPEAKER

The **speaker** is the voice you hear in a poem. This voice is not always that of the poet. Rather, the poet often creates a persona, or character, to be the speaker. Details in these poems will help you to identify who the speaker actually is as well as tell you more about him or her.

VOCABULARY DEVELOPMENT

PREVIEW SELECTION VOCABULARY

The following words appear in "Runagate Runagate" and "For My People." Look them over before you begin to read.

shackles (shak′əlz) *n.:* metal fastenings around wrists or ankles.

Enslaved people sometimes had ***shackles*** *to prevent them from running away.*

anguish (aŋ′gwish) *n.:* torment; extreme physical or mental pain.

The ***anguish*** *of being enslaved can hardly be described.*

dirges (durjez) *n.:* songs of mourning.

The sound of the ***dirges*** *from the funeral floated slowly across the water.*

disinherited (dis′in·her′it·ed) *adj.:* deprived of natural rights or privileges.

The ***disinherited*** *African Americans searched for something to call their own.*

hypocrisy (hi·päk′rə·sē) *n.:* deceit or insincerity; practice of pretending to believe in something that one doesn't.

The ***hypocrisy*** *of the store owner who pretended to support equal rights but would hire only white males was upsetting.*

IDENTIFYING WORD ORIGINS

Most words that make up the English language have their **origins** in older languages, such as Latin, Greek, Old English, or Germanic, for example. A dictionary entry will often trace a word's origins and meaning, showing you how its usage evolved as it was adapted into various languages. For example, the word *martial,* found in "For My People," comes from the Latin *martialis*, which is derived from the name of the Roman god of war, Mars.

Knowing the origin of the word can help you to "own it" and remember it more easily.

As you read these poems, be sure to look up unfamiliar words in the dictionary and check out their origins.

Runagate Runagate°

by Robert Hayden

FLUENCY

Read the boxed text aloud. Use your voice to convey the mood of desperation and fear in this stanza.

ANALYZE

What is the effect of Hayden's repetition of the conjunction *and* in lines 1–7?

INTERPRET

Re-read lines 13–18. What does the North represent? Why is it "mythic"?

VOCABULARY

shackles (shak′əlz) *n.:* metal fastenings on wrists or ankles.

I.

Runs falls rises stumbles on from darkness into darkness
and the darkness thicketed with shapes of terror
and the hunters pursuing and the hounds pursuing
and the night cold and the night long and the river
to cross and the jack-muh-lanterns beckoning beckoning
and blackness ahead and when shall I reach that somewhere
morning and keep on going and never turn back and keep on going

Runagate
Runagate
Runagate

Many thousands rise and go
many thousands crossing over
O mythic North
O star-shaped yonder Bible city

Some go weeping and some rejoicing
some in coffins and some in carriages
some in silks and some in **shackles**

Rise and go or fare you well

No more auction block for me
no more driver's lash for me

° **Runagate** (run′ə·gāt′) *n.*: a runaway or fugitive. The word *runagate* comes from the Middle English *renagat*, which means "apostate" or "villain." The Middle English word came from the Old French renegat, and that came from the Middle Latin *renegatus*. *Runagate* is related to the modern English word *renegade*, meaning "someone who rejects lawful or conventional behavior."

If you see my Pompey, 30 yrs of age,
new breeches, plain stockings, negro shoes;
if you see my Anna, likely young mulatto
branded E on the right cheek, R on the left,
catch them if you can and notify subscriber.
Catch them if you can, but it won't be easy.
They'll dart underground when you try to catch them,
plunge into quicksand, whirlpools, mazes,
turn into scorpions when you try to catch them.

And before I'll be a slave
I'll be buried in my grave

North star and bonanza gold
I'm bound for the freedom, freedom-bound
and oh Susyanna don't you cry for me
Runagate
Runagate

The Life of Harriet Tubman #20, 1940, by Jacob Lawrence.
©The Jacob and Gwendolyn Lawrence Foundation/Art Resource, NY

DRAW CONCLUSIONS

In the omniscient point of view, the speaker is "all-knowing" and not restricted to any time, place, or character. Which details in lines 1–29 suggest that the speaker is omniscient?

VOCABULARY

anguish (aŋ′gwish) *n.:* torment; extreme physical or mental pain.

COMPARE & CONTRAST

Compare the placement of the words in lines 35–36 with the words in lines 8–10. What does this placement suggest to you?

LITERARY FOCUS

Read lines 37–41 aloud. How does the transition from the long first line to the shorter subsequent lines affect your reading?

INTERPRET

Re-read lines 42–43. What did Harriet Tubman do for the runaways?

INFER

Re-read lines 42–52. What would happen if some of the runaways refused to keep going?

II.

Rises from their **anguish** and their power,
Harriet Tubman,

woman of earth, whipscarred,
a summoning, a shining

Mean to be free

And this was the way of it, brethren° brethren,
way we journeyed from Can't to Can.
Moon so bright and no place to hide,
the cry up and the patterollers° riding,
hound dogs belling in bladed air.
And fear starts a-murbling, Never make it,
we'll never make it. *Hush that now,*
and she's turned upon us, levelled pistol
glinting in the moonlight:
Dead folks can't jaybird-talk, she says;
you keep on going now or die, she says.

Wanted   Harriet Tubman   alias The General
alias Moses   Stealer of Slaves
In league with Garrison   Alcott   Emerson
Garrett   Douglass   Thoreau   John Brown°

Armed and known to be Dangerous

Wanted   Reward   Dead or Alive

Tell me, Ezekiel, oh tell me do you see
mailed Jehovah coming to deliver me?°

42. **brethren:** brothers (chiefly in religious use).
45. **patterollers:** patrollers, slave catchers.
55–56. **Garrison . . . Brown:** individuals active in the movement to abolish slavery.
59–60. **Ezekiel . . . me:** In the Bible, God appears to the prophet Ezekiel in glowing metal (here, the word *mailed* means "armored"). Ezekiel was commissioned by God to comfort the Israelites in captivity (Ezekiel 1:26–28; 2:1–10).

Hoot-owl calling in the ghosted air,
five times calling to the hants° in the air.
Shadow of a face in the scary leaves,
shadow of a voice in the talking leaves:

Come ride-a my train

Oh that train, ghost-story train
through swamp and savanna movering movering,
over trestles of dew, through caves of the wish,
Midnight Special on a sabre track movering movering,
first stop Mercy and the last Hallelujah.

Come ride-a my train
Mean mean mean to be free.

---

62. hants: variant of *haunts,* or spirits.

MEET THE WRITER

Robert Hayden (1913–1980) was born and raised in Detroit, Michigan. He attended Wayne University and earned his master's degree from the University of Michigan. He then taught English at the University of Michigan and Fisk University. Hayden wrote poems about Nat Turner, Harriet Tubman, Malcolm X, and Frederick Douglass, among others. While much of his poetry concerns African American history and the black experience, it is informed by a larger vision. When asked to define poetry, Robert Hayden said it is "the art of saying the impossible."

As a follower of the Baha'i faith, which teaches the spiritual unity of all humankind, Hayden rejected narrow racial categorizations—both for himself and his work. His poetry ranges from formal diction and traditional verse forms to informal diction and free verse. Hayden won the 1966 Grand Prize for Poetry in English at the First World Festival of Negro Arts in Dakar for his book *A Ballad of Remembrance*. In 1976, he became the first African American to serve as Poetry Consultant to the Library of Congress.

HISTORICAL CONTEXT

Hoot owl calls (line 61) were used as signals by leaders and travelers on the Underground Railroad.

WORD STUDY

Movering in line 67 is another term created by the poet. Use context clues to figure out its meaning.

INTERPRET

Why is the train described as being on a "sabre track" in line 69?

LITERARY FOCUS

What idea does the repetition of *mean* in the last line of the poem convey?

VOCABULARY

dirges (durjez) *n.:* songs of mourning.

LITERARY FOCUS

Read the second stanza aloud. What effect is created by the series of *-ing* verb forms?

ANALYZE

List the details in lines 10–20 that help you to identify the speaker.

For My People

by Margaret Walker

For my people everywhere singing their slave songs repeatedly:
their **dirges** and their ditties and their blues and jubilees,
praying their prayers nightly to an unknown god, bending
their knees humbly to an unseen power;

For my people lending their strength to the years, to the gone
years and the now years and the maybe years, washing ironing
cooking scrubbing sewing mending hoeing plowing digging
planting pruning patching dragging along never gaining never
reaping never knowing and never understanding;

For my playmates in the clay and dust and sand of Alabama
backyards playing baptizing and preaching and doctor and jail
and soldier and school and mama and cooking and playhouse
and concert and store and hair and Miss Choomby and
company;

For the cramped bewildered years we went to school to
learn to know the reasons why and the answers to and the
people who and the places where and the days when, in
memory of the bitter hours when we discovered we were
black and poor and small and different and nobody cared and
nobody wondered and nobody understood;

Barbecue, c. 1935, oil on canvas by Archibald J. Motley, Jr.
The Granger Collection, New York

For the boys and girls who grew in spite of these things to be
man and woman, to laugh and dance and sing and play and
drink their wine and religion and success, to marry their
playmates and bear children and then die of consumption and
anemia and lynching;

For my people thronging 47th Street in Chicago and Lenox
Avenue in New York and Rampart Street in New Orleans, lost
disinherited dispossessed and happy people filling the cabarets
and taverns and other people's pockets needing bread and
shoes and milk and land and money and something—
something all our own;

INTERPRET

Re-read lines 21–31. How does the speaker see the lives of the people?

VOCABULARY

disinherited (dis'in·her'it·ed) *adj.:* deprived of natural rights or privileges.

INTERPRET

Re-read the first stanza of the poem. Then read lines 37–43, noting the references to "dark of churches," "false prophet," and "holy believer." How would you characterize Walker's view of religion?

For my people walking blindly spreading joy, losing time being
lazy, sleeping when hungry, shouting when burdened,
drinking when hopeless, tied and shackled and tangled
among ourselves by the unseen creatures who tower over us
omnisciently and laugh;

For my people blundering and groping and floundering in the
dark of churches and schools and clubs and societies,
associations and councils and committees and conventions,
distressed and disturbed and deceived and devoured by
money-hungry glory-craving leeches, preyed on by facile
force of state and fad and novelty, by false prophet and holy
believer;

VOCABULARY

hypocrisy (hi·päk′rə·sē) *n.:* deceit or insincerity.

WORD STUDY

The word *fashion* in lines 44 and 46 comes from the Latin word *factus*—to make or do.

For my people standing staring trying to fashion a better way
from confusion, from **hypocrisy** and misunderstanding, trying
to fashion a world that will hold all the people, all the faces, all
the adams and eves° and their countless generations;

INFER

What is the speaker's tone in this last stanza? What does this tone reveal about the speaker?

Let a new earth rise. Let another world be born. Let a bloody
peace be written in the sky. Let a second generation full of
courage issue forth; let a people loving freedom come to
growth. Let a beauty full of healing and a strength of final
clenching be the pulsing in our spirits and our blood. Let the
martial songs be written, let the dirges disappear. Let a race
of men now rise and take control.

47. adams and eves: According to the Bible, Adam and Eve were the first man and woman (Genesis 2:7, 3:20). Walker here uses their names for a new race of people.

©Courtesy Estate of Gordon Parks/Library of Congress, #LC-USZ62-113572.

MEET THE WRITER

Margaret Walker (1915–1998) was born in Birmingham, Alabama. She grew up in a "talking" family, and the oral history of her people became an important part of her life at an early age.

Walker attended Northwestern University in Evanston, Illinois. After graduating in 1935, she worked for the Federal Writers' Project in Chicago. After four years, she left to do graduate work at the University of Iowa. The poems in her first volume of poetry, *For My People* (1942) were her master's thesis.

For My People won the Yale Younger Poets Award. The title poem had originally appeared in *Poetry* magazine in 1937 and had created a sensation. No African American writer had produced poetry like this. It was new not only in its expression of racial consciousness and protest, but also in its style.

Walker also published a best-selling novel, *Jubilee* (1966), which tells the story of a slave family and is based on stories Walker first heard told by her maternal grandmother. She did the extensive research for the novel while she was raising a family, teaching full time, and earning a Ph.D. at the University of Iowa.

Walker taught at colleges and for many years and served as the director of the Institute for the Study of the History, Life, and Culture of Black People at Jackson State University, Jackson, Mississippi. In summing up her life, the poet Amiri Baraka said, "She remained clear and beautiful, moving and prophetic."

EXTEND

With a partner, discuss the devices that the poet uses within the poem to help unify and maintain its flow? Then list some examples that you find through your discussion.

NOTES

Runagate Runagate • For My People

Reading Skills Identify the speaker and make inferences.

SPEAKER DETAILS CHART

Record lines and phrases from each poem that relate to the speaker. Then use them to make inferences about the speaker's identity.

POEM	DETAILS	INFERENCES ABOUT SPEAKER
"Runagate Runagate"		
"For My People"		

Runagate Runagate • For My People

VOCABULARY AND COMPREHENSION

A. Word Origins For each item below, fill in the blank with the appropriate word from the Word Box. Then, using a dictionary, write its definition.

WORD BOX

anguish
dirges
disinherited
hypocrisy

1. Greek *hypokrisis,* acting of a part ______________________
   Meaning: ____

2. Latin *dirige,* first words of the Latin prayer for the dead ______________
   Meaning: ____

3. *dis-* + *in-* Latin *heres,* heir ______________________
   Meaning: ____

4. Latin *angustia,* distress ______________________
   Meaning: ____

B. Reading Comprehension Answer each question below.

5. Why is the Underground Railroad called the "ghost-story train" in the poem "Runagate Runagate"?
   ____
   ____
   ____

6. In what way is the last stanza of "For My People" different from the others?
   ____
   ____
   ____

7. On a separate sheet of paper, write an essay that compares and contrasts the main ideas expressed by the speakers in "Runagate Runagate" and "For My People."

Vocabulary Skills
Use word origins.

BEFORE YOU READ

Still I Rise • Song for the Old Ones

by Maya Angelou

The Old People Speak of Death

by Quincy Troupe

In the poems of both Maya Angelou and Quincy Troupe, sound and meaning are intertwined. Their rhythm and their words absorb readers deeply into their poems.

LITERARY FOCUS: THEME

The **theme** of a work is the central idea or insight about human life that it reveals. Sometimes, the theme of a work is stated. Most of the time, however, the theme is implied.

To identify the implied theme of a poem, it is helpful to read the work more than once. Upon your first reading, decide what the subject of the poem is. The second time you read the poem, look carefully at the following elements and consider what they are telling you about its meaning:

- the attitude of the speaker toward the subject
- the central symbols and images
- the lines or words that are repeated

READING SKILLS: COMPARING AND CONTRASTING THEME

Comparing and **contrasting** the themes or messages of different poems can help you to understand them more fully. When you compare people or things, you show how they are alike. When you contrast people or things, you show how they are different. Note what Maya Angelou and Quincy Troupe have to say through their poetry. Consider the following elements of each poem as you read and compare and contrast their themes:

- the way each poem uses language
- the major figure in each poem (for example the "Fathers" in "Song for the Old Ones")

Literary Focus Understand theme.

Reading Skills Compare and contrast theme.

Vocabulary Skills Understand figurative language.

VOCABULARY DEVELOPMENT

PREVIEW SELECTION VOCABULARY

The following words appear in "Still I Rise," "Song for the Old Ones," and "The Old People Speak of Death." Look them over before you begin to read.

haughtiness (hôt′ē·nes) *n.:* arrogance; feelings of superiority.

*Her **haughtiness** prevented her from forming close friendships with others.*

withered (with′ərd) *adj.:* shriveled; shrunken.

*The old man's arms had become **withered** from lack of exercise.*

submission (sub·mish′ən) *n.:* the act of yielding or giving in.

*They chose **submission** rather than resistance.*

cunning (kun′iŋ) *n.:* skillful deception.

*They used their **cunning** to help them survive.*

residue (rez′ə·do͞o′) *n.:* part that remains or is left over.

***Residue** of their existence would remain long after they were gone.*

UNDERSTANDING FIGURATIVE LANGUAGE

Poets often use **Figurative language,** or phrases that describe one thing in terms of another. Figurative language can add interest to a poem and help convey meaning. They are not meant to be understood on a literal level. Common types of figurative language include the following:

- **Personification** gives human qualities to inanimate objects, ideas, animals, or machines. *Example: The bus groaned as it turned the corner.*
- **Similes** make comparisons using connecting words, such as *like, as,* or *than. Example: Standing on the hot pavement in the sun, I felt like a pancake on a griddle.*
- **Metaphors** make comparisons without connecting words. *Example: Her harsh comments were a slap on the face.*

As you read these poems, look for the ways in which the poets use figurative language to communicate their meanings and to convey the theme(s).

DRAW CONCLUSIONS

Read lines 1–4. Whom is the speaker addressing?

INTERPRET

Read lines 1–8 aloud. How would you describe the speaker's attitude?

COMPARE & CONTRAST

Re-read lines 9–10. Why does the speaker compare herself to the moon, sun, and tides?

VOCABULARY

haughtiness (hôt′ē·nes) *n.:* arrogance; feelings of superiority.

Still I Rise

by Maya Angelou

You may write me down in history
With your bitter, twisted lies,
You may trod me in the very dirt
But still, like dust, I'll rise.

Does my sassiness upset you?
Why are you beset with gloom?
'Cause I walk like I've got oil wells
Pumping in my living room.

Just like moons and like suns,
With the certainty of tides,
Just like hopes springing high,
Still I'll rise.

Did you want to see me broken?
Bowed head and lowered eyes?
Shoulders falling down like teardrops,
Weakened by my soulful cries?

Does my **haughtiness** offend you?
Don't you take it awful hard
'Cause I laugh like I've got gold mines
Diggin' in my own backyard.

You may shoot me with your words,
You may cut me with your eyes,
You may kill me with your hatefuhness,
But still, like air, I'll rise.

Does my sexiness upset you?
Does it come as a surprise
That I dance like I've got diamonds
At the meeting of my thighs?

Challenge-America, 1964 by Loïs Mailou Jones.
©Hirshhorn Museum and Sculpture Garden, Smithsonian Institution, Museum Purchase, 1977

Out of the huts of history's shame
I rise
Up from a past that's rooted in pain
I rise
I'm a black ocean, leaping and wide,
Welling and swelling I bear in the tide.

Leaving behind nights of terror and fear
I rise
Into a daybreak that's wondrously clear
I rise
Bringing the gifts that my ancestors gave,
I am the dream and the hope of the slave.
I rise
I rise
I rise.

ANALYZE

What is the promise implicit in the use of the metaphor in lines 33–34?

LITERARY FOCUS

Re-read lines 35–40. How does the speaker see herself?

EXTEND

Read "On the Pulse of Morning," the poem that Maya Angelou wrote for President Clinton on the occasion of his inauguration. Discuss with a partner ways in which that poem is similar to and different from "Still I Rise."

VOCABULARY

withered (wĭth′ərd) *adj.:* shriveled; shrunken.

ANALYZE

Re-read lines 1–6. What image of the old ones is created by the figurative language in these lines?

ANALYZE

Re-read lines 9–12. What do the old ones represent to the speaker?

NOTES

Song for the Old Ones

by Maya Angelou

My Fathers sit on benches
their flesh counts every plank
the slats leave dents of darkness
deep in their **withered** flanks.

They nod like broken candles
all waxed and burnt profound
they say "It's understanding
that makes the world go round."

There in those pleated faces
I see the auction block
the chains and slavery's coffles°
the whip and lash and stock.

Anna Washington Derry, 1927, oil on canvas, by Laura Wheeler Waring. Gift of the Harmon Foundation.
Smithsonian American Art Museum, Washington, DC / Art Resource, NY

11. **coffles** (kôf′əlz) *n.:* groups of enslaved people chained or tied together in lines.

My Fathers speak in voices
that shred my fact and sound
they say "It's our **submission**
that makes the world go round."

They used the finest **cunning**
their naked wits and wiles
the lowly Uncle Tomming
and Aunt Jemimas' smiles.°

They've laughed to shield their crying
then shuffled through their dreams
and stepped 'n' fetched a country
to write the blues with screams.

I understand their meaning
it could and did derive
from living on the edge of death
They kept my race alive.

19–20. lowly Uncle Tomming and Aunt Jemima smiles: The term *Uncle Tom* has been used colloquially to refer to a black person whose behavior toward white people is considered servile or "lowly." The term *Aunt Jemima* has been used at times to refer to a black woman who always appears to be happy and smiling (even when she isn't), particularly in the service of white people.

VOCABULARY

submission (sub·mish′ən) *n.:* act of yielding or giving in.

cunning (kun′iŋ) *n.:* skillful deception.

DRAW CONCLUSIONS

Re-read lines 17–20. Why did the old ones assume attitudes of humility and happiness?

EVALUATE

Examine lines 25–28. What is the speaker's feeling toward the old ones?

NOTES

MEET THE WRITER

Maya Angelou (1928–)

©AP Photo/Maya Angelou's Office via XM Radio, Nancy Robinson

"Growing up is painful for a Southern Black girl," writes Maya Angelou in her introduction to *I Know Why the Caged Bird Sings*, the first of her autobiographical books. At the age of three, she was sent to live with her grandmother in Stamps, Arkansas. Years later she vowed never to return to what she called the "grim, humiliating South." Reading books helped her escape and prepared her for a lifetime of writing. Angelou moved to California when she was a teenager, graduated from high school, and then went to New York to study dance. She joined a theatrical group and appeared in the folk opera *Porgy and Bess* on an international tour. She later returned to the United States to work for the civil rights movement.

Angelou is best known for her autobiographies, but she has also written poetry, screen plays, magazine articles, and appeared in the miniseries *Roots.* She has also presented her poetry on stage. One reviewer described her this way: "Angelou's statuesque figure, dressed in bright colors (and sometimes African designs), moves exuberantly, vigorously to reinforce the rhythm of the lines, the tone of the words." The entire nation was able to hear and see her read her poem "On the Pulse of Morning" at the inauguration of President Bill Clinton on January 20, 1993. She later said, "In all my work, what I try to say is that as human beings we are more alike than we are unalike. It may be that Mr. Clinton asked me to write the inaugural poem because he understood that I am the kind of person who really does bring people together."

The Old People Speak of Death

by Quincy Troupe

the old people speak of death
frequently now
my grandmother talks of those now
gone too° spirit
now less than bone

they speak of shadows
that graced their days with darkness
or either light speak of days & corpses
of relationships buried deeper
then **residue** of bone
gone now beyond hardness
gone now beyond form

they sing from ingrown roots
of beginnings those who have left us
& climbed through the holes we left in our eyes
for them too enter through

eye walk back now
through holes eye left in my eyes
for them too enter through too where
eye see them now darker than where roots begin
lighter than where they go
with their spirits
heavier then stone

4. **too** (to͞o) *adv.:* one common definition of the word means "excessively." Quincy Troupe uses the word to enhance the meaning and to play on the sound of the word *to* when spoken.

VOCABULARY

residue (rez′ə·do͞o′) *n.:* part that remains or is left over.

COMPARE & CONTRAST

Re-read lines 6–12 in this poem. With what are the old people in both Angelou's poem and this one associated?

INFER

Re-read lines 13–16. Where do those that have left go?

ANALYZE

Read lines 17–23 aloud. Note the play on the sound and meaning of "eye." What two ideas does Troupe want to suggest through this word?

ANALYZE

What images suggest new life and hope in lines 24–28?

LITERARY FOCUS

Re-read lines 29–36. What is the poet saying about the connection between the past and the present?

CONNECT

How do you feel Quincy Troupe's use of language adds to or subtracts from the reader's experience of the poem and theme?

& green branches will grow
from these roots darker than time
blacker than the ashes of nations
& wave in sun-tongued mornings
shadow the spirits in our eyes

they have gone now
with their spirits too fuse
with greenness enter stone & glue
their invisible faces
upon the transmigration° of earth
nailing winds & sing their guitar
voices through the ribcages
of our days
darker than where roots begin
greener than what they bring

the old people speak of death
frequently now
my grandmother talks of those now
gone too spirit
now less than bone

---

33. transmigration (trans′mī·grā′shən) *n.:* the movement from one place to another, or from one state of existence to another after death.

©Lynda Koolish

NOTES

MEET THE WRITER

Quincy Troupe, Jr. (1943–) was born in St. Louis where his father was a baseball catcher in the Negro Leagues. When Troupe was fifteen, he had a life altering experience after listening to a Miles Davis record on a juke box: "I put my nickel in and sat down and listened to it. It was great. I put another nickel in and listened to it again, and when I walked out of that fish joint [café] my life was kind of changed at that moment, hearing that music." Troupe would later become friends with Davis and collaborate with him on *Miles: The Autobiography* (1989), which won an American Book Award. Troupe also says that Davis was "the one that set me on the path to writing and using my imagination."

Troupe went to Grambling College on a baseball scholarship, but soon left. In the 1960s, he moved to Los Angeles and taught creative writing for the Watts Writers' Movement. He then began a long career of teaching at various colleges and universities. In 1972, he published his first book of poetry, *Embryo Poems 1967–1971*. It shows the influence of dialect and jazz in his work and contains one of his most moving poems, "Woke Up Crying the Blues," which is about the assassination of Martin Luther King, Jr. Troupe's second volume of poetry, *Snake-back Solos* (1978), won an American Book Award. In 2000, he published *Miles and Me*, a memoir of his friendship with Miles Davis. On the relationship between poetry and music, Troupe says, "At the base of American creativity is language . . . what black people can do with the rhythms and the words and musicians with the sounds coupled with the words is extraordinary."

Still I Rise • Song for the Old Ones • The Old People Speak of Death

Literacy Focus
Analyze themes.

Reading Skills
Compare and contrast poems.

COMPARE AND CONTRAST CHART

Each of these poems has a strong theme. Fill out the chart with examples and details that help you to identify and compare the themes.

	STILL I RISE	SONG FOR THE OLD ONES	THE OLD PEOPLE SPEAK OF DEATH
subject			
speaker's tone			
significant images/ symbols			
repetition of key words and lines			
theme			

Still I Rise • Song for the Old Ones • The Old People Speak of Death

VOCABULARY AND COMPREHENSION

WORD BOX
profound
submission
withered
cunning
residue
haughtiness

A. Figurative Language For each item below, fill in the blank with the appropriate word from the Word Box. Not all words will be used. Then underline the figure of speech in each sentence and identify it as a simile, metaphor, or personification.

1. Their ______________________ to authority was their ticket to survival.

   Figure of Speech: ______________________

2. His ______________________ hope sprouted new shoots when he heard the news.

   Figure of Speech: ______________________

3. The ______________________ heat extended its sticky embrace the minute we walked outside.

   Figure of Speech: ______________________

4. His ______________________ made him harder to find than a taxi during rush hour.

   Figure of speech: ______________________

B. Reading Comprehension Answer each question below.

5. To what does the appearance of the old ones in "Song for the Old Ones" testify?

   ____

   ____

6. From what perspective is the speaker in the last poem looking at the lives of the old people?

   ____

   ____

7. Compare and contrast the themes of two of the poems from this selection. Write your answer in a brief essay on a separate sheet of paper.

Vocabulary Skills
Understand and use figures of speech.

POEMS

BEFORE YOU READ

Facing It • Birds on a Powerline
by Yusef Komunyakaa

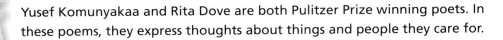

The First Book • Flirtation
by Rita Dove

Yusef Komunyakaa and Rita Dove are both Pulitzer Prize winning poets. In these poems, they express thoughts about things and people they care for.

LITERARY FOCUS: SIMILE

A **simile** is a type of figurative language that compares two things using a connective word such as *like, as, than,* or *resembles*. A simile employs imaginative comparison to help bring an image to life. Often, a simile compares two things that are not obviously alike. Here are some tips for interpreting a simile.

- Start by identifying the two things that are being compared. When the speaker in "Facing It" says that "My clouded reflection eyes me / like a bird of prey," the word *like* indicates that the speaker is comparing his own face to the face of a bird of prey, such as a hawk.
- Next, consider what you learn from the comparison. You can assume that the speaker of "Facing It" does not literally resemble a bird of prey. Instead, ask yourself: What qualities does a bird of prey possess that the speaker may share at this moment? A bird of prey is watchful, strong, cautious, and bold. Then ask: What does this suggest about the speaker's experience?

READING SKILL: VISUALIZING

Visualizing means creating in your mind an image of what you read. Visualizing enhances your understanding of your reading and helps you to connect it with your own knowledge. Because every reader's knowledge is unique, so is the way every reader visualizes. Your unique capacity to visualize makes your reading more meaningful.

- Start by picturing the details mentioned in the text, but don't stop there. Although mental images are primarily visual, they can arise from any or all of the senses. When the speaker in "Birds on a Powerline" brings his mother a cup of coffee, for example, you may visualize the shape of the cup and the color of the coffee, but you may also imagine the cup's warm smoothness and the coffee's earthy smell.

Literary Focus
Understand similes.

Reading Skills
Visualize aspects of poems.

Facing It

by Yusef Komunyakaa

My black face fades,
hiding inside the black granite.
I said I wouldn't,
dammit: No tears.
I'm stone. I'm flesh.
My clouded reflection eyes me
like a bird of prey, the profile of night
slanted against morning. I turn
this way—the stone lets me go.
I turn that way—I'm inside
the Vietnam Veterans Memorial
again, depending on the light
to make a difference.
I go down the 58,022 names,
half-expecting to find

FLUENCY

Read aloud lines 1–4. Is the pace quick or slow? What feeling does this suggest?

CONNECT

Recall a time that you observed your image on a reflective surface. How does this help you to visualize what the speaker sees in lines 8–13?

Vietnam Veterans Memorial, Washington, D.C.
©James P. Blair/CORBIS

"Facing It" from *Neon Vernacular* by Yusef Komunyakaa. Copyright © 1993 by Yusef Komunyakaa. Reproduced by permission of **Wesleyan University Press**.

ANALYZE

In lines 28–29 the speaker sees an arm disappear into the granite, as his own face faded into it in line 1. How might this phenomenon relate to feelings that come with revisiting memories at the memorial?

INTERPRET

Form a mental image of what the speaker describes in 29–31. Explain what is occurring.

my own in letters like smoke.
I touch the name Andrew Johnson;
I see the booby trap's white flash.
Names shimmer on a woman's blouse
but when she walks away
the names stay on the wall.
Brushstrokes flash, a red bird's
wings cutting across my stare.
The sky. A plane in the sky.
A white vet's image floats
closer to me, then his pale eyes
look through mine. I'm a window.
He's lost his right arm
inside the stone. In the black mirror
a woman's trying to erase names:
No, she's brushing a boy's hair.

Vietnam Veterans Memorial.
©David Muench/Corbis

Birds on a Powerline

by Yusef Komunyakaa

Mama Mary's counting them
Again. Eleven black. A single
Red one like a drop of blood

Against the sky. She's convinced
They've been there two weeks.
I bring her another cup of coffee

& a Fig Newton. I sit here reading
Frances Harper° at the enamel table
Where I ate teacakes as a boy,

My head clear of voices brought back.
The green smell of the low land returns,
Stealing the taste of nitrate.

The deep-winter eyes of the birds,
Shine in summer light like agate,°
As if they could love the heart

©GABRIEL BOUYS/AFP/Getty Images

LITERARY FOCUS

What does the simile "like a drop of blood" (line 3) contribute to the image of the birds?

ANALYZE

What details in the scene (lines 1–10) help you to form a mental picture of it?

8. **Frances Harper** (1825–1911): African-American poet and abolitionist.
14. **agate** (ag′it) *n.:* a type of hard, somewhat shiny rock.

VOCABULARY

luminous (lo͞o′mə·nəs) *adj.:* shining with light.

ANALYZE

The phrase "traveling shoes" (line 23) is an allusion to the spiritual "Death Came A-Knockin'," in which death asks a woman if she is ready to come with him; she indicates that she is by saying "[I've] got on my traveling shoes." What does this add to your understanding of how Mama Mary views the birds?

Out of any wild thing. I stop,
With my finger on a word, listening.
They're on the powerline, a **luminous**

Message trailing a phantom
Goodyear blimp. I hear her say
Jesus, I promised you. Now

He's home safe, I'm ready.
My traveling shoes on. My teeth
In. I got on clean underwear.

MEET THE WRITER

©James Keyser/Time Life Pictures/Getty Images

Yusef Komunyakaa (1947–) was born in Bogalusa, Louisiana, which he described as "a typical Southern town: one paper mill that dominated the place, and a public library that did not admit blacks." As a boy, he read the entire Bible—twice, and says that it had a major influence on his later writing, "The hypnotic Biblical cadence brought me close to the texture of language, to the importance of music and metaphor."

After graduating from high school, he joined the army and served in Vietnam. There, he was an information specialist and editor for *The Southern Cross*, a military newspaper. He says, "Every time anything happened within the area of operation, I found myself on a chopper, out to the action." He later received a Bronze Star.

After Vietnam, Komunyakaa returned to the United States, attended several universities, and began writing and publishing poetry. In *Copacetic* (1984) he uses blues and jazz forms in poems that explore his childhood in Louisiana. He tapped into his memory of Vietnam in *Dien Cai Dau* (1988), a title which means "crazy" in Vietnamese and was used by locals to describe U.S. soldiers. One reviewer said, "Komunyakaa's Vietnam poems rank with the best on that subject. He focuses on the mental horrors of war—the anguish shared by the soldiers, those left at home to keep watch, and other observers, participants, objectors, who are all part of the 'psychological terrain.'" The volume contains his often anthologized poem, "Facing It." ("It" refers to both the Vietnam Veterans Memorial and memory of the war.) Komunyakaa won the Pulitzer Prize for Poetry in 1994.

The First Book

by Rita Dove

Open it.

Go ahead, it won't bite.
Well . . . maybe a little.

More a nip, like. A tingle.
It's pleasurable, really.

You see, it keeps on opening.
You may fall in.

Sure, it's hard to get started;
remember learning to use

knife and fork? Dig in:
You'll never reach bottom.

It's not like it's the end of the world—
just the world as you think

you know it.

©Simon Jarratt/CORBIS

EVALUATE

What do lines 1–3 suggest about the poet's attitude toward reading?

CONNECT

Dove reminds readers that using a knife and fork was once difficult (lines 9–10). List three skills you found challenging when they were new to you but now seem natural. Then list three qualities that you think helped you to master these skills.

ANALYZE

What do you think Dove means by "the world as you think / you know it" (lines 13–14)?

LITERARY FOCUS

How does the simile "like a tulip" (line 5) help you to visualize the orange?

VOCABULARY

flares (flerz) *v.:* opens into a widening shape.

strewn (stro͞on) *adj.:* scattered.

CONNECT

What image of the night sky do you gain from "night strewn salt / across the sky" (lines 9–10)?

INTERPRET

What do you think Dove means in lines 18–19?

Flirtation

by Rita Dove

After all, there's no need
to say anything

at first. An orange, peeled
and quartered, **flares**

like a tulip on a wedgwood plate.
Anything can happen.

Outside the sun
has rolled up her rugs

and night **strewn** salt
across the sky. My heart

is humming a tune
I haven't heard in years!

Quiet's cool flesh—
let's sniff and eat it.

There are ways
to make of the moment

a topiary°
so the pleasure's in

walking through.

---

17. topiary (tō'pē·er'ē) *n.:* garden shrubbery that has been clipped into elaborate shapes.

©Tim Wright/CORBIS

NOTES

MEET THE WRITER

Rita Dove (1952–) was born in Akron, Ohio. Dove graduated with honors from Miami University in Ohio, received a Fulbright fellowship to attend the University of Tübingen in West Germany, and then completed her Master of Fine Arts degree from the Iowa Writers' Workshop.

In 1980, she published *The Yellow House on the Corner*. In that volume, the poem *"Ö"* contains the thought provoking lines: "You start out with one thing, end / up with another, and nothing's / like it used to be, not even the future."

Dove won the Pulitzer Prize for poetry for *Thomas and Beulah* (1986), which presents the story of her maternal grandparents' lives. She says, "It's not a dramatic story—nothing absolutely tragic happened in my grandparents' life. . . . But I think these are the people who often are ignored and lost." When Dove was asked what effect she hoped her poems would have on readers, she said, "In writing a poem, if the reader on the other end can come up and say: 'I know what you meant, I mean, I felt that too' then we are a little less alone in the world, and that to me is worth an awful lot."

Facing It • Birds on a Powerline • The First Book • Flirtation

Reading Comprehension Answer each question below.

"FACING IT"

1. Who is the speaker of the poem? Where is he?

___

___

2. Who, or what, does the speaker encounter?

___

___

"BIRDS ON A POWERLINE"

3. Describe how you visualized the birds on a powerline.

___

___

4. How does the speaker's mother respond to the appearance of the birds?

___

___

"THE FIRST BOOK"

5. What does the speaker of the poem urge listeners to do? Why?

___

___

"FLIRTATION"

6. Is the poem set in the past, present, or future? How might this fit its theme?

___

___

Reading Skills
Use visualization to aid comprehension.

BEFORE YOU READ

Living for the City by Stevie Wonder
Don't Believe the Hype by Public Enemy
The Evil That Men Do by Queen Latifah
In the Depths of Solitude by Tupac Shakur

From traditional spirituals and work songs to contemporary genres such as soul and hip-hop, meaningful messages have helped to define music for centuries. Artists such as Stevie Wonder, Public Enemy, Queen Latifah, and Tupac Shakur have all used music to convey ideas and feelings.

LITERARY FOCUS: EVALUATING MESSAGES IN MUSIC

When you identify the ideas presented in a song and form an opinion about them, you are **evaluating messages in music**. People may say that they not only hear music with their ears but feel it. For this reason, music and lyrics are a powerful means of conveying a message. It's up to you to decide whether or not you find that message truthful or convincing.

- Ask yourself: How does the song make me feel? The emotions that arise can help you to identify *what* ideas are being presented and whether you accept them.
- Consider *how* a message is conveyed. Notice words, images, rhythm, and sounds. For example, "Living for the City" starts with an image—"A boy is born in hard time Mississippi/Surrounded by four walls that ain't so pretty"—that launches a meaningful story.
- Think about *why* the artist is conveying this message. Sometimes the purpose may seem to be stated openly, as when Public Enemy says, "Don't believe the hype." Other times you may need to infer the meaning.

READING SKILLS: ANALYZING SOCIAL COMMENTARY

Any form of communication may include **social commentary**—commenting on society, often to call attention to injustice and promote change. The language used for social commentary depends on the artist's time and place, especially in popular music.

- As you read the lyrics of these songs and consider their messages, ask yourself what each artist is saying about the state of society. What problems are identified? What solutions are proposed?

SKILLS FOCUS

Literary Focus
Evaluate messages in music.

Reading Skills
Analyze social commentary.

Vocabulary Skills
Understand jargon and slang.

VOCABULARY DEVELOPMENT

PREVIEW SELECTION VOCABULARY

The following words appear in the songs. Look them over before you begin reading the lyrics.

epitome (ē·pit′ə·mē′) *n.:* the most accurate example of a type.

*Some fans call Stevie Wonder the **epitome** of a seventies soul singer.*

perpetrate (pur′pə·trāt′) *v.:* to commit an act, such as a crime.

*Queen Latifah has often spoken out against those who **perpetrate** violence.*

pondering (pän′dər·iŋ) *v.:* thinking deeply about.

*The poets' group spent the evening reading and **pondering** Tupac Shakur's lyrics.*

compromising (käm′prə·mīz′iŋ) *v. used as adj.:* willing to give up important things.

*Public Enemy held their political stance without ever being **compromising** or apologetic.*

UNDERSTANDING JARGON AND SLANG

One common aspect of African American popular music is inventive language, including **jargon** and **slang.** The terms *jargon* and *slang* are sometimes used interchangeably (that is, in place of one another) to describe nonstandard use of English. In general, however, jargon refers to words used within a particular group or profession, while slang refers to words used informally. For example, the word *beatboxing* (a percussive vocal style) could be considered jargon, while the word *hype* would be considered slang. Slang adds a playful element to many song lyrics.

- Using old words in a new way is a common type of slang. Often, you can readily grasp the meaning of this wordplay through its context. When Stevie Wonder describes the sister in the song as "sho 'nuff pretty," you can guess that the slang term "sho 'nuff" (from "sure enough") is used to mean "definitely."
- Newly invented words are another form of slang. They can make lyrics more authentic, more poetic, and more alive in the moment. As you read, consider the impact of the slang term, such as how it sounds when Public Enemy says "new jack" rather than "newcomer." Which is more memorable? Which speaks more directly to a contemporary audience?

Living for the City

by Stevie Wonder

A boy is born in hard time Mississippi
Surrounded by four walls that ain't so pretty
His parents give him love and affection
To keep him strong moving in the right direction
Living just enough, just enough for the city

His father works some days for fourteen hours
And you can bet he barely makes a dollar
His mother goes to scrub the floors for many
And you'd best believe she hardly gets a penny
Living just enough for the city

His sister's black but she is sho 'nuff pretty
Her skirt is short but Lord her legs are sturdy
To walk to school she's got to get up early
Her clothes are old but never are they dirty
Living just enough, just enough for the city

Her brother's smart he's got more sense than many
His patience's long but soon he won't have any
To find a job is like a haystack needle
Cause where he lives they don't use colored people
Living just enough, just enough for the city . . .

Lower Manhattan and Brooklyn Bridge at twilight.
©Rudy Sulgan/CORBIS

HISTORICAL CONTEXT

Mississippi has one of the highest poverty rates in the United States.

ANALYZE

Review lines 1–11. How would you describe the boy's parents and their values?

INTERPRET

What does line 14 tell you about the sister's character?

INFER

What does the simile "like a haystack needle" tell you about his job search? Why is it this way (lines 18–19)?

INFER

Bear in mind the young man's childhood as you read about his adult life in lines 21–24. How might this story be a form of social commentary?

His hair is long, his feet are hard and gritty
He spends his life walking the streets of New York City
He's almost dead from breathing in air pollution
He tried to vote but to him there's no solution
Living just enough, just enough for the city

I hope you hear inside my voice of sorrow
And that it motivates you to make a better tomorrow
This place is cruel no where could be much colder
If we can't change, the world will soon be over
Living just enough, stop living just enough for the city!!!!

ANALYZE

In lines 26–30, the artist switches from telling a story to addressing the listener. What effect does this have on how you understand the message?

MEET THE WRITER

Stevie Wonder (1950–) was born in Saginaw, Michigan. Blind almost from birth, he nevertheless became a brilliant composer and singer. He could play the harmonica by age five, started piano lessons at six, and was playing drums at eight. He wrote his first song at ten and had a rhythm and blues recording hit, "Fingertips—Part 2," when he was thirteen. Since then, he has created thirty-five albums with sales of more than 72 million dollars. He has won nineteen Grammys and a Lifetime Achievement Grammy in 1996. He used his celebrity status to help make Martin Luther King, Jr.'s, birthday a national holiday, and, as President Bill Clinton said, "In so many ways [Wonder] has helped to compose the remaining passages of Dr. King's legacy."

©Michael Ochs Archives/Getty Images

Don't Believe the Hype

by Public Enemy

Don't believe the hype

Back—caught you lookin' for the same thing
It's a new thing—check out this I bring
Uh-oh, the roll below the level
'Cause I'm livin' low
Next to the bass (c'mon)
Turn up the radio
They claim that I'm a criminal
By now I wonder how
Some people never know
The enemy could be their friend, guardian
I'm not a hooligan
I rock the party and
Clear all the madness, I'm not a racist
Preach to teach to all
'Cause some, they never had this
Number one, not born to run
About the gun
I wasn't licensed to have one
The minute they see me, fear me
I'm the **epitome**—a public enemy
Used, abused, without clues
I refused to blow a fuse
They even had it on the news
Don't believe the hype

Don't believe the hype

Yes—was the start of my last jam
So here it is again, another def jam

HISTORICAL CONTEXT

The term "public enemies" was first used by the Chicago Crime Commission in 1930 to identify the city's top criminals. It is now used for perceived threats to society.

ANALYZE

How do lines 8–10 connect with the song title?

VOCABULARY

epitome (ē·pit′ə·mē) *n.:* the most accurate example of a type.

FLUENCY

Read aloud lines 22–24 and listen for the long *u* sound. How does this affect the rhythm?

INTERPRET

What do lines 32–38 suggest about how the critics should be regarded? What do they suggest about how Farrakhan should be regarded?

EXTEND

Working in pairs, discuss the meaning of the metaphor "show the people what time it is" (lines 51–52). Then make a list of original metaphors that could express the same idea.

But since I gave you all a little something
That we knew you lacked
They still consider me a new jack
All the critics, you can hang 'em
I'll hold the rope
But they hope to the pope
And pray it ain't dope
The follower of Farrakhan°
Don't tell me that you understand
Until you hear the man
The book of the new school rap game
Writers treat me like Coltrane,° insane
Yes to them, but to me I'm a different kind
We're brothers of the same mind, unblind
Caught in the middle and
Not surrenderin'
I don't rhyme for the sake of riddlin'
Some claim that I'm a smuggler
Some say I never heard of ya
A rap burglar, false media
We don't need it, do we?
It's fake, that's what it be to ya, dig me?
Yo, Terminator X, step up on the stand and show the people
what time it is, boyyyyy!

Don't believe the hype

Don't believe the hype—it's a sequel
As an equal, can I get this through to you
My 98's boomin' with a trunk of funk
All the jealous punks can't stop the dunk

---

36. Farrakhan: Louis Farrakhan (1933–), American leader of the Nation of Islam.

40. Coltrane: John Coltrane (1926–1967), American jazz composer and saxophonist.

Comin' from the school of hard knocks
Some **perpetrate,** they drink Clorox
Attack the Black, because I know they lack exact
The cold facts, and still they try to xerox
The leader of the new school, uncool
Never played the fool, just made the rules
Remember there's a need to get alarmed
Again I said I was a timebomb
In the daytime, radio's scared of me
'Cause I'm mad, 'cause I'm the enemy
They can't come on and play me in prime time
'Cause I know the time, plus I'm gettin' mine
I get on the mix late in the night
They know I'm living' right, so here go the mike, psych
Before I let it go, don't rush my show
You try to reach and grab and get elbowed
Word to Herb, yo if you can't swing this
Learn the words, you might sing this
Just a little bit of the taste of the bass for you
As you get up and dance at the LQ
When some deny it, defy it, I swing bolos
And then they clear the lane, I go solo
The meaning of all of that
Some media is the wack
As you believe it's true
It blows me through the roof
Suckers, liars, get me a shovel
Some writers I know are damn devils
For them I say, "Don't believe the hype"
Yo Chuck, they must be on the pipe, right?
Their pens and pads I'll snatch

VOCABULARY

perpetrate (pur'pə·trāt') *v.:* to commit an act, such as a crime.

INFER

Line 59 is a great example of poetic license—an artist departing from conventional language use to create a particular effect. (For instance, "lack exact" is not grammatical, but it is effective.) What is said in these nine words?

INTERPRET

What do lines 80–86 say about the reliability of the media?

CONNECT

How might personal power result from a refusal to "believe the hype" (lines 95–96)?

ANALYZE

How does the short length of lines 105–111 support the message?

HISTORICAL CONTEXT

Red, black, and green (lines 99 and 109) are the colors of the Pan-African Flag, which was adopted in 1920 by the United Negro Improvement Association.

'Cause I've had it
I'm not an addict, fiendin' for static
I'll see their tape recorder and grab it
No, you can't have it back, silly rabbit
I'm goin' to my media assassin
Harry Allen,° I gotta ask him
Yo Harry, you're a writer, are we that type?

Don't believe the hype
Don't believe the hype

I got Flavor and all those things you know
Yeah boy, part two bum rush the show
Yo Griff, get the green, black, red, and
Gold down, countdown to Armageddon
'88 you wait the S-One's will
Put the left in effect and I still will
Rock the hard jams, treat it like a seminar
Reach the bourgeois, and rock the boulevard
Some say I'm negative
But they're not positive
But what I got to give
The media says this
Red black and green
Know what I mean
Yo, don't believe the hype

94. Harry Allen (1964–): *Village Voice* music journalist who defended Public Enemy's political stance.

©Michael Ochs Archives/Getty Images

NOTES

MEET THE ARTISTS

Public Enemy is a hip-hop group that started at Adelphi University on Long Island in 1982. The group's members included Chuck D, Flavor Fav, Professor Griff, and Terminator X. Public Enemy uses its songs to address social problems in the black community, racism, and government corruption. The group has been called controversial in part because some of their songs condone revolutionary tactics. Their second album, *It Takes a Nation of Millions to Hold Us Back*, brought them widespread success and has titles such as "Rebel Without a Pause," and "Prophets of Rage." Their song "Fight the Power," sums up their attitude and is featured in Spike Lee's film *Do the Right Thing*. Adam Yauch, from the band The Beastie Boys, says, "No one has been able to approach the political power that Public Enemy brought to hip-hop."

INTERPRET

The phrase "the evil that men do" comes from Shakespeare's Julius Caesar: "The evil that men do lives after them / The good is oft interred with their bones." Given the title, what is one message this song might explore?

GENERALIZE

In lines 3–10, what does the artist say she will bring "to the scene"? Does she expect to be respected?

The Evil That Men Do

by Queen Latifah

You asked, I came
So behold the Queen
Let's add a little sense to the scene
I'm livin' positive
Not out here knocked up
But the lines are so dangerous
I oughta be locked up
This rhyme doesn't require prime time
I'm just sharin' thoughts in mind
Back again because I knew you wanted it
From the Latifah with the Queen in front of it
Droppin' bombs, you're up in arms and puzzled
The lines will flow like fluid while you guzzle
You slip, I'll drop you on a BDP°-produced track

Queen Latifah rapping in Los Angeles, California, in 1990.
©Neal Preston/CORBIS

14. BDP: Boogie Down Productions, a hip-hop group.

From KRS° to be exact
It's a Flavor Unit° quest that today has me speakin'
'Cause it's knowledge I'm seekin'
Enough about myself, I think it's time that I tell you
About the Evil That Men Do

Situations, reality, what a concept
Nothin' ever seems to stay in step
So today here is a message for my sisters and brothers
Here are some things I want to cover
A woman strives for a better life
But who the hell cares
Because she's livin' on welfare
The government can't come up with a decent housin' plan
So she's in no man's land
It's a sucker who tells you you're equal
(You don't need 'em
Johannesburg° cries for freedom)
We the people hold these truths to be self-evident
(But there's no response from the president)
Someone's livin' the good life tax-free
'Cause some poor girl can't find
A way to be crack-free
And that's just part of the message
I thought I had to send you
About the Evil That Men Do

Tell me, don't you think it's a shame
When someone can put a quarter in a video game
But when a homeless person approaches you on the street

ANALYZE

Review lines 20–29. Why does the artist say that "It's a sucker who tells you you're equal"?

INFER

In lines 41–44, what values does the artist criticize?

15. KRS: the hip-hop MC of Boogie Down Productions known as KRS-ONE (Knowledge Reigns Supreme Overly Nearly Everyone).
16. Flavor Unit: a crew of MCs and DJs, including Queen Latifah, organized in the New York metropolitan area in the late 1980s.
31. Johannesburg: the largest city in South Africa; its black majority lived under racial segregation and white rule until 1994.

INFER

What does the artist mean by "the deaf, the dumb, the blind" (line 44)?

INTERPRET

In lines 47–54, what does the artist say about where the hope for peace resides?

EXTEND

In a small group, discuss the different perspectives and common themes that Stevie Wonder, Public Enemy, and Queen Latifah bring to their social commentary.

You can't treat him the same
It's time to teach the deaf, the dumb, the blind
That black on black crime only shackles and binds
You to a doom, a fate worse than death
But there's still time left
To stop puttin' your conscience on cease
And bring about some type of peace
Not only in your heart but also in your mind
It will benefit all mankind
Then there will be one thing
That will never stop you
And it's the Evil That Men Do

MEET THE WRITER

Queen Latifah (1970–   ) was born in Newark, New Jersey. In high school she played on two state championship basketball teams and also sang in a rap group. In 1989, she released *All Hail the Queen*, which contained "Ladies First," her signature song. Later hits included "Latifah's Had It Up to Here" and "Fly Girl." She played a role in Spike Lee's *Jungle Fever* and joined the cast of the sitcom, *Living Single*. In 1993 she released *Black Reign* which contained her hit "Unity," a song that demands respect for women. It won her a Grammy for Best Rap Solo Performance. Latifah continued acting and won an Academy Award Nomination for her performance in *Chicago*. In 2000 she published her autobiography *Ladies First: Revelations of a Strong Woman*.

Queen Latifah performing on *The Today Show* in 2004.
©Nancy Kaszerman/ZUMA/CORBIS

In the Depths of Solitude

Dedicated 2 Me

by Tupac Shakur

I exist in the depths of solitude
pondering my true goal
Trying 2 find peace of mind
and still preserve my soul
CONSTANTLY yearning 2 be accepted
and from all receive respect
Never compromising but sometimes risky
and that is my only regret
A young heart with an old soul
how can there be peace
How can I be in the depths of solitude
when there R 2 inside of me
This Duo within me causes
the perfect opportunity
2 learn and live twice as fast
as those who accept simplicity

VOCABULARY

pondering (pän′dər·iŋ) *v.:* thinking deeply about.

compromising (käm′prə·mīz′iŋ) *v. used as adj.:* willing to give up important things.

INTERPRET

Re-read lines 9–12. What stands in the way of the artist finding peace?

INFER

According to lines 13–16, what positive opportunity can arise from difficult challenges?

MEET THE WRITER

©Evan Agostini/Getty Images

Tupac Shakur (1971–1996) would tell interviewers that he was in prison before he was born because his mother, a member of the militant Black Panthers, was pregnant and in prison in 1971. While living in northern California Shakur became interested in rap and released two albums with the band Digital Underground. His first solo album, *2Pacalypse Now,* was released in 1991. Shakur began appearing in films such as *Juice* and *Above the Rim*, and his acting received rave reviews. But he was also having trouble with the law, and with violent rival rappers. What he called his "Thug Life" came to a sudden end when he was murdered by unknown persons in Las Vegas.

SKILLS PRACTICE

Literary Focus Evaluate messages in music.

Reading Skills Analyze social commentary.

Living for the City • Don't Believe the Hype • The Evil That Men Do • In the Depths of Solitude

CHART: EVALUATING MESSAGES IN MUSIC

Use the following chart to explore the messages in the four songs of this selection. In the middle column, summarize the message of the song. In the right-hand column, rate how effective you found the message on a scale of one to five (five means "very effective") and give one reason for your rating, based on evidence from the song.

SONG	MESSAGE	HOW EFFECTIVE? WHY?
"Living for the City"		1 2 3 4 5
"Don't Believe the Hype"		1 2 3 4 5
"The Evil That Men Do"		1 2 3 4 5
"In the Depths of Solitude"		1 2 3 4 5

Living for the City • Don't Believe the Hype • The Evil That Men Do • In the Depths of Solitude

VOCABULARY AND COMPREHENSION

WORD BOX

- epitome
- perpetrate
- pondering
- compromising

A. Jargon and Slang Fill in each blank below with the appropriate word from the Word Box. Underline all the examples of jargon or slang.

1. The DJ spent some time thinking and ______________________ which songs would be best in her mash-up.

2. People who ______________________ crimes are not cool.

3. The band that played at the dance was wicked and represented the ______________________ in popular music.

4. Taking everyone's opinion into account and ______________________ wasn't easy when half the group had already tuned out.

B. Reading Comprehension Answer each question below.

5. What does Queen Latifah offer in "The Evil That Men Do" as a solution for problems faced by society?

____

____

6. Which song do you feel had the most compelling message? Why?

____

____

7. Paraphrase what Stevie Wonder means by "living just enough for the city."

____

____

8. What do the songs in this selection show about artists' purposes in music? Write your answer in a brief essay on a separate sheet of paper.

Vocabulary Skills
Identify jargon and slang.

Writer's Workshop

PERSUASIVE WRITING

ASSIGNMENT

Write a persuasive essay on an issue that is important to you.

PURPOSE

To persuade

AUDIENCE

Your teacher and your classmates (or others who are interested in your topic)

STRATEGIES FOR SUPPORT AND ELABORATION

1. To develop your reasons, choose the following kinds of evidence that you find in sources you know are reliable:
   - facts and statistics
   - examples
   - analogies (comparisons)
   - anecdotes (brief stories)
   - quotes from experts
   - quotes from TV news shows, documentaries, and talk shows
   - surveys
   - interviews
2. Use mainly logical appeals to strengthen your essay.
3. Avoid emotional appeals.

PERSUASIVE ESSAY

When you try to **persuade,** you ask your audience to consider the validity of your opinions and ideas. At the same time, you must keep an open mind so you can understand, anticipate, and refute the arguments of those who disagree with you. You use persuasion in many different ways both in conversation and in writing. Examples include encouraging a friend or family member to go somewhere, applying and interviewing for admission to schools or extracurricular programs, writing a letter to a newspaper editor or an elected official, writing a review of a piece of literature, and posting your ideas about something on a message board. You also encounter persuasion in the form of advertisements.

In this workshop, you will write an essay to persuade readers to accept your opinion on a particular topic. To do this convincingly, you will need to provide reasons and evidence to support your position. You will also need to develop responses to counterarguments.

PREWRITING

1. **Choose a Topic**—Review your notes from the selections you've read in this book or check current news stories for topic ideas. Select an issue that is important to you.

2. **Formulate a Position**—After you've selected a topic, consider both the **pros** and the **cons** of the issue (the arguments for and against). Then decide what your position is on the issue, and write a one-sentence **opinion statement** clearly expressing your position. Use this statement to focus your thinking as you collect supporting data and organize your argument. If you change your position as you find more information, you can revise your opinion statement.

3. **Gather Support**—You'll need convincing **reasons** to support your position and reliable **evidence** to back up your reasons. Rely on logical appeals—reasons and evidence that are based on sound thinking. Watch out for faulty reasoning that uses misleading or irrelevant information. Also avoid emotional appeals that obscure or detract from the facts. (See the Strategies for Support and Elaboration in the side column for possible sources of information.)

State two or three strong reasons in support of your position. Then search for evidence to expand upon each reason. Look for recent facts and statistics in print sources (books, newspapers, magazines) and nonprint sources (the Internet, videotapes, TV shows, databases). Remember, an expert's opinion can add strong support to your argument. Consider conducting an interview either in person or by phone, mail, or e-mail.

In gathering your evidence from various sources, be careful to evaluate the validity of your information. Some Web sites and print sources do not provide accurate information. It is best to confirm all the information that you include in your essay in at least one additional source.

4. **Target Your Audience**—As you look for reasons to support your position, identify your **audience** and select evidence appropriately. Ask yourself these questions:
   - What is your audience likely to know about the topic, and what will you need to explain?
   - What concerns do you and your audience share?
   - What arguments might your readers make against your position (these are called **counterarguments**), and how can you refute them?

   While you were formulating your own opinion, you considered the pros and cons of the issue. Now, shape your argument to anticipate the possible objections of your audience. One strategy is to appeal to common ground on both sides of the argument and then logically work you way toward your position. Remember that many issues have compelling arguments on both sides. Your job is to present information that supports your position and refutes the opposition.

5. **Organize Your Argument**—After selecting the information you will use to support your position, you need to determine the best order in which to present it. For a persuasive essay, the most effective organization is usually **order of importance,** saving your strongest reason and evidence for last. Keep in mind, however, that this does not mean you can include weak or flawed information in the essay. All of your reasons should be based on sound thinking supported by solid facts. Your strongest reason will be the one that you believe will have the greatest impact on your audience. (See the outline in the side column for an example of a well-organized essay.)

PERSUASIVE ESSAY MODEL

First Paragraph
Introduction (includes opening remark and opinion statement)

↓

Second Paragraph
Reason #1
Evidence 1
Evidence 2

↓

Third Paragraph
Reason #2
Evidence 1
Evidence 2

↓

Fourth Paragraph
Reason #3 (strongest)
Evidence 1
Evidence 2

↓

Fifth Paragraph
Conclusion (reiterates reasons, rebuts counterarguments, and restates opinion)

EVALUATION CRITERIA

A good persuasive essay

- has an engaging opening and a clear opinion statement
- provides two or three strong reasons supported by evidence
- states counterarguments (opposition's reasons) and refutes them
- concludes with an effective restatement of the writer's opinion

DRAFTING

1. **Set Your Tone**—Aim for a confident, direct tone that comes from believing in the thoroughness of your research. Keep your voice active and do not stray from the topic. As you write, avoid wordiness and phrases like "in my opinion" and "I think." Also avoid words such as *might, maybe, probably,* and *perhaps* that will weaken your argument. Appeal to your readers with strong phrases such as "the facts show." Include citations for your evidence and verify each fact.

2. **The Three Parts of the Essay**
   - **Introduction** For a strong opening, try introducing your topic with any of the following: an amusing anecdote, a provocative question, a surprising fact, or an insightful quotation. Then present a clearly worded opinion statement about your topic.
   - **Body** The body is made up of your supporting reasons, each in a separate paragraph. Aim for two or three strong reasons. Include more reasons only if they will help your argument. Remember that the quality of your reasons is more important than the quantity. State each reason clearly and elaborate with facts that will sway your audience.
   - **Conclusion** In your conclusion, briefly reiterate the reasons that support your opinion, and, if appropriate, point out how they refute any counterarguments. Then end your essay by strongly restating your position.

EVALUATING AND REVISING

1. **Peer Review**—Exchange papers with a classmate and take turns slowly reading each other's essays aloud. Use the Evaluation Criteria in the side column as a guide to make suggestions for improvement. Discuss any confusing passages, wordiness, faulty reasoning, and lack of convincing support. Comment on the evidence that you each thought was the most persuasive.

2. **Self-Evaluation**—If you have time, put aside your paper for a day or two. Then, look at your work and the comments about it, and make whatever changes you think will improve your essay. Before completing your final draft, proofread for errors in grammar, usage, and mechanics. Make sure you used an appropriate style for incorporating quotations and identifying sources. Review how you have used your sources to make sure that you have not inadvertently used information without attributing it to the source.

Index of Authors and Titles

Numbers in italics refer to pages containing **Meet the Writers.**

(continued)

Vocabulary Development

Pronunciation guides, in parentheses, are provided for the vocabulary words in this book. The following key will help you use those pronunciation guides.

As a practice in using a pronunciation guide, sound out the words used as examples in the list that follows. Pay attention to the way the same vowel might sound in different words. For example, say "at" and "ate" aloud. Can you hear the difference in the way "a" sounds?

The symbol ə is called a **schwa.** A schwa is used by many dictionaries to indicate a sort of weak sound like the "a" in *ago.* Some people say that the schwa sounds like "eh." A vowel sounded like a schwa is never accented.

The vocabulary words in this book are also provided with a part-of-speech label. The parts of speech are *n.* (noun), *v.* (verb), *pro.* (pronoun), *adj.* (adjective), *adv.* (adverb), *prep.* (preposition), *conj.* (conjunction), and *interj.* (interjection).

To learn more about the vocabulary words, consult your dictionary. You will find that many of the words defined here have several other meanings.

at, āte, cär; ten, ēve; is, īce; gō, hôrn, look, tōōl; oil, out; up, fur, ə *for unstressed vowels, as* a *in* ago, u *in* focus; ′ *as in* Latin (lat′′n); chin; she; zh *as in* azure (azh′ər); thin, *the*; ŋ *as in* ring (riŋ)